The Age of Economic Measurement

The Age of Economic Measurement

Annual Supplement to Volume 33
History of Political Economy

Edited by Judy L. Klein
and Mary S. Morgan

Duke University Press
Durham and London 2001

Contents

Preface   1

The Reader's Essential Non-Guide to *The Age of Economic Measurement*   3
JUDY L. KLEIN AND MARY S. MORGAN

Perspective
Economics and the History of Measurement   4
THEODORE M. PORTER

A. F. W. Crome's Measurements of the "Strength of the State":
Statistical Representations in Central Europe around 1800   23
SYBILLA NIKOLOW

Make a Righteous Number: Social Surveys, the Men and Religion
Forward Movement, and Quantification in American Economics   57
BRADLEY W. BATEMAN

March to Numbers: The Statistical Style of Lucien March   86
FRANCK JOVANOVIC AND PHILIPPE LE GALL

Perspective
Reflections from the Age of Economic Measurement   111
JUDY L. KLEIN

Measuring Causes: Episodes in the Quantitative Assessment of
the Value of Money   137
KEVIN D. HOOVER AND MICHAEL E. DOWELL

Quantity Theory and Needs-of-Trade Measurements and Indicators
for Monetary Policymakers in the 1920s   162
THOMAS M. HUMPHREY

Leontief and the U.S. Bureau of Labor Statistics, 1941–54:
Developing a Framework for Measurement   190
MARTIN C. KOHLI

Richard Stone and Measurement Criteria for National Accounts   213
FLAVIO COMIM

Perspective
Making Measuring Instruments   235
MARY S. MORGAN

"Facts Carefully Marshalled" in the Empirical Studies of
William Stanley Jevons   252
SANDRA J. PEART

An Instrument Can Make a Science: Jevons's Balancing
Acts in Economics   277
HARRO MAAS

Perspective
Measurement, and Changing Images of Mathematical Knowledge   303
E. ROY WEINTRAUB

Fisher's Instrumental Approach to Index Numbers   313
MARCEL BOUMANS

Quantifying the Qualitative: Quality-Adjusted Price Indexes
in the United States, 1915–61   345
H. SPENCER BANZHAF

Contributors   371

Index   375

Preface

Since the late nineteenth century, measurement has been an integral part of economics. The metrics of the discipline lend it credence as a science, while contemporary debates illustrate the political significance of economic measurement (for examples, consider the 1996–97 U.S. congressional hearings on the Consumer Price Index, the symposium on measurement in the winter 1998 issue of the *Journal of Economic Perspectives*, and the recent attempts by the United Nations to construct a "Human Development Index"). Despite its importance, economic measurement has received remarkably little attention from historians of economics. The aim of the 2000 *HOPE* workshop was to account for the emergence and establishment of economic measurement as a critical element of modern economics. Participants wanted to understand what questions and problems created the drive to measurement and how economists reacted to the changing status of numbers in the discipline. The papers presented at the workshop explored the origins of economic measurement and the historical links between empirical observations, issues of public policy, changes in economic theory, and academic practice. Authors presented material from several countries in Europe and North America and concentrated on the time period from 1830 to 1950, which could well be labeled the "age of measurement" in economics.

The essays in this volume were first presented at a small intense workshop at Duke University on 28–30 April 2000. There were several stages of revision after the workshop in which authors developed points raised in the discussions and responded to reports by anonymous referees and suggestions from the editors.

We would like to thank the editors of *HOPE*—Craufurd Goodwin, Neil De Marchi, and Roy Weintraub—and the managing editor, Paul Dudenhefer, for their enthusiastic support of the workshop and this volume. We are also grateful to Shauna Saunders and other graduate students at Duke who contributed to the workshop, and we thank a number of referees who contributed reports on the papers. Finally, we thank all our authors for their patience in dealing with our editorial demands and for their hard work and creative engagement with our questions about measurement, both at the workshop and for this volume.

The Reader's Essential Non-Guide to *The Age of Economic Measurement*

Judy L. Klein and Mary S. Morgan

There is no editorial introduction or conclusion to this volume, nor is the book divided into labeled parts, nor is there any distinct chronology through the volume. The essays connect in different ways. We experimented with many orderings, intrigued by the trajectories of connection that each sequence suggested. In the end, we decided that section divisions and labels would constrain the way the reader might approach each essay and imply a narrower focus than we wanted to communicate about how we understood each contribution to this volume.

Instead, we have organized the volume to include several shorter essays that offer particular dimensions within which to think about the history of measurement in economics. These "perspective" pieces—Ted Porter's opening essay and contributions from Roy Weintraub and the two editors—form vantage points in a landscape, points where it is natural to pause and register both the path already traveled and the vistas ahead. Our hope is that the reader will experience these essays as a chance to draw breath and reconsider what is involved, rather than as dividing points that separate the other contributions. Taken together, these shorter perspectives and longer essays form our picture of the age of measurement. The linearity of books forced us to choose an order, one we trust the reader will find both harmonious and intriguing. We hope that you will find the same pleasure in making and tracing the measurement connections that we have experienced in editing this volume.

Perspective
Economics and the History of Measurement

Theodore M. Porter

In a classic historical essay on quantification in physics, Thomas Kuhn remarked on the use by social scientists of Kelvin's famous dictum on the decisive importance of measurement. Had it not carried the authority of physics, he argued, social scientists at the University of Chicago would never have chiseled it into the stones of their new building. Kelvin's phrase was displayed in abbreviated form as follows: "When you cannot measure, your knowledge is meager and unsatisfactory." Not inscribed was Frank Knight's gently satirical translation for social scientists: "If you cannot measure, measure anyhow" (Kuhn [1961] 1977, 178, 183; see also Merton, Sills, and Stigler 1984). Knight's version captures something fundamental about the motto that is a matter of less urgency for physicists, but reflects the particular ambitions and anxieties of the social sciences. The common presumption, implied also by the Chicago social scientists, was and remains that measurement and quantification were developed and proven first in physics and that the measurement activities of economists and psychologists have followed in this great scientific tradition. But this view fails to credit the practical purposes of measurement, which have been central to its history.

Themes from the Historiography

The understanding so often presumed of the arrangement of the sciences dates back to a formulation from about 1830 by Auguste Comte, whom

Correspondence may be addressed to Theodore M. Porter, Department of History, UCLA, Box 951473, 6265 Bunche Hall, Los Angeles, CA 90095-1473.

we have also to thank for the neologism *sociology*. He claimed as his discovery the doctrine that the sciences pass in turn through the three stages that lead to positivity. He listed the sciences in a hierarchical order, from abstract simplicity to concreteness and complexity: mathematics, astronomy, physics, chemistry, physiology, and sociology. Yet he firmly refused to privilege mathematics or measurement as motors of the progress of science. Sociology was to be a broadly historical discipline. Political economy and psychology had no place on his list—in part because he opposed their individualism, but more generally because he insisted on the need for a unified, integrative science of society rather than abstract, specialized ones.

Comte railed against a universal ethic of measurement, insisting that every science required its own special methods, which could never be reduced to those further up the hierarchy (Heilbron 1995). Far, then, from anticipating the campaign of the Chicago social scientists, Comte had defined an alternative ordering. Social science was more complex than the sciences of nature. It could, in a limited way, follow the model of physiology, whose decisive advance into the positive stage around 1800 followed from its rejection of mathematics and mechanics for a distinctively vitalistic perspective. Comte was far from alone in his philosophical tastes. From the late eighteenth century to the early twentieth, methodologically reflective pioneers of social science generally saw their charge not in terms of following the one true path of science toward mathematical exactitude but in terms of a consequential choice between mechanical and organic models, requiring more or less modification to be applied to society. Somewhat paradoxically, as we will see, measurement in social science was not decisively linked to physics. In political economy, especially, historicist and organic conceptions of the economy provided more encouragement to quantification than did abstract mechanical ones.

To pose the issue in terms of such broad conceptions, however, is to set out on the basis of grand and dubious assumptions about the character of scientific, including economic, measurement. It supposes that successful measurement is quintessentially the achievement of pure, basic, or disinterested science. In effect, it identifies theoretical understanding as the proper goal of science and values measurement for its contribution to the making of mathematical theories. The simplest version of this doctrine—that measurement is the first stage of mathematization, which proceeds by abstracting to general principles from quantitative data—has long seemed naive to historically informed interpreters of science.

Among the most acute of such interpreters was Alexandre Koyré, the French philosophical historian whose works inspired the first generation of professional historians of science in Britain and America. In a series of essays that have been collected in English under the title *Metaphysics and Measurement* (1968), he held up the mathematization of science as one of the great triumphs of the scientific revolution. Some of his best work concerned the mathematical achievements of Galileo. Legend presents Galileo as a great empiricist and depicts him atop the leaning tower of Pisa, testing Aristotelian doctrine by dropping balls of different weights. Koyré allowed that Galileo may well have rolled balls down inclined planes and chanted rhythmically as he counted beats of a pendulum; he insisted, however, that these measurements were not the basis for Galileo's mathematical law of falling bodies. The mathematization of science, Koyré argued, could never have been achieved in a Baconian, empirical way. Mathematical relationships in mechanics apply only to abstract bodies in geometrical space. Their discovery required, above all, working out the logical consequences of what natural philosophers like Galileo already knew. For this, the thought experiment was more valuable than actual manipulations of material objects. Experimental precision could not, and cannot, supply the premises of mathematical demonstration but can at best show these assumptions to be plausible.

Kuhn's essay on quantification in physics, which introduced some central themes he published a year later in *The Structure of Scientific Revolutions* (1962), takes a broadly similar view. Significantly, for present purposes, he wrote the essay for a social science colloquium at Berkeley, not long before he took a fellowship at the Center for Advanced Study in the Behavioral Sciences, and in many ways this essay was addressed to social scientists. Especially in the 1950s, many of them—though not, one may suppose, the economists—held to the faith that social science could ascend from systematic quantification to mathematized theory. Kuhn doubted this. As historian of physics, he rather disdained the indiscriminate Baconian efforts of experimenters outside the classical, mathematical traditions of geometrical optics, statics, and astronomy. A "second scientific revolution" (218), beginning at the end of the eighteenth century, had at last brought the formerly Baconian sciences of electricity, heat, and physical optics into physics by making them mathematical. Until about 1750, as Kuhn ([1976] 1977, 47) explained in a later essay, research in these fields was less like modern physics "than like those discoverable in a number of the social sciences today." Precise measurement began to appear in experimental physics around 1750, he proposed. By 1976 Kuhn took a more appreciative view of empirical measurement. He even allowed it some role in the advance of mathematical physics, though he interpreted it primarily as a parallel development associated with an increasingly sophisticated experimental practice. In his 1961 essay, Kuhn ([1961] 1977, 201) had been rather less charitable, insisting "that a quite highly developed body of theory is ordinarily prerequisite to fruitful measurement in the physical sciences," and, by implication, also in the social sciences.

The idea that measurement precedes exact or mathematical theory and provides its proper foundation has been maintained, often in defense of theoretical science, since at least the early nineteenth century. J. R. McCulloch (1825, 79–80), for example, explained the relationship between political economy and the emerging science of (social) statistics in these terms. In the 1950s, faith in the priority of measurement was more integral to sociology and political science than to economics. Kuhn's doubts about the campaign to seek a coherent framework of mathematical theory by assiduous measurement remain broadly convincing. But to frame the issue this way implies an unacceptably narrow view even of physics; for social science, it misses or dismisses virtually the whole history of measurement before the late nineteenth century and much of that history even in the twentieth. Kuhn's student John Heilbron began to define a larger role for physical measurement in his 1979 book on electricity in the seventeenth and eighteenth centuries. He published this work just as sociologists, philosophers, and historians of science were beginning to rediscover, as it were, the crucial importance of laboratories and experiments in the development of modern science (e.g., Collins 1985; Hacking 1983).

More recently, historians concerned with measurement and quantification have placed increasing emphasis on the practical, political, administrative, and economic role of numbers. That role cannot be understood as the consequence of developments in some "basic" science. It is rather a crucial dimension of the history of measurement, arguably its most crucial dimension. From this more practical standpoint, the history of economic and social measurement is intertwined with the history of measurement in natural science (Kula [1970] 1986; Frängsmyr, Heil-bron, and Rider 1990; Porter 1995). Even measurements of nature have often been framed within a larger project of economic quantification. The hierarchical understanding of economic measurement as following along in the great tradition defined by physics can be recognized as a fiction, indeed as part of a campaign for a different hierarchy: the primacy of academic economics (and social science) over administrative and reformist traditions of social inquiry. In this essay, I take seriously the applied tradition of practical measurement and use it to explore some relations of economic measurement to measurement of nature. I aim further to suggest some ways in which the applied tradition has framed also the self-consciously scientific campaign for more and better measurement.

Elements of a Periodization

Measurement to 1730

As Kuhn observed, some sciences were already mathematical in ancient times. What he called the "classical sciences" had arisen in Greece. But they were not really important sites for numerical measurement, in part because of the necessary abstraction, but also because the classical mathematical tradition was overwhelmingly deductive and geometrical, with little connection to precise or disciplined observation. In early modern Europe, to the seventeenth century and even beyond, geometry was more dignified than arithmetic, which was always tainted by associations with practical life and especially with the affairs of merchants (Swetz 1987). Geometry, reflecting its noble Greek sources, gave proofs worthy of philosophy and theology. Arithmetic was certainly useful, both in the marketplace and as a tool of astronomical calculation, but it lacked the certainty and the dignity of geometrical demonstration.

The practical purposes of measurement become clearer if we turn our attention to the study of the heavens, the most important object of arithmetic calculations through the Renaissance. Astronomy was a thoroughly heterogeneous endeavor. Physical accounts of the stars and planets were geometrical and yet causal: the planets were carried in their orbits by heavenly spheres. Quantitative astronomy deployed some devices of its own in modeling the heavens and aimed at prediction rather than deep explanation. There were two principal incentives in European astronomy to measure and calculate. One involved calendars, especially the dates of moveable church feasts such as Easter, while the other was astrological. In China and the Near East as well as in Europe, astronomical calculation was generally regarded as instrumental rather than philosophical. The Chinese were quite content to adopt the astronomy of Jesuit missionaries, as they had been to learn from Islamic astronomers, because nothing more was at stake in the use of these "western" astronomies than quantitative precision. In Europe, heliocentric astronomy would probably have created no trouble with the Church were it not that the Copernicans refused the role of mere calculators, claiming truth rather than mere convenience for the heliocentric mathematical system (Westman 1980). It was not for mathematicians to challenge the truths of physics, and still less of theology. The presumption involved might be compared to that of a modern government statistician who would propose a rival foundation for economic theory based on the official formulas used to measure money supply, production, trade, employment, and inflation.

The role of astrology points to other issues. This was by no means low status work, since astrologers cast horoscopes for kings, emperors, and popes. Deriving, ultimately, from pre-Greek Babylonian sources, and maintaining a problematical relationship to Christian doctrine, astrology was nonetheless very widely practiced in Renaissance Europe. While astrology was not synonymous with astronomy, most astronomers practiced it. It deployed the geometry of the heavens as a tool for making precise calculations of planetary motions so that the astrologer could determine the planets' positions at the moment of birth. Astrology was the most important site of quantitative precision through the sixteenth century. Astrological reasons, rather than merely astronomical ones, provided the principal incentive for applying measurement and calculation to the heavens. While it never worked perfectly, astrology was a disciplined strategy of prognostication, requiring meticulous calculation and supported by distinguished authorities. Measurement was not required here by the needs of pure science, but by practical demands. Some very accomplished astronomers, including Copernicus and Tycho Brahe, acquired the practice of precision in part through their involvement in what Robert Westman (n.d.) calls the "culture of prognostication."

The Impulse of Enlightenment: 1730–1830

As Kuhn suggested, the modern mania for measurement dates from the eighteenth century. In retrospect, it might well be seen as an aspect of the Enlightenment project, if indeed we can decide just what "Enlightenment" means in this context. Except for the Marquis de Condorcet, who became prominent only late in the century, none of the most famous philosophes—Montesquieu, Voltaire, Rousseau, Diderot, or even David Hume and Adam Smith—were serious practitioners of quantification, though some expressed themselves enthusiastically about numbers on occasion. After about 1830, statisticians would begin defending their science as an indispensable source of public information, but in eighteenth-century France, for example, social numbers were mostly controlled by functionaries, sometimes in alliance with savants, and were rarely made public (Brian 1994). A move toward centralized administration, in Britain and its colonies as well as on the European continent, defined one important nexus for the flourishing of measurement in the eighteenth century. Science, or natural philosophy, was of course another.

During the seventeenth century, in one of the fundamental developments of the Scientific Revolution, the relations of measurement and mathematics in astronomy slowly assumed a new form. Johannes Kepler, and then Newton, demanded a close fit between measurements and mathematical relations; Newton even derived his celestial mathematics from basic principles of a new mechanics. In the eighteenth century, theoretical questions sometimes drove advances in precision measurement, as in the midcentury conflicts over the shape of the earth. But these scientific efforts were enmeshed also in practical ones. The Cartesian elongated earth was not predicted by theory but derived from Cassini's surveys, undertaken to provide an accurate map of France (Konvitz 1987). The expeditions sent to Peru and Lapland to resolve the question of the earth's shape deployed the instruments and methods of surveying with as much precision as possible (Terrall 1992).

When Newton died in 1727, precise measurement was practiced only in a few rather narrow fields. Over the course of the next century, it became de rigueur in many sciences. This broad change in what we might call the ethics of scientific practice cannot be reduced to a single cause, yet the various causes and circumstances were not unconnected. On the institutional side, there were significant moves toward better educational opportunities and more definite career structures. From the intellectual standpoint, the expanded domain of mathematical theories provided both an incentive to quantify and a sharper specification of what to measure. These explanations, which complement each other, are both in a sense internalist since they involve looking inward at science. The economic aspect of measurement, by contrast, points outward. As a key dimension of the political and cultural situation of science, it supports a broader account of the expansion of measurement. This entails, first of all, the recognition of measurement as something practical and not only as an instrument in the pursuit of truth. In his more recent work, Heilbron (1990) emphasizes the use of measurement in the eighteenth century to advance the aims of centralizing states. As with astronomy, it is often difficult to know where basic science leaves off and applied work begins.

The metric system, devised under the French Revolution, illustrates by the utopian rationalism of its early advocates the interweaving of the diverse purposes and means of measurement. Its advocates wanted a universal system of interconversion, which was in fact partly achieved through a decimalized system of lengths, volumes, weights, temperatures, and, eventually, energies. Decimalized time never quite succeeded. Nor did the decimal system of angular measurements, one of the more immoderate ambitions of the metric system. To match angular measures with units of terrestrial distance, the meter was referred to the size of the earth. French savants proposed as its measure one ten-millionth of the distance from pole to equator. For this purpose, measuring expeditions were launched from Paris to the north and the south. The chaos of revolution and war added to the difficulty of the task, which was nevertheless sustained by a deep faith in the value of precision on the part of the astronomers Jean-Baptiste Delambre and Pierre-François Méchain. Precision was sustained institutionally by a much grander vision. The commission of weights and measures, charged with defining the metric system, included among its members Condorcet, Antoine-Laurent Lavoisier, and Pierre-Simon de Laplace, who apparently assumed the leadership role. Charles Gillispie (1997, 152) summarizes its ambition:

> Evidently the vision of a universal decimal system, embracing not only ordinary weights and measures but also money, navigation, cartography, and land registry, unfolded before the commissioners as they explored the prospect in the summer and autumn of 1790. In such a system, it would be possible to move from the angular observations of

astronomy to linear measurements of the earth's surface by a simple interchange of units involving no numerical conversions; from these linear units to units of area and capacity by squaring and cubing; from these to units of weight by taking advantage of the specific gravity of water taken as unity; and finally from weight to price by virtue of the value of gold and silver in alloys being invariant in composition through a rigorous fiscal policy.

And on it went, to the preparation of a decimalized land registry for tax purposes. Laplace's political economy was evidently not that of Anne Robert Jacques Turgot or of Adam Smith, but the aspiration to join science to commerce and administration is unmistakable, and dazzling.

The imbrication of economic and physical measurements in this period is illustrated also by the administration of German and Swedish mines. Cameralists are often, and with some reason, regarded as proto-economists, but they also wrote treatises on mining and agriculture and attempted even to measure with numbers and graphs the strength of states (see Sybilla Nikolow's essay in this volume). Late-eighteenth-century states sponsored research and education on a variety of related issues, such as worker health, forest regulation, and chemistry. Traditional reliance on the balance in mineral assaying, for unmistakably economic purposes, moved into universities and academies as part of this utilitarian order. Chemical studies of mineral classification, especially in Sweden, provided one nucleus for the French reformation of the chemical nomenclature. It aspired to define its simple substances operationally—that is, by the possibility of isolating and weighing them. Chemistry was far from a mathematical science in 1789, but it did become a science of precise measurement. Lavoisier would insist that competent practice required careful control and measurement so that reactants and products are always in balance (Porter 1981). This equality should be confirmed by reversing the analysis, resynthesizing the original products, and weighing them again.

Measurements of population and wealth were not quite systematic in early modern Europe, but they became increasingly common. Their prominence already in the seventeenth century provides further evidence that economic and political quantification was not merely derivative of developments in natural science. Here, as before, it is often difficult to distinguish administrative from scientific purposes in these activities. William Petty, founder of political arithmetic, was a prominent member of the new Royal Society of London when it was established in 1662. He was generous with advice to the king and remarkably bold in his endeavors to assign economic values to things——such as the lives of Irishmen. Petty, John Graunt, and others in this tradition often wrote from the standpoint of the crown, as if reckoning the value of royal property. In comparatively liberal England, this absolutist perspective fell from favor in the second half of the eighteenth century. Not so on the Continent. Swedish economic writers were particularly bold not only in counting the residents but also in assigning them a monetary value (Johannisson 1990). In Basel, the mathematician Daniel Bernoulli invoked the standpoint of "the state" in his remarkable paper of 1760 on the potential benefits of systematic smallpox inoculation. On the basis of simplifying assumptions about the incidence and mortality of smallpox as a function of age, he calculated from Edmond Halley's life table a hypothetical one that should prevail if smallpox were eliminated. He also reckoned that the age structure of the hypothetical population, including more adults in their productive years, would bring advantages to the state out of proportion to the simple increase in population (Bernoulli [1760] 1766).

Lavoisier too was involved in a form of political arithmetic. A chemist by disposition, he practiced tax farming as profession, which made him wealthy. Inspired, like Condorcet, by the reformist ministry of Turgot in the early 1770s, he shared with many in his generation of Enlightenment advocates a faith in agricultural improvement by scientific means. So it is not surprising that he should have worked for years on a survey of the territorial wealth of France. Eventually he published a partial report in 1791 for the Constituent Assembly, which he regarded as incomplete. This kind of work could not be controlled to the same extent as chemical experimentation. In an era of highly incomplete information, too many estimates and conjectures were involved. Yet, as with chemistry, he had a scheme for checking his economic figures: all results should be recalculated in another way from alternative data (Lavoisier [1791] 1988, 123–24). He declared that measurement was the only suitable basis for economic study. Every science, he explained, "has begun with discussions and metaphysical reasonings: theory is advanced, but the practical science remains in infancy." This "genre of combinations and calculations, of which I have attempted to provide some examples here, is the basis of all political economy" (113–14).

Many mathematicians were involved in estimating populations or even in the organization of censuses in the late eighteenth century, among them P. W. Wargentin in Sweden and Condorcet and Laplace in France (Brian 1994). After about 1790, censuses became common and then obligatory for any self-respecting modern government. For the first few decades, most were somewhat ramshackle. Yet in a way they culminated, even as they transformed, the Enlightenment campaign to comprehend populations and other resources, the better to manage them.

New Ideals of Exactitude: 1830–1900

All periodizations contain some arbitrariness. The history of measures is sufficiently heterogeneous to compound the problem. In the development of empirical social science, including social quantification, 1830 is perhaps the most satisfactory choice for a point of transition, even if the problematic of social order became acute after 1789 (Porter 2002). From about 1830 there occurred an enormous increase in the acquisition and use of quantitative information about nature, technology, and society alike. That date marks also, however, the appearance of a growing split between the measurement ideals of the physical and the social and economic sciences.

The mathematization of physics stretches over the whole period from about 1780 to 1830. By the latter date, Michael Faraday was anomalous in writing influentially about the theory of electricity without using the language of mathematics. The theories of heat, light, and magnetism had also become mathematical by this time. During roughly the same period, reporting precise measures in experimental physics became routine and then mandatory—not because experiment was subordinated to theory, but as an important strand in the evolving ethics of experimental practice (on these matters see Wise 1995). The quantification of natural history had been advancing since about 1730 or, at the latest, 1750. It was allied to Enlightenment territorial surveys, a bureaucratic initiative, but often expressed a quasi-romantic sensibility. One's experience of mountains could be heightened, as it were, by numerical measures of their elevations. Such was the perspective of the internationally celebrated naturalist and traveler Alexander von Humboldt, whose name has been attached by historians to the relentless quantification of the early nineteenth century (Cannon 1978). In this history, 1830 is again a date of some significance, because this is roughly when measuring campaigns became much more systematic and began to receive government support at an unprecedented level. Naturalists of the 1830s and 1840s prepared star charts, mapped coastlines, conducted geological surveys, compiled weather data, and charted the earth's magnetic field, often on a global (or cosmic) scale. At the same time, statistical collection became much more systematic and was organized in the leading European nations by permanent bureaus.

Systematic quantification even reached the humanities in the nineteenth century. In Germany, "precise measurements" were displacing "flowery descriptions" in archeology by the 1850s (Marchand 1996, 60). In the eighteenth century, this would have been eccentric. Ian Hacking (1990, 20) gives an example from the travels in 1777 and 1778 of Johann Bernoulli, of the famous mathematical clan, who, he writes, responded to a collection of Old Masters by taking out a yardstick and recording their dimensions. Considering his travel narrative as a whole, his use of measurement presents a different aspect, one that highlights the economic dimension of measurement and supports a later date for the triumph of systematic quantification. It is not clear that he carried a ruler at all on his travels. In Danzig he had wished he had one because of the astonishing detail in a very small ("maybe 20 inches high and 12 inches wide") Lebens Christi in pen and ink by Dürer (Bernoulli 1778–79, 1:297). The measurements to which Hacking refers, which Bernoulli recorded a few months later, may well reflect commercial practices: the paintings in question, the only ones in Bernoulli's six-volume travel narrative to which he attached measurements, had been recently purchased at auction. Or perhaps this is an instance of how the Enlightenment disciplined the extravagant and the erotic. The paintings are of such subjects as "a naked Venus" standing in a bush with Cupid and bees, "a golden necklace around her neck, and a thin diaphanous gauze covering her lower body" (2:197). As Hacking points out, Bernoulli was assiduous in estimating or inquiring about the populations of towns he visited. In Petersburg, he listed hundreds of paintings in the museum without any measurements, but he compiled a table of the prices of "foodstuffs and other necessities" (5:140–43) as an indication of the cost of living for expatriate academics such as Leonhard Euler.

By Koyré's and Kuhn's strenuous definition of scientific measurement, there was incomparably more of it after 1830 than there had been before 1730. In political economy, so tight a coupling of measurement and theory as they discuss for physics remained elusive. Even in physical science, this union was mostly limited to highly experimental branches and was uncommon or very limited in the campaigns of natural-historical measurement that, with statistics, produced most of the numbers in this quantitative age. Methodologically, physics was defined even in the later nineteenth century rather more by its insistence on precise measurement than by its commitment to mathematical elegance or rigor. The gradual triumph of the laboratory and of "nature's capacities" (Cartwright 1989) over the spontaneous productions of nature unconfined implied that the subject matter of the great natural historical measurement campaigns could no longer be part of physics. That redefinition encouraged physicists and philosophers to construe measurement, and indeed experimentation, more narrowly. In consequence, political economy was to become increasingly suspect as an "experimental science" by 1900.

Just as "nature" and "economy" were more and more sharply distinguished in the later nineteenth century, the Enlightenment intersection of political economy and natural science tended to narrow. It did not disappear. The crucial concept of "work," for example, was shared by energy physics and political economy from the end of the eighteenth century to the mid-nineteenth (Grattan-Guinness 1984; Wise 1989–90; Vatin 1993). The overlap of biology and social science was still more fundamental, more various, and more enduring. Yet the increasing autonomy of economic theory, a decisive feature in the distinctiveness of political economy, can be discerned from the active disapproval of some prominent naturalists and physical scientists. There was, indeed, a tradition of physicists and mathematicians who devoted significant efforts to political economy in the nineteenth century (Porter 1994). Some, like William Whewell, criticized Ricardian deductions, arguing instead for an empirical or historical economics. Others, such as A. A. Cournot, attempted to articulate the kind of mathematics that would support political economy as a measurement discipline. This meant attaining what the metric system had not, a quantitative standard of value, based perhaps on index numbers. Such efforts were at best modestly successful. After 1870, when economic theory began to be redefined in terms of the mathematics of individual utility, it became still less susceptible to measurement. Some of the founding marginalists, above all Jevons, were deeply committed to measurement, though he never showed how statistical numbers could be attached to his basic theory of political economy. Quantification was practiced more systematically by those who rejected deductive or mathematical approaches than by classical or neoclassical economists. In Germany, where it achieved its greatest academic coherence, statistical economics was virtually synonymous with historical

economics. The Germans strenuously opposed what they saw as the reductions implied by a social science grounded in physics, preferring a
historical approach that chose its metaphors from biology. As an alternative to deduction, they held up history and quantification.

This opposition to classical political economy also had a political
dimension and usually involved a moral opposition to laissez-faire or
Manchesterthum. Even those who supported the classical tradition—and
they were many, especially in Britain—rarely tried to imitate David Ricardo in their writings. As late as 1900, in the most professional outlet
for British economists, the *Economic Journal*, the writing was generally
descriptive or statistical, with few references to formal or mathematical
theory. Earlier, many political economists had been allied to the statistical movement, which grew up in the 1830s. Political economists and
"statists" collected figures and compiled tables to comprehend and manage the immense changes of the industrial era. Such numbers were often published by the financial press, in journals such as the *Economist*.
They concerned trade, labor, urbanization, poverty, crime, disease, and
illiteracy, problems that became increasingly urgent in Britain and then
northern Europe in the 1830s and 1840s, and in the United States after
the Civil War. These were issues affecting a whole society or economy.
To most investigators it made sense to study them as collective phenomena, statistically.

In a broad sense, this meant measurement. But statistics was a highly
empirical enterprise. A few ambitious quantifiers, like the Belgian
Adolphe Quetelet, hoped to measure the propensities of the "average
man" and to work toward the international standardization of statistical
categories so that rates of crime or suicide could be compared and their
differentials assigned to causes (Porter 1986). On the whole, however,
statistics meant the preparation and interpretation of tables, involving
measurement in a relatively loose sense. Even Quetelet, who was inordi-
nately fond of mechanical analogies to social processes, was largely unable to turn this perspective into the basis for measurement. As Stephen
Stigler (1999, chap. 2) has remarked, Quetelet's statistical practices were
less a matter of "social physics" than of social meteorology. Few economic or social quantifiers participated in the effort to comprehend the
causes of a less visible or more abstract sort that increasingly characterized experimental measurement in physics as well as theoretical writing in political economy. The attempt to define index numbers to measure the changing value of gold was perhaps an exception. Research on

economic cycles, as Morgan (1990) shows, meant also a search to find causes through statistical investigation, but not, in the nineteenth century, to measure them. Economics in this era was more quantitative than ever but did not yet take up systematically the construction and analysis of new entities through measurement.

Transformations of Measurement: The Twentieth Century

The articulation of a mathematical economics beginning about 1870 by William Stanley Jevons, Léon Walras, F. Y. Edgeworth, Alfred Marshall, Vilfredo Pareto, and Irving Fisher, among others, is often taken as an important transition in the field. Acceptance of neoclassical mathematics came rather quickly, even if its usefulness was contested, but its triumph in practice became decisive only in the 1930s and 1940s. Still, the late nineteenth century was a crucial period of discipline formation and the creation of university positions for the social sciences, especially in America (Ross 1991). Graduate degrees and specialized journals created a more favorable climate for new forms of theory and measurement. Eventually, "measurement without theory" would become problematic for theoretically ambitious economists, as mathematics became a necessary part of their training. Much "high theory" remained surprisingly remote from the measuring enterprise, but increasingly measurers developed tools to assign numbers to objects that could not be directly experienced, such as elasticities. They also adapted the tools of the new biometric statistics, and, integrating these with tools of their own, created the new field of econometrics. The study of time series, shared with meteorology, became an economic specialty (Klein 1997). With a regression equation, one could assign a measure to almost anything. One might say that economists tried to achieve with statistical manipulations what physicists did with increasingly elaborate and expensive experiments.

Yet a historical view shows important continuities as well as novelties in economic measurement, above all in the persistently close ties of economic measurement to administration and reform. That tie has, indeed, been itself a source of dynamism and change. Governments have taken on new functions, adopted new procedures of planning and budgeting, and faced publics and courts with changing standards of credibility and objectivity (Desrosières 2002). Mary Morgan (2002) has recently shown to what extent the history of twentieth-century economics can be framed in terms of the tools it has developed for modeling and measuring, often for political and administrative uses. These are by no means simply refinements of tools and strategies deployed in previous centuries. Yet there is a fundamental element of continuity. Notwithstanding the prominence of university social science and basic research, the modern history of economic measurement remains in important ways a practical one, a history of bureaucratic devices as well as scientific ambitions. Increasing technicality is not necessarily a mark of disciplinary autonomy; often it is an adaptation to this world of applications.

The twentieth-century essays in this volume reflect admirably that blend of ivory-tower and "real world" imperatives that have shaped economic measurement in the last century. Four of them address the uses of measurement in specific governmental agencies, in France, Britain, and the United States. Two others attend in some detail to the uses of economic measures by governments, and another essay provides an engagingly wide look at the mobilization of measures for purposes of public reform. A seeming exception is Boumans, who examines the mathematical dimension of measures. Even this article cannot escape the orbit of practical quantification, however, since Boumans's subject is Irving Fisher's work on index numbers. The main characters in these essays include many academic economists, but they also include mathematicians, state engineers, and professional employees of governmental agencies. Taken together, the essays tell a story of the increasing prominence of economists in government. Their growing role has led occasionally to clashes—such as in the U.S. Federal Reserve, which developed monetary measures long before economics Ph.D.s arrived on the scene. In many cases, the new government economists maintained close ties with economics as an academic field. There is a hint at least of a takeover here, but the process might best be characterized as one of mutual adjustment, of the reshaping of economics and government through reciprocal interactions.

If we were to look for comparable developments in the mathematical, natural, and engineering sciences, we might want to redirect our gaze from academic physics to fields like conservation biology, biomedical statistics, risk analysis, and environmental engineering. At the same time, we should not exclude the "basic" sciences. The twentieth century has opened up, especially in the social, medical, and engineering sciences, a more recondite domain of measurement, but at the same time it has drawn many such tools back into the realms of policy, regulation, and management.

The point here is not to insist on a radical split between the measuring activities of basic science and those in technology and administration, but to examine more closely their intersections. If the early history of measurement, from ancient times to 1830 or even 1900, was associated more closely with practical activities like forecasting, commerce, and administration than with pure science, we should not suppose that the hierarchy was simply inverted in the twentieth century. Where measurement and theory have been integrated, the integration has involved a mutual accommodation, often a difficult one, and has frequently required an intermediate level of calculation and modeling to translate between basic theory and experimental measurement. In the economic and social sciences especially, the impulse to make contact between practical measurement and the tools of theory has been driven by administrative demands as well as by academic expectations. These, to be sure, are sometimes in conflict, but this circumstance should not blind us to the manifold respects in which they have adapted to each other. The "age of measurement" is to be associated particularly with practices emerging in the borderlands. The significance of these developments for the evolution of states, economies, and societies makes the history of measurement itself something more than a narrow specialty and illustrates an influence that goes beyond the academic.

References

Bernoulli, Daniel. [1760] 1766. Essai d'une nouvelle analyse de la mortalité causée par la petite vérole et des avantages de l'inoculation pour la prévenir. *Histoire et memoires de l'Académie des Sciences*. Pt. 2:1–79.

Bernoulli, Johann. 1778–79. *Reisen durch Brandenburg, Pommern, Preußen, Curland, Rußland und Pohlen in den Jahren 1777 und 1778*. 6 vols. Leipzig: Caspar Fritsch.

Brian, Eric. 1994. *La mesure de l'état: Administrateurs et géomètres au XVIIIe siècle*. Paris: Albin Michel.

Cannon, Susan Faye. 1978. Humboldtian Science. In *Science in Culture: The Early Victorian Period*. New York: Science History Publications.

Cartwright, Nancy. 1989. *Nature's Capacities and Their Measurement*. Oxford: Clarendon Press.

Collins, H. M. 1985. *Changing Order*. Los Angeles: Sage.

Desrosières, Alain. 2002. Managing the Economy. In *Modern Social Sciences*, edited by Theodore M. Porter and Dorothy Ross. Vol. 7 of *The Cambridge History of Science*. Cambridge: Cambridge University Press.

Frängsmyr, Tore, John Heilbron, and Robin Rider, eds. 1990. *The Quantifying Spirit in the Eighteenth Century*. Berkeley: University of California Press.

Gillispie, Charles. 1997. *Pierre-Simon Laplace, 1749–1827: A Life in Exact Science*. Princeton, N.J.: Princeton University Press.

Grattan-Guinness, Ivor. 1984. Work for the Workers: Advances in Engineering Mechanics and Instruction in France, 1800–1930. *Annals of Science*, 41:1–33.

Hacking, Ian. 1983. *Representing and Intervening*. Cambridge: Cambridge University Press.

———. 1990. *The Taming of Chance*. Cambridge: Cambridge University Press.

Heilbron, Johan. 1995. *The Rise of Social Theory*. Translated by Sheila Gogol. Minneapolis: University of Minnesota Press.

Heilbron, John. 1979. *Electricity in the 17th and 18th Centuries: A Study in Early Modern Physics*. Berkeley: University of California Press.

———. 1990. The Measure of Enlightenment. In *The Quantifying Spirit in the Eighteenth Century*, edited by Tore Frängsmyr, John Heilbron, and Robin Rider, 207–42. Berkeley: University of California Press.

Johannisson, Karin. 1990. Society in Numbers: The Debate over Quantification in 18th-Century Political Economy. In *The Quantifying Spirit in the Eighteenth Century*, edited by Tore Frängsmyr, John Heilbron, and Robin Rider, 343–62. Berkeley: University of California Press.

Klein, Judy. 1997. *Statistical Visions in Time: A History of Time Series Analysis, 1662–1938*. Cambridge: Cambridge University Press.

Konvitz, Joseph. 1987. *Cartography in France, 1660–1848*. Chicago: University of Chicago Press.

Koyré, Alexandre. 1968. *Metaphysics and Measurement: Essays In Scientific Revolution*. Cambridge, Mass.: Harvard University Press.

Kuhn, Thomas S. [1962] 1970. *The Structure of Scientific Revolution*. 2d ed. Chicago: University of Chicago Press.

———. [1961] 1977. The Function of Measurement in Modern Physical Science. In *The Essential Tension*. Chicago: University of Chicago Press.

———. [1976] 1977. Mathematical versus Experimental Traditions in the Development of Physical Science. In *The Essential Tension*. Chicago: University of Chicago Press.

Kula, Witold. [1970] 1986. *Measures and Men*. Translated by Richard Szreter. Princeton, N.J.: Princeton University Press.

Lavoisier, Antoine-Laurent. [1791] 1988. *De la richesse territoriale du Royaume de France*. Edited by Jean-Claude Perrot. Paris: Editions du Comité des Travaux historiques et scientifiques.

Marchand, Suzanne. 1996. *Down from Olympus: Archaeology and Philhellenism in Germany, 1750–1970*. Princeton, N.J.: Princeton University Press.

McCulloch, J. R. 1825. *Discourse on the Rise, Progress, Peculiar Objects, and Importance of Political Economy*. Edinburgh: Archibald Constable.

Merton, Robert K., David L. Sills, and Stephen M. Stigler. 1984. The Kelvin Dictum and Social Science: An Excursion into the History of an Idea. *Journal of the History of the Behavioral Sciences* 20:319–31.

Morgan, Mary. 1990. *The History of Econometric Ideas*. Cambridge: Cambridge University Press.

————. 2002. Economics. In *Modern Social Sciences*, edited by Theodore M. Porter and Dorothy Ross. Vol. 7 of *The Cambridge History of Science*. Cambridge: Cambridge University Press.

Porter, Theodore M. 1981. The Promotion of Mining and the Advancement of Science: The Chemical Revolution of Mineralogy. *Annals of Science* 38:543–70.

————. 1986. *The Rise of Statistical Thinking, 1820–1900*. Princeton, N.J.: Princeton University Press.

————. 1994. Rigor and Practicality: Rival Ideals of Quantification in Nineteenth-Century Economics. In *Natural Images in Economic Thought: Nature Read in Tooth and Claw*, edited by Philip Mirowski, 128–70. Cambridge: Cambridge University Press.

————. 1995. *Trust in Numbers: The Pursuit of Objectivity in Science and Public Life*. Princeton, N.J.: Princeton University Press.

————. 2002. Ordering the Social. In *From Natural Philosophy to the Sciences: Essays on the Historiography of Nineteenth-Century Sciences*, edited by David Cahan. Chicago: University of Chicago Press.

Ross, Dorothy. 1991. *The Origins of American Social Science*. Cambridge: Cambridge University Press.

Stigler, Stephen. 1999. *Statistics on the Table: The History of Statistical Concepts and Methods*. Cambridge, Mass.: Harvard University Press.

Swetz, Frank. 1987. *Capitalism and Arithmetic: The New Math of the 15th Century*. La Salle, Illinois: Open Court.

Terrall, Mary. 1992. Representing the Earth's Shape: The Polemics Surrounding Maupertuis's Expedition to Lapland. *Isis* 83:218–37.

Vatin, François. 1993. *Le travail: Economie et physique, 1780–1830*. Paris: Presses Universitaires de France.

Westman, Robert. 1980. The Astronomer's Role in the Sixteenth Century: A Preliminary Study. *History of Science* 18:105–47.

————. n.d. Copernicus and the Crisis of the Bologna Prognosticators. Unpublished chapter.

Wise, M. Norton. 1989–90. Work and Waste: Political Economy and Natural Philosophy in Victorian Britain. *History of Science* 27:263–317, 391–449; 28:221–61.

————, ed. 1995. *The Values of Precision*. Princeton, N.J.: Princeton University Press.

A. F. W. Crome's Measurements of the "Strength of the State": Statistical Representations in Central Europe around 1800

Sybilla Nikolow

This essay provides insights into practices of statistical representations produced, published, and debated in the German-speaking territorial states in the period 1770–1830. Seventeenth- and eighteenth-century political arithmeticians, including John Graunt, William Petty, Johann Peter Süßmilch, and Daniel Bernoulli, had argued that one could gauge the wealth or power of a nation by counting people. August Friedrich Wilhelm Crome (1753–1833), professor of *Staatswissenschaften* und *Kameralismus* at the University of Gießen, in the liberal aristocratic state of Hessen-Darmstadt, took this argument several steps further by asserting that the ratio of people to geographic area was the "surest sign of culture" and by graphically comparing nations using that ratio. At the turn of the nineteenth century, the Enlightenment project of measuring population and wealth slowly became more systematic, driven by centralized states and bureaucracy (see the essay by Theodore Porter in this volume). An examination of Crome's contribution to state-crafting measurement highlights the nature of social science taught at German-speaking

Correspondence may be addressed to Sybilla Nikolow, Institute for Science and Technology Studies, University of Bielefeld, P.O. Box 100 131, D-33501 Bielefeld, Germany; e-mail: nikolow@iwt.uni-bielefeld.de. I would like to thank both editors for their encouraging comments on earlier versions of this essay. I also thank two anonymous referees for their careful reading of the essay and the contributors to this volume for a stimulating discussion in the workshop. My participation in the meeting at Duke University was made possible by a conference grant from the Royal Society, to whom I am grateful. All translations from the German are mine.

universities in this period as well as the heated controversy over the role of measurement and table making in the study of the state.

The part of Crome's work that has been almost completely forgotten by historians illustrates an interesting passage point in the history of state-crafting measurement. He used numerical terms to represent the knowledge of the territory within the tradition of geographical state description. His aim was to evaluate and compare internal and external power relations in Europe. He studied, compared, and related the size of the population, the area, the revenue income, and the military power and eventually systematized these figures as "the strengths of the state."

In the first part of my essay, I will show how Crome's statistical writings can be conceptualized within the German tradition of state description. Second, I will describe how and explain why he represented the state statistically and visually in the manner that he did. In the third part of my essay, I will demonstrate the implications of Crome's numerical abstractions as I discuss the contemporary scholarly criticism of the use of statistical numbers and tables in scholarship on the state. What the critics rejected as a reductive and mechanistic approach to the study of the state was for Crome a systematic abstraction. The reactions to Crome's ideas indicate that in some German-speaking states during Napoleon's occupation—and partly as a response to it—a more systematic and quantitative measurement of people and wealth resulted for the time being in a devaluation of statistics as a proper science. They show that the subsequent nineteenth-century academic dispute over the notion of statistics had already begun: should it be used to name a theoretical science taught at the universities or to label an administrative practice for managing the census?

The Place of Statistics in the Study of the State

The Academic System

Statistics was an empirical part of a body of knowledge on the territorial state that was conceptualized and taught as *Staatswissenschaften* and *Kameralwissenschaften* (or its synonym *Kameralismus*), a system of academic subjects including the social, political, and economic sciences in the German-speaking universities. Despite the fact that these studies included overlapping subjects and were taught in different places and by different scholars in different ways, historians have found striking similarities between them as they existed in the eighteenth century. *Staatswissenschaften*, literally translated as "sciences of the state," were the sciences of governing and included general philosophical subjects and law. In this curriculum students learned how to administer the territorial state and gained knowledge of the historical, empirical, and material constitution of the state as well (Bödecker 1990).[1] *Kameralwissenschaften* (in English, "cameralism"), was literally translated as the "sciences of the *Kammer*," the *Kammer* being not only the treasure chamber of the prince, but also the central organ for administering all sorts of sovereign revenues. *Kameralwissenschaften* was more obviously related to the future task of territorial administration, such as supervising the state's activities in agriculture, manufacturing, mining, forestry, accounting, and commerce. It included information not only on law and administration, but also on nature, technology, and applied mathematics (Tribe 1988). But as recent studies have demonstrated, the authors of works on both *Kameralwissenschaften* and *Staatswissenschaften* understood their tasks as contributions to the practice of governing the state rather than to a self-contained body of theory (Wakefield 1999; Lindenfeld 1997).

The Notion of the State and the Notion of Statistics

In this academic context, statistical descriptions were taught to enrich the historical, geographical, and philosophical analysis of the territorial state with empirical knowledge, and it was in this tradition that the state became an object of detailed observation and precise measurement. To understand the implications of this empirical study of the state, called "statistics" in the early modern period, we need to remember that the German notion of the "state" differed from the contemporary English or French notion. Despite the fact that around 1800 the modern state obtained, in central Europe as it did elsewhere, the status of a single acting subject with its own temporality and dynamic, the notion of the "state" was still used to combine three different, but not mutually exclusive, meanings. Derived from its Latin root, *Staat* was still related to *Zustand*, "status," "state," or "constitution" and denoting what constitutes a

---

1. Following Tribe 1988, 8, I tend to translate *Staatswissenschaften* by describing it as "sciences of governing" instead of using the literal translation as Lindenfeld 1997 does.

state as a distinctive country. *Staat* could mean the state as a territory, the state as a population (later conceptualized as the nation or the society), or the state as a power exercised by the ruling government (Koselleck et al. 1990).

Due to these multiple meanings of "state," statistics—whose definition derived from these notions in the German-speaking context—became a positivistic and empirical approach to those interrelated understandings of the state (Rassem 1980). Statistics in this sense was always the statistics of a country denoting remarkable facts about its territory and including the available empirical knowledge on the natural, social, legal, economic, and intellectual peculiarities that could be gathered and related to a territorial state and to the activities by a particular population and its ruling government (Hacking 1990, chap. 3; Nikolow 1994, chap. 1).

The Empirical Basis for State Descriptions

Statistical representations of the territorial state were always descriptions in respect to its status quo. In other words, statistics included the enumeration of the peculiarities of the existing state of affairs about countries. Here again the understanding of the state as a status or constitution affected the early modern meaning of statistics as a discipline distinct from history and geography (Lutz 1980; Seifert 1980). A publication was frequently described as statistical if it compared the characteristics of several countries at a particular moment. In terms of the material basis of these statistics, Crome witnessed a period of major change. At the end of the eighteenth century, statisticians could rely on numerous travel accounts to provide information on European states (Stagl 1995). Encouraged by the spirit of the Enlightenment, some states relaxed censorship restrictions on political and economic news. This was the case for some professors at the University of Göttingen in the Kingdom of Hanover for a certain period of time. August Ludwig Schlözer's reports, for example, inspired a new profession of political journalism (Zelger 1953).

Even before Napoleon's occupation, some states, such as Prussia in 1805, began to collect state data systematically in so-called statistical bureaus and publish them on an annual basis—obviously in an effort to reduce the public's mistrust of the census as a tool for control and intervention (Hacking 1990, chap. 4; Nikolow 1994, chap. 2). Around

1800 the practice of compiling and reorganizing already existing and published information became more and more associated with the work of statisticians (Seifert 1980). Statistics in this bureaucratic sense succeeded in becoming the empirical basis for governmental decisions, but its inclusion within politics worried some academic intellectuals—as the dispute over the use of statistical numbers shows. One has to take into account that the early modern notion of statistics, as an academic science in which peculiarities were enumerated, did not yet mean that these peculiarities had to be expressed exclusively by the use of numbers (Hacking 1990, chap. 3; Porter 1987, 352; Porter 1986, 23–24). Such eventually became the case, however, because of authors such as Crome who transformed statistical-geographical descriptions of the state into numerical and graphical representations.

Teaching How to Govern the Territorial State

Before Napoleon's occupation, the Holy Roman Empire consisted of a small number of large and powerful kingdoms, including Prussia, Bavaria, and Saxony, and a large number of small principalities, centrally directed by absolutistic sovereigns. Although their regional peculiarities were diverse, these kingdoms and principalities shared the opinion that the development of society and economy should flow exclusively from the state as the governing institution. Here a symbiosis of state and economy was characteristic (Tribe 1988). Furthermore, mercantilism in its eighteenth-century cameralistic and reformed version was not only an economic but also a political doctrine, having the formation of a strong state and a powerful administration as its goal. According to the practitioners of *Staatswissenschaft* and *Kameralismus* raised in the tradition of Enlightenment philosophy, the state as the governing body ought to provide the best possible conditions for the free development of its inhabitants. The state's activity should be directed toward establishing a social order and welfare similar to that which existed in the natural world.

The generation of scholars before Crome, among them Johann Heinrich Gottlob Justi, had already hoped to contribute to the instruction of future state officials in the proper arrangement of finances and government and political affairs (Wakefield 1999; Lindenfeld 1997; Tribe 1988). These scholars hoped this instruction would inspire the monarchs to balance their needs for revenue against the general welfare of their subjects, in order to increase the wealth of the country and to support the absolutist regime. The study of *Staatswissenschaften* and *Kameralismus*, including statistics, should contribute to these efforts. The proliferation of a "general knowledge of these various conditions and peculiarities of empires," as Justi (1755, 36) believed, should "show the influence and effect which these conditions have on the happiness, and strength and weakness of states." To meet this demand, a new class of officials had to be trained to possess at least a threefold expertise: legal, for administration; political, for the business of government; and economic- and political-financial, for directing the state's economy and trade (Tauscher 1956). The aim of statistical representations in the study of the state was to determine and evaluate various natural, social, economical, military, and intellectual resources within a territorial state and to balance power relations between its neighbors. As Bensaude-Vincent (1992) and Wise (1993) have shown for the French case, the balance was the epistemological model behind Antoine-Laurent Lavoisier's measurement projects in political economy and analytical chemistry (see also the articles by Theodore Porter and Harro Maas in this volume). As we will see, Crome extended the balancing notion beyond one country to make a Europe-wide comparison. For Crome, ideally the mutual power relationships between the countries should be counterbalanced and a high exploitation of land and labors would indicate the existence of an enlightened government.

Crome's Statistical Work

Crome's Background

Crome was a teacher before he became a professor. Like many other late-Enlightenment scholars who became innovative in the studies of the state, Crome had neither studied jurisprudence nor had an administrative career. He grew up in northern Germany and studied theology at the University of Halle. He worked first as a private teacher for princes and later became the instructor for history, geography, French, and statistics at the *Philanthropin*, an enlightened educational institution in the small principality of Anhalt-Dessau. According to the didactical principles that were developed and followed in this school, subjects such as geography, statistics, commerce, and accounting were understood as necessary, practical tools and favored in opposition to the teaching of the classics (Nikolow 1999). These radical ideas did not survive the later neo-humanistic attacks on education, but they became very influential in reforming the technical colleges in Prussia during the nineteenth century (Wagener 1936). At the *Philanthropin* the practical training was meant to contribute to a later active citizenship expected from representatives of occupations such as officers, entrepreneurs, or state officials. Crome (1833, 112, 138) gives the credit for his interest in *Staatswissenschaften*, *Kameralismus*, and statistics to the *Philanthropin*.

Crome was appointed professor at the University of Gießen because of his reputation as an author in the field, and this was not his only offer. He accepted the call to Gießen in 1787, when the academic status of this kind of empirical knowledge was still being debated. Traditionally *Staatswissenschaften*, including statistics, belonged to the academic disciplines taught by the philosophy faculty, while *Kameralwissenschaften* belonged to the faculty of law and all potential state officials had to undergo the study of law. Yet, the juridical faculty had in general the privilege of examining those subjects (Tribe 1998; Bleek 1972). In contrast to the study of jurisprudence, it was often doubted that empirical expertise, such as statistics that was necessary to work in state administrations, should and could be learned at the university at all; rather, state officials were expected to learn by doing in the *Kammer* or the *Bureau*. Nevertheless, some sovereigns succeeded in introducing these new subjects by founding state academies or special faculties in state universities such as in Gießen.

The first independent economic faculty was created at the University of Gießen; professors from other fields also contributed to the new department. Crome succeeded Johann August Schlettwein, who had found a niche in Gießen after the failure of his physiocratic experiment in the principality of Baden (Klippel 1994). When Crome arrived Schlettwein had already been gone two years, his department was closed, and there were hardly any students in the field—circumstances that illustrate the fragile position of economic and political studies within the academic system. Crome reintroduced these studies within the faculty of philosophy where he was finally appointed. He taught *Staatswissenschaften* and *Kameralismus*, including statistics and geography, and other applied subjects such as technology, economical zoology, agriculture, and forestry. In the field of statistics he regularly lectured on *Statistik der Europäischen Staaten*, a comparative description of the European powers by the use of statistical representations (Crome 1833, 159–74; Lenz 1957). After Crome arrived in Gießen, he used published accounts and intensified his research on the statistics of several countries. He also started to produce his own comparative books and maps in which he developed new ways to systematize the knowledge he had gained.

Two authors were of the most importance for Crome's own training as a statistician: Gottfried Achenwall (1719–1772) and Anton Friedrich Büsching (1724–1793). Both had been leading experts in the field of state description since the mid-eighteenth century. Crome read Achenwall in the 1770s and used his handbooks on the European states until he had produced his own. Achenwall is known for having lectured in German on these subjects and for then having established the discipline *Staatswissenschaft* in Göttingen. He introduced the notion of statistics as remarkable facts on the state (Achenwall 1752; Rassem 1980, 28). His notion of statistics was taught at the university and it was understood there as the exhaustive compilation of peculiarities describing the territorial state and the use of that information to formulate qualitative judgments about the land and the people.

Büsching went further in his state descriptions. He was actually trained in theology at the University of Halle and influenced by pietistic thought (Hoffmann 2000). After a short interlude as professor at the University of Göttingen, where he was attacked for his antischolastic thinking, he left academia for good. He remained a teacher and theologian and published several geographical volumes and respected travel accounts. If Achenwall is officially recognized as the father of statistics, Büsching gets credit at least for being the father of political geography. He made the political viewpoint a part of geography and the geographical viewpoint a part of the study of the state (Plewe 1957). In his *Neue Erdbeschreibung*, published in many volumes and editions through the second half of the eighteenth century, Büsching treats the "historia naturalis," the study of nature, parallel to the "historia civilis," the study of the society ([1754] 1770). Both were examined using measurable quantities only. Furthermore Büsching displayed his results in tables facilitating direct quantitative comparison between countries. Within this ordering, the society, namely the state population, occupied a special place—as it had in political arithmetic (Lutz 1980, 253). It was against this background that Crome later pleaded for a marriage between two, until then, distinctive fields of knowledge—namely, the study of the earth's shape (mathematical and physical geography) and the study of the population (the political arithmetic).

Thus, when Crome entered the field, he was able to base his state-crafting work on a new order of disciplines; among which statistics had become an increasingly distinctive field. Around 1800 natural history was coming to its end, beginning to be transformed into the new natural sciences; geography gradually became distinguished from statistics and history and became understood solely as mathematical and physical geography (including geodesy for instance); and, finally, statistics was separated from history (Seifert 1980; Lutz 1980). August Ludwig Schlözer (1804, 86), who succeeded Achenwall in Göttingen, clarified what had already taken place in the practice of state description: "History is moving statistics and statistics is stationary history." He defined statistics as a description of the state in terms of its status quo and described history as a process that could be studied by comparing statistics.

Books and Maps on Commodities

If Achenwall's definition of what should be called statistics in the academic context remained important for Professor Crome, Büsching's method of presenting information guided him in his research. Büsching was Crome's uncle, and Crome imitated his career to a certain extent. Büsching advised Crome to give up his initial hopes to practice theology in a Prussian parish after having left the University of Halle (Crome 1833, 24, 41). Moreover he encouraged Crome to improve earlier geographical descriptions of the states, as Crome eventually did with success.

Crome started to publish his own works while teaching at the *Philanthropin*. Among them were exhaustive geographical-statistical descriptions of certain principalities and states, written under commission, and more specialized handbooks on the production, consumption, and exchange of commodities, written for the use of merchants. Both kinds of books followed Achenwall's ambitious tradition of including all peculiarities. Among the latter was *Europens Produkte*, Crome's first comparative work, which first appeared in 1774 (fourth edition, 1805). In this work one could already see his efforts to analyze information in a systematic way. He made extensive use of two methods of representing information: first, he displayed numbers in tables, as Büsching did before him; second, he displayed results in maps in a geographical manner. Crome understood the notion of resources in a broader sense than did his predecessors. As we can see from this early work, the tables included not only an enumeration of natural resources, but also all manufactured products, geographical surface numbers, and the population for each European country. The attached and later separately published *Produktkarte* was a comprehensible and vivid display of the empirical material in the book (Nikolow 1999).[2] Of interest for the early history of thematic mapping, this addendum actually contained several parts; the map itself was displayed at the center and was framed by tables left and right and a legend at the bottom. By the use of signs, Crome indicated on the geographical grid for each country which products were produced, imported, and exported. The tables included lists of countries, surface areas and population by numbers, and the commodities by name. In comparison to other geological maps of his time, the references to land and people on the *Produktkarte* are unique. For that reason Arthur Robinson (1982, 55), the historian of thematic mapping, commented that it was "as much a general or reference map as it [was] thematic."

Ratio and Proportions as Tools for State Crafting

As we have already seen from his books and maps on commodities, Crome's understanding of resources includes social subjects such as the population number, economic subjects such as commodities, and geographical subjects such as surface areas. He continued to reflect on the relationship between these subjects in his later statistical works: *Ueber die Größe und Bevölkerung der sämtlichen europäischen Staaten* (1785), *Ueber die Kulturverhältnisse der Europäischen Staaten* (1792), *Allgemeine Übersicht der Staatskräfte von den sämtlichen europäischen Reichen und Ländern* (1818) and *Geographisch-statistische Darstellung der Staatskräfte von den sämtlichen, zum deutschen Staatenbunde gehörigen Ländern* (1820–25).

Crome aimed to relate two fields of knowledge of territories that had, until then, been treated as distinct: the *Länderkunde* and the *Größenkunde*. The *Länderkunde* was the study of the state territory and referred to its physical and political geography. The *Größenkunde* was the study of the number of the inhabitants, the main research topic of the political arithmeticians, and later led to the development of demography. The reason Crome joined these fields of knowledge was because he wanted

2. For a copy of the map, see Robinson 1982, 56.

to systematize all gathered information as he created an exhaustive, but also effective, evaluation of the territorial state. On the one hand, Crome wanted to include and highlight the population figures compared to earlier accounts, such as Büsching's, which were mainly focused on geographical elements. Crome (1785, 15) did this, because he believed that "the expansion of territory alone does not constitute the strength and bloom of a country; rather, it is the paucity or abundance of inhabitants who live there and who determine the various degrees of culture." On the other hand, Crome wanted to systematize the study of the state in a new way. Unlike previous works (such as Achenwall's), which enumerated all known details that could be related to the territorial state, Crome's work focused on its characteristic dimensions, basically the population size and the surface area, which were related to each other and to other state figures. Furthermore, Crome believed it no longer sufficient simply to compare the figures to each other. Instead he thought that both figures should be related and represented with their actual connections to each other made clear. Because this scheme included information from two realms of experience, land and people, a mediating dimension was needed. Crome found this dimension in the ratio of people to geographic area—without having the modern demographic notion of population density. In his 1785 book, he continued to present both figures, *Größe* and *Bevölkerung*, as distinct from each other. In his next book—published in 1792, by which time he was already teaching in Gießen—he introduced the ratio connecting the two figures and conceptualized it as a sign for the cultivation of its country. In his last two books (1818 and 1820–25), he carried his theory further by relating the ratio to financial figures and military forces.

Focusing on ratios instead of absolute numbers allowed Crome to put a gauge in the hand of statisticians enabling them to estimate the power of states beyond the actual particular differences in the categories of the statistical description. He had already announced this move to the ratio in his 1785 book by proclaiming his aim to evaluate the "cultural development of a country." He wanted to wrap up in this ratio everything "that presupposes mind and activity" (1785, 50). Crome's concern with the ratio served his intention of making the countries comparable and of determining the power relations between them.

Using examples Crome argued that one would assume France and Poland, countries of approximately the same size, to be similar in terms of "power, wealth and culture," but this similarity does not exist (222).

The "cultural development of a country" could not be exhaustively defined in the geographic area or in similar categories of the land—such as the fruitfulness of the soil, the geographic basis for agriculture and mining (222). He proposed instead to take the population figure and population politics into consideration. He did so by introducing the measurement of population and relating that to the surface area. Using published sources he calculated 895 people per square mile for Poland and more than 2,500 for France. He took both ratios as a starting point for the examination of the country's wealth and concluded the following about Poland from its comparison with France: "infinitely less life and activity," "less labouring hands," "much less handicraft flourishes," "less evidence of profitable trade, and the consequential luxury, from which later arts and sciences spring" (233). By adding tables containing different statistics on cities, manufactories, and soldiers, he underlined his argument that the power relation between the countries could be determined by using a direct comparison between national figures such as the ratio of people to geographic area.

From the *Größenkarte* to the *Verhältniskarte*

Crome's intention to merge the *Länderkunde* with the *Größenkunde* and to establish the ratio as a means for state-crafting comparison was complemented by his graphical work. All four of his statistical books included maps that were later published separately and translated into several languages. Their design was rather exceptional and unusual for thematic maps of the time, as he did not make use of the geographical grid. Rather, Crome's maps remind one of the display of diagrams and the presentation of facts in a tabular style found in the tradition of state descriptions. Tufte (1982, 43–44) attached the label "relational graphics" to the abstract design in a very similar chart by William Playfair included in Playfair's *Statistical Breviary* in 1801. One could place Crome's less familiar statistical maps within the same category.[3]

Crome's 1785 book was accompanied by the *Größenkarte von Europa*. This was a map in which he represented visually the area of the European territories by the use of superimposed squares, with Malta as

3. Thanks to Royston (1956), who has compared both authors, Crome now has a place in the history of the graphical representation of statistics. To explain this interesting conjunction, a thorough study of the similarities and differences in the disciplinary and cultural traditions to which they belonged would be necessary.

the smallest square in the very center and Russia as the largest (which he did not display to scale). His diagram displays the countries in order of their sizes. Because the squares were scaled, it was possible to compare them (and the countries they represented) by counting units and by comparing actual figures that had been written on each square. In the columns left and right of the diagram, he had already listed the ratio of people to geographic area for each country by indicating the average number of people who lived on each square mile.

In his later *Verhältniskarte von Europa*, which first appeared in his 1792 book, Crome also included a visual representation of this ratio, but in an indirect manner: below the superimposed squares, he drew bar charts for each country showing by bar length how much territory was divided between an average of 1,000 people in a given country. The bar charts were similar to the squares in the middle of his graph, which were almost concentrically arranged according to size (see fig. 1). We find Malta, with less space, displayed in the center; Norway and the Danish states on the left; and Iceland and Sweden on the right, both showing more space for the same number of inhabitants. This quantitative order could be appreciated at a glance. In the left-hand tables on the diagram Crome compared the proportional figures concerning the geographic area of each country, and in the right-hand tables he compared the proportional figures concerning the population size of each country. In the tables we find the comparison between France and Poland again. On the left their proportion in area is marked as "1." If one looks in the right-hand tables and follows the column of Poland to the line of France, the listing says "2 4/5," indicating that two and four-fifths more people live on the same surface area of France as in Poland. According to the indirect demonstration of the ratio in the bar charts, the French bar is shorter and displayed closer to the Maltese bar at the center of the diagram than is the Polish bar. The map should exemplify his argument in the book for the "proportional population of a state" to be seen as the "surest scale of culture" (Crome 1792, 2). For him this was a "main viewpoint" in which resources and income would no longer appear "as scattered fragments," especially if one put them "in context." Crome intended to systematize all peculiarities of the countries by absorbing them into one abstract system, a system that would enable him "to draw a true conclusion about the entirety" (5).

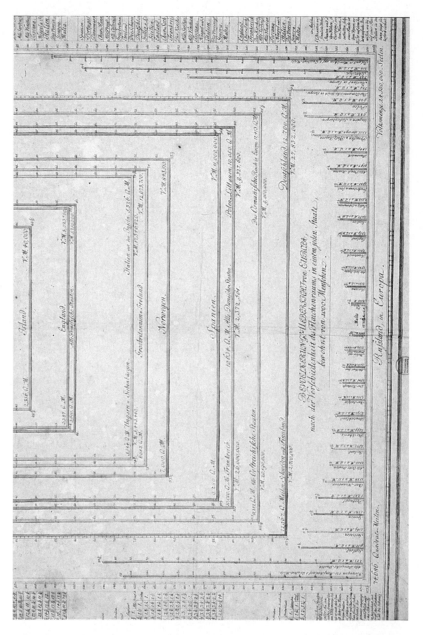

Figure 1   Bar chart at the bottom of the *Verhältniskarte*, taken from Crome n.d. This map is almost identical to the one that is included in Crome 1792. Reprinted by permission of the Kartenabteilung der Staatsbibliothek Preußischer Kulturbesitz, Berlin.

Crome's Later *Verhältniskarte* and the Measurement
of the "Strength of the State"

In the following years Crome further developed his abstract style to
represent graphically quantitative information about territorial states. A
completely new and final version of the *Verhältniskarte* appeared in connection with his later state-crafting books of 1818, 1820, and 1825. There
were several reasons the *Verhältniskarte* took almost twenty years to
complete—Crome had to fulfill his professorial and other duties, including negotiating with the Napoleonic garrison as representative of the university staff. Furthermore, it must have been almost impossible, around
1800, to get accurate data from the states due to the occupation and
wars of liberation. It docs not seem incidental that Crome finalized his
project only after 1815, the year when the Vienna Congress took place.
These agreements helped to create a new status quo for the central European states and provided the foundation, on economic grounds, for a
federal union between some major German states under the guidance of
the Prussian Kingdom. This was also the first step in the creation of the
German nation-state.

In his later state-crafting books and maps, Crome conceptualized what
he earlier called the "surest scale of culture" as the *Staatskräfte*. He basically systematized the way he made comparisons between the powers
by extending their earlier proportions to financial and military figures.
In his notion of *Staatskräfte*, he combined earlier cameralistic views on
the usefulness of a high population for the state with physiocratic ideas
on the land as source of income and liberalistic thoughts on the importance of handicrafts, commerce, and national wealth.[4] Crome evaluated
his figures by putting them into a qualitative and hierarchical order. The
general overview on the *Staatskräfte* he intended to give contained, as he
announced, "primarily the extent of the area and the counted number of
the people, along with their mutual relationships; further the fruitfulness
of the land by its cultivation and its agriculture; so also the products that
had been manufactured by industry and turned over in trading" (1818,
xii). The books on Europe and on the German Federation consisted only
of quantitative information, which he provided in the so-called general

4. Kirmes (1908) has studied Crome's economic theory. Strongly influenced by the general
trend to condemn all predecessors of the historical school, he devalued Crome's contribution
to the *Nationalökonomie*, the German political economy, as Roscher, the founding father of
this school, did earlier (1874, 649–51). It seems that Crome's combination of ideas was rather
typical for his time, place, and discipline (Tribe 1988, 1998).

tables for particular countries, including details for each resource. Each table contained columns for surface area, number of inhabitants, population density, state income, expenditures, and respective peculiarities.

The *Verhältniskarten* served as a guide to the basic figures in their mutual relationships. Here Crome no longer used bar charts to represent the population density, but circles. Furthermore he drew lines to show a state's income. He represented the extent in absolute value and as a per-person variable by the use of different colors. To explain his construction in detail, I am using a copy of its English translation that was engraved under the direction of A. Arrowsmith a year after its first publication (see figs. 2 and 3). As did the bars in the first *Verhältniskarte* from 1792, the circles represent the extent of surface area for every respective state in which 1,000 people lived. Here the Duchy of Lucca is displayed in the center, the Kingdom of Sweden at the far left, and the Russian Monarchy at the far right. The green tangents, placed on the right side of each circle, represent by length the actual number of people living in a state. The yellow tangents at the left of each circle represent the actual sum of the regular public revenue of each country as the wealth of the state. Finally, the blue lines, drawn downward from the center of each circle, indicate the quantity of florins that every individual, on average, contributed to the public revenue of the country (revenue again denotes the wealth of the state). In the left-hand table, Crome listed the combined results from the drawing. In the right-hand table, military details concerning land and sea power were listed, and these were differentiated by time of peace or war.

Crome (1818, xx) based the introduction of expenditures and military details into the statistical description of the territorial state on the liberal premise that these subjects "put a nation in the position to use its strengths in a safe and undisturbed way." Using the notion of *Staatskräfte*, Crome wanted to restrict the state's functions to protecting and governing the state population, now conceptualized as the nation. The state was expected to guarantee the unhindered development of its citizens. These views related to the local political discourse in which Adam Smith's ideas on the wealth of nations found a ready reception around 1800 in central Europe. (As we know from the sources, Crome came in contact with Smith's "improved system" via Satorious's translation, which was very influential for central European economic thinking at the beginning of the nineteenth century [Kirmes 1908, 111; Treue 1951]).

Figure 2   Statistical map from Crome 1819. This is the English translation of the map in Crome 1818. Reprinted by permission of the Kartenabteilung der Staatsbibliothek Preußischer Kulturbesitz, Berlin.

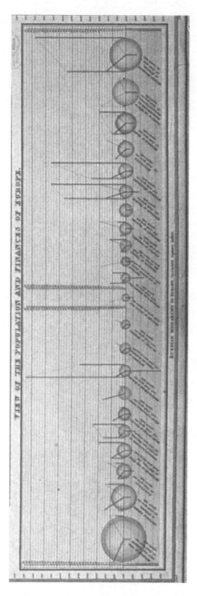

Figure 3   Detail of figure 2. Circles with tangents and lines representing the absolute and relative number of population and public revenue
of each country (from Crome 1819). This is an English translation of
the map that is included in Crome 1818. Reprinted by permission of the
Kartenabteilung der Staatsbibliothek Preußischer Kulturbesitz, Berlin.

Indeed, this reception inspired an economic discourse that was conceptualized under the notion of *Nationalökonomie*, the German version of political economy. In his later state-crafting work and in keeping with this new concept, Crome differentiated the "private property of the nation" from the "property of the state." He hoped thereby to make it impossible for "despotic regimes" to consume the national wealth, using it as a source to satisfy the state's needs (xvi). In the subtitle of his English map, he did not use the term "state revenue"; instead he used the notion of "public revenue" in summarizing expenditures and military assets. At Gießen, Crome (1833, 171–74) taught his "own system of *Nationalökonomie*" by discussing national resources independently of the treatment of politics, law, and finance when he considered the responsibilities of the state. He (1833, 174) claimed to have recommended this system to Ludwig Heinrich von Jakob, professor of economics in Halle (174). Jakob is now viewed as one of the founders of the new discipline of *Nationalökonomie* (Tribe 1998).

In Crome's hands *Staatswissenschaften* and *Kameralismus* became political and economical geography, and statistics were analyzed to construct the ratio of certain qualities and to compare the relative power of different countries. If many people lived in a territory, the cameralist Crome saw not a sign of poverty—as Thomas Malthus did in Scotland— but rather a sign of potential wealth: a large population denotes a high degree of the utilization of natural resources and indicates a high degree of land cultivation, the exercise of labor, trade, wealth, and welfare. In addition he borrowed the physiocratic idea that the use of land leads to wealth and from economic liberalism the assumption that productive work is paramount. For that reason he believed the impact of crafting and manufacturing commodities for the market should be included with such political-economic analyses.

Crome's new approach to such evaluations, unique and attributable to him alone, concerned how he abstracted his data and represented them numerically in tables and visually in maps. This innovation makes him important in a culture of measurement that underwent further developments in this direction in the statistical bureaus. Crome's abstractions separate him from his contemporaries, whose merely descriptive approach was typical for the statistical works of the time. Furthermore, he gave more credence to his representation of results in maps rather than to the information listed in the tables of his books. In announcing the final version of his *Verhältniskarte*, Crome stressed the extraordinary value of his graphical representations by referring to his book of tables merely as "commentaries" to the included map (1818, xi). In his statistical maps he established a new method of representing geographical, social, and economic facts. He employed a perspective on the peculiarities of the territorial state that provided a comprehensive and systematic picture of all its details while at the same time creating a general impression of its power. He used the ratio of people to geographic area as an instrument to abstract information from the actual empirical numbers published by officials and private collectors. As he argued in the case of the French Revolution, the mutual economic relationship between the European powers defined by and developed according to this ratio has changed very little, contrary to what one would expect. It seems that he valued his visual depictions over absolute and empirical numbers because they represented proportions that could be related back to the collected data; at the same time, they represented abstractions that he found stable enough to support more general conclusions. As the critics of numerical statistics would later show, to a certain extent we can interpret Crome's plea for the proportional view as an effort to purify his work from any contamination with local politics that one might expect from the use of public and private data.

Around 1800 central Europe witnessed a period of major change and disturbance within the political system, but it also saw the beginning of a number of far-reaching constitutional reforms that led to the modernization of the state and its bureaucracy. To take one example: Napoleon abolished the structure of numerous small principalities that had developed over time and founded the Kingdom of Westphalia as a buffer zone between Prussia in the East and France in the West. Other smaller states, such as those on the Rhine, joined pro-French federations—including Hessen-Darmstadt, where Gießen was located. These changes remained in place until the Vienna Congress of 1815 when, with the help of a statistical commission, the attempt was undertaken to equalize the imbalances causing and caused by war between the powers of France, Prussia, Russia and Austria.

Crome's state-crafting work was a part of the practice that Jacques Revel characterized as a particular continental tradition of producing and displaying knowledge of the territory (1991). The French example has been analyzed by Bourget (1988) and Brian (1994). Looking at these examples, it seems possible to include the German case and particularly

Crome within this picture. Therefore the continental tradition was developed as an alternative and complement to Britain's earlier and different technique of treating social and economic subjects of political arithmetic, although later in the nineteenth century they united to form a modern demographic understanding of statistics.[5] Revel (1991, 139–40) described the continental tradition in the following way: "Rather than being a series of numbers, this descriptive approach is used to draw on a monographic picture that includes all the aspects of a local situation and attempts to reconstruct the system of relations that unites them." Closely associated with the search for analogies, as was the practice of natural history, this approach did not involve abstract mathematics, but rather attempted "to reflect nature as faithfully as possible" to determine the "uniqueness of each place" through "the shifting interrelations of these various factors" (139–40). Although Crome followed Achenwall and Büsching in this tradition, the numerical abstractions of the *Staatskräfte* and his proportional view and graphical display of the territorial powers signified the importance both of precise measurement in this field and of a new understanding of statistics as a quantitative method for social science.

Noble Statisticians versus Ordinary Table Makers

The Background of the Debate

The numerical statistics published by Büsching, Crome, and others, such as the member of the Prussian statistical bureau and physiocrat Leopold Krug, were attacked by romantic critics. This attack took place in the scholarly literature between 1806 and 1811, between Napoleon's victory over Prussia and his defeat by the allies—a period of occupation and the wars of liberation in central Europe. The debate dealt with the question of whether quantification and table notation were the appropriate means to analyze and describe states and to communicate knowledge about them. In the dispute, the table was recognized as an indication of the new method of presenting geographical descriptions of the states. Its proponents were labeled as *gemeine Tabellenmacher*, literally

---

5. Although there were political arithmeticians in Germany in the eighteenth century, as the cases of the Prussian priest Süßmilch and the Baselian mathematician Daniel Bernoulli suggest, they do not seem to have taken part in the intellectual discussion on state measurement nor in the introduction of these subjects to the university.

translated as "ordinary table makers." While the table makers saw in tables an instrument with which to present information in a precise and orderly manner, their opponents rejected the use of tables as a working strategy.

This criticism came from philosophers and historians that were teaching at the University of Göttingen or closely related to it and to the—for dynastic reasons—pro-English government of Hanover. Because of Napoleon's occupation, it was expected that the university would be closed and/or transformed into a specialized school of training and that the English Kingdom of Hanover, once absorbed into the greater Westphalia, would be completely reorganized according to French and Prussian bureaucratic models (Kern 1987, 67–70). The table opponents from Göttingen and Hanover—Ludwig Heeren, Ernst Brandes, and Wilhelm Rehberg—formulated their criticism on the basis of the reductionistic perspective of modern statistics, in analogy to the similarly reductionist political proposals of which they were skeptical. They wanted to protect the study of the state, including its traditional statistical treatment, from materialism, empiricism, and political interference. The older qualitative statistical approach developed by Achenwall was described as a "noble" study, indicating its greater importance for the appreciation of the strength of the state. Schlözer, who had introduced a limited numerical measurement into the notion and practice of statistics, was already close to retirement and did not take part in the debate.

Recent historiography has treated the romantic criticism of table practices more seriously than it did before and has conveniently connected the debate to the discussion of the status of quantification in this period (Kern 1987; Johanisson 1990; Marino 1995; Lazarsfeld 1961, 292–94). But these historians have not focused on the subject of the debate directly; rather, they have only quoted the opponents and have often relied on citations chosen from older secondary literature, literature that presents us with a very restricted perspective on the history of statistics. The picture that we have thus gotten is still very selective, unsymmetrical, and not reflective of the participants' roles and work. With knowledge about the measuring activity of one of the so-called table makers—such as Crome, who furthermore displayed the strength of the European states in one map—we get a better idea of the grounds for criticism and how the discourse in the political sciences was shaped by the transformation of statistics into its numerical basis. The debate illustrates that measurement, as an academic discipline within these realms of knowledge, could not be simply accepted without resistance. The question became whether or not statistics as a scholarly subject could still remain in the realm of the university as an independent science and how it could be distinguished from the bureaucratic practice of the state if it became an activity of counting and measuring people, goods, and money. And as we will soon see from contemporary sources, the debate illustrated exactly the changes in the notion of state that were related to the new understanding of statistics.

Words versus Tables

The debates started in 1807 when Ludwig Arnold Heeren, philosopher of history and professor at the faculty of philosophy in Göttingen, wrote one of his frequent reviews for the *Göttingische gelehrte Anzeigen*, the journal in which the university professors commented on recent academic publications. In the review he praised a critical account of Wilhelm Rehberg, his former student and now state official in Hanover. This account described the mechanization of the state administration in Prussia, which was modeled after an army, as one of the causes of Napoleon's victory. In his review Heeren took up one of Rehberg's main points by claiming a similarity: that due to the making of tables, "the entire science of statistics," which had been until recently "one of the noblest and for the man as a citizen of the state, most interesting sciences," had become now "a skeleton" and "a cadaver" (1807, 1302).[6] For Heeren, by this means, the *sciences* of governing seem to have been killed by the use of tables. He believed the state to be a complex and living object, and therefore quantitative abstractions were inappropriate instruments for its appreciation.

Analyzing the state using measurements was criticized by Heeren and Rehberg because they assumed that the state was a living object and would have to be killed before it could be dissected. Studying the state at the university should, in their eyes, be done by synthesis rather than by analysis. The university itself should not follow utilitarian and political aims, but should, above all, train the future servants of the state in the moral qualities that were perceived as much more important. It was

6. Despite the fact that the reviews published in the *Göttingische Gelehrte Anzeigen* appeared anonymously, the ones I quote had all been identified as Heeren's, who then edited the journal.

not believed that one could derive general conclusions from the numerical representation of states alone. In the eyes of their critics, the modern statisticians would have to make themselves dependent on the shortsighted political views and ideological purposes of the governing rulers and state administrations in order to get the information they needed. In 1806, Heeren (1806, 834) had been even more explicit in his views, writing in the same journal: "according to our interpretation, it is the misuse of the table method, which would reduce everything to numbers, that not only stole the sprit of the study, but also had other practical consequences." He further emphasized his argument by juxtaposing the results of modern quantitative statistics against older qualitative statistics, commenting: "Here one had in several columns the number of square miles, earnings, inhabitants, and even the dear cattle before one's eyes, and so had one also the overview on the strengths of the state; but for national spirit, love for freedom, the genius and the character of great or small men at the top, there were no columns" (834). These characteristics were important to Heeren and could not be deleted from the academic study of the state on numerical grounds.

As already mentioned, Heeren was neither alone in his criticism nor in perceiving the link between the new method of studying the peculiarities of the territorial state and the rational reform of the state's administration. Rehberg (1807, 22) took up the statistical administrators' love of any details they counted and satirized the ideal of the statistical profession by painting a picture in which "one half of the inhabitants would be occupied to take the minutes of what the other half does. If nothing more would be accomplished at the end of an ideal statistical treatment, minutes would still be being taken and nothing of what had been produced would remain unnoticed." Similar to Heeren, Rehberg believed that if statistics were reduced to the practice of accounting, the quality and character of the people would not be taken into consideration. In observing the statistical practice in Prussia, Rehberg pointed out that "everything is accurately expressed by numbers: but also only numbers and proportions are given" (16). In making the difference explicit, he criticized that one did not know "how many people and products of all kinds one had to deal with; one did not know who these people were, how they were disposed, how they lived, what the land looked like" (16–17). The population figure, fundamental for Crome's evaluation, was for Heeren and Rehberg worthless. They both doubted that such important qualities could be reduced to numbers.

The State as a Machine and the Table Statisticians
as Laborers

The criticism was an attack against a zeitgeist that was defined as mechanical, rational, and industrial, and had been observed in states such as Prussia and, after the revolution, in France, but rejected elsewhere. Rehberg and Heeren were joined in their criticism by Ernst Brandes, another former student from Göttingen, Heeren's brother-in-law and Rehberg's colleague in Hanover. Inspired by Edmund Burke's critical "Reflections on the Revolution in France" (1790), Brandes (1808, 57) published a book similar to Rehberg's about the political situation in Germany, in which he too warned against the tendency to spread the "spirit of military mechanization" to the state administration. He called Prussia "a machine state" in which only the "skill" would count, but not "the whole person" (58). For him "the numerical statisticians," who were condemned to made "state tables" in the service of their governments, originated "from the slime of the machine-creature" (64). Implicit in this criticism was Brandes's and Rehberg's rejection of the French/Prussian model of administration, which they were forced to implement in Hanover during Napoleon's occupation.

In these attacks, the state—once in the hand of rational statisticians—figured as a machine. For Heeren ([Heeren] 1807, 1302) the state was something "more noble than a machine." He conceptualized the state as a complex, indivisible, and living object, and he believed its scientific representations should reflect such properties. In Germany at the turn of the nineteenth century, the heretofore positively charged metaphor of a machine began to have negative connotations, mainly attributed to it by representatives of the Romantic Movement. The metaphor was now widely used to indicate threats to the involvement and individuality of mankind. The state, which ought to function for the common wealth, began to appear a dangerous concoction with advantages for few (Sauer 1983). While the desirable state was envisioned using organic metaphors, its material and empirical descriptions were rejected as mechanistic reductions.

Even before the collapse of Prussia in 1806, the Romantics commonly compared its state political system to a machine. After 1806 the harshest criticism came from Adam Müller, scholar and frequenter of romantic circles, who developed an organic idea of the state in his Dresden lectures for officials and diplomats in 1808–9. The lectures were published as *Elemente der Staatskunst* and contributed to a practice of governing the state that he still conceived of as more an art than a science. His criticism of state rationalism was entwined with his criticism of the new manufacturing system and Adam Smith's concept of freedom (Hartung 1988; Hutter 1994). He tried to define the state in a new and positive way. For Müller (1809, 51) the state was not just "a manufacture"; it was also the "inner connection between the entire physical and spiritual wealth of the entire inner and outer life of a nation, . . . a great energetic, endlessly moving, and living entirety."

The Romantics imagined the state as a holistic being. To use numbers and tables as instruments to analyze it would mean first murdering its inhabitants and then dissecting them with a scalpel. Müller (51) believed that "from this entirety, science cannot provide a dead or stagnant picture" because "death cannot depict life, as stillness cannot depict motion." Embracing the rationalistic and analytic notions of the natural sciences, Müller would have—without being explicit about statistics—rejected Crome's numerical representations because they were depictions of a dead state—or to be more precise, of a state whose history had been artificially frozen.

Closely related to the negative image of the modern bureaucratic state as a machine was the idea that the table statisticians would make the study of the state a subordinated labor practice. Heeren ([Heeren 1807, 1300–1301) painted a picture of a master-servant interdependence between the statisticians and their political employers, imagining thus: "The former [the statisticians] teach the latter [the politicians] to make tables: and so the philosophers' stone was found! Now one could provide everything in numbers: Now all is so clear! One could boast of putting the entire state on one map sheet!" This was not seen as a relationship between equal partners. Brandes (1808) called them *Tabellenknechte*, literally translated as "table servants," denoting the statisticians' subordination to the governing ruler. Heeren (1807, 1301) too condemned them as "table makers" (*Tabellenmacher*) or "common statisticians" (*Gemeine Statistiker*), denoting their lower status in the profession, and he characterized their work as full of "pitiful and miserable trivialities." These notions relegated the statisticians to the same level as craftsmen, and the attack itself can be interpreted as an attempt to expel them from the "high kingdom" of science. As the Göttingian philosopher August Ferdinand Lueder (1812, 47) some years later presented the conflict, the whole purpose of the attacks was to make the scholarly world believe that one should distinguish the "high" and "noble" statisticians from the "common" and "low."

The Response

How the attacked statisticians—who had never been called by their real name and profession—reacted has not been reported in sources familiar to historians of statistics. Crome's and Krug's work provides us with some incidents that could be read as responses to the debate and allows us to draw some preliminary conclusions.

As editor of the journal *Germanien. Eine Zeitschrift für Staats-Recht, Politik und Statistik in Deutschland*, Crome clarified his position in the debate, explaining that "location, fertility, culture, education, and the nation's occupations, as well as the government and the administrations," had to be considered. But he gives "the surface area and the number of the population" more credit as basic variables ([Crome] 1811, 154). For Crome the population figure was more meaningful than other numbers. In his view the character and abilities of the citizens were not overlooked, even if not named in the tables, because he evaluated these categories indirectly by reflecting on the ratio of people to geographic area. He did not doubt the measurability of the state and its society. In his statistical approach, he assumed that the data he gathered and combined, allowed him to draw conclusions on state administration and policy. His opponents did not share his presuppositions about quantification in this realm because they conceptualized the state differently than he did.

For Crome this criticism was a purely philosophical reflection about how the state should exist ideally and not a contribution to realistic description. He supposed the table opponents wished to roll back efforts to enlighten the public. They would, he claimed, "reason about the so-called physiognomy of a country according to their fantasies" ([Crome] 1811, 154). In Crome's view, romantic enthusiasm was not compatible with scientific thought. The image of the "physiognomy of a country" was a popular notion of the time. In one of his reviews, Heeren demanded the drawing of "a clear idea of the physiognomy of each country" by the statisticians ([Heeren] 1806, 835). But while Crome seems to be skeptical of the physiognomic method of deriving inner dispositions from external appearances, Heeren seems to have been more optimistic. Crome used the notion of "physiognomy" to characterize a superficial and speculative way of gaining knowledge. Heeren might have seen in this method a technique for recognizing a familiar type by looking at the state descriptions from a distance. Such a distance was seen as necessary to prevent the observer from getting lost in the details.

The implicit assumption of precision that had been usually attributed to the publication of numbers was another issue that was being debated. It contributed to the mutual accusation that participants in the debate were not behaving as scientists should. Brandes (1808, 65) saw "meaningful imprecision in the details" because none of the "table laborers are able to deliver an approximation of true figures." Crome thought these objections "of little importance" as long as he could classify his opponents as "ignorant laymen" or "superficial and indolent statisticians" ([Crome] 1811, 154). In fact, he could deny his opponents' competence to judge statistical works because neither Heeren, Brandes, nor Rehberg were active in the field themselves—rather, they were merely reflecting on the consequences such methods would have for the state administration and for the training of state officials at the university.

The question of who was an amateur and who was an expert was highly debated. Leopold Krug, who was in the eyes of his Prussian government a layman because he lacked an academic education, was nevertheless the leading expert in the field (Hacking 1990, 30–32). Therefore it is not surprising that he judged his own table work by scientific standards: "If one means, as some have—that the circulation in a state and the yearly revenue of a nation cannot be reckoned in and determined by numbers, then one has confessed one's own weakness, but not the weakness of science. If the results were incorrect, there is no reason to doubt the method" (Krug 1805, vii–viii). Like Crome he believed that measurements in the realm of social science are possible and necessary, claiming, "Computations bring us closer to certainty" (vii–viii).

In his defense of numerical statistics, Crome also championed the public discourse on statistical information. Attacks on numerical statistics came from such countries, he wrote, "where certain aristocrats comfortably rule and would happily see that no statistical facts should be made known regarding their beloved states" ([Crome] 1811, 154). He assumed that critics there desired to restore conservative regulation (154). Here he sided with those who supported the transparency of state affairs and who saw in public numbers a means to oppose injustice and despotism. The supporters of the late Enlightenment movement in central Europe made statistics a catchword for the freedom of the citizen. Schlözer, for instance, asserted that despotism and statistics were mutually exclusive. Statistics works like a "barometer of civic freedom," he claimed (1804, 51–52). Statistics was for him the "empirical-sociological arm of a critical public" and an efficient tool for controlling the work of the government (Saage 1987, 52). Because of his temporary freedom from censorship he lectured on how to read and interpret statistical news and attacked the unenlightened behavior of certain rulers. As we know from his correspondence, he was much criticized for this practice, not least of all by his own colleagues in Göttingen. In 1774, as the political situation became unbearable even for his own government, his freedom from censorship was revoked (Frensdorf 1909, 77–80).

Crome became familiar with the practice of collecting and evaluating statistical news in the *Philanthropin*, where he supervised the students' reading of newspapers. Despite the fragile political situation in central Europe around 1800, Crome was certain that he would be on the prevailing side by projecting: "These gentlemen should consider that no amount of exertion can impede the spirit of the age and that it is no longer possible, in well governed states, to keep secrets from statistical data" ([Crome] 1811, 154). As Schlözer had, Crome saw in public numbers a proof of an enlightened government. His journal was explicitly designed to comment on some of these political reforms that certain German states had undertaken under the protection of Napoleon.

Conclusion

The debate over how reliable and sensible quantification was in this realm of knowledge took place in a turbulent political period in central Europe in which the notion of the state, together with the notion of statistics, underwent profound change. The controversy revealed that a new understanding of the state as effective bureaucratic machinery was underway. We know how the story went: in the peace after Napoleon's occupation, the European governments were enthusiastic about numerical figures and understood their published statistical accounts as representations of their actions (see Porter's essay in this volume). During that time, the older understanding of the state population was replaced by a notion of the nation as a community of citizens. Originally the empirical part of the sciences of governing and deeply connected to the old state, statistics finally became a social science by building itself around a conception of the population as nation. In addition, the population measurement itself became the major focus of nineteenth-century statistics (Porter 1986, part 1; Hacking 1990; Nikolow 1994). Crome had already related his measurement of the state exclusively to the estimation of the population figure. In the newer statistical treatments, the population figure was used to evaluate other data and was therefore prominent in representations of the state. This mechanistic approach therefore came to be criticized again by Romantics as portraying humans simply in terms of numbers.

The later history of measurement tells us that this conflict was never actually completely resolved. Certain actors reanimated it in certain moments of time. As Bradley Bateman's essay (this volume) demonstrates, almost one hundred years later a similar situation occurred. Social researchers then supported the ambitions of the Religion Forward Movement to produce more holistic and moral accounts of the society as an alternative to the more reductive approach to quantification later favored by academic social scientists and economists. Similarly the questions associated with the use of measurement applications for the management of the resources of empires in the nineteenth century (see also Sandra Peart's essay in this volume) were not fully resolved with the establishment of national institutions for measurement (see the articles by Martin Kohli and Flavio Comim in this volume). In practice the problems associated with the attempt to quantify resources for a whole society were negotiated by a societal consensus to trust numbers as symbols of an impartial knowledge produced by a community of professional experts (Porter 1995). As this episode on statistical representations shows, such a consensus was not yet established in central Europe around 1800, but liberal political thinkers like Crome and Krug were already thinking along these lines.

References

Achenwall, Gottfried. 1752. *Staatsverfassung der Europäischen Reiche und Grundrisse*. 2d ed. Göttingen: Johann Wilhelm Schmidt.

Bensaude-Vincent, Bernadette. 1992. The Balance: Between Chemistry and Politics. *The Eighteenth Century* 33.3:217–37.

Bleek, Wilhelm. 1972. *Von der Kameralausbildung zum Juristenprivileg. Studium, Prüfung und Ausbildung der höheren Beamten des allgemeinen Verwaltungsdienstes in Deutschland im 18. und 19. Jahrhundert*. Berlin: Colloquium Verlag.

Bödecker, Hans Erich. 1990. System und Entwicklung der Staatswissenschaften im 18. Jahrhundert. In *Die Wissenschaftskultur der Aufklärung*, edited by Reinhard Mocek. Halle, Germany: Wissenschaftliche Beiträge der Martin-Luther-Universität 18, A 123, 88–105.

Bourget, Marie-Noelle. 1988. *Déchiffrer la France. La Statistique Départementale à l' époche napoléonienne.* Paris: Éditions des Archives Contemporaines.

Brandes, Ernst. 1808. *Betrachtungen über den Zeitgeist in Deutschland in den letzten Decennien des vorigen Jahrhunderts.* Hanover, Germany: Gebrüder Hahn.

Brian, Eric. 1994. *La mesure de l'etat. Administrateurs et géomètres au XVIIIe siècle.* Paris: Albin Michel.

Büsching, Anton Friedrich. [1754] 1770. *Neue Erdbeschreibung.* Part 1. 6th ed. Hamburg: Johann Carl Bohn.

Crome, August Friedrich Wilhelm. n.d. *Verhältniskarte von Europa, welcher den Flächen-Inhalt und die Volksmenge der saemtlichen Europaeischen Staaten und Laender enthaelt.*

———. 1785. *Ueber die Größe und Bevölkerung der sämtlichen Europäischen Staaten. Ein Beytrag zur Kenntnis der Staatenverhältnisse und zur Erklärung der neuen Größen-Karte von Europa.* Leipzig: Weygandsche Buchhandlung.

———. 1792. *Ueber die Kulturverhältnisse der Europäischen Staaten, ein Versuch mittels Größe und Bevölkerung, den Grad der Kultur der Länder Europas zu bestimmen.* Leipzig: Weygandsche Buchhandlung.

———. 1805. *Europens Produkte mit einer neuen Produkten-Karte von Europa.* 4th ed. Tübingen, Germany: J. G. Cotta'sche Buchhandlung.

[———]. 1811. Review of *Vergleichende Übersicht des Areals und der Volksmenge, der Cessionen und Acquisitionen; des österreichischen Kaiserstaates, in den letzteren Jahren. Germanien* 4:153–60.

———. 1818. *Allgemeine Uebersicht der Staatskräfte von den sämtlichen europäischen Reichen und Ländern, mit einer Verhältniskarte von Europa, zur Uebersicht und Vergleichung des Flächen-Raumes, der Bevölkerung, der Staats-Einkünfte und der bewaffneten Macht.* Leipzig: Gerhard Fleischer dem Jüngeren.

———. 1819. *A Map of the Statistical Relations of Europe Serving as a View and Comparison of the Extent of Surface, Population, and Other Public Revenue of All States of Europe.* London: Engraved under the direction of A. Arrowsmith.

———. 1820–25. *Geographisch-statistische Darstellung der Staatskräfte von den sämtlichen, zum deutschen Staatenbunde gehörigen Ländern.* 2 vols. Leipzig: Gerhard Fleischer.

———. 1833. *Selbstbiographie. Ein Beitrag zu den gelehrten und politischen Memoiren des vorigen und gegenwärtigen Jahrhunderts.* Stuttgart: J. B. Metzler'sche Buchhandlung.

Frensdorf, F. 1909. Von und über Schlözer. *Abhandlungen der Königlichen Akademie der Wissenschaften zu Göttingen. Phil.-Hist. Klasse* 11.4.

Hacking, Ian. 1990. *Taming of Chance.* Cambridge: Cambridge University Press.

Hartung, Günter. 1988. Maschinen und Maschinenwesen aus Sicht der deutschen Romantiker. In *Willkommen und Abschied der Maschinen. Literatur und Technik. Bestandsaufnahme eines Themas*, edited by Erhard Schütz, 42–54. Essen, Germany: Klartext.

[Heeren, Ludwig Arnold]. 1806. Review of *Statistik der Europäischen Staaten*, bearbeitet von Conrad Mannert, and of *Statistik des Deutschen Reiches*, von Conrad Mannert. *Göttingische Gelehrte Anzeigen* 2.84:833–40.

————. 1807. Review of *Ueber die Staatsverwaltung Deutscher Länder, und die Dienerschaft der Regenten*, von Wilhelm Rehberg. *Göttingische Gelehrte Anzeigen* 2.131:1298–1308.

Hoffmann, Peter. 2000. *Anton Friedrich Büsching (1724–1793). Ein Leben im Zeitalter der Aufklärung*. Berlin: Berlin Verlag Arno Spitz.

Hutter, Michael. 1994. Organism as a Metaphor in German Economic Thought. In *Natural Images in Economic Thought: "Markets Read in Tooth and Claw,"* edited by Philip Mirowski, 289–321. Cambridge: Cambridge University Press.

Johanisson, Karin. 1990. Society in Numbers: The Debate over Quantification in 18th-Century Political Economy. In *The Quantifying Spirit in the Eighteenth Century*, edited by John L. Heilbron, Tore Frängsmyr, and Robin E. Rider, 343–61. Berkeley: University of California Press.

Justi, Johann Heinrich Gottlob von. 1755. *Staatswirthschaft*. Vol. 1. Leipzig: Bernhard Christoph Breitkopf.

Kern, Horst. 1987. Schlözers Bedeutung für die Methodologie der empirischen Sozialforschung. In *Anfänge Göttinger Sozialwissenschaft. Methoden, Inhalte und soziale Prozesse im 18. und 20. Jahrhundert*, edited by Hans Georg Herrlitz and Horst Kern, 55–71. Göttingen: Vandenhoeck and Ruprecht.

Kirmes, Alfred. 1908. *August Friedrich Wilhelm Crome. Ein Beitrag zur Geschichte der deutschen Nationalökonomie*. Bern, Switzerland: Buchdruckerei Gustav Grunau.

Klippel, Diethelm. 1994. Johann August Schlettwein and the Economic Faculty at the University of Gießen. *History of Political Thought* 15.2:203–27.

Koselleck, Reinhard, Werner Conze, Hans Boldt, and Diethelm Klippel. 1990. Staat und Souveränität. In vol. 6 of *Geschichtliche Grundbegriffe*, edited by Otto Brunner, Werner Conze, and Reinhardt Koselleck, 1–154. Stuttgart: Klett-Cotta.

Krug, Leopold. 1805. *Betrachtungen über den National-Reichtum des preußischen Staats und über den Wohlstand seiner Bewohner*. 2 vols. Berlin: Johann Friedrich Unger.

Lazarsfeld, Paul L. 1961. Notes on the History of Quantification in Sociology. Trends, Sources, and Problems. *Isis* 52:277–333.

Lenz, Friedrich. 1957. Die Wirtschaftswissenschaften in Gießen. Ein Beitrag zur Geschichte der politischen Ökonomie. In *Ludwigs-Uni. Justus Liebig-Hochschule 1607–1957. Festschrift zur 350-Jahrfeier*, 375–96. Gießen: Justus Liebig Hochschule.

Lindenfeld, David F. 1997. *The Practical Imagination: The German Sciences of State in the Nineteenth Century.* Chicago: University of Chicago Press.

Lueder, August Ferdinand. 1812. *Kritik der Statistik und Politik nebst einer Begründung der politischen Philosophie.* Göttingen: Vandenhoeck und Ruprecht.

Lutz, Gerhard. 1980. Geographie und Statistik im 18. Jahrhundert. Zur Neugliederung und Inhalten von "Fächern" im Bereich der historischen Wissenschaften. In *Statistik und Staatsbeschreibung in der Neuzeit vormehmlich im 16.–18. Jahrhundert,* edited by Mohammed Rassem and Justin Stagl, 249–62. Paderborn, Germany: Ferdinand Schöningh.

Marino, Luigi. 1995. *Praeceptores Germaniae. Göttingen 1770–1820.* Göttingen: Vandenhoeck and Ruprecht.

Müller, Adam Heinrich. 1809. *Die Elemente der Staatskunst.* Vol. 1. Berlin: J. D. Sander.

Nikolow, Sybilla. 1994. Statistiker und Statistik. Zur Genese der statistischen Disziplin in Deutschland zwischen dem 18. und 20. Jahrhundert. Ph.D. diss. Technische Universität Dresden.

———. 1999. Die Versinnlichung der Staatskräfte. Statistische Karten um 1800. *Traverse. Zeitschrift für Geschichte. Revue d'Histoire* 6.3:63–82.

Playfair, William. 1801. *Statistical Breviary Shewing on a Principle Entirely New, the Resources of Every State and Kingdom in Europe.* London: T. Bensley.

Plewe, E. 1957. Anton Friedrich Büsching. *Herman Lautensach-Festschrift. Stuttgarter Geographische Studien* 69:107–20.

Porter, Theodore M. 1986. *The Rise of Statistical Thinking, 1820–1900.* Princeton, N.J.: Princeton University Press.

———. 1987. Lawless Society: Social Science and the Reinterpretation of Statistics in Germany, 1850–1880. In vol. 1 of *The Probabilistic Revolution,* edited by Lorenz Krüger, Lorraine J. Daston, and Michael Heidelberger, 351–75. Cambridge, Mass.: MIT Press.

———. 1995. *Trust in Numbers: The Pursuit of Objectivity in Science and Public Life.* Princeton, N.J.: Princeton University Press.

Rassem, Mohammed. 1980. Stichproben aus dem Wortfeld der alten Statistik. In *Statistik und Staatsbeschreibung in der Neuzeit vornehmlich im 16.–18. Jahrhundert,* edited by Mohammed Rassem and Justin Stagl, 17–31. Paderborn, Germany: Ferdinand Schöningh.

Rehberg, Wilhelm. 1807. *Ueber die Staatsverwaltung deutscher Länder und die Dienerschaft der Regenten.* Hannover, Germany: Gebrüder Hahn.

Revel, Jacques. 1991. Knowledge of the Territory. *Science in Context* 4:133–61.

Robinson, Arthur H. 1982. *Thematic Mapping in the History of Cartography.* Chicago: University of Chicago Press.

Roscher, Wilhelm. 1874. *Geschichte der National-Oekonomik in Deutschland.* München: R. Oldenburg.

Royston, Erica. 1956. A Note on the History of the Graphical Representation of Data. *Biometrica* 43:241–47.

Saage, Richard. 1987. August Ludwig Schlözer als politischer Theoretiker. In *Anfänge Göttinger Sozialwissenschaft*, edited by Hans Georg Herrlitz and Horst Kern, 13–54. Göttingen: Vandenhoeck and Ruprecht.

Sauer, Liselotte. 1983. *Marionetten, Maschinen, Automaten. Der künstliche Mensch in der deutschen und englischen Romantik*. Bonn: Bouvier.

Schlözer, August Ludwig. 1804. *Theorie der Statistik, nebst Ideen über das Studium der Politik überhaupt*. Göttingen: Vandenhoek und Ruprecht.

Seifert, Arno. 1980. Staatenkunde—eine neue Disziplin und ihr wissenschaftstheoretischer Ort. In *Statistik und Staatsbeschreibung in der Neuzeit vormehmlich im 16.–18. Jahrhundert*, edited by Mohammed Rassem and Justin Stagl, 217–44. Paderborn, Germany: Ferdinand Schöningh.

Stagl, Justin. 1995. *A History of Curiosity: The Theory of Travel, 1550–1800*. Chur, Switzerland: Harwood.

Stollberg-Rilinger, Barbara. 1986. *Der Staat als Maschine: Zur politischen Methaphorik des absoluten Fürstenstaates*. Berlin: Duncker & Humblot.

Tauscher, Anton. 1956. Kameralismus. In vol. 5 of *Handwörterbuch der Sozialwissenschaften*, edited by Erwin von Beckerath, 463–67. Stuttgart: Fischer.

Treue, Wilhelm. 1951. Adam Smith in Deutschland. Zum Problem des "Politischen Professors" zwischen 1776 und 1810. In *Deutschland und Europa. Historische Studien zur Völker- und Staatenordnung des Abendlandes*, edited by Werner Conze, 191–233. Düsseldorf: Droste.

Tribe, Keith. 1988. *Governing Economy: The Reformation of German Economic Discourse 1750–1840*. Cambridge: Cambridge University Press.

———. 1998. Natural Law and the Origins of Nationalökonomie: L. H. von Jakob. In *The Rise of the Social Sciences and the Formation of Modernity: Conceptual Change in Context, 1750–1850*, edited by Johan Heilbron, Lars Magnusson, and Björn Wittrock, 189–205. Dordrecht: Kluwer Academic Publishers.

Tufte, Edward R. 1982. *The Visual Display of Quantitative Information*. Cheshire, Connecticut: Graphic Press.

Wagener, Werner. 1936. Die Standes- und Berufserziehung in der Pädagogik der Philanthropisten. Ph.D. diss., Handelshochschule Leipzig. Borna-Leipzig: Robert Noske.

Wakefield, André R. 1999. The Apostles of Good Policy: Science, Cameralism, and the Culture of Administration in Central Europe, 1656–1800. 2 vols. Ph.D. diss., University of Chicago.

Wise, Norton. 1993. Mediations: Enlightenment Balancing Acts, or the Technologies of Rationalism. In *World Chances: Thomas Kuhn and the Nature of Sciences*, edited by Paul Horwich, 207–56. Cambridge, Mass.: MIT Press.

Zelger, Renate. 1953. Der Historisch Politische Briefwechsel und die Staatsanzeigen August Ludwig v. Schlözers als Zeitschrift und Zeitbild. Ph.D. diss., Ludwigs-Maximilians-Universität München.

Make a Righteous Number: Social Surveys, the Men and Religion Forward Movement, and Quantification in American Economics

Bradley W. Bateman

As Theodore Porter suggests in the introductory essay to this volume, one of the impulses that first drove people to measure economic phenomena was an ethical impulse to understand rapidly evolving modern societies. But whereas Porter's concern is largely with European economists, such as the table statisticians that Sybilla Nikolow (this volume) describes in her essay, a similar story might also be told in American economics· it was not primarily a desire to imitate natural scientists that led early American economists to attempt the measurement of social phenomena, but rather a moral curiosity to more fully understand the world unfolding around them.

A prime example of this can be seen if we look at the work encouraged by Richard T. Ely, widely known as the father of American economics for his role in founding the American Economic Association. Together with a generation of men that included Henry Carter Adams, Simon Nelson Patten, and E. A. Ross, Ely helped to found not only

Correspondence may be addressed to Bradley W. Bateman, Department of Economics, Grinnell College, Grinnell, Iowa 50112. I would like to thank the Lilly Foundation for its support during the writing of this essay. I thank Stanley Hauerwas, Michael Lienesch, and Steve Leonard for questions and suggestions that helped me while drafting the essay. Ruth Grant, Mary Morgan, Victoria Brown, and Michael Lienesch each read early drafts of the essay and saved me from embarrassing errors. Derek Brown, Thomas Christiano, Stanley Hauerwas, Abe Hirsch, Sam Kerstein, Judy Klein, Robert Moats Miller, Malcolm Rutherford, Shauna Saunders, Chris Sellers, Nancy Tomes, Einar Thomassen, and an anonymous referee also read earlier drafts and provided me with helpful comments. Karen Carroll gave me immeasurable help by copyediting several early drafts of the essay. Any remaining errors are mine alone.

the American Economic Association (AEA), but the historical school of American economics as well. All of these men, and most of the others who helped found the AEA, were ardent advocates of a brand of liberal Protestantism known as the Social Gospel. So intense was their ethical impulse that they were known to their contemporaries more often as the "ethical economists" than they were as "historical economists."

The purpose of this essay is to tell a multilayered story about one of the most important types of measurement with which the ethical economists were involved—the social survey. In order to explain the forces that drove the social survey to prominence and made it such an important part of the ethical economists' work, the essay is built as a series of overlapping explanations of four intertwined worlds: the social survey movement, American Protestantism, Progressive politics, and American social science. These intertwined worlds were not static, however, and over the first two decades of the twentieth century each underwent significant changes. Thus as we move through them, we will see how the social survey came to be seen very differently during and after the Progressive Era.

The essay concludes with a reflection on the particular way that the forces that swept the social survey off the stage of American social science shaped the transition from historical economics to Institutionalism.

At the Center: The Men and Religion Forward Movement

Our story begins in an unlikely place: the Men and Religion Forward Movement of 1911–12, which was at that time the largest Protestant evangelization effort ever undertaken in the history of the United States. Between its kickoff on Sunday, 24 September 1911, and its conclusion on Sunday, 28 April 1912, the Movement presented over nine thousand addresses to 1.5 million men in the seventy-six largest cities of the United States. A "Committee of 100" men in each community followed a template designed by the Movement's founders and organized an eight-day event for the community. Many high profile men and women were associated with the Movement and appeared on platforms around the country to speak: Washington Gladden, Walter Rauschenbusch, Jane Addams, and William Jennings Bryan. The revival was designed to last only a few months, at which time the Movement would dissolve and men who had been evangelized were to work within their local churches to further the Movement's goal of the increased participation of men and boys in church life.[1]

The Movement's leaders, a group called the Committee of 97, worked for sixteen months to prepare for the revival, and it was organized to operate with impressive bureaucratic efficiency. In part this was because the man who worked most to organize the Movement, Fred B. Smith, was already a highly successful administrator in the Young Men's Christian Association (YMCA); in part it was because prominent businessmen like J. P. Morgan, Cyrus McCormick, John D. Rockefeller, Jr., and John Wanamaker played leading parts in organizing and funding the Movement (Gorrell 1988, 156). Each city's campaign was to consist of eleven committees, each of which had a well-defined role to play in preparing for and running the eight-day event.

It was by no means unusual for a revival to be well organized and, in fact, revivals by the end of the nineteenth century were so well organized that people already referred to the "machinery" of the revival (McLoughlin 1959). But the Men and Religion Forward Movement had special features that no previous revival had employed.[2] One of these was an explicit effort to use the press as a means of promoting the event. The Committee of 100 in each city was to have a Publicity Committee, whose work was of "the utmost importance," but whose duties were "not to be limited to advertising" (Men and Religion Forward Movement 1911, 10). Thus, while the Committee was to prepare traditional advertising for such venues as laundry lists, hotel menus, billboards, streetcars, and stationery, it was also to "furnish varied and live copy" (10–11) each week to the local newspapers to insure maximal exposure for the Movement. As the actual event approached, the articles fed to the press were to increase and the Committee was to arrange for daily press coverage during the eight days of the revival.

As it turned out, however, the content of those press releases was to include not only announcements of the speakers and revivalists to be

1. Just as there are many ways to view the rise of measurement in the social sciences, there are many ways to view the Men and Religion Forward Movement. Two of the interesting ways to consider it, but which are not considered in this essay, are from the perspective of women's studies and in comparison to the contemporary Promise Keeper's movement. For a treatment from the point of view of women's studies, see Bederman 1989. For a comparison to the Promise Keeper's movement, see Allen 2000.

2. Gail Bederman (1989, 441) says that the leaders took the drive for efficiency and bureaucracy to "hitherto unknown lengths, organizing the entire revival like an up-to-date, rationalized corporation."

involved, but also social statistics about the community in which the event was to take place. In each of the seventy-six cities in which an eight-day event was held, a large-scale effort was undertaken to measure the "social and religious statistics" of the city. This social survey was the responsibility of the Social Service Committee of each of the Committees of 100, and the directions for carrying it out involved the most detailed instructions in the Movement's *Program of Works*, the manual published to lay out the directions for executing the revival in each city. Each city was to have an individual who coordinated the social survey, which was to be undertaken by several means. For example, information from the census, from police records, and from church rolls was to be collected (see fig. 1). But men in each church were also to survey the neighborhoods around their churches to collect information, among other things, about the residents, the number of saloons, the number of motion picture theatres, the number of dance halls, and the number of playgrounds.[3] All of this information was then to be channeled through the Publicity Committee to the press to impress upon the men and boys of the city the need for Christian social service.[4]

This part of the Movement's strategy turned out to be its most successful; many more men turned out for the social service lectures and programs than they did for the traditional evangelism or Bible study. The original organizers of the Movement had not even planned to have a social service component in the Movement, and once they were persuaded to include it, they believed that it would only be a "minor feature" (Smith 1936, 97).[5] There are many ways to explain this popularity, as we will discuss below, but the important point here is that the survey work had very high visibility and that it was seen as central to the entire Men and Religion Forward Movement.[6]

3. See Stelzle 1912 and Cocks 1912 for information on the full range of statistics that were collected in the local surveys.

4. The information from the seventy-six surveyed cities was also compiled and published by Charles Stelzle, the Movement's Dean of Social Service, in *American Social and Religious Conditions* (1912).

5. There are two excellent, first-hand sources on the uncertain dynamics of the Social Gospelers within the Men and Religion Forward Movement: Stelzle 1926, 154 and Smith 1936, 97.

6. Although it is not central to the argument at this point, it is also worth noting that the social service program of the Movement led to considerable constructive action, including campaigns against prostitution and dance halls, the construction of playgrounds, and the exposure of public officials involved in "social vice."

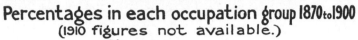

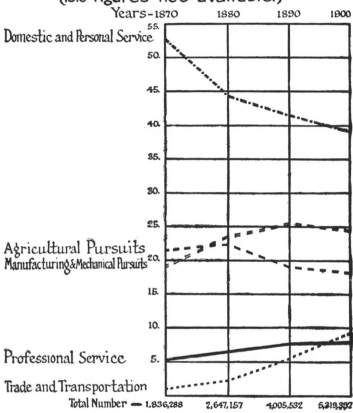

NOTE.—Figures in chart refer only to women and girls over ten years of age.

Figure 1   This graph from Stelzle 1912, 86, shows the way in which the information collected from the social surveys of the Men and Religion Forward Movement was presented to the public

To fully understand this high public profile, however, requires seeing the Men and Religion Forward Movement and the use of social surveys in several different contexts. Four of these contexts—the social survey movement, American Protestantism, Progressive politics, and American social science—are separate but overlapping circles, each of which illuminates the role of the social survey in the Men and Religion Forward Movement as well as filling in a larger picture of the trajectory of measurement in the early twentieth-century American social sciences.

The First Circle: The Social Survey Movement

When the leaders of the Men and Religion Forward Movement settled on conducting a survey in each of the seventy-six cities in which they were to stage a revival, they were drawing on an idea in very good currency that had recently been imported from late Victorian England. Although statistical societies had become common in the first half of the nineteenth century in England, the social survey movement began there in 1886 when the wealthy ship owner Charles Booth responded to the "incendiary" claim, made by the Marxist Social Democratic Federation in London, that one quarter of the working class in London lived in dire poverty.[7] Booth had long attended meetings at Toynbee Hall and Oxford House and was well acquainted with settlement house workers, but his politics were conservative and he wanted to make an "objective, scientific investigation" (Zimbalist 1977, 74) to determine the true state of the working class. He was to spend seventeen years on his study and publish seventeen volumes between 1889 and 1903 under the title *Life and Labour of the People in London*. He spent a fair part of his fortune on the survey, employing hundreds of people to help him compile a massive empirical account of how the working people of London actually lived. The process transformed Booth, who discovered that the correct figure for those living in dire poverty was actually closer to one third, but it also ignited a movement to document social conditions. Before Booth had finished his widely publicized project, B. Seebohm Rowntree was to publish his canvass of the working-class districts of York, *Poverty: A Study of Town Life* (1901). The first major American social survey, however, was *Hull House Maps and Papers* (1895), undertaken by Florence Kelley, Jane Addams, and the residents of Hull House and published by Richard T. Ely in his series *Library of Economics and Politics*.[8]

7. Quoted in Zimbalist 1977, 74. Theodore Porter (1986, 30–39) provides the best short history of the rise of the "private statistical societies" in Britain.

8. See Sklar 1991 on Ely's role in the final production of the Hull House volume.

In the United States, the social survey movement grew quickly, in part because it represented a constructive move in an old but sterile debate over poverty. After the Civil War, American concern with poverty had centered largely around a debate on the causes of poverty. Much of this debate was public, such as the commonly repeated refrain of the temperance advocates that poverty was the result of alcohol consumption or Henry George's contention that poverty was the result of the concentration of land ownership. But it was also an academic debate between the Social Darwinists and classical economists, on the one hand, who argued that poverty was not subject to social amelioration, and the advocates of the new "scientific charity" such as the Stanford economist Amos Griswold Warner, on the other.[9] Against this contentious backdrop, efforts to measure the actual extent and impact of poverty seemed like a reasonable step forward.

The real arrival of the social survey movement in America occurred with the famed Pittsburgh Survey that was launched in 1907. The Pittsburgh Survey was undertaken as a project of the new magazine *Charities and the Commons*, which had been created in 1905 through the merger of *Charities*, the magazine of the New York Charity Organization Society, and *The Commons*, the magazine of the Chicago settlement house movement, edited by Graham Taylor.[10] After the new magazine published a piece on slum conditions in Washington, D.C., in 1906, a group of people from Pittsburgh approached the magazine with a request for a social survey of their city. The Russell Sage Foundation, established in 1907, provided $27,000 for the conducting of the survey and another $20,000 for its publication.[11] The Pittsburgh Survey lasted for two years and resulted in six books.[12]

The Pittsburgh Survey also provided an important link between American economics and the social survey movement. One of the high profile advisers to the Survey was John R. Commons, who had been Ely's graduate student in the 1880s at Johns Hopkins and who had joined Ely on the faculty of the University of Wisconsin in 1904. Commons employed

9. For a history of this debate, see Zimbalist 1977. For a history of the rise of "scientific charity," see Lubove 1965. Interestingly, Amos Griswold Warner's classic *American Charities* (1894) appeared in the same series as *Hull House Maps* (*Library of Economics and Politics*, edited by Richard T. Ely).

10. Both Richard T. Ely and John R. Commons had been contributors to *The Commons*. See Chambers 1971, 26.

11. For the most complete history of the Pittsburgh Survey, see Chambers 1971.

12. A list of these books can be found in Zimbalist 1977, 124–25.

several of his graduate students to work on the Survey and he trained a whole cadre of social surveying economists in his work on later surveys.[13]

One of the books that resulted from the Survey, Crystal Eastman's *Work Accidents and the Law* (1910), nicely illustrates the nature of contemporary quantitative work as well as the reform nature of the genre. Eastman's research was exhaustive. She recorded the details of every man injured, maimed, or killed in the Pittsburgh steel industry between 1 July 1906 and 30 June 1907. She recorded their salaries, the facts of their family life, the death benefits paid out to their family (if any), and, as backdrop to all of this, she included detailed descriptions of the work the men in steel mills did, including descriptions of the machinery they worked on (with photographs), descriptions of the ethnic makeup of the steelworkers' communities, and descriptions of the railroads and coal mines involved in the local industry. All of this information was presented in dramatic fashion, beginning with a frontispiece, the "Death Calendar in Industry for Allegheny County," which showed a red cross for each of the 526 industrial deaths during the year marked on a black and white calendar. This was followed by pie charts showing that more than 50 percent of the families of men killed in accidents received less than $100 in death benefits and that fewer than 25 percent received $500 or more. Eastman accompanied the tables showing the amounts paid out (if any) for loss of limbs and eyes with a photograph of Meunier's statue "The Puddler," with the ranges for each limb (e.g., loss of a leg, $0–225) drawn into the photograph with arrows (see fig. 2). All this information was meant to shock, and it did. So it only seemed natural that the final chapter of the book, "Legislation," should unself-consciously begin, "On the facts set forth, legislative interference is warranted, and the question becomes, How shall we legislate? To which question there are, speaking in most general terms, two answers offered" (Eastman 1910, 207).

These six books were not the only result of the Pittsburgh Survey, however. Another outcome was that the editor of *Charities and the Commons*, Paul U. Kellogg, decided to change the name of the magazine to the *Survey* in 1909. In this guise the magazine became the national focus for the social survey movement and a leading voice in the Progressive

---

13. Steven R. Cohen (1991) discusses the group of social surveying economists who trained under Commons.

movement.[14] In 1911, when the Men and Religion Forward Movement's *Program of Work* was published, it included this suggestion to the men in each of the seventy-six cities responsible for conducting the social surveys, "Read carefully during the period of preparation *The Survey*, the official weekly periodical of the Charity Organization Society, 105 East 22nd Street, New York, with whose publishers special cooperative arrangements have been made" (Men and Religion Forward Movement 1911, 37).[15]

The Second Circle: American Protestantism

These arrangements between the Men and Religion Forward Movement and the *Survey* would not have surprised anyone at the time. Many of the people who had been instrumental in both *Charities* and *The Commons* were explicitly defined in the public eye as Christians, and one of the steadiest voices in the stream of criticism of American industrialism during the previous twenty years had been the advocates of the Social Gospel.[16] Thus the tone of moral and social reform in the social survey movement was very much part and parcel of the move among liberal Christians to address the many problems associated with the transition from entrepreneurial capitalism to corporate capitalism; this meant that the suggestion to read the *Survey* and to incorporate its insights was not an appropriation of the methods of a secular movement, but an effort to develop a set of common Protestant concerns.

For at that same moment, the Social Gospel was in the ascendancy in American Protestantism. Following the Civil War, American Protestantism had begun its long split into what Martin Marty has labeled "two party" Protestantism. One of these parties, the private party, focused on individual salvation. When leaders in this party, such as Dwight Moody, looked at the urban slums, they saw the appropriate Christian response as offering to individuals the personal redemption of rebirth in Jesus Christ.

14. Chambers 1971 is the definitive history of the *Survey*. The magazine continued publication until 1952.

15. In 1910 Paul U. Kellogg, the *Survey*'s editor, served with Charles Stelzle, the Movement's Dean of Social Service (together with Josiah Strong), on a Commission on the Church and Social Service that had been convened to investigate a steel strike in South Bethlehem. This strike had arisen out of the workers' anger at being forced to work on Sundays.

16. The prevalence of the liberal Protestant impulse in the emerging Progressive response to corporate capitalism is further illustrated by the fact that Jacob Riis was also an advocate of the Social Gospel.

Meunier:
The Puddler

O to $200.

O to $300.

O to $225.

O to $100.

VALUATIONS PUT ON MEN IN PITTSBURGH IN 1907

Actual amounts paid as compensation by employers to twenty-seven workmen
permanently injured in Allegheny County, April, May, June, of that year

For loss of an eye,........ $200, $150, $150, $100, $75, $50, $50, $48, 0, 0, 0.
For loss of an arm,........ $300,   0,   0.
For loss of two fingers,.... $100, $100,   0,   0,   0,   0,   0.
For loss of leg,........... $225, $175, $150, $100, $55,   0.

[For relative significance of these figures see Chapter VIII.]

Figure 2   This figure showing the meager compensation paid to vic-
tims of industrial accidents (Eastman 1910, facing p. 126) illustrates the
vivid way that the early social surveyors communicated their findings

Protestants like Moody believed that "efforts to improve the world were
largely futile" (Marty 1984, 316). Thus Moody did not want to amelio-
rate the social conditions he saw in the cities, he wanted to save souls.

"I look on this world as a wrecked vessel. God gave me a life-boat and said to me, 'Moody, save all you can'" (317).

The alternative Protestant response to this lifeboat mentality came from the second party of American Protestantism, the "public party," as Marty called it. This group, which we now refer to as the adherents of the Social Gospel, believed that the appropriate Christian response to the poverty and inequality around them was to reform society through the creation of new social institutions. The difference between these two groups is often cast in terms of their outlooks on the millennium. The members of the private party believed that they lived in premillennial times, before the return of Jesus Christ and his one thousand-year reign. As they climbed into their lifeboats, they were preparing to wait out the storm until his return. The Social Gospelers, on the other hand, when they looked around themselves, believed that the millennium had already come and that their job was to begin building the Kingdom then and there. Thus the sense of agency for Protestants in these two groups could not have been more different.

Until the twentieth century, however, the public party had clearly been in the minority. Not until the first decade of the twentieth century did the advocates of the Social Gospel begin to dominate the discourse in the Protestant churches.[17] In 1908 thirty-three Protestant denominations, representing eighteen million church members, formed the Federal Council of Churches, which, in turn, established the Committee on Church and Social Service in the same year. In 1912, the same churches signed on to the Social Creed of the Churches, a document originally passed by the Methodists, which committed them to such social reforms as the abolition of child labor, the ten-hour work day, and the six-day work week.

To fully understand the dispute between the private and the public Protestants, and so what was at stake for each group, we must under-stand that both groups saw America as a Protestant nation. In different ways they each saw America as the place where the Reformation of the Church was to take its final form, and where the Kingdom of God would

17. An astute reader of an earlier draft of this essay asked why this turn to the Social Gospel took place in American Protestantism. The simplest answer would be that the turn was a part of the larger response in American society to the news of more poverty and the abuses of the trusts. Since the liberal Protestants who defined the Social Gospel were also a leading force in the Progressive movement, it seems reasonable to say that the same forces that defined the rise of the Progressive movement also defined the rise of the Social Gospel. See the next section of the essay for more discussion on this point.

ultimately be created on this earth.[18] Thus, Walter Rauschenbusch, the
great theologian of the Social Gospel, could write *Christianizing the
Social Order* (1912) to express his belief that the amelioration of the
nation's social ills was a matter of Christian redemption as much as it
was a political matter. For the Social Gospelers, the political redemption
of the nation was inseparable from its Christian redemption. Marty is
then quite correct to call the two groups *parties*, for they did each see
themselves as offering a different future for the American polity.

It is against this background that one must place the Men and Religion
Forward Movement, for it began very much as a vehicle for the private
party but instead became a successful instrument of the public party.[19]
The original organizers of the movement were men concerned with the
salvation of individual souls, and their financial supporters had in mind a
traditional revival culminating in an altar call for men ready to be saved.
But when Fred B. Smith was backed into inviting Raymond Robins, one
of the most prominent Social Gospelers, to lead a twenty-minute devo-
tional at one of the organizational conferences for the Movement in 1910
(after several years of trying to avoid meeting him), he was impressed by
two things: that Robins actually preached from the Bible and that "by the
close . . . he had captured the heart and mind of every man in the audito-
rium" (Smith 1936, 94). This led Smith to invite Robins to formally join
the Movement as an organizer for the social service committees. Initially
Smith did not think that much would come of his invitation. Much to
his surprise, then, the social service component to the Movement "went
steadily to the front." In part this was attributable to the leadership of
men like Charles Stelzle and Raymond Robins; it also reflected, however, the interests of the men who participated in the revival, and this
in turn reflected the tone of the times. Reform had taken center stage in
American politics, and people were interested in hearing about the needs
of those around them. In *Christianizing the Social Order*, Rauschenbusch captured nicely the way in which social reformation, politics, and
Christian nationalism mixed naturally in the minds of liberal Protestants
at the time of the Men and Religion Forward Movement:

18. The best source for understanding the force of the idea of the Kingdom of God in American history is still Niebuhr 1937.

19. The best treatment of the struggle for the soul of the Movement is in Bederman 1989.
I have been unable to locate any extant discussion of the reaction of the corporate heads who
helped finance the Movement to its "capture" by the Social Gospelers.

It has been a terrible process of national education. If in 1890 a prophet, personally conducted and introduced by an archangel, had predicted accurately one half of the facts which are now common knowledge, public opinion would have dismissed him with incredulity.

It is proof of the moral soundness of our people that when they did understand, there was a revulsion of feeling. The standards of collective morality rose almost with a snap. Some men died broken-hearted when they found themselves fixed by the stern gaze of this new moral feeling. Others are to-day looking in this new light at the fortunes they gathered by the old methods, and are wishing that their hands were emptier.

Sin is the greatest preacher of repentance. Give it time, and it will cool our lust in shame. When God wants to halt a proud man who is going wrong, he lets him go the full length and find out the latter end for himself. That is what he has done with our nation in its headlong ride on the road of covetousness. Mammonism stands convicted by its own works. It is time for us to turn.

We are turning. (Rauschenbusch 1912, 4–5)

The primary instrument of the new "national education" that had led to this turn was the social survey. What the people had been unwilling to hear from an archangel, they were now hearing, and accepting, from the social surveyors.

The Third Circle: Progressive Politics

When Rauschenbusch said that the nation had responded "with a snap" to the new information about social conditions, he was probably providing an accurate description of how it seemed at the time. The Social Gospel had been preached for thirty years by the turn of the century but still had not gained dominant status within the Protestant churches. Nor, following the collapse of Reconstruction, could it be said that reform politics had commanded center stage in American politics. But after the turn of the century, things had unexpectedly, perceptibly changed. Theodore Roosevelt, the reforming governor of New York, had been put on the Republican ticket in 1900 as the vice-presidential candidate "partly as a favor to New York's Republican political boss, Thomas C. Platt, who worried about tentative proposals Roosevelt had floated to increase corporate regulation and taxation" and who had wanted him out of the state and out of the way (Diner 1998, 213). Roosevelt was well known as a war hero and an imperialist, but he had not been put on the ticket with any serious intention that the party would pursue reform if McKinley and he were elected. Thus when McKinley was assassinated in 1901, Roosevelt moved only cautiously toward reform, out of a sense that he did not have an electoral mandate. Only in his own campaign for the Presidency in 1904 did he bring reform to the center of his electoral platform.

But in the eight years between 1904 and 1912, when Rauschenbusch was writing, the Progressive Era had come fully into its own. Now the many voices for reform and institutional change that had emerged in the late nineteenth century, particularly during the depression of the 1890s, had found expression in electoral victory. In fact, by 1912, the same year that Roosevelt bolted from the Republican Party to run for the presidency against William H. Taft and Woodrow Wilson, there were no candidates who did not advocate some form of Progressive reform. It should not be surprising that Rauschenbusch felt that the tide was turning.

Progressivism, however, was never a single, well-defined idea. In response to the historiographical puzzle of how to define American Progressivism, Daniel T. Rodgers has suggested that it consisted of three intertwined discourses: the discourse of antimonopolism, the discourse of social bonding, and the discourse of social efficiency. "Together they formed not an ideology but the surroundings of available rhetoric and ideas—akin to the surrounding structures of politics and power—within which progressives launched their crusades, recruited their partisans, and did their work" (Rodgers 1982, 123).

Rodgers identifies the Social Gospel as being at the root of the discourse of social bonding, or what we might call the language of "interdependence" that was evolving in turn-of-the-century America to replace the old language of individualism. For the first time since the Revolution, Americans were faced with a set of social structures, such as corporate capital, and social outcomes, such as the large-scale poverty revealed by the social surveyors, that led them to seriously question the ability of the individual to successfully navigate the world on self-initiative. In fact, individuals with too much power were widely seen as the cause of many of the changes in American society. Thus prominent Social Gospelers such as Ely were quick to rail against individualism and offered their vision of a Christian nation as a new way to "bond" the nation together to work for the amelioration of the worst social problems. What Rauschenbusch described as the sin of Mammonism, Ely described as the sin of individualism.[20]

As Rodgers argues, Progressivism was not one thing through time, and the three discourses were to play different roles as time went on. Antimonopolism had been the first language of Progressivism and the one that had propelled it onto center stage in Roosevelt's 1904 campaign.[21] But the people who were drawn into this discourse were largely liberal Protestants who belonged to the Republican Party. Thus they brought the discourse of social bonding and the presuppositions of the Social Gospel with them into the discourse on monopolistic control in the American economy. Two of the prominent examples of this "double discourse" were Richard T. Ely and John R. Commons, both of whom were prominent advocates of the Social Gospel during the 1890s, were active in reform circles, and wrote and taught about monopoly.

In addition to the fact that many individuals drew from, or participated in, more than one of these discourses, it is also widely recognized that there was a shift in primary emphasis during the Progressive Era (1900–1917) from the discourse of social bonding to the discourse on social efficiency. Whereas the early Progressive period was very clearly marked by explicit Christian rhetoric, after 1912 the more prominent public rhetoric came to be a secular message of social control and efficiency. In many regards this shift is explained well in Rodgers's schemata, for one element of it was a shift in the rhetoric of the Social Gospelers themselves. Without experiencing any loss of faith, many liberal Protestants after 1905 began to talk increasingly in the language of democracy. Initially this discourse explained democracy itself as the ultimate form of the freedom they believed to be inherent in Protestant faith (especially as against their perception of an authoritarian Catholicism). Rauschenbusch was a vocal proponent of this conflation of Christianity and democracy. But it was not long before many adherents of the Social Gospel began to speak of the virtues of democracy without explicit reference to Christianity at all. And when the public discourse turned increasingly to social control and efficiency, the same liberal Protestants

20. Thomas Haskell (1977) offers the most succinct treatment of how "interdependence" came to dominate the discourse of American higher education and displaced the older language of individualism.

21. Mary S. Morgan (1993) offers a good survey of the evolving concern with monopoly in late-nineteenth-century America.

spoke openly, but in secular terms, of the advantages of efficiency for democracy.

The intertwined languages of social bonding and social efficiency were not just a matter of two conflated rhetorics, however. During the second decade of the twentieth century, a strong secular movement advocating social efficiency emerged within Progressivism. This group has also been called the "scientific Progressives."[22] Two of the most prominent political statements of this new outlook were Herbert Croly's *The Promise of American Life* (1909) and Walter Lippmann's *Drift and Mastery* (1914). From the point of view of business, Frederick Taylor and Elton Mayo, the two most prominent advocates of improving industrial management in order to achieve higher productivity, were leading proponents of this emerging idea of social efficiency. "The language of social efficiency offered a way of putting the Progressives' common sense of social disorder into words and remedies free of the embarrassing pieties and philosophical conundrums that hovered around the competing language of social bonds" (Rodgers 1982, 126).

This impulse, to create a language of efficiency that would allow Progressives to talk about social waste, budgeting, and the improved management of factories, came from many sources. As the quotation from Rodgers above suggests, for many people there was certainly an embarrassment over, if not an impatience with, the arguments that moral progress was actually taking place.[23] For academics and intellectuals, this impatience manifested itself in a growing interest in pragmatism, "the belief that decisions should be made on the basis of experience rather than in accordance with traditional secular or religious ideals" (Rodgers 1982, 115). And in the population at large, there was a growing number of non-Protestants, people for whom the idea that democracy was a Protestant ideal had no weight at all. For many of these people, who were disaffected with the idea of a Protestant nation, the call to a

22. See Danbom 1987. Julie Reuben (1996) has shown that the turn to a public rhetoric of science and efficiency was matched by a turn in the newly emerging research universities from seeing the religiously oriented social sciences as the moral center of undergraduate education to assigning this role to the natural sciences.

23. See Danbom 1987, 100–111 for examples of the growing skepticism that people were actually becoming any more moral during the Progressive Era. As Danbom and others have argued, it was bound to become a problem for Christian Progressives that so much of their rhetoric depended on the idea of moral regeneration and that they had so little to offer by way of concrete policy proposals. The argument that institutions could be reformed with a more determined application of the Golden Rule was a weak reed at best.

better and more efficient use of resources offered a compelling alternative to the Social Gospel.

Thus, when Rauschenbusch said that the nation was turning, he was more correct than he realized. For while it was undoubtedly true that the nation had experienced a quick and startling turn to Progressive electoral politics during the previous twelve years and that advocates of the Social Gospel had been among the most prominent voices calling for a new politics, it was also true that the ground was about to shift under the Social Gospelers' feet. The years 1913–16 have appropriately been termed the "high tide" of Progressivism, but by 1912, when Rauschenbusch wrote, the discourse of social efficiency was already crowding against the discourse of the Social Gospel (Diner 1998, 223–32). Thus, as Rauschenbusch wrote, another turn was just over the horizon.

The First World War would mark not just the end of Progressive politics, but the end of an era. The grim reality of the war signaled the demise of the hopeful outlook in electoral politics as well as in the churches, where the Social Gospel also quickly lost its purchase on American culture. And, as we will see, the demise of Progressive politics and the Social Gospel led to a change in the status and understanding of the social survey movement. The Men and Religion Forward Movement would stand, in retrospect, as marking the heyday of a certain phase of the social survey movement.

By 1926 the changed nature of American society was all too clear to the social surveyors. In that year the *Survey* published a print symposium to address the question "Where Are the Pre-War Radicals?" which included contributions from twenty-two of the most prominent Progressives. Only a few of the participants, such as Eugene V. Debs and Norman Thomas, had been radicals, but they had all been at the forefront of the movement for Progressive reform as politicians, journalists, lawyers, and social activists. None of them, however, denied that times had changed. Part of the change in the tone of the times came from the emergence of the new political determination of the unions. Seeing the bargaining advantage created by America's entry into the First World War, over 750,000 workers had gone on strike in 1917 after the declaration of war. This newfound militancy carried over after the war as "workers struck everywhere after the armistice, as management rolled back not only wages but wartime union gains" (Diner 1998, 241). The idea that well-educated, upper-middle-class Progressives could serve as the voice for laborers took a beating in the face of the unions' growing clout.

But, at an even more basic level, the war had subverted the assumptions of human rationality and fundamental human decency common to all the strands of Progressive discourse. As Ida Tarbell (1926, 558), the famed muckraker, said in the *Survey* symposium, Progressives "knew little about human beings, and what as individuals and herds they can be counted on to do under certain circumstances."

The First World War and its aftermath had been a part of yet more "national education." And just as the education provided by the social surveyors had helped lead to one turn for the nation, this new education had helped lead to yet another turn.

The Fourth Circle: American Social Science

The story of American social science in the first two decades of the twentieth century very much shadows the history of Progressive politics. On one level, of course, the two were intimately intertwined; many of the early American social scientists were active participants in Progressive reform.[24] On another level, the Social Gospel heavily underpinned both during the first decade of the century, and both still had many of these Social Gospelers in their ranks during the second decade.

Thus it should be no surprise that just as the discourse of social bonding was supplanted by that of social efficiency in Progressive politics during the second decade of the twentieth century, so it was also in American social science. Likewise it is no surprise that just as the First World War helped to gut Progressive electoral politics, so too it helped to weaken the Progressive impulse in American social science (Ross 1991, Smith 1994, Reuben 1996). The turn away from Progressivism in the social sciences was different than in electoral politics, however; unlike in the political arena, there was no truly conservative force in social science to supplant the Progressives. Instead, in an effort to distance themselves from their previous leanings, the social scientists openly turned against what now seemed to have been an overly optimistic rhetoric of reform and moral transformation and embraced a call for more "scientific" work.[25]

24. Diner (1980) offers an excellent window into the way in which academic social scientists were involved in reform movements and reform politics.

25. Everett 1946 is still probably the best treatment of the way that moral reform underpinned the whole generation of early evangelical economists, including Henry Carter Adams, J. B. Clark, and Simon N. Patten. See also Bateman 1998 and Bateman and Kapstein 1999.

There was apparent by the 1920s an increasingly sharp line between research done with a reformist and ameliorative purpose on
the one hand and research with a scientific purpose on the other. This
was a period in the development of the social sciences in the United
States at which two tendencies were apparent. One was the thrust toward the much more extensive empirical study of the contemporary
world, evident in psychology, economics, political science and sociology alike. . . . At the same time, such social scientists were insis-
tent that their investigations were conducted in a scientific spirit, that
is, they were part of a wider scientific enterprise which included the
building of theory and the understanding of general processes. (Bulmer 1991, 305–7)

Many people have referred to this change as the turn to "scientism"
by American social scientists after the First World War, and it is clear
that, after 1918, economists, political scientists, and sociologists all did
embrace a new public rhetoric in defense of their empirical and statistical work, replacing their former moral fervor with calls for a "scientific"
treatment of data.[26] As Dorothy Ross has perceptively pointed out, however, this turn was largely rhetorical, and did not necessarily indicate a
total loss of faith in the possibility of social improvement. After all, the
Americans had come out of the war in better shape than any other country. Even if the social scientists were now embarrassed by their former
naiveté and lived amidst the ruins of Wilson's pious rhetoric, the United
States was now in a unique position in the world. However, the social scientists had to adapt themselves to the new national tone of "normalcy"
and "realism" if they hoped to secure the professional gains that they had
begun to make.

For economists the turn to scientism is nowhere more obvious than in
the emergence of "Institutionalism" after 1918.[27] As Malcolm Rutherford (1997) has recently pointed out, there was no self-identified school
of Institutionalists until the end of the second decade of the twentieth
century, and the school's greatest moment came in the 1920s when a

26. Both Bannister 1987 and Ross 1991 deal extensively with the turn to scientism. This
turn away from the older moralism and pietism of American social science toward a more "objective" scientific posture may well explain the change that Biddle (1999) notes in the style of
empirical argument around 1920.

27. See Rutherford 1997 on the emergence of the larger school of Institutionalism after
1918. Rutherford 1999 is an excellent analysis of the changing conception of "science" in Institutional economics.

cadre of younger men, including Wesley C. Mitchell, Walton Hamilton, J. M. Clark, and Robert F. Hoxie, drew on the earlier work of Thorstein Veblen and John R. Commons in shaping a new program in American economics.[28]

The best example of this turn within economics is Mitchell's effort to scientize economic management through his work with the National Bureau of Economic Research, the Commerce Department, and several philanthropic organizations. Mitchell, Herbert Hoover, Beardsley Ruml, Mary Van Kleeck, and Henry Dennison all had a vision of a data-driven effort at the level of the firm and the industry that would lead to better management and, hence, to greater economic stability (Alchon 1985, Barber 1985). This dream fit the times perfectly. It honored the prerogatives of privately owned capital, it was "scientific," and it offered a "sober," hard-eyed hope for a better future. It is no wonder that Institutionalism seemed to have such a bright future and was able to attract so much funding during the 1920s.

"In the Scientific Spirit": The Beginning of the End of the Social Survey Movement

By the 1920s the American social landscape looked quite different than it had in 1895, when Richard T. Ely had published *Hull House Maps and Papers* in the *Library of Economics and Politics* series. Progressive politics had come and gone, American social science had shed its rhetoric of moral reform, and the Social Gospel had been eclipsed after the First World War. The same currents that had caused these changes had also changed the ground under the social survey movement. What had served as the seedbed for empiricism in economics, sociology, social work, and political science came to be seen in quite a different light.[29]

Initially, the social survey was seen as adaptable to the changing times. In 1915, in the heyday of the discourse of social efficiency, John Gillin, a rising star in rural sociology at the University of Wisconsin, argued that the social survey could now be turned into a method for making

---

28. Yuval 1998 is also helpful in this regard, although from a different perspective. Samuels 1998 treats the intellectual origins of Institutionalism in Veblen's and Commons's writings at the turn of the century.

29. Of these four contemporary disciplines, only the literature in the history of economics fails to mention the role of the social survey in its early history. Converse 1987 is the best history of the ways that the social survey influenced later academic survey research.

the accurate measurements that would be necessary for improving social efficiency in the same way that accounting methods had been used for improving business efficiency:

> Never as now have men put the test of efficiency to political, economic, and social movements and agencies. In business, cost of production and distribution cannot longer be ignored or guessed at; they must be known. Thousands of dollars are spent by business and industrial firms every year for advice as to how the wastes of business may be eliminated. Business organization is judged by its success in so coordinating the forces it employs that there may be the minimum of friction and waste. The efficiency movement, so-called, has produced remarkable results in commercial and industrial organizations.
>
> The social survey is an expression of this same movement in the social as distinguished from the economic realm. The social survey is an endeavor to take stock of certain phases of the community which bear upon that community's welfare. (Gillin 1915, 605)

Gillin, in his essay, which appeared in the *Publications of the American Statistical Association*, goes on to argue for several improvements in the conduct of social surveys. John R. Commons had already argued for one of these improvements in another of the American Statistical Association's journals during his work on the Pittsburgh Survey: the standardization of the measurement of social conditions so that comparisons could be made between different cities.[30] Thus, at this point, the social survey was still seen as an important quantitative method in the social sciences, but one that should now be used for improving social efficiency, not for driving moral reform and political mobilization.

Only five years later, however, Gillin had come to see the social survey very differently. In 1918 Gillin had been asked to chair a committee of the American Sociological Society on the "standardization of research." The committee published reports, written by Gillin, in 1919

---

30. John R. Commons (1909, 320) actually makes a succinct and elegant point that presages J. M. Clark's later work on overhead costs. Commons says that, with a set of standard measures for social conditions, it would be possible to calculate the "profit and loss" of the "trade longevity of the workman" in a standard way that would allow for seeing how national resources could best be used for the maintenance of the labor force. Presumably, it is this type of social calculation and the discovery of such possibilities for welfare improvements that would define the social, as opposed to economic, efficiency that Gillin refers to in the quotation in this paragraph. Since Gillin's article draws from the statistical ideas in Commons's earlier article, this inference seems reasonable.

and 1920, the first of which was little more than an enumeration of the current work being undertaken at several American universities and colleges. But the next year Gillin wrote a longer report calling for "a determination at all costs to apply the scientific method to social phenomena of all kinds" (1920, 232). Whereas only five years earlier it had been sufficient to call for refinements in the social survey that would have made it more suitable for use as a tool for identifying possible improvements in social efficiency, now the entire enterprise of surveying needed to be recast in a new scientific guise. Julie Reuben has chosen to refer to this turn in the publicly stated intentions of social scientists as "objectivism" rather than "scientism." The point of her distinction is to capture the idea that the crux of the change in their work had as much to do with a shift in the *meaning of* science as it did with a *turn to* science. Social scientists before the First World War had referred to their work as scientific, but that had meant that it was empirical in the broad sense of collecting data. Now it would be important for them to take an unbiased, or value-free, point of view toward that data and to use it to reveal causal relationships and seek unprejudiced explanations for the social phenomena they studied. Thus for Reuben the turn was less a turn to science than to a new value-neutral, or value-free, approach to the analysis of data.

In the new world of scientism, the old work of the social surveyors was still valuable for helping with the collection of descriptive statistics, but now social scientists needed to think first and foremost about what they would *do* with the data that the surveyors collected. The collection and presentation of statistics by themselves was no longer a worthwhile endeavor for social scientists: "It is perfectly apparent by this time that the Promised Land of wholesome social life cannot be seen clearly by eyes dimmed with easy tears; nor can the call to constructive social work be heard above the thumping of a fluttery heart. Social reform of any and every kind must be thought out and carried through in the scientific spirit" (Gillin 1920, 232). Thus Gillin's committee was now less interested in trying to reform how the social survey was conducted than they were in getting past it. Data from the surveys was still important, and Gillin was careful to make an explicit nod to the valuable funding available from the Russell Sage Foundation and other philanthropists, but his real emphasis was on the development of a new scientific ethos.

At the Birth of Institutional Economics

When the organizers of the Men and Religion Forward Movement embraced the social survey and put it at the center of their well-organized, nationwide revival in 1911 and 1912, they gave it an exposure and force that it had never had. A million and a half men came out to hear the message generated by the seventy-six surveys that the Movement organized, and millions more read about the results in the newspaper articles that the Publicity Committee of the Movement generated in each of the seventy-six cities. What was happening must surely have seemed like the fulfillment of Walter Rauschenbusch's (1907, 209) claim from five years earlier, that "for the first time in religious history we have the possibility of so directing religious energy by scientific knowledge that a comprehensive and continuous reconstruction of social life in the name of God is within the bounds of human possibility."

With or without the publicity of the Men and Religion Forward Movement, the social survey would have always been explicitly identified with the evangelical economists and the Social Gospel (see fig. 3). But by the time that social scientists started to distance themselves from the social survey, the central discourse of Progressivism had become social efficiency, and the critiques of the earlier methods tended to talk about "eyes dimmed with easy tears," rather than about Christianity itself, when they criticized the optimistic and hopeful tone that had defined their earlier work. The emotionalism and the "temporary excitement" of the revival were certainly on their minds when they thought about the nature of the tool upon which they had once pinned so much hope. The larger American society was distancing itself from the Social Gospel and the Progressive movement after the First World War, and social scientists were going to have to make the same break if they wanted to participate in the public discourse and secure their own professional gains. At this point the social survey was too closely associated with the past to be redeemed.

In some ways this outcome may seem inevitable. Irmela Gorges has told a very similar story about the social survey in Germany: how it began in the *Verein für Sozialpolitik* as a tool of social reform and the subsequent debates that led to the development of a "value-free" form of the survey (1991). Likewise Franck Jovanovic and Philippe Le Gall show in their essay on Lucien March (this volume) that similar problems regarding the interpretation of social statistics arose in France early in

Courtesy of the Scranton Tribune-Republican.

Figure 3   This early cartoon from the *Survey* (vol. 30, no. 5) shows the way in which the social surveyors' viewpoint was inextricably linked to the church

the twentieth century. Many scholars have noted the close relationship between the rise of the liberal state and the collection of social statistics, and there is, likewise, a rich literature about the transformation of the early statistical projects into some form of modern statistical "science." But because there is already an ample literature on the connecting threads between the earlier form of the social survey in America and the later, more statistically sophisticated variants developed in sociology and political science, it seems more appropriate to dwell in conclusion on some of the particular ways that the forces that led to the demise of the social survey helped shape American economics.[31]

As noted above, the strong turn against moral reform and Progressive politics that carried the social survey out of American economics was a part of the same current that brought Institutional economics into being. For many decades Institutionalism has been characterized as having started with the work of Thorstein Veblen and John R. Commons at the end of the nineteenth century. But while it is undoubtedly the case that the men who first self-identified as Institutionalists in the second decade of the twentieth century drew inspiration from Veblen and Commons, it is also the case, as Malcolm Rutherford has pointed out, that Mitchell, Hoxie, Walter Stewart, and the others saw themselves as undertaking something new and different. It seems reasonable to describe one sense of that newness as moving beyond the "historical" economics that Ely and Commons had propounded. Just as the younger economists wanted to move beyond the embarrassingly "easy tears" of the social survey, they also wished to move beyond the whole project that had been defined by the evangelical impulse firing the earlier work of Ely, Commons, Simon Nelson Patten, and Henry Carter Adams.

This is not to say that they were not interested in social amelioration, but by the 1920s American economists were being carried by exactly the same trends that were redefining the sense of proper scientific analysis in every other American social science. It is particularly interesting to note, however, that in economics the part of the move that involved abandoning the social survey had the unintended result of purging the serious study of poverty from the discipline for at least forty years. Not until the 1960s, when government funds from the War on Poverty programs were used to establish the Institute for Research on Poverty at the University of Wisconsin, would economists undertake sustained empirical analysis of American poverty. The empirical work undertaken by Mitchell and the other Institutionalists in the 1920s focused very narrowly on business, finance, and manufacturing.

This move to a more narrow conception of the topics studied in empirical work in economics coincided with the final split between sociology and economics in American social science. Since at least the 1890s, men

---

31. See Converse 1987 for an excellent treatment of the transition to more statistically sophisticated forms of survey research.

who had once defined themselves primarily as economists, such as E. A.
Ross, had been redefining themselves as sociologists as they shifted the
focus of their work. But the divide between the disciplines had continued to remain permeable for at least two more decades. Commons, for
instance, had held a chair of sociology at Syracuse in the 1890s; as late as
1919, Gillin had included Commons's social survey work in his annual
reports on the state of current research in sociology. But after 1920, questions of poverty began to fall solely within the purview of sociology and
social work, rather than economics, as the disciplines made their final
split. When sociologists "scientized" and "objectivized" their discipline
after 1918, they continued to include poverty in their legitimate field of
inquiry; they merely insisted on developing a scientific approach to its
study. Economists, on the other hand, would appear to have abandoned
the study of poverty when they abandoned the social survey. There is
undoubtedly more to this story than can be covered in this essay, but
one way to understand the two sides of this split is to see them as two
variants in the reaction against the influence of the Social Gospel and
Progressivism in American social science.

References

Alchon, Guy. 1985. *The Invisible Hand of Planning: Capitalism, Social Science, and the State in the 1920s*. Princeton, N.J.: Princeton University Press.
Allen, Larry Dean, II. 2000. A Comparative Analysis of the Men and Religion Forward Movement and Promise Keepers. Ph.D. diss., Boston University.
Bannister, Robert C. 1987. *Sociology and Scientism: The American Quest for Objectivity, 1880–1940*. Chapel Hill: University of North Carolina Press.
Barber, William J. 1985. *From New Era to New Deal: Herbert Hoover, the Economists, and American Economic Policy, 1921–1933*. Cambridge: Cambridge University Press.
Bateman, Bradley W. 1998. Clearing the Ground: The Demise of the Social Gospel Movement and the Rise of Neoclassicism in American Economics. In *From Interwar Pluralism to Postwar Neoclassicism*, edited by Mary S. Morgan and Malcolm Rutherford. *HOPE* 30 (supplement): 29–52.
Bateman, Bradley W., and Ethan Kapstein. 1999. Between God and the Market: The Religious Roots of the American Economic Association. *Journal of Economic Perspectives* 13.4:249–58.
Bederman, Gail. 1989. "The Women Have Had Charge of the Church Work Long Enough": The Men and Religion Forward Movement of 1911–1912 and the Masculinization of Middle-Class Protestantism. *American Quarterly* 41.3:432–65.
Biddle, Jeff. 1999. Statistical Economics, 1900–1950. *HOPE* 31.4:607–51.

Booth, Charles. 1902–3. *Life and Labour of the People in London*. London: Macmillan.

Bulmer, Martin. 1991. The Decline of the Social Survey Movement and the Rise of American Empirical Sociology. In *The Social Survey in Historical Perspective, 1880–1940*, edited by Martin Bulmer, Kevin Bales, and Kathryn Kish Sklar. Cambridge: Cambridge University Press.

Chambers, Clarke A. 1971. *Paul U. Kellogg and the Survey: Voices for Social Welfare and Social Justice*. Minneapolis: University of Minnesota Press.

Cocks, Orrin G. 1912. The Scope and Value of the Local Surveys of the Men and Religion Movement. *Proceedings of the Academy of Political Science* 2.4:63–70.

Cohen, Steven R. 1991. The Pittsburgh Survey and the Social Survey Movement: A Sociological Road Not Taken. In *The Social Survey in Historical Perspective, 1880–1940*, edited by Martin Bulmer, Kevin Bales, and Kathryn Kish Sklar. Cambridge: Cambridge University Press.

Commons, John R. 1909. Standardization of Housing Investigations. *Journal of the American Statistical Association* 11:319–26.

Converse, Jean. 1987. *Survey Research in the United States: Roots and Emergence, 1890–1960*. Berkeley: University of California Press.

Croly, Herbert. 1909. *The Promise of American Life*. New York: Macmillan.

Danbom, David. 1987. *The World of Hope: Progressives and the Struggle for an Ethical Public Life*. Philadelphia: Temple University Press.

Diner, Steven J. 1980. *A City and Its Universities: Public Policy in Chicago, 1892–1919*. Chapel Hill: University of North Carolina Press.

———. 1998. *A Very Different Age: Americans in the Progressive Era*. New York: Hill and Wang.

Eastman, Crystal. 1910. *Work Accidents and the Law*. New York: Charities Publication Committee.

Everett, John R. 1946. *Religion and Economics: A Study of John Bates Clark, Richard T. Ely, and Simon Patten*. New York: King's Crown Press.

Gillin, John L. 1915. The Social Survey and Its Further Development. *Publications of the American Statistical Association*, n.s., 14.111:603–10.

———. 1919. Report of the Committee on the Standardization of Research of the American Sociological Society. *Papers and Proceedings of the American Sociological Society* 14:252–59.

———. 1920. Report of the Committee on the Standardization of Research of the American Sociological Society. *Papers and Proceedings of the American Sociological Society* 15:231–41.

Gorges, Irmela. 1991. The Social Survey in Germany before 1933. In *The Social Survey in Historical Perspective, 1880–1940*, edited by Martin Bulmer, Kevin Bales, and Kathryn Kish Sklar. Cambridge: Cambridge University Press.

Gorrell, Donald K. 1988. *The Age of Social Responsibility: The Social Gospel in the Progressive Era, 1900–1920*. Macon, Ga.: Mercer University Press.

Haskell, Thomas. 1977. *The Emergence of Professional Social Science*. Urbana: University of Illinois Press.

Lippmann, Walter. 1914. *Drift and Mastery: An Attempt to Diagnose the Current Unrest*. New York: M. Kennerley.

Lubove, Roy. 1965. *The Professional Altruist: The Emergence of Social Work As a Career, 1880–1930*. Cambridge: Harvard University Press.

Marty, Martin. 1984. *Pilgrims in Their Own Land: 500 Years of Religion in America*. Boston: Little, Brown.

McLoughlin, William G. 1959. *Modern Revivalism: Charles Grandison Finney to Billy Graham*. New York: Ronald Press.

Men and Religion Forward Movement. 1911. *Program of Work*. New York: Association Press.

———. 1912. *Messages of the Men and Religion Forward Movement*. 7 vols. New York: Association Press.

Morgan, Mary S. 1993. Competing Views of "Competition" in Late Nineteenth Century American Economics. *HOPE* 25.4:563–604.

Morgan, Mary S., and Malcolm Rutherford. 1998. American Economics: The Character of the Transformation. In *From Interwar Pluralism to Postwar Neoclassicism*, edited by Mary S. Morgan and Malcolm Rutherford. *HOPE* 30 (supplement): 1–26.

Niebuhr, H. Richard. 1937. *The Kingdom of God in America*. New York: Harper and Row.

Porter, Theodore. 1986. *The Rise of Statistical Thinking, 1820–1900*. Princeton, N.J.: Princeton University Press.

Rauschenbusch, Walter. 1907. *Christianity and the Social Crisis*. New York: Macmillan.

———. 1912. *Christianizing the Social Order*. New York: Macmillan.

Residents of Hull House. 1895. *Hull House Maps and Papers: A Presentation of Nationalities and Wages in a Congested District of Chicago, Together with Comments and Essays on Problems Growing out of the Social Conditions*. New York: Crowell.

Reuben, Julie. 1996. *The Making of the Modern University: Intellectual Transformation and the Marginalization of Morality*. Chicago: University of Chicago Press.

Rodgers, Daniel T. 1982. In Search of Progressivism. *Reviews in American History* 10:113–32.

Ross, Dorothy. 1991. *The Origins of American Social Science*. Cambridge: Cambridge University Press.

Rutherford, Malcolm. 1997. American Institutionalism and the History of Economics. *Journal of the History of Economic Thought* 19.2:178–95.

———. 1999. Institutionalism as "Scientific" Economics. In *From Classical Economics to the Theory of the Firm: Essays in Honour of D. P. O'Brien*, edited by Roger E. Backhouse and John Creedy. Cheltenham, U.K.: Edward Elgar.

Samuels, Warren, ed. 1998. *The Founding of Institutional Economics: The Leisure Class and Sovereignty*. London: Routledge.

Sklar, Kathryn Kish. 1991. Hull House Maps and Papers: Social Science As Women's Work in the 1890s. In *The Social Survey in Historical Perspective, 1880–1940*, edited by Martin Bulmer, Kevin Bales, and Kathryn Kish Sklar. Cambridge: Cambridge University Press.

Smith, Fred B. 1936. *I Remember*. New York: Revell.

Smith, Mark C. 1994. *Social Science in the Crucible: The American Debate over Objectivity and Purpose, 1918–1941*. Durham, N.C.: Duke University Press.

Stelzle, Charles. 1912. *American Social and Religious Conditions*. New York: Revell.

———. 1926. *A Son of the Bowery: The Life Story of an East Side American*. New York: Doran.

Tarbell, Ida M. 1926. Where Are the Pre-War Radicals? *The Survey* 40.9:558.

Warner, Amos Griswold. 1894. *American Charities: A Study in Philanthropy and Economics*. New York: Crowell.

Yuval, Yonay. 1998. *The Struggle over the Soul of Economics: Institutionalist and Neoclassical Economists in America between the Wars*. Princeton, N.J.: Princeton University Press.

Zimbalist, Sidney E. 1977. *Historic Themes and Landmarks in Social Welfare Research*. New York: Harper.

March to Numbers: The Statistical Style of Lucien March

Franck Jovanovic and Philippe Le Gall

La réalité n'est qu'un vestige dans l'immense étendue des possibilités.
Celles-ci ne forment pourtant point un chaos.
—Lucien March, "Statistique" (1924)

The development of economic thought in France has long been characterized by a local idiosyncrasy: the tradition of *ingénieurs économistes*.
Through their grappling with economic problems that confronted the
public sectors and with concrete issues tied to the constructive problems
undertaken by the state, engineers have often shown signs of originality and savoir faire—it has even been claimed that they "do economics while others talk about it" (Caquot 1939, quoted in Divisia 1951,
x). In any case, these engineers laid the foundations of microeconomics
(Ekelund and Hébert 1999), committed themselves in an early mathematization of economic issues (Kurita 1989) and, in a sense, paved the way
for econometrics (Hébert 1986).

But these French engineers also developed an indisputable talent for
measurement in economics, exemplified by their work on costs. Their involvement in measurement and more generally in statistics became particularly apparent around 1900: the Statistique Générale de la France

Correspondence may be addressed to both authors at GRESE, Université Paris I Panthéon-
Sorbonne, Maison des Sciences Economiques, 106–112 Boulevard de l'Hôpital, 75013 Paris,
France; e-mails: jova@univ-paris1.fr and phlegall@univ-paris1.fr. We are grateful to Judy
Klein and Mary Morgan for encouraging us to join this project and for commenting exten-
sively on earlier drafts. The paper also benefited from helpful comments from the workshop
participants and an anonymous referee.

(SGF), the main government statistical agency of the time, even became an engineers' fortress. Although the SGF remained small in comparison with other European statistical bureaus, the work it achieved during the early twentieth century remains impressive in two areas: the collection of data and the elaboration of explanations of what had been measured. Lucien March (1859–1933) deserves special attention in the engineers' involvement in statistics and economic measurement. He entered the École Polytechnique in 1878, became an engineer in the Corps des Mines, and was head of the SGF from 1899 to 1920.[1] March finds no easy home in our contemporary schemes, in the sense that he breaks with standard classifications. He reshaped the French statistical system, imported the new statistical techniques devised by British biometricians, investigated the field of time-series analysis, contributed to the spread of eugenics in France, promoted lectures in statistics at a time when they remained scarce, and made noteworthy incursions in economics and demography. Last, but not least, he developed a philosophy of science based on measure that—in some respects—illustrates the importance of the state in developing measurement, as the essays in this volume by Theodore Porter, Flavio Comim, and Martin Kohli suggest.

In this essay we will dissect March's methods of statistical research. We were motivated at the outset by the fact that his full contribution to the history of statistics has received scant attention. Our essay originates from two other concerns, both related to his specific approach to statistics. First, we would like to suggest that econo-engineers should be defined not only by their technical innovations but by their "non-mathematical arguments" as well, as Keiko Kurita (1989, 8) suggests. Indeed, their general training and practice sometimes led them to "take a detached view of their field" (Divisia 1951, 141) and to develop epistemological frameworks that remain underappreciated in the contemporary literature. Second, in debates that have recently occurred in the field of macroeconometrics, several protagonists—for instance, Summers (1991)—have questioned the usefulness of contemporary theory and called for more empirical inquiries and epistemological foundations. On this point, past episodes can afford enlightening lessons: several engineers of the nineteenth century and of the first half of the twentieth century based their practice of statistical economics on well-shaped

1. March had no academic position. Yet it should be noted that in 1920, he became involved with Emile Borel in the creation of the Institut de Statistique de l'Université de Paris, which played an important role in the training of statisticians in France (Desrosières 1993).

epistemological arguments—and such arguments, developed by scholars who are reputed to be advocates of mathematization, quantification, and measurement, could certainly be instructive. We found that March directly addressed both concerns. He carefully elaborated new tools for the statistical work in the social sciences and rooted them in an epistemological framework and in worldviews that were at the same time creating the scope and inscribing the limits of statistics. This association of statistics with worldviews delineates what we label March's statistical style.

We analyze this style in three steps. The first section of the essay deals with the way March viewed statistics—its nature, properties, and range of application. We will see that statistics was approached as an objective and scientific way to deal with complex phenomena and collections of heterogeneous facts. In the second section, we focus on March's concrete contributions to statistics in two areas: statistical methods and their application to economics. We will demonstrate that his work is characterized by the search for methods that could make possible the discovery of regularities at work in a complex and changing world and that he constantly pressed the limits of his own results. The last section sheds some light on March's worldviews and how they assigned a precise role to statistics. His was a means of approaching, measuring, and taming a social world characterized by an epistemic uncertainty, and his work is only meaningful in the frame of this epistemology that defines the scope and limits of statistics.

On Numbers and Measurement: Delineating Statistics

From the very beginning of his scientific career, March carefully tried to identify the nature and the frontiers of statistics. Such was not an easy agenda: at a time when the application of statistical procedures to the social sciences was controversial in France (Ménard 1980) and statistics was even derided (Porter 1995), March suggested that statistics was a path based on precise and scientific criteria, a path that various disciplines should follow.

Statistics as *Une Langue Commune*

March (1924, 341) thought that the identification of the territory of statistics resulted from the identification of the limits of the experimental method:

> The methods that suit the experimental sciences, and that are based on the possibility of isolating one circumstance among all those that coexist in a phenomena, do not perfectly apply to the observational sciences, in which a fact can never be reproduced in the way it had been originally produced, and where the invariability of the adjacent circumstances, with the exception of one, can never be realized.[2]

Thus, "when we do not control the main circumstances of observation, the statistical method is to be applied" (March 1930b, 9), and the scientist can only observe the facts "as they appear" to him (11). Statistics was thus a substitute for the experimental method. March shared here the views of other social scientists of the time: Mary Morgan (1990) indeed suggests that the use of statistics, especially by economists and the first econometricians, was based on similar arguments and that more generally this problem "arose in other social sciences and in natural sciences where controlled experiments were not possible" (9).

Although these views were not original, March's arguments deserve attention. In various textbooks he explained that, in contrast to the experimental method, statistics was concerned with complex phenomena and heterogeneous collections:

> These facts are generally ruled by complex influences that remain impossible to separate or to control at will. They arise from the shock of circumstances that we do not master and often from intentional facts whose scattering and capriciousness disconcert. . . . The phenomena that are studied are often influenced not only by causes that operate in the scope of observation (for instance, the health of workers in the case of wages), but also by causes that largely preceded observation (for instance, those relative to heredity, habits, and traditions in human societies). In short, the complexity of the range of observation is particularly important in the studies of collections of living beings or of social facts. (1930b, 145)

At that stage, March's thought moved in two directions.

2. All translations from the French are ours.

First, given its complexity, the human world could only be observed and knowledge of it required data. This requirement can be illustrated by the institutional role March played in France at the turn of the century. In 1892 he joined the Office du Travail (OT), which had been created the previous year to study the various elements of labor.[3] At that time the SGF was a department of the OT.[4] This connection was not by chance: it was necessary for the OT to get precise information on national economic structure as well as on individuals, and such information could be collected through censuses that fell within the scope of the SGF. The SGF reported regularly on demography and economics (industrial structures, wages, and so forth) and collected data for various ministries and administrations; some of their findings were published in the associated review, the *Bulletin de la Statistique Générale de la France*. The work these agencies achieved during this period was impressive, especially that concerning the collection of data, and a large part of the work is largely to be attributed to March (Huber 1937).

But March's concept of "observation" requires more precise definition. To him, social scientists had "to describe carefully and to measure as exactly as possible the facts to be observed" (1924, 331). Consequently, statistics and measurement were closely associated: "the method of statistics intervenes when we want to measure" (1908, 290). March's historical survey of the development of statistics directly led him to believe that "the development of a lot of sciences has followed the creation or the improvement of instruments of measure that made possible immediate and objective determinations of what was studied" (1924, 326). Otherwise stated, just as he defined statistics on a basis of exclusion, he identified its range of application through the elimination of nonmeasurable phenomena, such as those of psychology (1924, 332)   and we guess that March never appreciated the "calculus of pleasures and pains" discussed by Harro Maas in this volume. Yet statistics has a wide range of application, as March's applied work illustrates. March's work mainly concerned demography and economics and is a hymn to statistics: it was constantly based on measurable phenomena or on phenomena that he helped to make measurable, such as unemployment (Topalov 1994). Perhaps less known is his involvement in eugenics. From an institutional point of view, he contributed to the creation in 1912 of a French society

3. On the history of the OT, see Luciani 1992.
4. The history of the SGF is rather meandering, in the sense that it is characterized by a successive dependency on various ministries and administrations (see Marietti 1947).

devoted to the promotion of eugenics, the Société Française d'Eugénique, and in various papers he remained open about his eugenic beliefs.[5] From a methodological point of view, this involvement is perfectly understandable given the other issues he tackled: eugenics involved a quantification and a measurement of the hereditary makeup of individuals, "a reduction of people to numbers" (MacKenzie 1981, 34).

Second, March saw such a gathering of data and measurements as a unique means to approach the social world. Some regularities could then be unveiled, and statistics aimed precisely toward the discovery of signs of constancy, of order within the chaos of complex phenomena: "Because the human mind does not easily understand a complex or variable group, it can only exert its power for generalization through the reduction of complexity to more simple notions, of variables to something constant. The method of statistics tends toward that" (1924, 327). This idea was not highly original: March here exemplifies the nineteenth-century use of statistical methods in which relationships were extracted from varying measurements (Porter 1986). It should be remarked, however, that he rejected the belief that Nature was basically a simple machine.

March thus saw statistics as closely associated with observation and measurement. It offered a means of condensing heterogeneous data and of identifying regularities in mass phenomena; statistics was defined in "Statistique," a masterly paper published in 1924, as *la pléthométrie*. It was also *une langue commune* (1924, 363), applying to large territories and to a large diversity of objects. Just like Karl Pearson, March believed that statistics "provided the proper discipline to reasoning in almost every area of human activity" (Porter 1995, 20). The foundations of March's statistical ambitions need now to be explored.

Objective Foundations of Measurement and Statistics

March exposed the way statistics could extract regularities in a way that could achieve a scientific status. Statistics was defined as a three step process including observation, the determination of results, and interpretation and forecasting. This final step was believed to be unduly influenced by personal and *subjective* judgments and was thus excluded

5. See, for instance, March 1929. See Carol 1995 and Desrosières 1993 and 1998 on March's involvement in eugenics.

from the range of science. By contrast, the scientific status of the first two steps was based on their *objectivity*: statistics "helps one to reduce conjectures and gain precision in the objective dimension of the results of observation—and consequently to increase the scientific value of these results" (March 1924, 364).

The scientific dimension of the first step, that of observation, originates in the elaboration of nomenclatures and in the training of collectors. Both were seen as making statistics objective, in the sense that they contribute to "the elimination of particular and personal influences" (337). Nomenclatures as such deserve little attention, but to remark that March believed that they became objective tools as soon as their structure was detailed in such a way that it minimized the collectors' doubts.[6] Interestingly, he also advocated the need for homogeneous nomenclatures at the international level: nomenclatures should be "universal conventions" (1930b, 5), standardized tools that exclude judgment. In that sense, he had in mind a kind of objectivity associated with distance, one that transcends frontiers and hints at Porter's similar analysis of quantification as "a technology of distance" (1995, ix). The search for objectivity in the collection of data was also at work on the collectors' side: "The observer has to indicate no personal tendency; his impartiality has to be absolute" (March 1924, 330). March (328) stressed the need for the training of collectors, who have to be "impartial," "honest," and "competent"— such "morality" would lead to a reduction of errors in the collection of data. Thus he thought that careful and objective measurement was a prerequisite for scientific work in statistics.

The second step in the process of statistics was the determination of results—that is, the extraction of constant results from measurements. Once more, objectivity was at work: aggregate results aimed at identifying what individual cases share in common (342) while transcending personal behaviors. To reach this goal, the statistician had to use appropriate tools: graphs, index numbers, the correlation coefficient, and the principle of compensation associated with the normal law. March recognized that this law was beneficial and that "the use of more or less elementary mathematical schemes makes possible the determination of objective values" (1909, 255); yet he also believed that it was "an ideal model" (255) or a "bold hypothesis" (1912c, 378), and other kinds of

---

6. The collection of data was not a purely observational process: it was preceded by a priori beliefs (March 1930b, 36).

distributions were available for use (1908, 293). The key to this puzzle is to be found in his belief that science needs conventions: the Gaussian law was "precious since it establishes the practical unity of [a] group" (1909, 255–56)—it was a "frame" that sets precise limits (1910, 485). Similar arguments were developed concerning the correlation coefficient and index numbers. Although these tools could—and should—be criticized, they were parts of the conventional language of science and made possible the coordination of scientific activities; such routines work toward objectivity.

These two steps in March's process of statistics formed an objective and scientific path from heterogeneous, individual, and complex facts toward aggregate results. This statistical path in science deserves two further comments. First, March constantly insisted on the need for identifying—and also for overcoming—the limits of every component of these steps. It is striking to note that his whole work leaves space for criticism—for what he labeled "scientific criticism" (1924, 323)—which was, for instance, associated with the search for more realistic conventions. Second, March stressed the need for the elaboration of a precise and simple vocabulary. A precise vocabulary, in the sense that any confusion should be banished. For instance, "one has to regret that words such as *probability* and *correlation*, which possess a well-determined meaning in mathematical language and in logic, are used differently in statistics" (1909, 262). As we will see below, March harshly criticized the assimilation of correlation with causality practiced by several statistical economists of the early twentieth century. Otherwise stated, March claimed that we cannot demand too much of the tools used in statistics or ask for more than their hypotheses stipulate. He continued to advocate the use of simple vocabulary to help avoid misunderstanding and because he hoped that statistical tools could be used by nonspecialists, (for instance, businessmen) as well.

Graphs, Coefficients, Barometers: March's Measurement Implements

Now we will analyze the manner in which March approached and practiced statistics in his concrete work. We will here suggest that his contribution to the elaboration of statistical tools for the social sciences as well as for his own economic work, especially on business cycles, perfectly illustrates how he extracted regularities from heterogeneous data and how he pressed the limits of such attempts.

Fechner and Pearson Revisited: New Tools for the Comparison of Socioeconomic Time Series

Today March remains known for his study devoted to the comparison of socioeconomic variables, *Les représentations graphiques et la statistique comparative* (1905). This work aimed at presenting two kinds of tools that he considered useful for such an enterprise: graphic representations and mathematical indices, which he called *indices de dépendance*.

Here March's analysis of these indices deserves special attention.[7] *Les représentations* opened with Gustav Fechner's indices,[8] which March pedagogically exposed and applied to various examples, including the relationship between marriage and birth rates in France and the relationship between several financial variables such as the Banque de France cash balance and discount rate. He then presented "improvements" to Fechner's indices and moved toward Pearson's coefficient of correlation. But the use of these indices led him to face a problem relative to time: "In the previous studies, we have supposed that we dealt with annual changes. But it frequently appears that, in the changes that affect statistical facts, we can distinguish various phases. We will distinguish yearly changes, changes relative to several years (for instance, decennial changes), secular changes, and of course changes relative to periods inferior to one year" (1905, 32). March thus recognized that using a tool devised outside the social sciences required adaptation. Actually the correlation coefficient could not be immediately used by economists, since economic laws did not deal with variability within the population, "rather, socio-economic data often consisted of single observations . . .

---

7. As explained below, March saw these indices as closely connected to graphs.

8. March presented two coefficients of dependency devised by Fechner. The first one is $i = (c - d)/(c + d)$, where c is the "number of agreements" (i.e., cases in which the two series move in the same direction) and d is the "number of disagreements" (i.e., the opposite case). However, "this index does not take into account the magnitude of the compared differences" (1905, 26). March also referred to another coefficient, defined as $I = (C - D)/(C + D)$, where C is the sum of the products of the values of both variables when their variation reveals an "agreement" and D is the sum of the products of the values of both variables when their variation reveals a "disagreement." However, this index "does not sufficiently take into account the amplitude of the compared variations" (1905, 27).

connected together to form a time-series which exhibited variability over time. Available correlation techniques were not designed with such time-series in mind" (Morgan 1997, 49). March recognized the difference between biometrics and the social sciences, and therefore the question was: Which of several units of time should be correlated? As Judy Klein (1997, 229) noted:

> The earliest writers saw the time-correlation problem as isolating the different components and correlating only similar components of two or more variables. It was usually of greater interest to economists to investigate correlation of short-term oscillations, in particular the movement through the trade or business cycle. Economic statisticians recognized that the correlation coefficients of unmanipulated observations only indicated a relationship between the secular changes.

And as March (1905, 32) stated, "In a careful analysis of the conditions of dependency between two statistical series, we have to calculate the coefficient of dependency between annual changes as well as between long-term changes—for instance, decennial changes." Here we should note that the 1905 study contained new techniques that could solve the time problem. March suggested that correlation of first differences could be used to capture the correlation of short-term changes,[9] whereas the correlation of long-term changes was based on a ten-year moving average. He applied the method to the relationship between the marriage and birth rates in England and also introduced lags in the analysis. But the study also contained a new method of time-series decomposition (independently developed by Reginald Hooker in 1901 and John Norton in 1902)[10] that enabled him to isolate short-term changes defined as the deviations from a moving average representing the trending factor: "In order to offer a greater precision to our analysis," he wrote, "we have to decompose the changes that are studied. . . . We can determine a coefficient of dependency between: (1) the *courbes interpolées* or *courbes moyennes*; (2) the differences between the observed numbers and these *courbes moyennes*" (1905, 34). He applied this

9. A similar method was independently suggested by Reginald Hooker in 1905. See Klein 1997 and Morgan 1990.

10. See Klein 1997. Note that in 1863, Jules Regnault, a largely neglected French economist, formulated the basis of such a decomposition in his modeling of the stock market (Jovanovic 2000; Jovanovic and Le Gall 2001).

decomposition to the study of the relationship between the marriage rate and unemployment (36).

Les représentations undoubtedly deserves a special place in the history of econometrics and time-series analysis. Several of March's other contributions also illustrate the intersections of his work with econometrics, for instance his parametric estimation of a distribution of wages (March 1898). Moreover, two statisticians trained by March, Henri Bunle and Marcel Lenoir, also wrote econometric treatises.[11] However, an econometric interpretation of March's economic work would be misleading: he had a greater predilection for other statistical strategies, as his construction of a business barometer suggests.[12]

March and Business Cycles: On Barometric Indexation

In the 1920s March attacked the challenging task of measuring business cycles. He constructed a French business barometer—barometers defined as "time-series representations of cyclical activity" (Morgan 1990, 57)—based on index numbers and considered an equivalent to the Harvard barometer.[13]

Although March postulated that business cycles were complex in the sense that they resulted from "innumerable and very different economic facts" (1923, 252), he believed that they could be analyzed with the help of index numbers, "instruments of observation and analysis" and "instruments of measurement" (277). But such numbers were also "conventions" (253) or instruments of international comparison. March thus adopted indices that were counterparts of those on which the previously constructed barometers were based: the price of financial instruments (A),[14] the wholesale prices $(B1)$, the British wholesale prices $(B2)$, and

11. On Bunle 1911 and Lenoir 1913, see Chaigneau and Le Gall 1998, Desrosières 1993, Hendry and Morgan 1995, and Morgan 1990.

12. March's research path can here be contrasted with that of Hooker (on Hooker, see Klein 1997; Morgan 1990, 1997). Around 1900 both examined similar problems, but March's work took an almost opposite direction and became concerned with historical time. This helps explain why the correlation coefficient was of little importance in the papers he published after 1905.

13. On a history of business barometers, see Armatte 1992.

14. During the 1910s, the statisticians of the SGF became interested in the influence of the stock market fluctuations on economic activity, and Lenoir led the study of that issue. In a first step, he developed in 1919 the first long-term indices relative to the French stock market. This included the construction of two indices: an index relative to bonds (including 17 securities)

the Banque de France discount rate (*C*). He thus ended up with *ABC* curves in Warren Persons's Harvard style (see Morgan 1990). March's barometer, shown in figure 1, illustrates the cycles in France, England, and the United States. The barometer suggests the ways the various curves are related within the cycles—their "*successions*," in March's own words. It also suggests a kind of international regularity: March remarked that "the *ABC* curves in England reveal the same pattern [as those in the United States]: the oscillations of speculation precede those of prices, which are themselves followed by the oscillations of the discount rate" (177). These successions, however, were less apparent in the case of France.

March's index numbers approach remains at times ambiguous. On the one hand, he seemed to view them as physical measurements of variables (277), as in the price index work of Wesley Clair Mitchell and Irving Fisher (see Spencer Banzhaf's article in this volume)—and the purpose was to get measures of their movements through time. On the other hand, the important thing about March's measurement approach was not the numbers as such (compared to the point of the exercises discussed by Marcel Boumans [this volume] and Banzhaf [this volume]) but rather the search for graphic indicators that could establish facts about economic phenomena and make possible the discovery of regularities, in the style of Mitchell's business cycle work. Then the existence of such regularities had to be verified by the *indices de dépendance*: "These movements can be usefully compared to each other . . . in order to search for possible links. I have already exposed in the Société [de Statistique de Paris] adequate methods to reach this aim" (263).[15] This means that March believed that graphs and indices were two complementary technologies that should be used hand in hand.

March's views on cycles deserve two comments. First, he thought that index numbers could not "be considered as precise" (277) and could not take into account the whole range of circumstances—this was to him a major difference between measurement in economics and measurement

---

and an index relative to stocks (including 186 securities, decomposed in twenty-five sector-based sub-indices). In a second step, he constructed after 1919 several indices complementary to those previously mentioned and some monthly indices as well. This work by Lenoir deserves two brief comments. First, it illustrates the role of the SGF in constructing instruments that make possible the observation of economic activity. Second, his work was closely associated with graphs used to infer some of the relationships between the stock market and economic activity.

15. He made here no use of correlation.

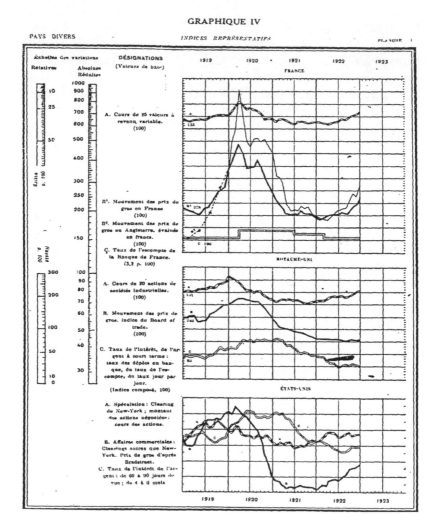

Figure 1   March's barometer (1923, 276)

in some of the natural sciences (277–78). However, he believed that a large variety of indices could help in narrowing uncertainties (278–79). Second, the complexity of business cycles was grounded in the belief that their origins could not be traced back to a single cause: "Cyclical fluctuations cover phenomena of very different origins: meteorological accidents (drought, frost, flooding, and so forth), social accidents (wars, strikes), or monetary phenomena" (271). March did not use the term "fluctuation" by chance. He rejected the possibility of strictly periodic cycles because economic conditions were changing in such a way that the length of cycles was expected to vary; business cycles were seen as recurrent but not strictly periodic. From that point of view, his cycle approach strongly differs from William Jevons's and Henry Moore's social astronomy (see Sandra Peart's essay in this volume and Le Gall 1999). Moreover, some of the phenomena influencing economic conditions could not be quantified and measured (March 1923, 270). This meant that institutions, history, and so forth were significant and consequently that partial theories should be considered cautiously.

Similar conclusions can be drawn from a paper March published in 1912 on a statistical and graphical test of the quantity theory of money (considering the 1783–1910 period). March doubted the relevance of such a simple relationship and believed that "other factors have to be taken into account" (1912b, 114). His approach to monetary issues can here be contrasted with the episodes in the quantitative assessment of the value of money analyzed by Kevin Hoover and Michael Dowell (this volume) and Thomas Humphrey (this volume). A common concern of the authors they study was the search for causes, and some of them referred to John Stuart Mill's emphasis on a single main cause[16]—although Mill thought that no one such cause could be extricated empirically from a multitude of significant causes (Peart this volume). By contrast, March found it necessary from the start to take into account the whole range of circumstances; he developed a taste for a statistical approach that left no room for abstraction[17] and that could respect the complexity of the real world. He believed that statistics made possible the derivation of empirical regularities in the social world; we suggest, however, that such regularities could not be considered laws.

16. According to Zouboulakis (1990), Mill and the economists of the "Ricardian tradition" had to demonstrate the relevance of an analytical approach which was based on the isolation of economic phenomena. Their proof rested on an argument—the "composition of causes"—directly taken from mechanics: when an effect depends on a concurrence of causes, these causes must be studied one by one and their laws separated in order to obtain, eventually, the law of the whole phenomena. See also Le Gall and Robert 1999.

17. By contrast, "Mill thought that abstractions were necessary to the scientific pretensions of political economy because they would reveal the true nature of economic activity to us," although "he did not think that that was all you needed in order to explain things in the economy" (Morgan 2000, 153).

March's views on economic cycles and on the quantity theory show that he became more interested in the *composition* problem—the interweaving of phenomena, which was to him the fundamental issue in the social sciences—than in the *decomposition* problem, although he remains known for his technical contribution to the latter. We also see that March, even while he practiced statistics, which he saw as a methodological path to observe the social world, constantly put forward the limits of his exercises. To understand such a combination, we should examine the association he made between statistics and his epistemological views.

Approaching the Lost World: Epistemological Foundations of Statistics

We believe that March's statistical work cannot be separated from his epistemological views: the various limits he put forward—those in measurement and statistics—in both his theoretical and applied work originate in precise worldviews. March believed that the world was intrinsically complex, characterized by epistemic uncertainty, and out of reach—a kind of lost world. However, this does not mean that he excluded realism from the range of science and of statistics: he believed statistics offered a means of approaching—and taming, in the sense of Ian Hacking (1990)—the world and of allowing decision making in human societies.

Correlation, Historical Time, and Causality:
March Attacks

March carefully delineated the range of application of the method of correlation: it was a tool that took no account of the time dimension and could not be considered to measure causal relationships.

He realized that a correlation coefficient cannot be sufficient to analyze the relation between variables, it makes possible the quantification of the intensity of their association, but it leads to a loss of information in the sense that it negates historical time. March thought that history mattered within the social world, that various circumstances could never be considered constant: "Economic laws, like every general formula, remain valid only during a certain period and under precise circumstances" (1912b, 112). However, unlike correlation, graphs illustrate economic movements over time:

From the point of view of descriptive statistics, [graphs] present . . .
the schematic picture of facts that can be measured. From the point
of view of comparative (or analytical) statistics, they show the reciprocal relations between facts and can help in the discovery of what is
constant in these relations. Moreover, they simplify the comparison
of the various phases of a phenomenon, they reveal irregularities and
anomalies. (1905, 4)

This conviction led March to proclaim that correlation and graphs should
not be separated—and this was the methodological path he followed
when studying business cycles, as seen above. This idea originated in the
1905 study, whose title was suggestive: *Les représentations graphiques
et la statistique comparative*. If that study is today known for including pioneering ideas about correlation, it also contains long discussions
about graphs that remain neglected. Yet its originality lies in the association of both tools providing a "control" for each other: "The alliance
of graphic processes and calculus makes possible a precise analysis of
the links between facts, as far as we can evaluate the appearances and
the particularities that can be measured. The result is a method of investigation and control that should be recommended" (40). Morgan gives
precision to the different roles of correlation and graphs: correlation was
seen as a measure of the strength of an atemporal relation between variables, whereas "the arguments based on graphs were employed to justify explanations of specific historical time series" (1997, 73). She indeed
suggests that "While the introduction of the correlation coefficient could
be regarded as in some sense a significant technical advance, most economic statisticians continued [at the turn of the century] to use graphic
methods extensively. . . . Correlation . . . does not tell you the history of
the variable or help you to explain what has happened, nor even help you
predict a time series; it is a complementary, not a replacement, technology" (74–75).

If correlation was thus associated as a complement to graphs, it was
dissociated from causality. As early as 1905, March pointed out a basic difference between the *indices de dépendance*—including Pearson's
correlation coefficient—and causality, a basic difference[18] that he carefully explained from the early 1910s through to his 1930 blueprint, *Les*

---

18. Of course with correlation, no dependency is explicit—just a co-relationship. Yet recent
histories of econometrics and of statistics show that at the turn of the century, several scholars
read causality into correlation (see below).

principes de la méthode statistique. His arguments largely originate in Pearson's positivist thought, as his translation into French of the third edition of *The Grammar of Science* suggests. That book, as well as the rest of Pearson's work, was an indictment of causality. Pearson believed that we cannot gain access to causes; instead, we perceive correlations:

> Nowhere do we find perfect lawlikeness, he stressed. Everywhere we find correlations. That is, even in mechanics there is always some unexplained variation. This should cause us no distress. The possibility of science depends only in the most general way on the nature of the phenomena being investigated. A correlation, after all, is not a deep truth about the world, but a convenient way of summarizing experience. Pearson's conception of science was more a social than a natural philosophy. The key to science he found not in the world, but in an ordered method of investigation. For Pearson, scientific knowledge depended on a correct approach, and this meant, first of all, the taming of human subjectivity. (Porter 1995, 21)

March and Pearson were led to believe that causality was a "pure concept" or a "conceptual limit" whose realism had to be questioned in each particular case. This idea was expressed by March in his preface to Pearson's book:

> The author of the *Grammar* adopts Hume's idea according to which no internal necessity, and consequently no absolute regularity, exists between cause and effect. The succeeding events [*successions*] never reappear in an identical way; the notion of causality is once more a borderline notion [*notion-limite*] that exceeds sensible experience. A more or less close *statistical* agreement exists only between the changes of the cause and those of the effect (1912a, v).

This concept of *notion-limite* indicates that for March there was an epistemological barrier to grasping all causal influences in concrete cases. Along with Pearson, March claimed that causal relationships were just simple and particular "images" of the world (1931, 475)—"simplicity of nature is ultimately a simplification introduced by a mysterious power, the mental mechanism" (1912a, iv)—that should leave room for recognition that the universe was not so simple and was rather inaccessible. Consequently, the general case became a "space in between": absolute independence and dependence were just borderline cases, whereas the general rule was the continuum of intermediate situations—that is, "the various degrees of association" (Pearson 1912, 200). Correlation was precisely the adequate tool for measuring the association between two variables, but there was no possibility it could help one infer the existence of a causal relation.

At that stage we can see that March's approach contrasts with the unwavering faith of other authors using correlation, including Moore[19] and Hooker (Morgan 1990; Le Gall 1999). Moreover this differentiation of causality and correlation strongly influenced the subsequent French pioneers of econometrics—and in a more formal fashion, Lenoir (Chaigneau and Le Gall 1998). Furthermore, in order to avoid confusions generated by previous studies such as Moore's, March rejected the use of the word *correlation* in his applied work and had a predilection for the words *covariation or concomittance*, which were to him free of notions of causality.[20]

Both the alliance of correlation and graphs and the dissociation of causality from correlation find their explanations in a worldview that reserves a particular place for history and that denies the possibility of the successful search for causal relationships.

Measuring and Taming the Lost World

A key to this worldview is to be found in March's belief in the "variability"[21] and the "complexity" of the world, to use his own words. Although some regularities and even a certain determinism could be unveiled by statistics (March 1924, 351), March thought that Nature—and especially the human world—was characterized by permanent change, by epistemic uncertainty. No absolute determinism ruled society in the sense that man permanently acts on reality and that social facts depend on a human will that cannot be understood (1924, 350). Thus history matters and "variability" was permanently at work. Moreover, a large variety of phenomena were interconnected in such a way that knowledge of them was unattainable—and here we find an explanation of March's rejection of the search for causal relationships.

---

19. In a review of *Laws of Wages: An Essay in Statistical Economics* (1911), March harshly criticized Moore's assimilation of correlation and causality (see 1912c, 368).

20. Yet in the 1905 paper, March still used the word *dépendance* for "reasons of euphony" (18).

21. In this he remained close to Mill's view that hardly any two cases are exactly similar (see Peart this volume).

But how does one deal with such a world? March thought that the social scientist could not understand it, and he rejected the construction of "pseudo-realities," to use a contemporary word, that aimed at modeling and reproducing the universe[22] and that belonged only to the range of "images." Indeed, he claimed that no "anthropomorphism" (1908, 294) could exist between a theoretical world—in the sense of an abstract model—and the real world: "Certainty or scientific evidence results from an accordance between thought and itself. . . . Scientific certainty only exists in the world of concepts" (1912a, iii). In other words, March was delineating a frontier between the real and inaccessible world and any theoretical world, where certainty can prevail but has no realistic counterpart. "Pseudo-realities" were certain in the sense that they obey formal rules of logic, but given the inaccessibility of the real world, they could never be satisfying: "a theory is only satisfying if it covers [*embrasse*] the whole facts" (1909, 258). Understanding the way the universe functioned was thus out of reach.

However, there was no renouncement of studying reality per se at work here. The world could not be exhaustively understood, but it could be approximately observed and measured. Here we understand the pivotal role of statistics for March: it was the unique way to approach reality. His worldviews thus paved the way for the kinds of studies that open the door to a large variety of indicators:

> In physical meteorology, we never obtain the best forecasts on the basis of a single look at the barometer, but on the basis of observations of the thermometer, the hydrometer, and the weather vane. I doubt that a single index that would be a synthesis of these four observations could be more useful than four indications taken separately. . . . Similarly, in the observation of business movement, we have to avoid a unique basis; it is useful to examine the whole basis. (1923, 281)

Such an increase in the number of measures could lead to a convergence toward more certain knowledge. However March also developed a more pessimistic idea: scientists would like to believe in such a convergence—we interpret this belief as a convention—but "the unknown and the known increase jointly" (1912a, v). In addition the social scientist could never be certain that he has reached reality: the regularities he extracted

---

22. The argument remains close to the distinction between statistics and the experimental method.

could have been different in another context, with other tools. "Reality is just a trace [*vestige*] in the large set of possibilities" (1924, 346); in that sense, statistics was only the expression of possibilities—it afforded means to study facts, but it remained impossible to infer that we had reached reality.

Such an epistemological view was a watershed. March was rejecting nineteenth-century beliefs, and in a more formal fashion, the deterministic conception of the social world. Previous statisticians or economists (such as Adolphe Quetelet, Regnault, or Moore) based their studies on the belief that simple and deterministic laws were at work—that, after all, Nature was driven by only a few wheels. This also explains the mathematical modeling of the human world that is to be found in the work of some of these authors. By contrast March rejected mathematical economics. He perceived a complexity at work in reality, and he believed this complexity should lead to a reorientation of statistical work: statistics was not a means to approximate determinism anymore, but should now aim at approaching and measuring an evasive Nature. In a sense March's thought illustrates the way the development of statistics began to tame chance at the turn of the century; statistics made chance amenable to analysis and brought it under control—as Ian Hacking emphasized when he showed how Francis Galton's tools represent "a fundamental transition in the conception of statistical laws" (1990, 181). Moreover, recent work by Giorgio Israel (1996, 2000) suggests that the erosion of determinism in science around the turn of the century made room for kinds of instrumentalism—in the sense that the aim of science became more the reproduction than the understanding of reality.[23] Yet March never rejected the study of reality: he maintained along with nineteenth-century scientists the idea that science should reveal something about reality—indeed, such a belief was the reason he remained opposed to the development of instrumental models. Nevertheless, the social world was seen as intrinsically complicated, making the task of science and statistics immensely difficult.

Statistics, in taming chance, had become a means to measure the world. But it was also a means to improve the human lot and environment. These views originate in March's perception of forecasting. Straightaway it should be noted that forecasting is characterized by a form of paradox: it is the ultimate aim of statistics but at the same time it

23. Such an analysis perfectly fits the history of econometrics (Le Gall 2001a).

marks the end of science. Indeed, March believed that forecasting was a subjective exercise: the various users of statistical studies—businessmen or governments—have to interpret statistical regularities according to their own aims. It was taken for granted that statistics offered a fragile knowledge relative to a complex object. Forecasting was thus based on conjectures relative to what has happened and to what will happen and necessarily involved "personal judgment" (March 1923, 280). In March's words, it was "*un art*" (1931, 475) characterized by "*la liberté de se déterminer*" (1930a, 269)—and was the moment when science stops. Once more, this idea is to be contrasted with the appreciation of forecasting found within the deterministic paradigm, in which the discovery of laws was synonymous with the discovery of what the future had in store. In March's statistical work we see now both chance tamed and cracks in determinism. But this "end of science" does not reduce the usefulness of forecasting, and March's barometer is here an enlightening case study. Although the label is somewhat misleading,[24] the barometer was an instrument of prediction. It was a tool to be used by governments and businessmen: for instance, forecasting based on an analysis of the curves could aid in reasoning and decision making within the firm. An illustration can be found in the fact that a barometer makes possible the determination of the moment when "the prices will be the most attractive" (March 1931, 473). More generally, forecasting was a means to lessen risks, to dominate the environment, to aid community reasoning within a firm or a nation: "*administrer c'est prévoir*" (1930b, x) was March's motto.[25] Statistics was thus seen as a means of measuring but also of taming and shaping the social world.

Conclusion

March's statistical style can be understood as the search for tools and indicators that make possible an approximate measurement of the social

---

24. The visual language of the graphs provides not just an indicator of where the economy is going (as a barometer), but a whole picture of what it has gone through. March's "barometer" was not just an instrument of observation but more nearly an instrument of current indication and prediction.

25. We do not believe here that this emphasis on using statistics for prediction rather than explanation was exclusively influenced by his practical work for the government. We more generally suggest that it was associated with and resulted from well-shaped epistemological views.

world—a quest that was only meaningful with respect to precise epistemological views. His involvement in measurement was closely associated with the belief that a unique research path existed in the social
sciences. Observation formed the path, and it generated knowledge per
se.

Our history of March's statistical style can illuminate the way the relations between measurement, statistics, and economics were perceived
in France during the early twentieth century, and the characteristic style
of French thinking about economic statistics. March's statistical style—
which, in certain respects, shares much in common with the American
statistical parades of the 1910s and with the approach of the National
Bureau for Economic Research and Mitchell—can explain the lack of
recognition of the contributions to pre-probabilistic econometrics that
arose at the SGF during the early 1910s (particularly those of Bunle
and Lenoir, both of whom finally followed March's statistical path). But
March's stamp was deeper: his statistical style flourished in France and
contributed to a particular approach to public statistics. Between 1920
and World War II, the SGF—then run by Michel Huber, who had been
largely trained by March—followed this approach. After World War II
the INSEE[26] developed a method associated with national accounting
that largely remained impervious to mathematical methods and to the
Cowles approach and their methods of statistical inference, which were
seen as a conservative practice based on the observation of the past (Malinvaud 1991). In some respects, that strategy was a wider feature of
French economic thought during the period (Le Gall 2001b).

Yet, beyond this historical influence, we believe that March deserves
a particular attention for his emphasis on the epistemological foundations of the statistical work to be done in economics, an emphasis that
followed three precepts. First, he constantly stressed the need for criticism, sometimes in a pre-Popperian style. All of his work was constantly an occasion for the identification of limits. Second, his approach
to the world remained wise. He claimed that scientists could never completely master the way the social world was functioning and, for that
reason, would have to remain aware of their own limits and possibilities. Third, he was adamant that science has a precise aim: the knowledge of the world and of mankind and the improvement of the human

---

26. The Institut National de la Statistique et des Études Économiques. The SGF became the
INSEE in 1946.

lot. Yet, as Israel convincingly explains, during the twentieth century, science progressively became dominated by another factor: its own language, in the sense that it became more concerned with the construction of its own models than with inquiries into the objects it was supposed to explain. Such an approach is perfectly exemplified by the construction of "pseudo-realities" in economics. However, and although our contemporary context strongly differs from that of the early twentieth century, March reminds us that "science offers means and not the ends of action" (Israel 2000, 196). We can still draw lessons from March's statistical style.

References

Armatte, Michel. 1992. Conjonctions, conjoncture et conjecture: Les baromètres économiques (1885–1930). *Histoire et mesure* 7.1–2:99–149.

Bunle, Henri. 1911. Relation entre les variations des indices économiques et le mouvement des mariages. *Journal de la Société de Statistique de Paris*. 52:80–93.

Carol, Anne. 1995. *Histoire de l'eugénisme en France: Les médecins et la procréation, XIXe-XXe siècles*. Paris: Le Seuil.

Chaigneau, Nicolas, and Philippe Le Gall. 1998. The French Connection: The Pioneering Econometrics of Marcel Lenoir (1913). In *European Economists of the Early 20th Century: Studies of Neglected Thinkers*, edited by W. J. Samuels. Cheltenham, U.K.: Edward Elgar.

Desrosières, Alain. 1993. *La politique des grands nombres: Histoire de la raison statistique*. Paris: La Découverte.

———. 1998. Lucien March (1859–1933): A Pioneer of Quantitative Economics. In *European Economists of the Early 20th Century: Studies of Neglected Thinkers*, edited by W. J. Samuels. Cheltenham, U.K.: Edward Elgar.

Divisia, François. 1951. *Exposés d'économique: L'apport des ingénieurs français aux sciences économiques*. Paris: Dunod.

Ekelund, Robert B., and Robert F. Hébert. 1999. *Secret Origins of Modern Microeconomics: Dupuit and the Engineers*. Chicago: University of Chicago Press.

Hacking, Ian. 1990. *The Taming of Chance*. Cambridge: Cambridge University Press.

Hébert, Robert F. 1986. Emile Cheysson and the Birth of Econometrics. *Œconomia—Economies et sociétés*. 10:203–22.

Hendry, David F., and Mary S. Morgan. 1995. *The Foundations of Econometric Analysis*. Cambridge: Cambridge University Press.

Huber, Michel. 1937. Quarante ans de la Statistique Générale de la France. *Journal de la Société de Statistique de Paris*. 78:179–214.

Israel, Giorgio. 1996. *La mathématisation du réel: Essai sur la modélisation mathématique*. Paris: Le Seuil.

———. 2000. *Le Jardin au noyer: Pour un nouveau rationalisme.* Paris: Le Seuil.

Jovanovic, Franck. 2000. L'origine de la théorie financière: Une réévaluation de l'apport de Louis Bachelier. *Revue d'économie politique* 110.3:395–418.

Jovanovic, Franck, and Philippe Le Gall. 2001. Does God Practice a Random Walk? The "Financial Physics" of a French 19th Century Pioneer, Jules Regnault. *European Journal for the History of Economic Thought* 8.3. Forthcoming.

Klein, Judy L. 1997. *Statistical Visions in Time: A History of Time Series Analysis, 1662–1938.* Cambridge: Cambridge University Press.

Kurita, Keiko. 1989. La pensée économique des ingénieurs des Ponts et Chaussées dans la période de l'industrialisation de la France. Ph.D. diss., Université Panthéon-Sorbonne (Paris I).

Le Gall, Philippe. 1999. A World Ruled by Venus: On Henry L. Moore's Transfer of Periodogram Analysis from Physics to Economics. *HOPE* 31.4:723–52.

———. 2001a. Les représentations du monde et les pensées analogiques des économètres: Un siècle de modélisation en perspective. *Revue d'histoire des sciences humaines.* Forthcoming

———. 2001b. Twentieth Century French Economic Thought in Historical Perspective. In *The Columbia History of Twentieth Century French Thought*, edited by L. D. Kritzman. New York: Columbia University Press.

Le Gall, Philippe, and Olivier Robert. 1999. David's Family and the Flat-Earthers. In *Research in the History of Economic Thought and Methodology*, vol. 19, edited by W. J. Samuels and J. Biddle. Stamford, Conn.: JAI Press.

Lenoir, Marcel. 1913. *Etudes sur la formation et le mouvement des prix.* Paris: Giard et Brière.

———. 1919. Le mouvement des cours des valeurs mobilières françaises depuis 1856. *Bulletin de la Statistique Générale de la France* 9:65–92.

Luciani, Jean, ed. 1992. *Histoire de l'Office du Travail.* Paris: Syros.

MacKenzie, Donald A. 1981. *Statistics in Britain, 1865–1930.* Edinburgh: Edinburgh University Press.

Malinvaud, Edmond. 1991. *Voies de recherche macroéconomique.* Paris: Odile Jacob.

March, Lucien. 1898. Quelques exemples de distributions des salaires. *Journal de la Société de Statistique de Paris* 39:193–206, 241–48.

———. 1905. *Les représentations graphiques et la statistique comparative.* Nancy: Berger-Levrault.

———. 1908. Remarques sur la terminologie en statistique. *Journal de la Société de Statistique de Paris* 49:290–96.

———. 1909. De l'application des procédés mathématiques à la comparaison de statistiques. *Bulletin de l'Institut International de Statistique* 18:254–64.

———. 1910. Essai sur le mode d'exposer les principaux éléments de la théorie statistique. *Journal de la Société de Statistique de Paris* 51:447–86.

———. 1912a. Note du traducteur. In *La grammaire de la science*, 3d ed., by Karl Pearson. Paris: Félix Alcan.

———. 1912b. L'influence de l'accroissement du stock monétaire sur les prix. *Journal de la Société de Statistique de Paris* 53:111–15.

———. 1912c. La théorie des salaires: A propos de l'ouvrage du Professeur Ludwell Moore: Laws of Wages. *Journal de la Société de Statistique de Paris* 53:366–83.

———. 1923. L'étude statistique du mouvement général des affaires. *Journal de la Société de Statistique de Paris* 64:251–81.

———. 1924. Statistique. In *De la méthode dans les sciences*. Paris: Félix Alcan.

———. 1929. Démographie. In vol. 22 of *Traité d'hygiène*, edited by L. Martin and G. Brouardel. Paris: Librairie Baillière.

———. 1930a. Les éléments instructifs des prévisions économiques. *Bulletin de l'Institut International de Statistique* 24:268–82.

———. 1930b. *Les principes de la méthode statistique*. Paris: Félix Alcan.

———. 1931. La statistique et le mouvement des affaires. *Bulletin de l'Institut International de Statistique* 25:470–78.

Marietti, Pascal-Gaston. 1947. *La Statistique Générale en France*. Rufisque, Senegal: Imprimerie du Gouvernement.

Ménard, Claude. 1980. Three Forms of Resistance to Statistics: Say, Cournot, Walras. *HOPE* 12.4:524–41.

Morgan, Mary S. 1990. *The History of Econometric Ideas*. Cambridge: Cambridge University Press.

———. 1997. Searching for Causal Relations in Economic Statistics. In *Causality in Crisis? Statistical Method and the Search for Causal Knowledge in the Social Sciences*, edited by V. R. McKim and S. P. Turner. Notre Dame, Ind.: University of Notre Dame Press.

———. 2000. Explanatory Strategies for Monetary Policy Analysis. In vol. 1 of *Macroeconomics and the Real World*, edited by R. E. Backhouse and A. Salanti, 141–54. Cambridge: Cambridge University Press.

Pearson, Karl. 1912. *La grammaire de la science*. 3d ed. Paris: Félix Alcan.

Porter, Theodore M. 1986. *The Rise of Statistical Thinking 1820–1900*. Princeton, N.J.: Princeton University Press.

———. 1995. *Trust in Numbers: The Pursuit of Objectivity in Science and Public Life*. Princeton, N.J.: Princeton University Press.

Summers, Lawrence H. 1991. The Scientific Illusion in Empirical Macroeconomics. *Scandinavian Journal of Economics* 93.2:129–48.

Topalov, Christian. 1994. *Naissance du chômeur, 1880–1910*. Paris: Albin Michel.

Zouboulakis, Michel. 1990. *La science économique à la recherche de ses fondements: La tradition épistémologique ricardienne, 1826–1891*. Paris: Presses Universitaires de France.

Perspective
Reflections from the Age of Economic Measurement

Judy L. Klein

In this perspective, I use six images to sketch a chronology and economic history of the age of economic measurement. These six images are not from canonical works in the history of economics. Rather they are drawn from fertile "borderlands" (see Theodore Porter's essay in this volume), "trading zones" (Galison 1997), or "bridges" between commercial, political, and scientific arithmetics (Klein 1997). The six visualizations bear witness to the eras in which they were crafted and reflect the important studies discussed in other essays in this volume.

Playfair's Inquiry into the Propensity of Nations to Decline

A few years after Adam Smith published his *Inquiry into the Nature and Causes of the Wealth of Nations*, William Playfair published several tracts examining the causes of the *decline* of nations. Playfair used what he described as a "linear arithmetic" to examine these causes—almost every publication of his is graced with stunning colorful graphs including area charts, line graphs, bar graphs, and circular charts. He was the first to publish several of these forms of presenting commercial data (he

Correspondence may be addressed to Judy L. Klein, Department of Economics, Mary Baldwin College, Staunton, VA 24401; e-mail: jklein@mbc.edu. I thank Mary Morgan for her comments on earlier drafts, the participants of the Age of Measurement workshop for their thought-provoking presentations, and Princeton University Press for permission to reproduce George Dantzig's linear programming timetable.

argued that he was the first to apply the principle of geometry to matters of finance), and his stained copper-plated charts were well received by the Academy of Science in France, German writers, and at least Thomas Jefferson in the newly formed United States. Playfair acknowledged the difficulty of separating the permanent and accidental causes for national decline voiced by contemporary writers such as Edmund Burke. He asserted, however, that his "mode of painting" could isolate and capture the essence of permanent causes (1786, 5).

Playfair thought that his inquiries would be of particular interest to those in his own country because England had risen "high above the natural level assigned to it by its population and extent" (1805, v). In his late-eighteenth-century publications, Playfair was particularly concerned that England's trade deficit and the level of its national debt—incurred in fighting the American War of Independence, the war with the Republic of France, and the war with Napoleon (the latter being addressed in his later work)—could spell the beginning of the end for its commercial strength. Most of the graphs in his 1786 *Commercial and Political Atlas* and his 1801 *Statistical Breviary* visually displayed measurements of national exports and imports (with deficits stained in red) or government revenues, expenditures, and debt. The price of wheat was the other major focus of Playfair's charts (see Klein 1995)—between one-third and one-half of family expenditures at that time went to wheat flour or bread, and no other important price fluctuated so greatly. For Adam Smith (see the article by Kevin Hoover and Michael Dowell in this volume), Playfair, Sir George Shuckburgh Evelyn, and other late-eighteenth-century writers, tables or graphs of time series of the price of wheat spoke to the changing value and well-being of labor and to the balance between the agricultural and manufacturing sectors.

The graph I wish to highlight here is his "Universal Chart of Commercial History" (fig. 1). Playfair (1805) wanted to capture the "propensity" of all wealthy and commercially powerful nations to decline to states of desolation and poverty. He asserted that national phenomena were "exempt from accidental vicissitudes" because "number and magnitude reduces chances to certainty" (xii). Accident could only appear to be a cause for the decline of wealth of nations; a nation had to be ripe for ruin. It was the cause of this "ripeness" that Playfair addressed in his essay. In his graph he used dimension, without number or magnitude, to indicate the general course of the rise and fall of the wealth of nations that had been distinguished for their prosperity and power. The chart

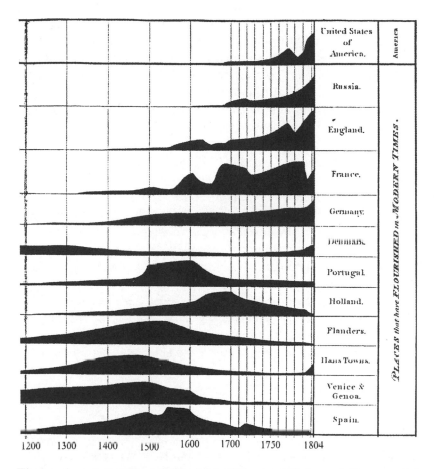

1200   1300   1400   1500   1600   1700   1750   1804

Figure 1   A portion of Playfair's "Chart of Universal Commercial History" (1805, frontispiece). This portion begins in A.D. 1200, ends in 1804, and covers only those commercial empires that "flourished in modern times." Playfair etched the area of each empire, which indicated commercial strength and its duration, from historical narrative.

begins midway through the height of the Egyptian empire in 1500 B.C. and ends in A.D. 1804. Time series of internationally consistent estimates from national income accounts were not available until over 140 years later. Playfair measured without numbers, boldly asserting that "for a very accurate view, there are not materials in existence; neither would it lead to any very different conclusion, if the proportional values were ascertained with the greatest accuracy" (1).

In his Royal Statistical Society discussion of William Guy's 1879 essay "On Tabular Analysis," William Stanley Jevons lamented that a sterile, graphless eight decades separated Playfair's inauguration of linear arithmetic and Jevons's own economic graphs. Playfair's charts, however, embody the state of economic measurement of his era. Numbers existed for extensive time series in the price of wheat, and in the service of empire building, there were shorter, regularly tabulated numbers on trade flows and government expenditures and the occasional declaration of population (see Playfair 1801 and Sybilla Nikolow's essay in this volume). There were no magnitudes to measure the wealth of nations other than the mercantile proxy of tables of exports and imports. The economic well-being of nations, however, was a key concept in the political economy of the day, and it was to the goal of nation building (or empire building or nation preserving) that statistical inquiries were usually directed. Although graphs were unusual in these inquiries (see Nikolow's discussion, this volume, of August Crome's charts as an exception to this), a few pamphlets with statistical tables were published. Around 1800 this interest in the general course and general causes of the rise and fall of the wealth of nations dominated interest in the course and causes of short term changes. As to the latter "fluctuations to which nations are liable," Playfair asserted (1805, vii), "it would be absurd to enter into any theory about them."

Von Thünen's Geometric Landscape

In 1826 the German agriculturalist Johann Heinrich von Thünen published *The Isolated State with Respect to Agriculture and Political Economy*. Although his formal education at agriculture colleges had included mathematics and some political economy—Adam Smith in particular— von Thünen was a farmer and a parliamentarian, not a professor. His treatise on the isolated state is considered an early masterpiece in deductive reasoning and optimization methods. Chapter 1 on the "hypothesis" begins: "Imagine a very large town, at the centre of a fertile plain which is crossed by no navigable river or canal. Throughout the plain the soil is capable of cultivation and of the same fertility. Far from the town, the plain turns into an uncultivated wilderness which cuts off all communication between this State and the outside world" ([1826] 1966, 7).

What place does this imagining and von Thünen's comparative statics have in our view of the age of economic measurement? Von Thünen's

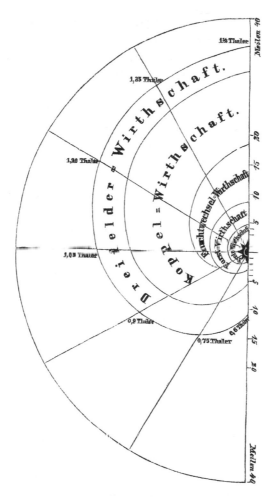

Figure 2   Von Thünen's (1826, 393) diagram of the relationship between the price of wheat in thalers (measured as an angle) and the extent of various forms of cultivation from the town center (measured as a radius). The radius of the full circle represented forty miles. So, for example, when the price of wheat was 0.6 thalers, all forms of cultivation extended to only ten miles from the town center, and the longer fallow, three-field (*dreifelder*) system was found only between five and ten miles from the town center. When the price of wheat was 1.5 thalers, cultivation extended to thirty-five miles from the town center.

semicircular layout for relating forms of cultivation to the price of wheat (reproduced in fig. 2) is a good illustration of the relationship between magnitude and mathematics in the days when agriculture dominated production, canals and rivers dominated commerce, and the price of wheat dominated many other measures of value. Auguste Comte (see Porter this volume), a European contemporary of von Thünen, asserted that mathematics developed as a means of measuring magnitudes *indirectly*. Among the educated in von Thünen's day, the chief form for this indirect imputation of magnitude was Euclidian geometry (see Roy Weintraub and Marcel Boumans's essays in this volume).

In von Thünen's schematic diagram, the price of wheat is measured as an angle. A viewer starting at six o'clock (where the price of wheat is 0.6 thalers) and proceeding up to noon (where the price of wheat is 1.5 thalers) will notice that the radius for cultivation increases, as do the radii of the systems of cultivation characterized by shorter fallow time and more intensive use of the land. In the translated words of von Thünen ([1826] 1966, 217): "The diagram illustrates the effect of the Town grain price on the extension of the cultivated plain. Only the radius of the cultivated area and of the individual concentric rings is marked; so if we wished to draw a representation of the Isolated State for a given grain price, say 1.05 thalers, . . . we would have to measure the distance between the Town and the point 1.05 with a compass, and draw a circle of this radius around the Town."

Although this serves as an example of nonempirical, indirect measurement, we will see that in the twentieth century, geometric models in economics were sometimes invested with empirical input.

The Manchester Statistical Society's Studies of the Dark Days

Several decades after Playfair questioned the reasonableness of examining short-term fluctuations, these same fluctuations were the chief objects of the economic investigations of the Manchester Statistical Society. The society was formed in September 1833 (a couple of years before the London Statistical Society, which took its example from Manchester). Four decades later a newly elected president of the society, Thomas Wilkinson, used the opportunity of his 1875 inaugural address to reflect on the turning point of the 1830s, which he saw as the beginning of a new epoch (see Porter this volume, Cullen 1975, and Ashton

1934). Before that time, canals and coaches had been the chief means of transport, and postage and daily newspapers had been expensive luxuries. In 1836 the newspaper duty was reduced to one penny, and the twice-weekly *Manchester Guardian* became affordable to many. In 1837 direct railway service from Manchester to London began. The population of Manchester had increased 45 percent between 1821 and 1831, and the cholera epidemic of 1832 had stimulated interest in epidemiology. In 1832, the Manchester member of Parliament helped to establish the Statistical Office of the Board of Trade. McCulloch's *Dictionary of Trade* (1832) and *Statistical Account of the British Empire* (1837), extended familiarity with economic and demographic data. Other changes that Wilkinson thought relevant to the founding of the statistical society were the abolition of the slave trade in 1833, the opening up of trade with the East to all merchants (resulting from the end of the East India Company monopoly), the 1834 poor law legislation, and the beginning in 1834 of a system of national education. The latter issue was a major focus of many of the earlier studies of the society; in its first few years members put money and energy into gathering their own data through extensive surveys on education, sanitation, and the condition of the working classes (see Bradley Bateman's discussion of the social survey movement in this volume). As public authorities began taking over the tasks of collecting and analyzing data on these subjects, the society became more interested in "the laws which regulate the creation and diffusion of wealth" (Wilkinson 1875, 20). From the time of the society's first publication of its transactions in 1853, articles on economic statistics comprised a sizeable share.

The membership of the society included bankers, physicians, captains of industry, barristers, schoolmasters, civil servants, merchants, actuaries, and the occasional professor. It is obvious from the praise he received in many of the presentations published in the transactions that Professor William Stanley Jevons was a star of the Manchester Statistical Society. He was particularly appreciated for bringing theory and deductive logic to bear on the inductive investigations of the society. The banker John Mills, for example, praised Jevons's careful comparison of the rise in prices from 1851 with the previous three decades of declining prices (discussed by Hoover and Dowell, Sandra Peart, and Harro Maas in this volume):

The two periods selected as the areas of the comparison, could only have been chosen in the light of an *hypothesis* which was a deduction from a known increase in the commodity which is the common standard of the values in exchange of all other commodities. From the first ascertained fact that one side of the scale was being depressed by additional weight, he deduced the conclusion that the opposite scale must rise; and at this point the inductive statistical process commenced by way of verifying the theoretical anticipation. . . . the ultimate result of the statistical enquiry was to show an actual average rise of prices of about 10 percent. The remarkable investigation cited here as a beautiful typical illustration of the use of hypothesis in this class of enquiries, may suffice to show the mode in which theoretical Political Economy and Statistics co-operate and render a reciprocal service. (Mills 1871, 7–8).

This reciprocal service was particularly in demand in the society's concern with economic fluctuations. Over the course of decades, several members of the society sought for and refined measurements that could shed light on financial crises. For example, in an article presented before the society titled "Banking Statistics as a Measure of Trade," George Pownall argued that the banking interest had been neglected in public data (1876, 22). He claimed that information on "the ebb and flow of trade," "the lost link, the missing key" was "hidden in the books of the London and country banks" (22). Pownall called for publication of weekly data on the total turnover of all banks in key cities in order to determine the extent and locality of depression: "We could watch it as we now read a weather glass" (31; see Franck Jovanovic and Philippe Le Gall's essay in this volume on Lucien March's search for such a commercial barometer). Pownall declared that tables of exports and imports were insufficient, that only the weekly returns of all banks could "tell us a story of the dark days" (34).

The society did have at hand the weekly returns of the Bank of England with which to begin telling a story of those dark days. Starting with William Langton's presentation during a time of depression in 1857, the society crafted its own measurement of mercantile debt and plotted and tabulated the data to decipher the story of the dark days within the decades, within the year, and within the quarter (settlement days for taxes and dividends). After Langton's retirement from the society, the project was taken up by Henry Baker (1876) and A. W. Flux (1895).

Over the four decades that this project spanned, Langton, Baker, and Flux presented tables and graphs of weekly observations on the balance of the commercial community's indebtedness to the Bank of England constructed from the Bank's returns from 1844 to 1894. According to Wilkinson's recollection (1875, 21), Langton had "developed a theory of a tide in the requirements of commerce, occurring quarterly from the fiscal system existing in this country, annually as a result of the seasons, and decennially from moral causes."

In his initial presentation, Langton included a table and two charts showing the balance of account between the Mercantile Public and the Bank of England. Langton, chief cashier for Heywood Bank and a founder of the Manchester and Salford District Provident Society, used weekly Bank of England returns to construct a commercial balance of account which compared bills discounted and temporary advances by the Bank with the "other securities" and "other deposits" of the Bank (see Thomas Humphrey's essay in this volume for a discussion of banking and bills of exchange). If the aggregate value of the former two exceeded the latter two, the trading public was indebted to the bank, and the line in the charts would be above zero. If other securities and other deposits exceeded the two items indicating credit extended to merchants, then the Bank was indebted to the public and the lines fell below zero. This accounting strategy was thus directed toward measuring a balance that would indicate whether "the mercantile community are in a condition of ease, with unemployed funds at call, or whether their necessities require them to lean for assistance on the Bank of England" (Langton 1857, 9; on accounting measurement strategies, see also McCloskey 1993 and the articles in this volume by Mary Morgan and Flavio Comim).

A small part of Langton's chart indicating the behavior of this measure through the quarter is reproduced in figure 3. It looks remarkably similar to the high-low-close charts used nowadays for daily stock returns, and it may well be the earliest precursor to these. For each quarter, the heights of the ends of a line indicated the lowest and highest values observed in the thirteen weekly returns, the height of the bisecting horizontal line indicated the mean weekly balance for that quarter, and the slant of the line indicated the direction of change over the quarter. This was a pioneering marshalling of the facts. After plotting and examining this constructed measure of a commercial balance of account for every quarter from the third quarter in 1844 to the fourth quarter in 1857 and

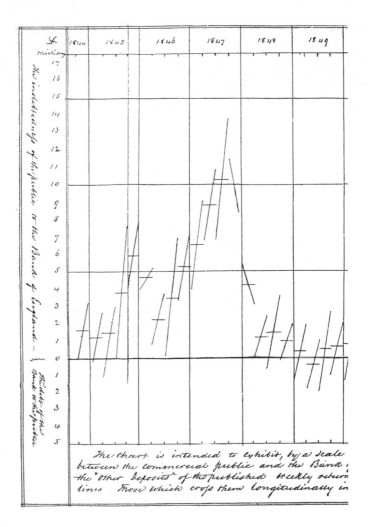

Figure 3   A portion Langton's (1857) chart of the quarterly fluctuations of the balance of account between the commercial public and the Bank of England. For each quarter, the ends of the slanted lines show the extreme weekly values of the quarter, measured in millions of pounds sterling; the height of the horizontal line indicates the mean weekly value of indebtedness; the direction of the slant indicates whether commercial indebtedness increased or decreased over the course of the quarter. Values above zero indicate commercial indebtedness, values below zero indicate the net debt of the Bank of England to the public. The entire chart spanned the years 1844 to 1857.

after examining his plot of weekly values (not shown), Langton (1857, 10–11) concluded:

> It has an annual increment and collapse, and is doubtless connected with the action of the seasons upon trade. In the midst of other disturbances, this wave may be traced in the magnitude of the operations of the third and fourth quarters, and the almost invariable lull in the second quarter of each year; the third quarter being generally marked by rapid increase in the demand for accommodation at the Bank. The culmination point of the movement, originating in the third quarter of the year, appears to be a moment favorable to the bursting of those periodical storms, in which the commercial difficulties of the country find their crisis.
>
> These disturbances are the accompaniment of another wave, which appears to have a decennial period, and in the generation of which moral causes have no doubt an important share.

The decennial wave and the tendency of periodic storms bursting forth in the fourth quarter, when the accumulated commercial debt had to be settled, were later taken up by others in the society, including John Mills and William Stanley Jevons. The work of Mills and Jevons has been well documented in the history of economics, but Langton's constructed balance, indicative of the accounting strategy that was to be so effective in economic measurement, his ingenious charts, and the updated tables and innovative diagrams of Henry Baker and A. W. Flux illustrate the directed curiosity and confidence brought to bear on economic measurement in British learned societies in the latter half of the nineteenth century.

Municipal Statistics on Parade

By the end of the nineteenth century, collecting, tabulating, and reasoning with economic measurements was a very public and even popular enterprise extending far beyond the confines of national government departments and sessions of learned societies. Patricia Cohen (1999) has documented the measurement pursuits of the mid-nineteenth-century temperance and antiprostitute movements in the United States, and Bateman (this volume) has examined the late-nineteenth-century social survey movements in Britain and the United States. By 1914 some institutional research groups were taking up the highlighted causes and the numbers generated by the surveying efforts of grassroots religious organizations and private charities. In these studies the seasonal economic fluctuations were usually of more concern to the researchers than the cyclical fluctuations. For the poor, making it through the dark days of the year posed as much if not more of a challenge then making it through the dark days of a trade cycle. The New York Baptist preacher of the social gospel Walter Rauschenbusch had, for example, lamented that in the rush season of commerce, young women were worked to the point that exhaustion threatened their potential for future reproduction; in the slow seasons of the commercial year, these same young women were unemployed and tempted by vice to procure an income (1908). Examples of formal research institutions taking up the issues of women's employment (see also Peart's discussion of Jevons's research in this volume) and the deleterious social effects of seasonal fluctuations in employment include Sidney Webb's seminar on Social Investigation and Research at the London School of Economics (e.g., Webb and Freeman 1912), the Boston-based Women's Educational and Industrial Union studies of the economic relations of women (e.g., Perry 1916), and the studies of the New York City Bureau of Social Statistics.

From 1914 until 1918 the socially conscious Mitchel administration governed New York City and established, with funding from private charities, a municipal Bureau of Social Statistics. The functions of the bureau were to measure, determine possible causes of, and recommend "efficient" solutions to destitution in the city. A new political administration closed down the bureau in 1918, but in that year Isaac Max Rubinow published the measurements of the bureau's "dependency index" in the *American Economic Review*. The measurement strategy used was one of measuring relative change; as Rubinow explained, the purpose of the index was not to measure the total amount of existing dependency or relief given, but only the fluctuations. The bureau used the index instrument because it was familiar to "not only every serious student of social science but even many progressive business men" (Rubinow 1918, 714). The dependency index was a composite of indices measuring monthly changes in family care, homelessness, the use of municipal lodging houses, foster child care, dispensary use, chattel loans, and free burials in Potters Field. Among the findings of the measurement exercise was a major rise in dependency in the winter months, such that

Figure 4   The parade of statistical exhibits by the municipal employees of New York City on 17 May 1913 (Brinton 1914, 343)

dependency in January was 39 percent above the average for a year and 82 percent above the level for a typical September.

The extent to which social and economic measurements were accepted during the Progressive Era in the United States and a form in which they were made accessible are illustrated in figure 4. On 17 May 1913 thousands of people viewed and cheered the horse-drawn floats of graphs constructed by the municipal employees of New York. In his classic text on *Graphic Method for Presenting Facts*, Willard Brinton (1914, 343) described the parade: "The progress made in recent years by practically every city department was shown by comparative models, charts, or large printed statements which could be read with ease from either side of the street. Even though the day of the parade was rainy, great crowds lined the sidewalks. There can be no doubt that many of the thousands who saw the parade came away with the feeling that much is being accomplished to improve the conditions of municipal management."

According to Brinton, the graph that most impressed the crowds was the one showing a decline in the death rate due to improvements in sanitation and nursing methods. The Great War that soon followed and the worldwide influenza epidemic of 1918 no doubt shook this confidence in the progress of civilization aided by measured social action.

Kitchin's Trade Cycle Chart

As with all major wars, World War I generated inflationary booms in most of the participating countries as well as in their colonies. For Britain and the United States, the expected, prolonged deflationary bust did not begin immediately after the war. Indeed in the first quarter of 1920, businessmen, journalists, and some economists were speculating figuratively and literally on endless prosperity. In the autumn of 1920, prices in Britain fell within two months to the armistice level marked in 1918. Wesley Mitchell called it the first worldwide recession, and the swiftness with which deflation dampened speculative excesses reinforced the Federal Reserve's resolve to adhere to a real bills view of the way the world worked (see Humphrey this volume). This "great economic storm," which began in Japan in May 1920 and "was to sweep over the world," set the tone for the *Annual Financial and Commercial Review* published by the London *Times* on 28 January 1921. In addition to the leader on finance and trade in 1920 and reports on individual industries, exchanges, colonies, and countries, the annual review included a pull-out chart constructed by Joseph Kitchin showing the history of trade cycles from 1783 to 1920 (partially shown in figs. 5a and 5b).

The title of Kitchin's essay that accompanied the chart was "Trade Cycles Chart: The Past as a Guide to the Future, A Study in Economics." Kitchin's analysis in the chart and in the essay captures several characteristic features of the state of economic measurement in that key cross section of the first worldwide recession. The first was the synergy between financial and academic presses. This large chart was intended not only for inclusion in the annual *Times* supplement, but the newspaper also expected many to purchase special copies, suitable for framing, at a price of one shilling each. The extent of the chart's circulation is evident in the debate between Nikolai Kondratiev (1922) and Leon Trotsky (1923) a few months later (see also Klein 1999b). This chart also illustrates some boundary crossing at that time between the financial press and universities. Kitchin was a businessman and a writer for the financial press, but his statistical prowess impressed Arthur Bowley at the London School of Economics. Bowley made extensive use of Kitchin's

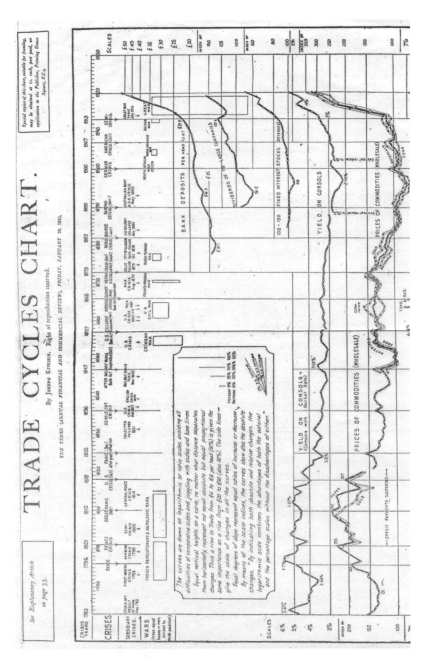

Figure 5a   The top one-third of Kitchin's "Trade Cycles Chart" (1921). The time series start in 1783 and end in 1920. Kitchin plotted per capita values for the British economy on logarithmic scales.

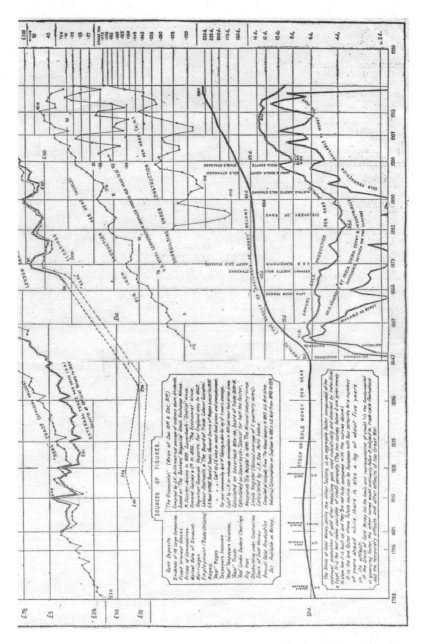

Figure 5b   The bottom one-third of Kitchin's "Trade Cycles Chart" (1921). Kitchin organized the chart so that the primary causes of economic fluctuations, world production and stock of gold, were at the foot of the chart.

measurements, and Kitchin later published some of his own work in the Harvard-based *Review of Economic Statistics* (see, for example, Bowley 1922 and Kitchin 1923). In the autumn of 1920, Professor C. Ottolenghi of Turin had suggested the establishment of a European statistical "observatory," with headquarters in London. Although an official observatory was never established, the *Manchester Guardian* published several supplements, with contributions from journalists and professors in Britain, Italy, France, Germany, and Belgium on "European Reconstruction Numbers." This cooperative measurement effort inspired a 1922 conference at which representatives from the Universities of London, Cambridge, and Harvard committed themselves to constructing national indices of economic conditions. It was also in the early 1920s that business cycle institutes were established in at least eight countries (see Morgan 1990, 56–72).

Another feature captured by Kitchin's analysis was the logarithmic scale, which renders percent changes rather than levels of change (the monetary value of differences from one period to the next) comparable. William Stanley Jevons's ratio charts in the 1860s initiated the application of this instrument. Within academic forums, Alfred Marshall (1885), Vilfredo Pareto ([1896–97] 1964), Bowley (1901), and Irving Fisher (1917) had written about the usefulness of ratio charts, but there had also been articles about them in the financial and popular science press (see Brinton 1914). During World War I, the U.S. government's Joint Committee on Standards for Graphic Representation had urged the use of ratio charts in government and business reports. As Bowley (1922, 146) described it, the ratio chart had been the "subject of organized propaganda" in the United States, but Kitchin was bringing it to the breakfast tables of the educated masses in Europe with merely a small boxed explanation.

A third feature was the decomposition of time series. Kitchin (1921, 35) explained that there were two classes of movements depicted in his linear arithmetic: the "fundamental or basal movements (primary) and the trade cycles or oscillatory movements (secondary)." In a later study, Kitchin went on to decompose the oscillatory movements into minor cycles of forty months' duration (sometimes called Kitchin cycles) and major trade cycles of seven to eleven years (1923).

Kitchin's chart and essay captured causal structure. Kitchin organized his series so that the primary cause of change, the stock of gold money, was on the bottom; readers were supposed to gradually move their eyes up the causal structure from gold to shipbuilding and pig iron production, then to London clearing house returns, to wages, employment, marriage rates, interest rates, and finally, to bank deposits. Kitchin saw the stock of gold money as the basis of credit and the "governing factor" of the fundamental movement. He challenged the reader to visually smooth out the other curves to eliminate the fluctuations due to wars and trade cycles and see that they followed this fundamental movement of gold stock. In Kitchin's chart we can see the remarkable rise in the stock of gold and in prices in the 1850s, in contrast with previous decades of declining prices, that inspired William Stanley Jevons to construct a price index to measure the influence of the increase in the gold stock (see section on Manchester Statistical Society above, Hoover and Dowell this volume, Peart this volume, and Maas this volume). We can also see evidence of the 1857 financial crisis that inspired Langton's investigation into commercial debt.

The periodization of the fundamental movement is evident in Kitchin's analysis. Kitchin pointed out that smoothing several series to eliminate the trade cycle illustrated a general stagnation from 1783 to 1851, a rise from 1851 to 1873, stagnation from 1873 to 1894 and a rise from 1894 to 1913. This dating closely matched other contemporary attempts at periodization (see, for example, Layton 1920 or Kondratiev 1922). And finally, we see from Kitchin's chart and essay the impact of wars. Where possible, Kitchin began his data series at the close of England's wars with America, France, and Spain in 1782–83. He argued that wars had been a major influence on economic movements and the only wars comparable in influence (as measured by losses of men divided by world's population) to the Great War just passed were the Napoleonic Wars that began in the 1790s. The curves for Kitchin's sixteen-plus variables are sandwiched between the war boxes at the top, measuring the losses and duration of wars, and the world stock of gold money curve at the bottom of the chart.

Dantzig's Schema of the Birth of Linear Programming

Partly because they have so affected economies, wars have also been a key spur to the development of economic theory and economic measuring instruments. Wars evoke concerted thought and action on public finance—note the intense developments in monetary theory with the

Bank of England's suspension of species payment during the Napoleonic Wars (see Hoover and Dowell this volume and Klein 1997, 73–85) or the stimulus to national income accounting of John Maynard Keynes's *How to Pay for the War* (see Comim this volume). Wars also cause inflation, which in turn inspires new methods of measuring value—the first documented attempts to tabulate indexed time series were during the Napoleonic Wars. World War I shipbuilding needs inspired the first U.S. "cost-of-living" index, as opposed to just a wholesale price index (see Spencer Banzhaf's article in this volume). War necessitates massive mobilization of resources and often gives way to shocking demobilization in its aftermath. It was for this reason the Bureau of Labor Statistics took up Wassily Leontief's input-output analysis in the 1940s (see the essay by Martin Kohli in this volume).

World War II and the Cold War also shaped development in economics through government employment of economists called upon to apply their statistical training and their science of economizing to the allocation of resources within military operations and through government financing of economic research in such forums as the British Office of Operational Research, the U.S. Statistical Research Groups at Columbia and Princeton, the Office of Naval Research, or the RAND Corporation (see Schelling 1960, Wallis 1980, Friedman and Friedman 1998, Mirowski forthcoming, Klein 1999a, Klein 2000a, and Klein 2000b). These defense-related research groups were well-endowed borderlands where military strategists, mathematicians, logicians, physicists, and economists shared and shaped measurement techniques and strategies.

The visual image that brings this broad sweep of the age of measurement to a close is George Dantzig's schematic diagram of the chronological influences on linear programming (see fig. 6). In the course of his planning for U.S. Cold War military activities in 1947, Dantzig, with input from Leonid Hurwicz and Tjalling Koopmans of the Cowles Commission, developed the simplex algorithm for mathematically framing and computing the solutions for a system of linear inequalities such that costs for an activity, subject to resource constraints, would be minimized. This exercise in optimization yields accounting prices or shadow prices (the simplex multipliers) that measure the value of inputs even in cases where prices do not exist. I will return to a discussion of the implications of this measurement feat, but first I will explore the history behind this novel measuring instrument.

TABLE 2-1-I

LINEAR PROGRAMMING TIMETABLE: ORIGINS—INFLUENCES

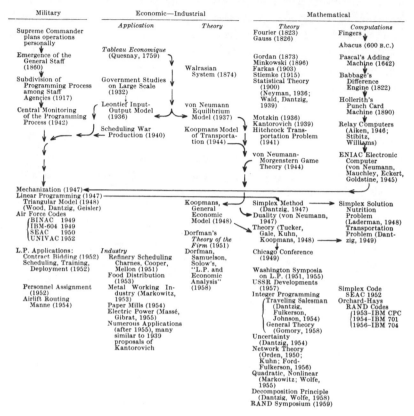

Figure 6   Dantzig's (1963, 13) timetable illustrating the influences on, and the subsequent influence of, linear programming and the simplex method

Dantzig's schematic diagram depicts the variety of influences on the formulation of linear programming and the simplex method and how it in turn influenced those same disciplines. The black arrows illustrate direct causal influence. Given the resource allocation thrust of linear programming, some might see John von Neumann's 1932 model of general equilibrium theory as a direct precursor to linear programming, but in Dantzig's scheme the direct arrow to linear programming comes from Leontief's input-output model rather than from von Neumann's equilibrium model. Dantzig described the latter as a *qualitative* mathematical model, the purpose of which was "to make valid logical deductions from the assumption" (1963, 17). In this way von Neumann's use of mathematics in his equilibrium model was similar to that of von Thünen. The results were hypothetical magnitudes for demonstrable purposes only. As Dantzig saw it, Leontief's input-output table was a key leap from qualitative mathematical models to quantitative models in the service of economics:

> To appreciate the difference between a purely formal model and an empirical model, it is well to remember that the acquisition of data for a real model requires an organization working many months, sometimes years. After the model has been put together, another obstacle looms—the solution of a very large system of simultaneous linear equations. In the period 1936–1940, there were no electronic computers; the best that one could hope for in general would be to solve twenty equations in twenty unknowns. Finally there was the difficulty of "marketing" the results of such studies. Hence, from the onset, the undertaking initiated by Leontief represented a triple gamble. (17)

Dantzig (18) credits the war-inspired Bureau of Labor Statistics with extending "the scope, accuracy, and area of application" of Leontief's input-output tables (see Kohli this volume). Indeed Dantzig saw World War II and the Cold War as the major stimuli for this extension, due to the government's need for large-scale planning, funding for research into applied mathematics, and underwriting of computer design and construction. In the summer of 1947, Dantzig and his colleagues in the Air Force-funded Project SCOOP (Scientific Computation of Optimum Programs) generalized Leontief's descriptive interindustry model, which had a singular set of outputs, to describe a variety of output scenarios and to provide the criterion for choosing the optimal one. In 1949 Koopmans organized a Cowles Commission conference on linear programming, generating considerable interest in and further research on this subject in the economics community (see Koopmans 1951 and, for example, Dorfman, Samuelson, and Solow 1958). Linear programming was a normative approach to resource allocation: it told the user the optimal activity mix—the least-cost network for shipping from factories to distributors, the best food basket for maximizing nutrients subject to a budget constraint, or the cheapest blend of alloys subject to specifications.

Although the simplex method that initiated linear programming is a computational algorithm, Dantzig did not adopt it as a solution to a system of linear inequalities until he had tried it out in different geometries and found it an efficient solution process (see Boumans this volume and Weintraub this volume on different geometries). Using the simplex method, investigators descend the edges of a convex polyhedron, vertex by vertex, until they reach a minimum. Von Neumann was the first to point out that in the course of solving the original problem through this vertex-to-vertex descent, one creates a dual programming problem. In cases of resource allocation, the multipliers used to solve this second problem are imputed prices of the components such that total cost is minimized, with relative scarcity and relative contribution to total activity accounted for. Linear programming thus measures optimal prices in systems in which there are no markets to determine prices. These imputed values were called "accounting prices" or "shadow prices" or "imaginary prices." Economists working in centrally planned economies, development policy, large corporations, and military planning were quick to take up this new way of measuring nonmarket determined prices, whose relative values would have ideally arisen from decentralized competitive markets.

Stephen Enke's 1954 RAND-funded report on the economics of fissionable material for atomic bombs illustrates the promise that the newly discovered method of measuring shadow prices held out to U.S. military planning:

> In the case of atomic bombing, a system can perhaps be devised that is expected to maximize the number of targets destroyed per unit of fissionable material used. However, this may require such a lavish employment of delivery aircraft that the product of the "last" plane is zero. As aircraft are costly, this can hardly be a minimum budget system. In all these instances the operations analyst has the task of estimating the various combinations of inputs that will supposedly achieve a given military output. However, the determination of the most economic combination depends upon the values of the various inputs. It is here that the economist can contribute the principles of value determination and the logic of economizing. In these ways, too, economists can aid in determining the proper production, use, and allocation of the fissionable materials U^{235} and PU^{239}, because these problems involve economic suboptimizations. (1954, 217–18)

Enke asserted that a price system, "even an imaginary one," would aid in decision making for the production and distribution of atomic bombs:

> Linear programming provides a means of handling a number of these small optimizations and the institution of shadow prices may well permit a decentralized method of solution. Despite the secrecy that surrounds it, fissionable material is pre-eminently an economic good, and economists with the necessary clearances should be capable of important contributions to national defense. (231)

Conclusion

It appears that we have come a long way from an observed, localized market price of wheat to a shadow price of Uranium[235]. But is our vertex-to-vertex descent down Dantzig's convex polyhedron to conjure up imaginary prices so different from our wedge-by-wedge ascent up von Thünen's convex polyhedron to measure intensity of land use from an imaginary town center? Certainly the barriers to entry in terms of mathematical notation and vocabulary increased over the decades covered by this essay, and the measurement of shadow prices was the end product of a well-funded, well-staffed concerted effort rather than the result of the musings of a gentleman farmer or a financier. Also, the normative quality of Dantzig's optimization stands in stark contrast to the descriptive qualities of von Thünen's deductions or Playfair's charts. Playfair's "linear arithmetic," however, and Dantzig's "linear programming" were both acts of measurement for empire building. They both tweaked the correspondence of magnitude, dimension, and empirical observation: Playfair gave dimension to something that had been observed, at least through historical narratives, but not measured. In their determination of shadow prices, linear programmers measured values that had not been observed.

We also see the thread of common measuring strategies that Mary Morgan discussed in her essay (this volume). Linear programming, for example, makes use of weighted-average and balancing strategies. We can see the effectiveness of the accounting strategy in Playfair's trade deficit charts, in Langton's balance of commercial indebtedness, and in Stone's refinement of national income accounts. Over this 150-year period, certain techniques also show remarkable resilience and flexibility. For example, the relative change technique appears within a variety of economic measuring instruments including index numbers, ratio or logarithmic charts, and the geometric mean. Indeed, if one had to choose a single data manipulation technique to summarize nineteenth-and twentieth-century capitalism, the simple percent change/rate-of-growth calculation would be a good candidate. We also see the importance of geometry to framing the measurement process or expressing, comparing, and verifying economic measurements. A less obvious, but still important, insight we can gather from this panoramic vista of the age of economic measurement is that many key developments in economic measurement have occurred at the edges where the habitat of the economics discipline gives way to other biomes. These borderland innovations have in turn been inspired by economic factors themselves—including Old-World appropriations of New-World gold, financial crises, poverty with its accompaniment of social agitation, and war.

References

Ashton, T. S. 1934. *Economic and Social Investigations in Manchester, 1833–1933: A Centenary History of the Manchester Statistical Society*. London: King.

Baker, Henry. 1876. Observations on a Continuation Table and Chart, Shewing the "Balance of Account between the Mercantile Public and the Bank of England"; 1844–75, with a Special Reference to its Course in the Years 1866–75. *Transactions of the Manchester Statistical Society*, session 1875–76, 203–21.

Bowley, Arthur L. 1901. *Elements of Statistics*. London: King.

———. 1922. An Index of British Economic Conditions 1919–22. *The Review of Economic Statistics* 4 (supplement 2, June): 145–56.

Brinton, Willard C. 1914. *Graphic Methods for Presenting Facts*. New York: Engineering Magazine Company.

Cohen, Patricia Cline. 1999. *A Calculating People: The Spread of Numeracy in Early America*. New ed. New York: Routledge.

Cullen, M. J. 1975. *The Statistical Movement in Early Victorian Britain: The Foundations of Empirical Social Research*. New York: Harvester Press.

Dantzig, George B. 1963. *Linear Programming and Extensions*. Princeton, N.J.: Princeton University Press.

Dorfman, Robert, Paul A. Samuelson, and Robert Solow. 1958. *Linear Programming and Economic Analysis*. The RAND Series. New York: Macmillan.

Enke, Stephen. 1954. Some Economic Aspects of Fissionable Material. *Quarterly Journal of Economics* 68.2: 217–32.

Fisher, Irving. 1917. The "Ratio" Chart for Plotting Statistics. *Publications of the American Statistical Association* 15.118: 577–601.

Flux, A. W. 1895. Fifty Years' Accounts of the Bank of England. *Transactions of the Manchester Statistical Society*, session 1894–95, 69–96.

Friedman, Milton, and Rose Friedman. 1998. *Two Lucky People: Memoirs*. Chicago: University of Chicago Press.

Galison, Peter. 1997. *Image and Logic: A Material Culture of Microphysics*. Chicago: University of Chicago Press.

Guy, William A. 1879. On Tabular Analysis. *Journal of the Statistical Society of London* 42.3: 644–62.

Keynes, John Maynard. 1940. *How to Pay for the War: A Radical Plan for the Chancellor of the Exchequer*. Toronto: Macmillan.

Kitchin, Joseph. 1921. Trade Cycles Chart. The Past as a Guide to the Future. A Study in Economics. *The Times Annual Financial and Commercial Review* 28 (January): 35, 38–39.

————. 1923. Cycles and Trends in Economic Factors. *The Review of Economic Statistics* 5.1: 10–16.

Klein, Judy L. 1995. The Method of Diagrams and the Black Arts of Inductive Economics. In *Measurement, Quantification and Economic Analysis*, edited by Ingrid Rima, 98–139. London: Routledge.

————. 1997. *Statistical Visions in Time: A History of Time Series Analysis, 1662–1938*. Cambridge: Cambridge University Press.

————. 1999a. Controlling Gunfire, Inventories, and Expectations with the Exponentially Weighted Moving Average. Unpublished. Mary Baldwin College.

————. 1999b. The Rise of "Non-October" Econometrics: Kondratiev and Slutsky at the Moscow Conjuncture Institute. *HOPE* 31.1:137–68.

————. 2000b. Economic Stabilization Policies and the Military Art of Control Engineering. Unpublished. Mary Baldwin College.

————. 2000a. Economics for a Client: The Case of Statistical Quality Control and Sequential Analysis. In *Toward a History of Applied Economics*, edited by Roger E. Backhouse and Jeff Biddle. *HOPE* 32 (supplement): 27–69.

Kondratiev, Nikolai Dmitrievich. 1922. *Mirovoe Khoziastvo i Ego Kon'iunktury vo Vremia i Posle Voiny*. Vologda, Russia: Oblastnoe Otdelenie Gosudartsvennogo Izdatelstva.

Koopmans, Tjalling C., ed. 1951. *Activity Analysis of Production and Allocation*. New York: John Wiley.

Langton, William. 1857. Observations on a Table Shewing the Balance of Account between the Mercantile Public and the Bank of England. *Transactions of the Manchester Statistical Society*, session 1857–58, 9–22.

Layton, Walter T. 1920. *An Introduction to the Study of Prices*. London: MacMillan.

Marshall, Alfred. 1885. On the Graphic Method of Statistics. *Journal of the Royal Statistical Society* 50:251–60.

McCloskey, Donald. 1993. Schelling's Five Truths of Economics. *Eastern Economic Journal* 19.1 (winter): 109–12.

Mills, John. 1871. Inaugural Address on the Scope and Method of Statistical Enquiry, and on Some Questions of the Day. *Transactions of the Manchester Statistical Society*, session 1871–72, 1–16.

Mirowski, Philip. Forthcoming. *Machine Dreams: Economics Becomes a Cyborg
Science*. Cambridge: Cambridge University Press.

Morgan, Mary S. 1990. *The History of Econometric Ideas*. Cambridge: Cambridge
University Press.

Pareto, Vilfredo. [1896–97] 1964. *Cours d'économie politique*. In *Oeuvres complètes
de Vilfredo Pareto*, edited by G. H. Bosquet and G. Busino. Geneva: Droz.

Perry, Lorinda. 1916. Millinery as a Trade for Women. Women's Educational and Industrial Union, Department of Research. Vol. 5 of *Studies in Economic Relations
of Women*. New York: Longmans Green, and Company.

Playfair, William. 1786. *The Commercial and Political Atlas*. London: J. Debrett.

————. 1801. *The Statistical Breviary: Shewing on a Principle Entirely New The
Resources of Every State and Kingdom in Europe; Illustrated with Stained
Copper-Plate Charts, Representing the Physical Power of Each Distinct Nation
with Ease and Perspicuity*. London: T. Bensley.

————. 1805. *An Inquiry into the Permanent Causes of the Decline and Fall of
Powerful and Wealthy Nations*. London: Greenland and Norris.

Pownall, George H. 1876. Banking Statistics as a Measure of Trade. *Transactions of
the Manchester Statistical Society*, session 1876–77: 21–36.

Rauschenbusch, Walter. 1908. *Christianity and the Social Crisis*. New York: Macmillan.

Rubinow, Isaac Max. 1918. Dependency Index of New York City, 1914–1917. *American Economic Review* 8.4: 713–40.

Schelling, Thomas C. 1960. Economic Reasoning and Military Science. *American
Economist* 4.1: 3–13.

Trotsky, Leon. 1923. O Krivoi Kapitalisticheskovo Razvytya. *Vestnik Sotsialistich-
eskoi Akademii*, no. 4:5–12.

von Thünen, Johann Heinrich. 1826. *Der isoleierte Staat in Beziehung auf
Landwirtschaft und Nationalökonomie*. Darmstadt: Wissenchaftliche Buchge-
sellschaft.

————. [1826] 1966. *von Thünen's Isolated State*. Translated by Carla M. Warten-
berg. Oxford: Pergamon Press.

Wallis, W. Allen. 1980. The Statistical Research Group, 1942–1945. *Journal of the
American Statistical Association* 75:320–30.

Webb, Sidney, and Arnold Freeman, eds. 1912. *Seasonal Trades*. London: Constable
and Co.

Wilkinson, Thomas. 1875. Inaugural Address on the Origin and History of the
Manchester Statistical Society. *Transactions of the Manchester Statistical Society*
1875–76: 9–24.

Measuring Causes: Episodes in the Quantitative Assessment of the Value of Money

Kevin D. Hoover and Michael E. Dowell

> Historische Kaufkraftvergleiche schweben also immer mehr oder
> weniger in der Luft.
> —Wilhelm Röpke, *Die Lehre von der Wirtschaft*

Money and Measurement

Nothing is more familiar than the value of money. Every time we buy a book or a beer or note the price of a computer or a car, we simultaneously update our information about the value of money expressed in units of books, beer, computers, or cars. Money is nevertheless not like these physical goods. Value (or price) and quantity are separate characteristics for physical goods. A copy of Keynes's *General Theory* is the same book whether it costs $10 or $10,000. But a ten-dollar bill is, in a relevant sense, a different thing when a copy of the *General Theory* costs $10 than when it costs $10,000. That the *real* quantity of money depends on the prices of goods was understood well before the dawn of modern economics. It is sometimes not enough to evaluate that real quantity with respect to a book, a pint of beer, a computer, or a house. Both because it is a useful portmanteau statistic and because it plays a causal role in our theories of the macroeconomy, we sometimes need to know the real quantity of money with respect to goods in general—that is, we need to know the general price level.

Correspondence may be addressed to Kevin D. Hoover, Department of Economics, 1 Shields Avenue, University of California, Davis, CA 95616; e-mail: kdhoover@ucdavis.edu.

We are now so familiar with the idea of price indices that the idea of a general price level no longer appears problematic. But consider the recent discussion of the measurement of the Consumer Price Index (CPI), particularly in the wake of the December 1996 report of the Advisory Commission to Study the Consumer Price Index (commonly known as the Boskin Commission [Boskin et al. 1996]). Getting the right value for the price indices is important on several dimensions. There is a scientific interest in, for example, measuring the real Gross Domestic Product (GDP) or productivity growth. If the price indices are too high, we appear less prosperous and productive than we really are. Real GDP and productivity data, as well as inflation data that are based directly on the price indices, affect the policy actions of the central bank and so have important consequences for the future prosperity of the country. And they affect various index-linked payments in pensions and contracts, thereby affecting the distribution of income and government finance.

The Boskin report concluded that the CPI overstated inflation by 1.1 percentage points. While some commentators disputed the particular estimates, almost no one observed what a conceptually odd conclusion the report had drawn. Index numbers reduce the changes in prices of many goods to a single summary statistic. There is no unique, correct way to make that reduction. Although there are better and worse ways to make it, the class of theoretically admissible indices is infinite. To conclude that the CPI overstates *true* inflation by a precise amount is implicitly to claim that there is a precisely true price index, a unique value of money—but there is no such true index.

The problems of what the value of money is and how to measure it are not new. Both classical political economists and policymakers in the eighteenth and nineteenth centuries faced the same problems that we do today, albeit in an era much less rich in economic data and statistical understanding. They were perhaps less complacent about how to address the problems; for, although index numbers appeared during the same period, they had not yet come to dominate the thinking about the general price level. The goal of this essay is to look back to this earlier time and to a selection of classical authors to ask, What did they mean by the "value" of money? And how did they measure it?

There is, of course, a logically prior question that should be related to the conception of the problem at hand: what *is* measurement? We shall take measurement to mean the assignment of a quantitative value to a conceptually quantifiable variable, in our case the value of money, on the basis of empirical data. Assigning values to distance with a yard-stick or to temperature with a thermometer epitomize measurement. In these cases, measurement consists of placing an instrument (the yard-stick or the thermometer) in a physical relationship with the thing to be measured. For any interaction between the instrument and the thing to be measured to produce a useful result, we must maintain certain theoretical (and generally not directly testable) commitments. We assume, for instance, that the yardstick is rigid or that the mercury expands linearly. We must also assume that the system of measuring instrument and measured object are isolated in the sense that any interfering causes are trivial or have been shielded away or that we have a systematic method of compensating or accounting for their influences.

Although the same features of theoretical presuppositions and the need for isolation or compensation arise in economic measurement, there is rarely anything that corresponds to a tangible measuring instrument such as a yardstick or thermometer. Money and goods can be counted and prices recorded, but often these raw data are not the aspects of the economy that we seek to measure. Raw data are inputs to a process of manipulation in accordance with theoretical presuppositions—a process that assigns a number to a quantity that may not be directly observable to the senses, even in principle.

Indirect measurement is characteristic of many physical sciences as well as economics. Yet it raises the question of the difference between measurement and inference. The inferential distance between the thermometer and body temperature seems short compared to that between a spectroscopic photograph and the temperature of the sun or between a set of prices for thousands of goods and the value of money. Nevertheless we suggest the distinction between measurement and inference is heuristic rather than essential. We typically expect measurements to appeal to a different set of theoretical presuppositions than those at stake in the investigation at hand. If the linearity of the expansion of mercury with temperature was the question, we would not expect measurements made with a mercury thermometer to decide it. Related to this, we expect measurements to be transferable beyond the particular theoretical context in which they are made. Thus, we not only expect the fact that we measure the temperature of water to be 90°C to imply that an ice cube dropped into the water will melt, but also that we can calculate the rate at which it will melt based in part on transferring the measured temperature into the appropriate thermodynamical equations. Transferability is related to the notion that the measured variables are *real* characteristics. (See Spencer Banzhaf's essay in this volume for a discussion of conceptions of measurement and the value of money in the twentieth century.)

To address the question of measuring the value of money, we will examine some of the writings of Adam Smith, the Bullion Committee of 1810, Thomas Tooke, and William Stanley Jevons. Our purpose is limited. Each of the three individuals has written extensively on prices and money, and the Bullion Committee's report involved as authors and positive or negative critics many of the most important British economists of the day (e.g., David Ricardo). Our concern is neither with the totality of any of the author's works nor with the details of the monetary controversies in which they were involved except insofar as they directly affect our central purpose—understanding the motivations, problems, and pitfalls that each author faced in a particular empirical investigation aiming to quantify the value (or changes in value) of money. We also recognize that we may have been able to illustrate these issues with other authors or other works. We take an episodic rather than a systematic approach. For each author, taking the Bullion Committee as one, we examine a single text or part of a text, focusing on the concept of the value of money and the strategies used for measuring that value. Despite the episodic approach, there is nonetheless some continuity in the discussion. These authors can be read as carrying on a conversation. To one degree or another, the later authors comment on the earlier, and the problems that motivate each author's work are related to the those addressed by the earlier authors in a connected historical sequence.

Adam Smith's "Digression Concerning the Variations in the Value of Silver"

While Smith discusses his general notions of value and money in book 1, chapters 4 and 5 of the *Wealth of Nations*, his attempt to quantify changes in the value of money does not occur until book 1, chapter 11, "Of the Rent of Land" in the "Digression Concerning the Variations in the Value of Silver" (Smith [1776] 1981, 195–259).[1] The "Digression" sits in the midst of a discussion of the value of produce from land that always pays rent relative to land that sometimes does and sometimes does not pay rent. The general tendency, Smith argues, is for the produce of

---

1. Page references are to the Glasgow edition of the *Wealth of Nations*.

the land other than food to rise in value as the overall wealth of society rises. For goods that are not easily transportable (e.g., quarry stone), the relevant market is more or less local. But for silver, which is easily transported, the relevant market is the whole world. The value of silver in the world will depend on the proportion between supply, driven by accidental discoveries of new mines, and demand, driven by general economic development. Smith seeks to show that over four centuries the balance between supply and demand has shifted so that three distinct episodes can be discerned—each characterized by a particular general direction of the price of silver or, equivalently, the value of money.

The main purpose of Smith's investigation appears to be a detached scientific one: does the behavior of silver illustrate his understanding of the course of the value of nonagricultural produce over time? Smith ([1776] 1981, 200 and passim) also wishes to provide empirical evidence against the crudest version of the quantity theory of money. In the crude version, whenever the quantity of precious metals increases, so do prices. Smith objects that the stock of money naturally increases in a prosperous country, but that much of it is absorbed by the increased trade and the increased demand for silver and gold in luxury manufactures, so that prices need not increase.[2] To make his case, he needs to measure the actual change in the value of silver.

Near the end of the "Digression," Smith ([1776] 1981, 258) goes on to suggest two further practical purposes for understanding the value of money: (1) to help judge accurately the state of the economy—prosperous or otherwise; and (2) to give information on cost-of-living adjustments for public servants (cf. Jevons 1863, 81–85; Cannan 1925, 67). (We presume that he exempts private employees on the ground that the market will set their wages appropriately.)

Conceptually, what is the value of money? is an easier question for Smith than for later authors. Since he holds a labor theory of value, the price of silver relative to labor is the true measure: "Labour, it must be remembered, and not any particular commodity or sett of commodities is the real measure of value both of silver and of all other commodities" ([1776] 1981, 206). This seems clear enough, but Smith is, in fact, not completely consistent, partly for reasons that are hard to fathom and

2. A similar position is taken by the Bullion Committee. See the disussion of the Bullion Committee Report below.

partly for reasons that reflect theoretical presuppositions that guide his measurement strategy.

Immediately before the "Digression," Smith ([1776] 1981, 194) defines a fall in the value of silver as consisting in the fact that an amount of it would "purchase or command a smaller and a smaller quantity of labour, or exchange for a smaller and a smaller quantity of corn, the principal part of the subsistence of the labourer." Here corn appears to be as much a measure of the value of silver as labor itself, yet we know that labor is more fundamental than corn in Smith's account of value. In practice, Smith judges the value of silver from the silver price of corn. Why not collect wage rates rather than corn prices, as Tooke ([1838–57] 1972, 1: 55–56) would later argue would have been more consistent with Smith's analysis?[3]

The answer is not obvious, but we speculate on two considerations. First, Smith ([1776] 1981, 49, and book 1, chaps. 8 and 10) understands that labor and wages are heterogeneous across occupations. In contrast, what heterogeneity there is in corn is resolvable through straightforward, conventionally agreed upon adjustments. Second, Smith does not believe that the reward to labor measured in necessaries and luxuries is truly a constant (51). In his view wages are higher in an advancing state than in a declining state and may, in fact, fluctuate as well as trend. Thus, even if in some metaphysical sense labor is everywhere equally valuable, the question that forms the core of the *Wealth of Nations*—what makes a nation prosperous?—is a question about why some countries are rich in the necessaries and conveniences of life and others poor. Smith is shrewd enough to understand that knowing the labor value of silver (i.e., the nominal wage) without knowing about prices cannot answer that question.

Why then focus on corn and not "a sett of commodities"? It might seem that Smith has answered this question with the observation that corn is the largest part of the typical worker's subsistence. In fact, his answer is based more on his theory of how relative prices develop over time (Smith [1776] 1981, 206). He observes that the average supply and demand for any produced goods are on average nearly equal over long periods of time. Cattle are essential to corn production—both as a source of manure and as draft animals. Over time, technological improvements

---

3. References to Tooke's *History of Prices* ([1838–57] 1972) are by volume number and page number.

raise corn production and tend ceteris paribus to reduce the price of corn. But rising productivity also raises the demand for cattle; the price of cattle increases as cattle production has to be moved off waste land onto arable land to meet this demand. Smith argues that the increased input price more or less offsets the productivity gain in corn production, rendering the price of corn in terms of labor nearly constant.

The question of changing relative prices arises again in Smith's discussion of cost-of-living adjustments for public servants. Here he notes that corn governs the profit rate in agriculture and that the price of other vegetable crops should fall on trend relative to corn while the price of butcher's meat rises ([1776] 1981, 258). Similarly, he expects to see falling real prices of manufactured goods (260–64). Thus for Smith, corn serves as an index—not in the modern sense of a weighted average, but rather in the sense of a neutral commodity that indicates where labor stands against commodities in general. Smith recognizes that the composition of the commodity bundle is likely to shift systematically over time with secular trends in relative prices.

The nature of the theoretical conception underlying Smith's advocacy of the corn price as the standard measurement of the value of silver points to the measurement of secular trends rather than year-to-year fluctuations. Smith ([1776] 1981, 228; 216) observes that the stock of precious metals is so large relative to the flow of new production that there is little year-to-year variation in supply. In contrast, the corn supply is highly variable from year to year. Corn is, therefore, a poor measure of short-run fluctuations in the value of silver or labor.

Smith's conceptual and theoretical framework is developed in passing as he encounters interpretive issues. In contrast, the bulk of the "Digression" is devoted to quantitative assessment of the changing value of silver. Smith seeks accurate data on corn prices. In the time before statistics were kept purposefully for economic analysis, this is no easy task. Smith puts together his raw data from a hodgepodge of sources: contemporary accounts in letters and other documents that record prices incidentally, old price-control statutes, contract prices, and the actual accounts of corn markets. Many of these data cannot be taken at face value but must be adjusted or interpreted. For example, Smith ([1776] 1981, 197) considers a price-control statute from 1262 in which the price of bread is tied to the market price of corn. He regards the middle price of the table as the normal price of corn on the assumption that the law treated probable price variations symmetrically. In another case, he observes that recorded conversion prices in cases in which landlords can take their rent in either money or corn are likely to be set at about half of the usual market price (200). Similarly, Smith must be careful to adjust weights and measures: reported corn prices must be adjusted for the relative proportions of wheat and barley (e.g., 210), while circulating silver coin must be adjusted for the degree to which it is degraded relative to standard coin (e.g., 212–13).

Collating and cleaning the data are only the start of the measurement process. The essential element is what we might today refer to as "signal extraction": how can the secular trend in corn prices be discerned in the pattern of year-to-year fluctuations? Smith observes that prices in unsystematic sources, such as letters or memoirs, are often extreme prices, since they were remarkable for their novelty. It would be wrong, he argues, to infer from the fact that the lowest prices in ancient times were much lower than the lowest prices today or from the fact that the highest prices in the thirteenth century were much higher than the highest prices today that in either case the *normal* prices were also much lower or higher ([1776] 1981, 203).[4]

Smith adopts two strategies for signal extraction. The first is time-series averaging. For example, in the case of the earliest data (1223–1601), Smith ([1776] 1981, 268–71) reduces the raw data to twelve-year averages before drawing his conclusions about secular price movements. We can regard the averaging as an example of isolating the measuring apparatus from interfering causes through a strategy that renders these causes trivial, as discussed above.

The second strategy is to account for each of the interfering causes one by one in order to select only those corn prices that do not reflect special, transitory circumstances. Much of Smith's discussion of the data after 1570 employs this strategy. In the seventeenth century he appeals to circumstances such as the Civil War to account for the high price of corn in 1648 or the export bounty to account for the high price of corn in 1688 (Smith [1776] 1981, 212). An account of this sort, however, shifts the question somewhat, for Smith is no longer merely measuring the exchange value of corn. Rather, he is attempting to distinguish between changes in the exchange value that can be attributed to changes in silver and changes that can be attributed to some other cause. Both the shift

---

4. In modern terminology, the mean and the variance of prices are likely to show considerable independence.

from measurement of the value of money *simpliciter* to measurement of the *causes* of changes in the value of money and Smith's strategy of attributing to changes in the supply of silver whatever changes in the value of money are left over once all other factors are accounted for recur in the other episodes that we shall consider presently. It is convenient to give Smith's strategy the anachronistic name "the method of residues" (see Mill 1851, 404).[5]

The Report of the Bullion Committee of 1810

By the time of the publication of the Bullion Report (Cannan 1925), Britain had moved from the silver standard, with which Smith is concerned, to a gold standard. In 1797 during one of the panics of the Napoleonic Wars, the Bank of England, at the direction of the government, suspended the convertibility of its notes (paper pounds sterling) into gold. This was intended as a strictly temporary measure but was in fact renewed successively until convertibility was finally resumed in 1821. The Bullion Committee was a response to the inflation in the second half of the first decade of the nineteenth century. The committee's report sought to demonstrate that the cause of the inflation was the excess issue of Bank of England paper notes and to refute alternative theories of the inflation. Although the report was motivated by a general rise in prices, its terms of reference were limited to determining the cause of the high price of gold bullion. The main conclusion of the committee was that Britain should resume convertibility.

Unlike Smith, the Bullion Report is unburdened by any conceptual commitment to a deep account of value. The only value that explicitly concerns the committee is the exchange value of the paper pound in terms of gold or vice versa or indirectly with precious metals in other monetary systems through the foreign exchanges. There is no doubt that bullion prices in 1810 were substantially higher than the mint price of £3 17s. 10½ d. per ounce, mint price being that price at which the mint would convert gold bullion into legal tender coin. As a result, gold coin ceased to circulate, as it was completely supplanted by cheaper paper money. So far, no serious measurement issues arise. The deeper question,

---

5. The method of residues is described in Mill's (1851, 405) fourth canon: "Subduct from any phenomenon such part as is known by previous inductions to be the effect of certain antecedents, and the residue of the phenomenon is the effect of the remaining antecedents."

however, was to what extent the rise in price of bullion was attributable to the policy of the Bank of England. The tricky problem is, then, one of measuring causes.

The alternative explanations for the high price of bullion focused on the disruptions to international trade and public finance as a result of the prolonged war with France. One argument was that the immediate need for gold to support the armies in the field had drained gold away from England, driving up its price. The committee rejects the conceptual basis for this argument (Cannan 1925, 10).[6] It admits that there is little gold in Britain but contends that gold cannot be considered scarce when as much can be had as desired for those willing to pay its high price. In effect the committee argues that goods are not scarce so long as their supply is infinitely elastic at their market price—a very modern conception of scarcity. And merchants assure the committee that gold is in fact freely available at the market price.

The committee is not, however, content with a conceptual argument. It seeks to measure the degree to which the rise in the price of bullion is attributable to the Bank of England. Its measurements are underpinned by a modified specie-flow mechanism.

The pure specie-flow mechanism (e.g., that attributed to David Hume) assumes that consumers seeking the cheapest goods send gold to countries with low prices and that the gold circulating as money drives up prices until the goods of the receiving (or home) country are no longer cheap relative to the sending (or foreign) country. The modified specie-flow mechanism recognizes that the transport of gold is costly and that business between countries can be more effectively conducted through the exchange of merchants' bills drawn on the banks and denominated in the currencies of the different countries. The home country, with relatively cheap goods, then finds itself with an increasing stock of bills drawn on the foreign country. With an excess supply of such bills, their price falls, which is reported as a rise in the home country's (or a fall in the foreign country's) exchange rate.

Variation in the exchange rate is limited, however, since it can never diverge for long from the ratio of the gold content of the coin of the two countries adjusted for the cost of actually transporting the gold. The key idea is effective arbitrage. In this respect, the theory of the Bullion Committee resembles the modern corporate finance literature in that it

6. Page references are to Cannan's (1925) reprint of the committee's report.

concerns end states rather than causal processes. In particular, the committee never attempts to provide any detail of the process through which excess Bank of England notes affect prices. Thus, while its theory is compatible with versions of the quantity theory of money, it is quite different from those versions, such as Milton Friedman's (a century and a half later), that attribute price increases to wealth effects and the consequences of portfolio rebalancing. The committee in fact rejects the notion that there is a fixed relationship between the quantity of money, the level of economic activity, and the price level such as might be reflected in a stable velocity of circulation. It states:

> But the quantity of currency bears no fixed proportion to the quantity of commodities; and any inferences proceeding upon such a supposition would be entirely erroneous. The effective currency of the Country depends upon the quickness of circulation, and the number of exchanges performed in a given time, as well as upon its numerical amount; and all the circumstances which tend to quicken or retard the rate of circulation, render the same amount of currency more or less adequate to the wants of trade. (Cannan 1925, 57)

The committee's approach to measurement is straightforward and relies heavily on the modified specie-flow mechanism. With currencies convertible into gold, the price of gold should be the same everywhere and the currencies should trade at par—that is, in the ratio that reflects their relative gold content. With the pound sterling inconvertible, the committee assumes that since bullion remains available everywhere (this is the importance of their particular conceptualization of scarcity), the real price of bullion is the same everywhere and the real exchange rate is at par. Any excess of the nominal over the real price of bullion or any fall in the nominal exchange rate below par is, then, a direct measure of the effect of the excess paper pounds.

This measurement strategy is more difficult to implement in practice than the bare outline suggests. Unlike Smith, the Bullion Committee has relatively good data on exchange rates and gold prices themselves; the gold and foreign exchange dealers are a regular part of the merchant community and support circulars such as *Lloyd's Lists* and *Wettenhall's Course of Exchange* for business purposes (Cannan 1925, 8–9). Even with such data, there are at least two complications to consider. First, the par values for exchange rates are based on the assumption that coinage of the various countries is at its full legal weight. Actual deviations from par must account for the fact that coins of the various currencies may be clipped or worn to different degrees (Cannan 1925, 23–24).[7] Second, the legal standard in some countries is gold and in other countries silver, requiring that calculations of par also account for the price of silver relative to gold.

More significantly, the Bullion Committee has a sophisticated understanding of the limits of its theoretical framework. Its strongest conclusions are delivered only under the assumptions that transport, handling, and conversion costs for bullion and coin are zero and that arbitrage is perfect and speedy. Most of the effort of measurement in its report is directed at setting bounds to these costs or limits to the effectiveness of arbitrage. The strategy is counterfactual. Supposing that there were no inconvertible paper money, how much could the price of bullion differ from the price of coin? And how much could the exchange rate vary from par?

The coinage of some countries—although not Great Britain—was subject to seigniorage. Loss to wear and tear for British coin is limited to 1.11 percent by legal tender statutes, although the committee estimates this loss to be less than 1 percent (Cannan 1925, 13–15). Legal restrictions on exporting gold derived from melting British coin—restrictions not easily enforced—add a premium of 3–4 shillings per ounce to bullion legal for export. Counting these and other costs, the committee estimates the largest difference possible between coin and bullion at 5 percent of the value of coin. It cites the experience in the years before 1797 as confirming that limit.[8]

Similarly, relying on the testimony of merchants, the committee recognizes that the cost of transporting bullion, including insurance, fluctuates with the military situation but does not exceed 7 percent (Cannan 1925, 25).

Some data are dismissed as outliers by appeal to violations of the ceteris paribus conditions of the modified specie-flow mechanism. For example, the military situation in Portugal resulted in a substantial balance of payments deficit with England and an exchange rate 13½ percent in

---

7. Smith ([1776] 1981, 43–44) also addresses the "debased coin."

8. The committee did recognize one factor that would tend to cause the price of coin to rise above that of bullion. The opportunity cost measured as the lost interest for the period over which the bullion is being minted into coin is estimated at less than 1 percent. The committee also assumes this percentage is falling as the operation of coining bullion becomes more efficient (Cannan 1925, 12–14).

favor of England. This situation is treated as anomalous. The excess demand for British bills had become so high and the exchange rate so favorable to England that the price differentials between England and Portugal had reached the point at which it was profitable to ship bullion. Equilibration through actual shipments of bullion is a slower process than equilibration through the trade in merchants' bills. And the market was too disordered to equilibrate in the usual manner as it would have in a politically and economically more stable situation.

Once all the factors by which the actual specie-flow mechanism in the real world differs from the ideal theory are taken into account, the measurement strategy of the committee is the same as that employed by Smith: whatever cannot be accounted for otherwise is attributed to the excess of paper money (the method of residues). The committee concludes that bullion is 15 to 16 percent above its mint price; at most, 5½ percentage points of that difference can be attributed to other causes than excess paper. The foreign exchanges stand 16 to 20 percent below par, and at most 7 percentage points can be attributed to the costs of actually shipping bullion. Between 9½ to 13 percentage points of the rise in the price of bullion is attributed to excess paper currency.

Thomas Tooke's *History of Prices*

The first volume of Tooke's monumental six-volume *History of Prices* was published in 1838—over a quarter century after the report of the Bullion Committee—and seventeen years after the resumption of convertibility. The first two volumes examined prices before and after the period of the paper pound. Tooke's aim was to bolster the case for the Banking School, which advocated that the currency be convertible and that banks freely discount "real bills" of good quality and short duration. The Banking School believed that paper money could not be inflationary in such an institutional environment. The last volume of the *History* (written with William Newmarch) was not published until 1857—thirteen years after the Banking School was vanquished by the Bank Charter Act of 1844. This act institutionalized the operating procedures for the Bank of England, procedures advocated by its arch-rival, the Currency School.[9] (See Thomas Humphrey's article in this volume for

9. The Bank Charter Act divided the Bank of England into an issue department and a banking department. The issue department was required to fully back any notes in excess of £14 million with bullion or coin (Andréadès [1909] 1966, 289).

a discussion of the role of the Federal Reserve's allegiance to the real bills doctrine in its choice of what to measure in the 1910s to 1930s.)

The scope of Tooke's investigations into the value of money rivals that of Smith, and his attention to factual detail considerably exceeds Smith's. Yet his purposes are less detached: Tooke sought to refute the empirical basis for one set of monetary policies and to establish that of another. His concern for topical problems in monetary policy helps to explain his short-run focus.[10] Smith identified trends; Tooke hopes to explain year-to-year variation. His is not a descriptive task but one of causal assignment. The question is *"Whether, in the altered proportions between money and the objects exchanged by it, the variations of prices, consequent on those altered proportions, originated in, and were dependant upon, alterations in the quantity of money on the one hand, or in the cost of production, and the accidents affecting supply, on the other"* (Tooke [1838–57] 1972, 1:154; emphasis in original).

That the requisite measurements aim to establish causes, not merely to describe relative prices, is central to Tooke's enterprise. He draws a distinction between the "depreciation of currency," which he defines as the mismatch between the actual metallic content of coin and the mint regulations or between paper money and the coin that it is supposed to represent, and the "depreciation of money," which he defines as a fall in value of money owing to an increase in its quantity "indicated by, and commensurate with, a general rise in prices of commodities and labor" (Tooke [1838–57] 1972, 1:119–23). The Bullion Committee addressed the depreciation of the currency, but Tooke believes that the relevant question for his time is the depreciation of money.

Unlike Smith or the Bullion Committee, Tooke's conception of the value of money is fuzzy in its essence:[11]

> Of variations in the value of the standard itself there is no infallible criterion. Variations, therefore, in the value of the standard, if they occur, can only be inferred from variations of considerable extent and duration, in the bullion prices of commodities and labour, in cases in which these variations do not, according to the widest induction of facts, admit of being accounted for, by circumstances which have influenced

---

10. Tooke does not deny that there are secular trends in prices; it is just that they are not what interests him in the context of monetary policy.

11. Although Tooks's conception of the value of money was "fuzzy," it is again an application of the method of residues.

the prices of the commodities and labour in question, independently of the supposition of any alteration in the quantity or rate of circulation of the currency. ([1838–57] 1972, 1:125)[12]

Tooke brings a wide range of information to bear on the question of the changing value of money, but it remains unclear what process he uses to aggregate it and draw firm conclusions. There may be some element of truth in the view (which might be taken by any modern-day economist) that Tooke was simply a fact grubber who has outrun the resources of his statistical methods. Yet, this is not the whole story.

Tooke was aware of the existence of index numbers. He cites, for instance, Arthur Young's crude cost-of-living index (Tooke [1838–57] 1972, 1:226n). Despite his familiarity with the idea, price indices play no part in the *History of Prices*. A price index would not in any case have necessarily captured Tooke's conception of the general price level. He states his conception directly: "It is the quantity of money constituting the revenues of the different orders of the state, under the head of rents, profits, salaries, and wages, destined for current expenditure, according to the wants and habits of the several classes, that alone forms the limiting principle of the *aggregate of money prices*,—the only prices that can properly come under the designation of *general prices*" ([1838–57] 1972, 3:276). Tooke's conception is rather closer to the current one of national income or to John Maynard Keynes's "aggregate demand price" than it is to the CPI or other index number for prices.

Tooke's conception of general prices is well suited to the theoretical presuppositions on which his measurement strategy is based. The first two volumes of the *History* aim to refute the view of the Currency School that the decline in prices from the resumption of convertibility in 1821 up to the time Tooke is writing was the result of a reduction in Bank of England paper notes. The Currency School was regarded as the intellectual successor to the Bullion Committee. So it is surprising that Tooke ([1838–57] 1972, 1:4, 123–7) fully supports the analysis, the measurements of depreciation, and the policy conclusions of the Bullion Committee as well as Ricardo and other "bullionists." His objection to the Currency School is, as he characterizes it in his *Inquiry into the Currency Principle* ([1844] 1959, 6), that it adopts a crude version of the specie-flow mechanism, in which prices are determined by gold flows

---

12. Tooke's reference to "variations of considerable extent and duration" should not be taken in context to imply a focus on secular changes in prices.

and all gold is treated as if it were coin and, therefore, part of the circulating medium, without any account of the mechanisms through which such flows might affect demand or the costs of production. What is more, Tooke ([1844] 1959, 67–73) charges the Currency School with arbitrarily treating Bank of England notes as a perfect substitute for coin, irrespective of whether they are convertible or not, and unaccountably distinguishing between these notes and other financial assets used in trade, including merchants' bills and country banknotes. The Bullion Committee was no more specific in its description of the mechanism of price change than the Currency School, but its adherence to the *modified* specie-flow mechanism in which actual gold flows are secondary and its agnosticism with respect to the proportionality of prices to money are more consonant with Tooke's own views.

Tooke's main theoretical objection to the Currency School can be cast positively as the key to his own approach. In his definition of general prices cited above, as well as in the practical judgments he makes throughout the *History*, it is clear that Tooke believes that, when examined from the point of view of causal processes, money is never the *proximate* cause of price changes. At best, money affects prices indirectly through incomes and expenditure and, therefore, through demand or interest rates (which he regards as part of the cost of production and supply, though only in the long run) ([1844] 1959, 69–72, 81; [1838–57] 1972, 1:115, 2:347, 5:583–4).

Tooke's approach is fine-grained and critical. He tries to show that his opponents' theories are inconsistent with the data examined broadly. For example, relying on the idea that increases in the money stock should scale prices generally upward, Tooke (e.g., [1838–57] 1972, 1:232) offers evidence that some prices rise and others fall. At a minimum, he makes the point that price change is unlikely to be monocasual, that it is net effects that are observed, and that some decomposition is necessary (e.g., 1:124–5). In this and other respects, his approach is similar to Smith's; yet Tooke criticizes in detail Smith's empirical account of the progress of the value of silver. He questions, for instance, Smith's adjustments to the quantity data on corn, which were meant to account for its variable quality (Tooke [1838–57] 1972, 1:23). More importantly, he criticizes Smith's measuring strategy. He argues that Smith is inconsistent in defining value in terms of labor and then declining to use the money wage as data on the changing value of silver: the money price of "common day labour" is, Tooke (1:56) writes, "a better criterion than corn, of the value of the precious metals." And he goes on to point out that laborers consume many other commodities than corn. As we have already observed, Smith's justification for focusing on corn prices was more subtle than simply that corn forms the largest portion of a worker's subsistence. So, to some extent, Tooke misses Smith's point.

More tellingly, Tooke criticizes Smith's strategy of isolating changes in corn prices resulting from changes in the value of silver from those resulting from supply conditions in agriculture. Smith averaged his data into twelve-year blocks, hoping to cancel out year-to-year fluctuations. Tooke ([1838–57] 1972, 1:59 and passim) demonstrates through a year-by-year analysis that the seasons show long cycles of successive good and bad years.[13]

The measurement strategy, which Tooke also employs for later periods, is exemplified in his reanalysis of Smith's account of the seventeenth and eighteenth centuries. Tooke examines each price change and attempts to give an adequate explanation in nonmonetary terms. Only the unexplained residual can be attributed to monetary factors—the method of residues again, and applied relentlessly.

It is surprising, and apparently inconsistent, given Tooke's criticism of Smith's focus on corn, that Tooke himself mainly cites corn prices. In the early volumes of the *History*, wage rates and the prices of other commodities are sometimes mentioned, but only corn prices are examined systematically. In the later volumes, other prices are cited more frequently, but corn dominates. Tooke ([1838–57] 1972, 1:5–6) identifies the sources of price changes as (1) the seasons, (2) the vicissitudes of war, (3) monetary conditions, (4) changing population, and (5) technical progress. The last two he dismisses as operating too slowly to be important for the short-term changes in the value of money that interest him. In this conclusion, he clearly demonstrates how his purposes are different from Smith's.

Appealing to Charles Davenant's empirical law, which shows that the price of corn is highly sensitive to small variations in the size of the harvest, Tooke ([1838–57] 1972, 1:10–12) places the greatest explanatory weight on the seasons—that is, on changing supply conditions.[14] While he sometimes cites data on the stocks of wheat and other grains, he

13. In the language of modern time-series analysis, Tooke shows that that there is a near unit root in the seasons, so that reversion to the mean is a slow process for which twelve-year averages are too short.

14. See the article on Davenant in *Palgrave's Dictionary* (1925).

appears to lack any *systematic* source of information on quantities of grain. The appeal to Davenant's law is more an argument for the plausibility of large price swings than the basis for measurement. Indeed, though Tooke acknowledges the need to compose causes in order to compute the *net* effects on prices, he provides no basis for quantitatively implementing such a composition. He writes as if it is enough to show that when prices are abnormally high, the harvest was abnormally low, to demonstrate that any monetary explanation is unnecessary for any part of the price change.

A similar lack of a technique for quantitative assessment plagues Tooke's appeal to the data on price changes for a wider spectrum of goods. At best he is able to point out instances when goods typically do or do not rise and fall in price together. He does draw quantitative conclusions, but the technique is opaque. For example, at one point he cites his own testimony to Parliament on the fall of prices for forty non-agricultural commodities, which he estimates to be 40 percent ([1838–57] 1972, 2:88). The reader is left to puzzle where the number might have come from. Arnon (1990, 17) characterizes Tooke as a sort of idiot savant (our words, not Arnon's) who, deeply immersed in the data, was able to draw conclusions about the general direction of prices—conclusions that a modern statistician would have drawn using index numbers. Tooke had argued, for example, that prices in 1810 and 1811 had fallen, whereas the bullionists had argued that they had risen. Arnon's index numbers support Tooke.

Tooke's failure to provide aggregate measures of changing prices is, as we have already argued, at least in part justified by his own conception of the value of money. The interaction of his strategy of treating each price change as sui generis with his theoretical presupposition that money affects prices only indirectly is nearly self-validating for his view that monetary conditions in fact affected prices very little. He was, as we have noted already, willing to agree with the Bullion Committee that the inflation in the second half of the first decade of the nineteenth century was the result of an excess issue of inconvertible paper. Symmetrically, he was willing to concede that part of the price fall after the resumption of convertibility in 1821 could also be attributed to the change in monetary regime—but no more than to the degree of divergence in value between paper and gold (that is, about 6–7 percent in his estimation). Other than that case, with no technique of decomposing price changes, Tooke is content to show that any time prices change, there is some nonmonetary factor operating in the right direction. It is hard to see that any residue could be left for which monetary explanation would be requisite.

William Stanley Jevons's "A Serious Fall in the Value of Gold"

Although William Stanley Jevons's "A Serious Fall in the Value of Gold" (1863) was written only a few years after the final volume of Tooke's *History*, it belongs to a different intellectual world. The great monetary-policy debates of the first half of the nineteenth century had been resolved in practical political terms in favor of the Currency School. Jevons's concerns are, in many ways, closer to Smith's than to the Bullion Committee's or Tooke's. The operation of the banking system and the problems of paper currencies are hardly mentioned. The focus is on the metallic standard. New supplies of gold had been discovered in California and Australia. Jevons's question was to what degree these affected the value of money. Although he was not concerned with the course of the value of money over centuries as Smith had been, he was, in contrast to Tooke and the Bullion Committee, concerned with the permanent changes—secular rather than cyclical (to use a modern terminology that Jevons would have appreciated).

Jevons's conception of the value of money is strictly exchange value: "All that is meant by a fall in the value of gold, is the fact that more gold is now usually required to purchase an article than in former years" (1863, 18). Like Tooke, Jevons was aware of the essential ambiguity of this definition: "Value is a vague expression for potency in purchasing other commodities" (20). If gold becomes less potent in its ability to purchase some commodities and not more potent with respect to others, then its value has certainly declined. The standard (to use later terminology) is Pareto dominance. But given that Pareto dominance is rarely exemplified in the economy, Jevons strikes a pragmatic pose: if the increases in prices of goods predominate over the declines, then the value of gold is said to fall. Anticipating the results of his investigations, he writes: "I regard the fall in the value of gold as conclusively proved, although the exact nature of the problem is left amid the obscurities of economic science in general" (21). Jevons is thoroughly modern in his desire to provide a precise numerical answer to an intrinsically vague question.

Jevons's theoretical presuppositions are partly statistical and partly economic. On the statistical side he begins with the notion, vaguely justified by appeals to probability, that a price rise is more likely to occur as the result of a change in the quantity of gold if the prices of many goods rise relative to gold rather than the price of just one. The idea is that the supply conditions of the various goods are independent, so that in any reasonable aggregation they should cancel out, where the supply conditions of gold affect the price of all goods relative to gold and so will not cancel out.[15] (For a more detailed discussion of this point, see Harro Maas's essay in this volume.)

Like Smith and Tooke, Jevons acknowledges that prices will be affected by changing conditions of supply and demand for each good. Since he wishes to determine the permanent component of price change caused by changes in the stock of gold, he must eliminate the effects of cyclical variation.[16] In contrast with the earlier authors, Jevons is keenly aware of the trade cycle. He argues that ideally one would like to compare prices at the same relative point across different trade cycles. Practically, however, he recognizes that cycles have different lengths, so that it is generally impossible to locate the precisely analogous point in different cycles (1863, 34–35). Instead, he suggests comparing the averages across cycles. In this approach, he appeals to the same notion of cancellation of transitory influences through time that we argue motivated Smith to look at twelve-year averages. But Smith's averages covered periods with arbitrary end points, whereas Jevons needs to date the beginnings and ends of the particular cycles. He does this by looking at the time series for interest rates, appealing to his own theory of how interest rates vary with the trade cycle (36).

Jevons's strategy for measurement is to exploit the independence of transitory variation both across commodities and over time. He constructs index numbers. Index numbers are not original to Jevons; his novelty lies in applying them to the problem of the value of money.[17] His

15. Jevons (1867, 153) further clarifies the point, arguing that given the complexities of the measurement problem "we can only attack them by the use of averages, and by so trusting to probabilities." With fifty commodities, "the probability is almost infinite" that individual causes will cancel.

16. "At the same time, we shall be put on our guard against mistaking any temporary fluctuation due to excessive investment or credit, for the effect of gold depreciation. . . . To eliminate such disturbances in our comparisons of prices before and after the gold discoveries, we might compare the prices at corresponding points of the commercial tide" (Jevons 1865, 34).

17. In another article, Jevons (1865, 119–20) suggests that index numbers would have helped Tooke and William Newmarch to reduce and render more interpretable the mass of price data in the *History*. As we noted above, Tooke knew about index numbers in a general way. Jevons's first reference is to a tabular standard of value due to Evelyn in 1798. Chance

index numbers are simple geometric averages of the prices of a selection of thirty-nine major (and, subsequently, of an additional seventy-nine minor) commodities (1863, 38–41, 51). (For a more detailed account of Jevons's methodology in constructing his index numbers, see Sandra Peart's article in this volume. For a discussion of his choice of the geometric mean, see Maas this volume.) Jevon's data is mainly drawn from *The Economist*. He is aware of many of the issues regarding the appropriate methods of weighting different prices familiar in modern treatments of index numbers (1863, 21). But Jevons lacks information on the quantities of commodities. He argues that his separate examination of major and minor commodities amounts to a demonstration that his main conclusions are insensitive to weightings (57). Using these indices, Jevons is able to compare price changes between cycles for the period before the discovery of gold in California through 1862. Hc concludes that prices in general have risen 9 to 15 percent over that period and that this price rise could be caused only by changes in the stock of gold.[18] (See Peart this volume for a discussion of the reactions to Jevons's conclusions.)

Like the earlier authors, Jevons adopts strategies of isolation and compensation. The cross-sectional averaging process implicit in the construction of his index numbers is one such strategy, as is the use of business cycle averages of the index numbers themselves. He also makes adjustments to the data—for example, to cotton prices affected by the American Civil War—to account for special circumstances unrelated to gold (1863, 26–27).

The assumption of independence is crucial if his averages are to eliminate disturbing influences. And while Jevons investigates possible lack of independence among the minor commodities, noting for instance that bar iron, pig iron, and tinned iron plates, which appear as individual commodities are effectively a single commodity (1863, 54), he never offers any detailed support for the notion that the only source of interdependent price movement must come from changes in the gold supply.[19] In particular, he does not confront the possibility raised by Smith

---

(1966) finds the earliest example of an index number in 1675. While Smith did not use index numbers himself, much of his data is drawn from William Fleetwood, whom Chance (109) credits with having been aware of all the elements of index numbers.

18. The range of estimates corresponds to the range of price indices that he computes.

19. Jevons also believes that technological progress can affect the value of gold independently of the supply of gold, but he expects the effects to act too slowly to interfere with his measurements over the chosen time horizon.

that secular changes in relative prices might undermine the ability of the index numbers to extract the monetary signal from the economic noise.[20] It may be true that as matters of pure data processing, Jevons's index numbers are, as he writes, "independent of any assumptions as to the cause of the fall in the value of gold" (58–59). Nevertheless, his choice of how to construct them and how to manipulate them is guided by his theoretical assumptions and his ultimate purpose of identifying the cause of the decline of the value of gold with its changing supply.

In constructing his index numbers Jevons, like the previous authors, employs the method of residues. Because it differs from modern practice, it is easy to misunderstand Jevons's approach and to regard it as positively characterizing changes in the value of money rather than subtracting away nonmonetary influences. Unlike modern economists, Jevons does not argue that his index number captures the change in the value of money in a neutral way that could be used as an input into a study of the causes of that change. Rather he claims that, in the very construction of the index number itself, the nonmonetary causes have cancelled out. The index number is itself a residue—whatever would not cancel—and is a measure of the monetary causes of changing prices.

Both Tooke and Jevons appeal to the method of residues. Given Tooke's theoretical assumptions, the method of residues all but guarantees that little of the change in prices will be attributed to money. Jevons seems to speak directly to Tooke's measurement strategy when he writes:

It may seem to some persons that the best and perhaps only way to ascertain whether and why prices have altered, is to examine the circumstances of the demand and supply of each article. I do not hesitate to say that the whole inquiry would be thrown into confusion by any such attempt, and that for the particular purposes of our inquiry it is better not to know the details concerning the articles. If you are able to explain the rise or fall of one commodity by circumstances unconnected with gold, and throw it out of the inquiry, you must do the same with others, or else the impartial balance of the inquiry is overthrown. . . . A searching inquiry into the conditions of supply and demand of every article would result in every one being thrown out as

20. He offers a decomposition of price changes into a trend and an idiosyncratic relative price component that depends on mean reversion in the relative price component. The necessary mean reversion is an untestable identifying assumption.

unworthy of reliance as a measure of the value of gold. (1863, 58)[21]

Jevons's conclusion, although it is antithetical to Tooke's, bears the same self-validating quality: best to leave some proportion of the change in prices unexplained, for that proportion is what is attributable to gold, and otherwise nothing would be attributed to gold.

Measuring the Value of Money in Historical Context

It should come as no surprise that we found that the measurement strategies of each of the authors reviewed are imbued with theoretical presuppositions and are shaped by the author's particular conception of the value of money. This conclusion is inevitable because it reflects our own methodological presupposition. Although it was not obvious beforehand, rereading the four authors with the question "How did they try to measure?" squarely in mind made us realize just how different their investigative aims and conceptions of the value of money are. To some extent this was not obvious to the authors themselves. Tooke seems to talk past Smith in his detailed criticism of Smith's measurements. He betrays little recognition of how much Smith was concerned with secular rather than short-run change and with a desire to address the causes of prosperity rather than just the causes of price change.

A focus on causes is common to all the authors. One might think that there is a neutral description of the changes in the value of money on which all could agree as a preliminary to debating the causes. Both Jevons and Tooke are explicit in claiming that this is so. But the practice of all the authors belies their protestations: each has devised a measuring strategy that aims to reveal the quantitative significance of particular causes of changing prices. Both Tooke's and Jevons's measurement strategies very nearly build their qualitative—if not quantitative—conclusions into their measuring systems.

A final point, not obvious at the beginning, is that all the authors identify the monetary causes of price change through the method of residues: whatever is left after all the other factors are accounted for must be attributable to money. Why measure negatively? We end with a conjectured answer. The very notion of the general value of money is a fuzzy one. It

---

21. This view is contradicted by Jevons himself when he adjusts the data for the effects of the American Civil War on cotton prices. It appears Jevons is willing to throw out some observations.

is hard to be precise about what it is conceptually. Therefore it is equally hard to know what in the world to measure that might correspond to it. But it is feasible to measure some things in the world that it is not. Whatever is left must include the value of money.

References

Andréadès, A. [1909] 1966. *History of the Bank of England: 1640 to 1903*. 4th ed. New York: Kelley.

Arnon, Arie. 1990. What Thomas Tooke (and Ricardo) Could Have Known Had They Constructed Price Indices. In *Perspectives on the History of Economic Thought*. Vol. 4, *Keynes, Macroeconomics and Method*. Edited by D. E. Moggridge. Brookfield, Vt.: Edward Elgar.

Boskin, Michael, et al. (Boskin Commission). 1996. *Toward a More Accurate Measure of the Cost of Living: Final Report to the Senate Finance Committee from the Advisory Commission to Study the Consumer Price Index*. Washington, D.C.: U.S. Congress.

Cannan, Edwin. 1925. *The Paper Pound of 1797–1821: A Reprint of the Bullion Report*. 2d ed. London: P.S. King & Son.

Chance, W. A. 1966. A Note on the Origin of Index Numbers. *The Review of Economics and Statistics* 48.1:108–110.

———. 1996. Some Suggestions for Complicating the Theory of Money. In *Interactions in Political Economy: Malvern after Ten Years*, edited by Steven Pressman. London: Routledge.

Jevons, William Stanley. 1863. A Serious Fall in the Value of Gold Ascertained, and Its Social Effects Set Forth. In *Investigations in Currency and Finance*, 13–118. New York: Kelley.

———. 1865. The Variation of Prices and the Value of Currency Since 1782. In *Investigations in Currency and Finance*, 119–50. New York: Kelley.

———. 1867. The Depreciation of Gold. In *Investigations in Currency and Finance*, 150–59. New York: Kelley.

———. [1884] 1964. *Investigations in Currency and Finance*. New York: Kelley.

Mill, John Stuart. 1851. *A System of Logic, Ratiocinative and Deductive: Being a Connected View of the Principles of Evidence and the Methods of Scientific Investigation*. 3d ed. Vol. 1. London: John W. Parker.

Davenant, Charles R. 1925. In *Palgrave's Dictionary of Political Economy*, edited by Henry Huggs, C. B. Inglis and R. H. Inglis, 483–85. London: Macmillan.

Smith, Adam. [1776] 1981. *An Inquiry into the Causes and Consequences of the Wealth of Nations*. Glasgow ed. Edited by R. H. Campbell and A. S. Skinner. Indianapolis, Ind.: Liberty Fund.

Tooke, Thomas. [1838–57] 1972. *A History of Prices and the State of the Circulation from 1793 to 1837*. 5 vols. New York: Johnson Reprint Corporation.

———. [1844] 1959. *An Inquiry into the Currency Principle: The Connection of the Currency with Prices and the Expediency of a Separation of the Issue from Banking*. London: London School of Economics and Political Science (University of London).

Quantity Theory and Needs-of-Trade Measurements and Indicators for Monetary Policymakers in the 1920s

Thomas M. Humphrey

It is no accident that the age of measurement in economics coincides with the rise of central banking, for that epoch produced the statistical indicators that central bankers employ in conducting monetary and credit policy. So plentiful did the indicators become that officials were often forced to choose among them. At other times, however, choice was hardly an option. Instead, legal, institutional, or analytical considerations dictated which indicators policymakers would use. These considerations became especially important in the 1920s and early 1930s when U.S. gold holdings were sufficiently large to relax the constraint of the international gold standard and permit domestic control of the money stock and price level. At that time, two rival sets of indicators clamored for acceptance by Federal Reserve System (Fed) policymakers.

One set of indicators, consisting of the money stock, the price level, and the real rate of interest, was appropriate for an activist, ambitious central bank that endeavored to stabilize the price level and smooth the business cycle. The other set consisted of measures of aggregate output, type and amount of commercial paper in bank portfolios, levels of

Correspondence may be addressed to Thomas M. Humphrey, Federal Reserve Bank of Richmond, P.O. Box 27622, Richmond, VA 23261; e-mail: Tom.humphrey@rich.frb.org. I am extremely grateful to the editors, Judy Klein and Mary Morgan, for their constant encouragement, penetrating criticisms, and valuable suggestions in the writing of this article. For a different treatment of some of the topics discussed here, see the companion essay "The Choice of a Monetary Policy Framework: Lessons from the 1920s," in the fall 2001 issue of the *Cato Journal*.

short-term nominal rates of interest, and volume of member bank bor-rowing at the discount window. This set was appropriate for a passive, decentralized, noninterventionist system of autonomous regional reserve banks serving local commercial banks and their borrowers by accom-modating automatically all productive demands for loans over the cy-cle while preventing credit from flowing into speculative uses. In other words the second set of indicators was appropriate for the type of bank-ing system mandated by the 1913 Federal Reserve Act.

Fed policymakers accepted the latter set of indicators because they had little choice in the matter. The 1913 Federal Reserve Act required them to do so. The act established a system of twelve independent but co-operating regional reserve banks whose job was to "accommodate com-merce and business" by "furnishing an elastic currency" and "affording a means of rediscounting commercial paper." Accommodation and re-gional autonomy were the watchwords. The act said nothing about sta-bilization as a policy goal or about a single central agency charged with the duty of achieving that goal.

Nevertheless, by the mid-1920s there were voices—some within, but most without, the Federal Reserve System—claiming that the Fed should have learned that stabilization, not accommodation, was its overriding responsibility and that certain statistical measurements were available to help it accomplish that task. Accordingly, these same voices advo-cated that the Federal Reserve Act be amended to make stabilization the chief responsibility of the system, with power given to a single central authority to unify, coordinate, and synchronize the policy actions of the individual reserve banks.

But the Fed rejected these suggestions and clung to the notion that ac-commodation, not stabilization, was its duty and that the proffered mea-sures were irrelevant to the discharge of that duty. The result was that the Fed spurned those measures and the quantity theoretic or monetary-approach-to-the-business-cycle framework that featured them in favor of an entirely different framework. Composed of the real bills or needs-of-trade doctrine (also known as the commercial loan theory of banking), that latter framework had nonmonetary forces driving the price level just as it had output and the needs of commerce determining the money stock.

Since the doctrine taught that (1) money created by loans to finance real production rather than speculation has no influence on prices, (2) causality runs from prices and output to money (rather than vice versa, as in the quantity theory), and (3) the central bank in no way possesses control over money, there was no reason for the Fed to accept a theory asserting the opposite.[1] Indeed, as previously noted, throughout the 1920s officials and economists located at the Federal Reserve Board and certain regional reserve banks went out of their way to reject the quantity theory and its notions that the price level and real output could and should be stabilized through money stock control.

The initial phase of the Great Depression starkly revealed the consequences of the Fed's choice of policy frameworks. The depression put the rival frameworks, or theories, to the test. When quantity theory indicators—money stock, price level, and real rates of interest—became available, they signaled to quantity theorists that monetary policy was extraordinarily restrictive and likely to precipitate a contraction. The real bills or needs of trade indicators—member bank borrowing and nominal market rates of interest—indicated to proponents of the Fed's doctrine that policy was remarkably easy; therefore the Fed had already done all it could do to stop the slump. Guided by these indicators, the Fed did nothing to arrest and reverse the monetary contraction that was pushing the economy into depression.

Indeed, far from being alarmed by the monetary contraction, the Fed saw it as precisely what the real bills doctrine prescribed in an environment of falling output and employment. For the slumping levels of those variables meant, according to the doctrine, that less money and credit were required to finance them. Likewise, the price deflation accompanying the slump was interpreted as indicating not that money and credit were tight, but rather that the speculative excesses of the stock market boom of 1928–29 were being purged from the economy.

In brief, real bills indicators were telling the Fed early in the depression that it was doing the right thing and that its policy was sound. In actuality, however, the opposite was true, and the real bills indicators were leading the Fed astray. Those indicators, although accurate and precise, nevertheless wreaked havoc because they were embodied in a framework instructing the policymakers to let the supply of money and credit vary procyclically rather than countercyclically.

---

1. Conversely, there was every reason for Fed officials to endorse a doctrine that implied that their policies, being passive and automatic, could never be the cause of inflation or deflation. Such a doctrine promised to exonerate officials from blame for these phenomena and perhaps accounts for its appeal to them.

The story of the rival theories and their constituent policy indicators is instructive for at least four reasons. First, it illustrates how different statistical gauges can yield conflicting policy signals. Second, it indicates that theory necessarily precedes measurement in the sense that central bankers must have an analytical framework before they can determine the relevant indicator variables to measure. Third, it also reveals the corollary proposition that policymakers observe only what they are predisposed to see. That is, it shows that their chosen analytical framework dictates the very indicators to which they will respond.

Finally, it indicates that theories superficially similar in some respects can differ fundamentally in others. In the case of the quantity theory and the real bills doctrine, it shows that while both recognized that money stock growth in excess of output growth might be inflationary, they disagreed over the cause. The quantity theory attributed inflation to the resulting excess aggregate spending. But the real bills doctrine attributed it to the wrong kind of spending—namely, spending for speculative, as opposed to productive, purposes.

These two theories also yielded opposite predictions regarding the optimal cyclical behavior of the money stock. The real bills doctrine, stressing as it did that output generates the very money necessary to purchase it off the market, held that money should vary procyclically, rising with production in booms and falling with it in slumps. By contrast, the quantity theory, holding as it did that output is independent of money in long-run equilibrium but influenced strongly by it at cyclical frequencies, implied that money should vary countercyclically in the interest of economic stabilization.

The following paragraphs discuss the development and application of the two theories and their associated policy indicators in the 1920s and early 1930s. Three themes emerge. First, quantity theory indicators, although implied or foreseen as early as 1911, had to evolve through several stages of statistical work before emerging as serious candidates in the mid-1920s. Second, much the same can be said for the real bills doctrine. It too had to undergo several modifications and applications in the period 1914–28 before it could feature member bank borrowing and market interest rates as key policy guides. That the Fed was willing to countenance these modifications rather than switch to the quantity theory testifies to its allegiance to the doctrine. Third, the doctrine's failure to signal the onset of the Great Depression indicates that the Fed had allied itself with a causal framework inappropriate for measuring and controlling, for stabilization purposes, the nation's money supply.[2]

Quantity Theory Framework

The distinguishing characteristic of the quantity theoretic or monetary business cycle framework that vied unsuccessfully for the Fed's acceptance is easily described. It consisted of a causal chain running from Fed policy to bank reserves to the money stock and thence to general prices and output. Its transmission mechanism also featured a secondary, self-reinforcing feedback loop running in reverse direction from prices to money via inflation-induced demands for loans, demands which banks supply by creating new checking deposits. It implied that the Fed could control the money stock and thereby stabilize prices and smooth the business cycle. By the mid-1920s a vigorous empirical tradition had developed around the model. Key names in this tradition included Simon Newcomb, John Pease Norton, Edwin W. Kemmerer, Irving Fisher, Warren M. Persons, Carl Snyder, and Holbrook Working.

It was Newcomb, a renowned astronomer and part-time economist, who, in his 1885 *Principles of Political Economy*, suggested that David Ricardo's $P = MV/T$ equation of exchange might serve as an empirical framework to examine money's effects on the economy.[3] Newcomb also suggested an idea that John Norton, in his *Statistical Studies in the New York Money Market*, would later incorporate into the most comprehensive and disaggregated version of the equation ever published, namely the notion that the total stock of circulating media could, in principle, be divided into its separate components—coin, paper currency, demand deposits—each with its own velocity coefficient (1902, 1–12).[4] Inspired by Newcomb, Kemmerer, in his 1907 *Money and Credit Instruments in*

2. See also Kevin Hoover and Michael McDowell's essay in this volume on examples of links between causal frameworks and measuring instruments from the history of monetary theory.

3. Ricardo ([1810–11] 1951–55, 311) stated the $P = MV/T$ equation as follows: "Put the mass of commodities of all sorts [T] on one side of the line,—and the amount of money [M] multiplied by the rapidity of its circulation [V] on the other. Is not this in all cases the regulator of prices [P]?"

4. Besides containing terms for each type of coin and currency in circulation and their velocities, Norton's equation included notation for bank reserves, the deposit expansion multiplier, proportion of maximum allowable deposits banks actually create, velocity of deposits, and the discounted and full maturity values of bank loans—all for the four different classes of banks existing in the United States in 1902.

Their Relation to General Prices, and Fisher, in his 1911 *The Purchasing Power of Money*, elaborated upon Newcomb's suggestions in at least five ways.

Kemmerer and Fisher incorporated variables representing checking deposits (M') and their velocity (V') into the equation to obtain $P = (MV + M'V')/T$. Then, constructing pioneering time series—series that required new forms of measurement—of index numbers for each of the equation's elements, they combined these individual series into a single series for the entire right-hand side of the equation.[5] The resulting magnitude, $(MV + M'V')/T$, gave them an estimate of the hypothetical or predicted price level P which they compared with an independent price index series representing the actual observed price level.[6]

Visually comparing graphed curves of the two series over the period 1878–1901, Kemmerer concluded that the fit passed the ocular test closely enough to verify the quantity theory. When Warren Persons questioned this conclusion by calculating the correlation coefficient for Kemmerer's series and reporting it as a meager 0.23 with a probable error of 0.13 (1908, 289), Fisher, in response, demonstrated that the coefficient for the two series for the different period 1896–1909 was a whopping 0.97, indicating a very close fit ([1911] 1913, 294).

Further support for Fisher came when he and Persons applied link-relative and proportional-first-difference techniques of trend removal to Fisher's original series (Fisher [1911] 1913, 295; Persons 1911, 827–28). Doing so, they found that the correlation remained fairly high even when the series were cleansed of serial correlation. Fisher argued that these correlations, together with his finding that discrepancies between

5. Kemmerer's and Fisher's pathbreaking time-series estimates of the exchange equation's components constituted milestones in the statistical measurement of economic variables. Following Fisher ([1911] 1913, 430–88) but without going into detail, we can summarize these measurements as follows: For Kemmerer, M (defined as currency in the hands of the public) = currency outside the Treasury minus the vault cash of reporting banks; $V = 47$ (a calibrated constant); $M'V' =$ bank clearings multiplied by a factor of 2.86; $T =$ simple average of population, merchandise exports and imports, freight carried by railroads, and twelve other indicators of trade; $P =$ weighted average of the index numbers of wages, railroad stocks, and wholesale commodity prices, with weights of 3, 8, and 89 percent, respectively. For Fisher, $M =$ Kemmerer's measure minus the estimated vault cash of nonreporting banks minus the revisions of estimated gold stock; $V =$ (money deposited in banks + wage bill)/money in circulation; or M' = individual deposits subject to check; $V' =$ volume of transactions settled by check/individual deposits subject to check; $T =$ average of index numbers of quantities of trade in various lines. For P, see following note.

6. Fisher constructed his independent price index series as a weighted average of the wholesale prices of 258 commodities, hourly wage rates, and the prices of forty stocks.

the actual and hypothetical price series predicted the direction of movement of the former as it gravitated toward the latter, verified the quantity theory.

Still, skeptics could maintain that Fisher's work (and Kemmerer's as well) consisted of attempts to confirm the equation of exchange rather than the quantity theory. They could further maintain that because the equation is an accounting identity—and with its velocity term defined as $V = PT/M$, a tautologically truistic one at that—accurate measurement of its constituent variables could result in no disparity between the computed and actual price levels that constituted its opposite sides. If so, then high correlation between the two price series indicates merely the absence of measurement error rather than the validity of the quantity theory.

To forestall such criticism, Fisher argued that the identity, when combined with "supplementary knowledge" of the behavior of its constituent variables, allowed him to confirm statistically that the price level P was indeed determined by velocity-augmented money per unit of real output MV/T as the quantity theory held ([1911] 1913, 157). That is, he held that with velocity defined independently of the other variables so that the equation becomes nontautological, the price level adjusts to equate the real or price-deflated money stock M/P to the real demand for it, this real demand being the fraction $1/V$ of real transactions T the public wishes to hold in the form of real cash balances.

With the empirical quantity equation in place, New York Fed statistician and economist Carl Snyder—that rarest of birds: a Fed quantity theorist—and the University of Minnesota economist Holbrook Working applied it to establish the direction of causation between money (defined by them as demand deposits) and prices at secular and cyclical frequencies (Snyder 1924, 699, 710; Working 1923 and 1926). Secularly, they found the long-run path of prices to be determined jointly by the trend rates of growth of money, velocity, and trade. Of these trend growth rates, that of velocity appeared to be essentially 0 percent whereas that of trade was approximately 4 percent. They concluded that the money stock must expand secularly at the trend rate of trade growth to stabilize the price level.

In short, Snyder and Working had established that with velocity trendless, the price level evolved secularly at a percentage rate equal to the difference between the growth rates of money and trade. By contrast, at cyclical frequencies trade seemed to have a negligible influence on the price level whose variations apparently stemmed largely from variations in money alone. Evidently short-term oscillations of trade mattered little for prices because they were accommodated by corresponding oscillations in velocity. To Snyder, this finding—that velocity cyclically covaried in unison with trade to neutralize the mutual influence of both—meant but one thing. It meant that the ratio of the two variables could be replaced by a constant term k in the equation of exchange $P = kM$, implying that money contemporaneously determined prices at every point of the cycle.

For Working, however, things weren't quite that simple. His data series told him that while money did indeed determine prices over the cycle, it did so with a lag rather than contemporaneously. In his interpretation, the resulting lagged adjustment of prices to changes in the money stock necessitated compensating cyclical changes in the velocity-to-trade ratio to keep the exchange equation in balance. Evidently Snyder's k ratio, rather than being an absolutely fixed constant, exhibited transitory deviations from its trend equilibrium level with momentarily sticky prices accounting for the deviations. Due to temporarily inflexible prices, monetary shocks initially disturbed the k variable, driving it from equilibrium. With inflexibility quickly vanishing, corrective price-level changes then occurred to eliminate the deviation and restore the k ratio to trend.

To estimate the lead-lag relationship between money and prices implied by this result, Working correlated lagged and contemporaneous measures of the price level on detrended money (1923, 1926). He found that such correlations, though high for all lag lengths up to a year, were highest at six to eight months. This result was consistent with his other finding that money led prices by twelve months at the lower turning point of the cycle and by nine months at the upper turning point. Here seemed to be strong statistical evidence of money-to-price causality.

Fisher's Definitive Version of the Model

To Working's analysis of money's cyclical price-level effects, Fisher added his seminal and definitive account of the output and employment effects. In essence, he equipped the framework with an output-inflation/price-surprise relationship to argue that unanticipated price changes caused by monetary shocks were responsible for fluctuations in real interest rates and therefore in output and employment as well. Towering above the rest, his empirical contributions to the monetary theory of the cycle are to be found in his three remarkable journal articles of 1923, 1925, and 1926. But he had already sketched the underlying theory in his classic 1911 volume, *The Purchasing Power of Money*. There he argued that whereas money stock changes have no permanent, enduring effect on real output and employment, they do affect those variables temporarily over periods lasting perhaps as long as ten years. To account for these transitory real effects, Fisher appealed to two concepts first enunciated in his 1896 monograph "Appreciation and Interest," namely the distinction between real and nominal interest rates and the notion of asymmetrical expectations between business borrowers and bank lenders. The first concept defines the real rate of interest as the difference between the nominal observed rate and the expected rate of price inflation or deflation. The second concept says that business borrowers, by virtue of being entrepreneurs, possess superior foresight and so anticipate and therefore adjust to actual inflation or deflation faster than do bank lenders. According to Fisher, inflation lowers the real rate as seen by borrowers. Bankers, however, being slower than their customers to adjust their inflationary expectations, see a higher real rate of interest. Deflation works analogously to raise the real rate seen by borrowers more than it does the real rate seen by bankers.

Fisher ([1911] 1913, 55–73) attributed business cycles to such real rate movements. An increase in the money stock sets prices rising both directly and also indirectly through the price-money-price feedback loop referred to above. Because nominal interest rates adjust more slowly to inflation than do the expectations of entrepreneurs, real rates as seen by the latter group fall. (Similarly, real wages, rents, and raw material costs also fall as their nominal values fail to adjust for inflation as fast as do the expectations of entrepreneurs.) Such real rate falls, raising as they do the expected rate of profit on business projects financed by bank loans, spur corresponding rises in investment, output, and employment. As the expansion proceeds, banks run up against their reserve constraints. Moreover, they even begin to lose reserves as depositors, needing additional coin and currency to mediate a rising volume of hand-to-hand transactions, withdraw cash from their checking accounts. To protect their reserves from such cash drains, banks raise their nominal loan rate until it catches up with and then surpasses the rate of inflation. Real rates rise, thereby precipitating the downturn. Causation runs from money to prices to real rates to output and employment.

Having sketched his theory, Fisher then sought its empirical verification (see also the articles by Marcel Boumans and Spencer Banzhaf in this volume for a discussion of the price indices Fisher constructed to explore causal links). Citing Working's 1923 estimate that money stock changes over the period 1890–1921 had temporally preceded price level changes by about eight months, he took this finding as constituting strong evidence of money-to-price causality (Fisher 1925, 199). To establish corresponding price-to-output causality, he correlated distributed lags of rates of price-level change with an index of the physical volume of trade (1925).[7] Likewise, to establish price-to-employment causality, he correlated distributed lags of rates of price change and employment (1926). Finding a high correlation of .941 for the first set of series and .90 for the second, he concluded that "the ups and downs of [output and] employment are the effects . . . of the rises and falls of prices, due in turn to the inflation and deflation of money and credit" (792).

Here was his statistical confirmation of the trade cycle as a monetary phenomenon receptive to a monetary cure. Cycles, in other words, stem from price level movements caused by misbehavior of the money stock. It follows that monetary policy, properly conducted, could stabilize the price level and, in so doing, eliminate the business cycle as well. Policymakers had but to observe and react to the price level. Its deviations from target would trigger corrective monetary responses that would restore it to target. The price level itself was the main gauge of monetary policy. If the policymakers desired supplementary indicators of monetary tightness or ease, they could observe the money stock and real interest rates—the remaining chief variables of Fisher's analysis.

The Fed's Framework

Fisher's cycle model spotlighted the money stock, price level, and real interest rate as indicators. It linked these indicators through a causal chain running from the Fed to real activity, with the Fed actively initiating the causal sequence. The Fed determined the money stock. The money stock determined the price level directly and also indirectly

7. Fisher employed at least three weighting schemes to distribute the lag. The first used linearly declining monthly weights for eight-month intervals. The second used a unimodal sequence of lag coefficients to weight the past rates of price change. The third and most ambitious scheme distributed the lag according to the density function of a lognormal distribution (see Chipman 1999, 192–94). All schemes yielded high correlation coefficients.

through the dynamic price-money-price feedback loop that operates during transition periods between long-run monetary equilibria. The price level, or rather its rate of change, temporarily moved the real rate of interest. Movements of the real rate influenced output and employment. The cycle admitted to both a monetary cause and a monetary cure. The Fed, by stabilizing the price level, could smooth the cycle as well.

By contrast, economists at the Federal Reserve Board in the 1920s adhered to the real bills doctrine in which causation ran in the opposite direction from prices and real activity to money, with the Fed occupying a passive, accommodative role (Laidler 1999, 18; Yohe 1990, 486). In the Fed's framework, seasonal and cyclical movements in real activity drive business demands for bank loans. Since banks supply loans in the form of check-deposit money subject to a fixed fractional reserve requirement, these same movements lead to corresponding changes in bank demands for reserves, reserves borrowed from the Fed. The Fed passively accommodates these demands by discounting bank paper. In so doing, it contributes seasonal and cyclical elasticity to the money stock.

The Fed's framework did not come ready-made, however. Like the quantity theory whose elements, though assembled or foreseen as early as 1911, only became fully coordinated into an empirical framework with Fisher's output-inflation correlations of the mid-1920s, the real bills doctrine had to go through at least five overlapping stages, or developments, before it emerged in the form which the Fed employed to conduct policy in the initial phase of the depression. First came the pure or pristine version of the doctrine itself, which Fed officials —board economists Adolph G. Miller, Walter W. Stewart, and Emanuel Goldenweiser; reserve bank governors George W. Norris, James B. McDougal, George J. Seay, and John U. Calkins; founders and architects of the Federal Reserve System Carter Glass and H. Parker Willis—inherited from nineteenth-century Banking School economists. It was this version that the above named officials, once freed of their World War I preoccupation with selling bonds for the U.S. Treasury, found necessary to reformulate to purge it of ambiguities and inconsistencies. Missing from that inherited version were the notions of legal reserve requirements and of central banks as providers of reserves. Consequently, the second stage saw Fed economists in the period 1919–22 correcting those omissions by incorporating into the doctrine a representation of the central bank's rediscount function. Third and fourth, respectively, came the 1923 application of the doctrine to derive real-bills guides to policy and, in the stabilization hearings of 1926–27 and 1928, to reject quantity theory guides. Fifth came the attempt starting in 1923 to reconcile the doctrine with the newly discovered technique of open-market operations. Such operations, constituting as they did activist, discretionary policy intervention, conflicted with the doctrine's notion of policy as a passively accommodating and automatically self-correcting affair. The resulting reconciliation saw member bank borrowing and market interest rates emerge in the mid- to late 1920s as the doctrine's key policy indicators.

Original Doctrine Reformulated

The first step of the developmental process came with the passage of the 1913 Federal Reserve Act directing the Federal Reserve System to allow trade to flourish by providing the necessary credit. Written into the act was the prototypal version of the doctrine which the Fed inherited from its nineteenth-century Banking School predecessors. That version consisted of a rule gearing money (and credit) to production via the short-term commercial bill of exchange, thereby ensuring that output generates its own means of purchase and that money adapts passively to the legitimate needs of trade (Mints 1945, 206–7, 284). The rule implied that money could be neither excessive nor deficient when issued against short-term commercial paper arising from real transactions in goods and services. More precisely, the rule implied that so long as banks lend only against bona fide commercial paper, the money stock will be secured by, and will automatically vary equiproportionally with, real output such that the latter will be matched by just enough money to purchase it at existing prices.

During the six years following the end of the war, Federal Reserve System founders and architects Glass and Willis, together with board economists Stewart, Miller, Goldenweiser and others, sought to spell out explicitly the logic of the foregoing implications and give them an exact and systematic formulation (Laidler 1999, 192–95; Yohe 1990, 486). They realized that doing so would remove ambiguities clouding earlier statements of the doctrine, statements that Lloyd Mints, the leading expert on the doctrine's history, described as "invariably brief, incomplete, and frequently not consistent" (1945, 206). Correcting those statements and getting the doctrine right became the first order of business. It was absolutely essential to articulate precisely the framework that the Federal Reserve Act had mandated as a policy guide and to spotlight its indicator variables in sharp relief. In their reformulation, Fed officials did four things.

First, they defined the needs of trade as the value of inventories of working capital, or goods-in-process, the production of which is financed by bank loans. As discussed below, Fed officials measured the needs of trade, or nominal output, by using the board's index of industrial production to capture its physical product component and the Bureau of Labor Statistics's wholesale price index to represent its nominal dollar component. They further assumed that each dollar's worth of goods-in-process generates an equivalent quantity of paper claims in the form of commercial bills which business borrowers pledge as collateral to back their loan demands. They then observed that these loan demands pass the real bills test (since they are secured by claims to real goods) and therefore qualify for matching supplies of bank loans. They finally noted that since banks supply loans in the form of banknotes and checking deposits the sum of which comprises the stock of bank money, the supply of loans must equal that money stock.

From the foregoing they drew four conclusions. First, provided banks lend only against short-term commercial bills arising out of transactions in real goods and services, stocks of money and credit (i.e., loans) must conform to the needs of trade. Second, since those needs are by definition the same as the value of goods-in-process, the money stock is ultimately secured by the latter such that when those goods reach the market they will be matched by just enough money to purchase them at existing prices. Third, no monetary overhang can persist to spark inflation after the goods are sold. Instead, producers use their sales proceeds to pay off their loans and the money returns to the banks to be retired from circulation. Here is the concept of the self-liquidating loan that constitutes the bedrock principle of the reformulated doctrine. Only if loans were made for speculative purposes would monetary overhang persist. Such loans, being nonproductive, finance no real output to generate the sales revenue leading to their retirement. Consequently, the loans and the money issued by way of them remain outstanding. The limitation of loans to self-liquidating uses rules out this pathological case. In short, inflationary overissue is impossible provided money is issued on loans made to finance real, rather than speculative, transactions. Fourth, with prices taken as given and determined by nonmonetary considerations, the money stock and volume of bank credit must vary in step with real production.

Here was the essence of the reformulated real bills doctrine (see Federal Reserve Board 1924, 29–39 for an articulation of this doctrine). Its distinctiveness lay in its treatment of prices and output as given exogenous variables when, as Fisher had claimed, they move under the influence of changes in the money stock itself.[8] Accordingly, when the Fed came to measure output and prices, it did so not with the Fisherian intention of attributing movements in those variables to an excess or deficient money stock. Rather it did so in order to estimate, or predict, the supply of real bills it would be called upon to rediscount so that member banks might accommodate business demands for credit.

Augmenting the Doctrine

With the Federal Reserve Act authorizing reserve banks to rediscount bank paper, a new element entered the real bills version of the monetary transmission mechanism. Step two of the reformulation of the real bills framework saw Fed founders and economists in the late 1910s and early 1920s recognize this element by incorporating a representation of the rediscount function into the framework. The rediscount function, of course, was useful to banks who, facing a mandatory legal reserve ratio, had to obtain the necessary reserves to back the money and credit required by the needs of trade. The Fed enabled them to do so by rediscounting the commercial paper they had acquired from their customers. By limiting the type of paper eligible for rediscount, the Fed ensured that reserves were just sufficient to underwrite production without promoting speculation. Nonborrowed sources of reserves, including inflows of gold and currency, were dismissed as superfluous. Ideally, the discount window supplied all the reserves necessary to meet the needs of trade.[9] And it did so at a discount rate normally aligned with or below short-term market interest rates so as to pose no barrier to accommodation.

The significance of these propositions cannot be overestimated. Here was the view, dominant at the Federal Reserve Board in the early 1920s, of the Fed as passive accommodator rather than active initiator of

8. Fisher, of course, never denied that nonmonetary causes such as autonomous changes in trade might also change prices. Nevertheless, as David Laidler (1991, 80) observes, "the overwhelming impression left by Fisher's account of the empirical evidence is that variations in the quantity of money are the principal cause of price level fluctuations."

9. In Wheelock's (1991, 13) words, "The Real Bills Doctrine implied that rediscounts alone would provide sufficient liquidity to accommodate commerce and meet financial emergencies. No [other sources of reserves] were necessary."

changes in economic activity. Here was the idea that causation runs from output and prices to loans to bank money, with the Fed supplying the necessary reserves. Standing at the end of the causal queue, the Fed cannot force money on the economy. It merely supplies reserves on demand. Of course it may influence this demand through changes in its rediscount rate. Still, it must accept all real bills tendered it at the prevailing rate. The contrast with the quantity theory could hardly have been more pronounced.

Making the Doctrine Operational

Step three of the reformulation saw board economists—some newly hired when the Federal Reserve System's main research office, with Walter Stewart appointed director in July 1922, was moved from New York to Washington—give the doctrine operational content by defining its variables so that they could be measured and serve as policy guides. As previously mentioned, output was defined as aggregate physical product as measured by the board's own monthly index of industrial production. Dating from December 1922 and constructed from data on output in manufacturing and mining, this index, principally the work of Walter Stewart and Woodlief Thomas, had forerunners in the production indexes developed by Wesley Clair Mitchell for the War Production Board in 1917, by Carl Snyder for the New York Fed in 1918–20, and by Stewart himself in 1921 before he left Amherst College to go to the board. The board gave this index pride of place in its collection of statistical measures for two reasons. The index quantified the Federal Reserve Act needs-of-business criterion. It also represented the strategic variable that, according to the real bills doctrine, drove all other variables—loans, bills, money stock—in the credit mechanism.

Likewise, the board defined productive loans as bank credit advanced solely to finance the production and marketing of goods in the agricultural, industrial, and commercial sectors of the economy. (The board also published, in its monthly *Bulletin*, figures on what it regarded as speculative lending—notably loans to brokers and dealers, real estate loans, and long-term capital investment loans.) As for the assets securing, or backing, productive loans, the board defined real bills as paper pledged as collateral for such loans and eligible for rediscount at the Fed. The exact counterpart of productive loans, such bills constituted evidence of their soundness. Here was the Board's belief that the type of paper banks acquire in making loans describes and governs the particular use of the borrowed funds. Here was its conviction that real bills signify and measure productive credit just as non-real bills denote speculative credit.

This belief—that type of collateral corresponds to use of borrowed funds—was not shared by all. As early as 28 November 1922, Benjamin Strong of the New York Fed, in a talk to the Graduate Economics Club at Harvard, opposed the belief on the grounds that the very fluidity of credit across uses and instruments rendered it fallacious (Chandler 1958, 197–98). With credit fungible, banks and their customers could borrow on real bills to finance speculation. Conversely, they could borrow on speculative paper—stocks, bonds, and mortgages—to finance production. If so, then type of paper is independent of purpose of loan, and there is no assurance that credit advanced on real bills will remain in productive channels. But many Fed officials, notably Miller and reserve bank governors Calkins, McDougal, Norris, and Seay, disagreed with Strong and throughout the 1920s continued to argue that the form of collateral denotes the particular use of the borrowed funds.

As for the money stock, the Fed thought so little of it as a strategic variable that it published no series on it before 1941. True, the Federal Reserve Board did collect data on the currency and demand deposit components of the money stock. And it even published information on these individual components, including (1) monthly figures on currency in circulation, (2) a series on weekly reporting member banks that contained substantial detail on deposits, and (3) a semi-annual all-bank series that one could use to establish benchmarks of monthly deposit estimates based on those of reporting member banks. But the board never assembled these components into a single comprehensive measure of the money stock. Indeed it had little reason to do so. Guided as it was by the real bills doctrine, the board saw money creation as simply a by-product, or secondary side effect, of bankers' loan decisions. To the board, loans, not money, were what mattered. Provided banks made the right kind of loans, the money stock would take care of itself.

The final step in the board's effort to make the doctrine operational involved defining the price level as measured by the wholesale price index. The Board attributed movements in this latter index either to the long-term operation of exogenous real forces, notably technological progress or resource scarcity, or to short-term speculation—that is, to nonproductive uses of money and credit. Accordingly, secular price changes were ascribed either to cost-reducing productivity growth or cost-enhancing capacity limitations. Likewise, short-term rises in the price level were seen as evidence of a speculative withholding of goods from the market in anticipation of the higher future prices they might bring. And short-term falls in the price level were seen as the inevitable consequence of the bursting of the speculative bubble as goods were dumped on the market at fire sale prices. The Fed's inclination was to do little to interfere with these latter price falls. Instead it regarded them as necessary to purge the economy of its preceding speculative excesses. The upshot was that the Fed watched the price index for evidence of speculation and its aftermath rather than for evidence that money was plentiful or tight.

Policy Guides in the Board's *Tenth Annual Report*

With these definitions and interpretations in hand, Stewart, writing (with Miller's support) in the board's famous *Tenth Annual Report* (Federal Reserve Board 1924), specified two policy guides designed to ensure that the volume of money and credit was neither excessive nor deficient. These were the celebrated quantitative and qualitative tests, respectively.[10]

The quantitative test focused on the ratio of credit (or money) to trade. (Again, the board's index of industrial production measured trade's real, or output, component and the wholesale price index its nominal, or price, component.) The test consisted, in the words of Friedman and Schwartz (1963, 253), of a "marriage of the traditional real bills doctrine and an inventory theory of the business cycle." The real bills component stated that money and credit are optimally supplied when variations in their quantity match corresponding variations in nominal product or income (Hardy 1932, 77; Reed 1930, 62). In other words, money and credit would exhibit desirable elasticity when they rose and fell in procyclical fashion with the dollar value of real output whose financing they supported (Hardy 1932, 78–79).

The inventory theory component added the proviso that money and credit should so behave only as long as they finance no speculative

10. For critical evaluation of these tests, see Friedman and Schwartz 1963, 252–53; and Mints 1945, 265–68. For more sympathetic treatments, see Hardy 1932, 74–80; Reed 1930, 59–64; West 1977, 195–98; and Wicker 1966.

inventory accumulation (Hardy 1932, 77).[11] That is, money and credit should not finance production destined for speculative stockpiling rather than for final sales. The danger is that such stocks of commodities eventually would be dumped on the market to depress prices and real activity. Evidently, the sharp boom-bust cycle of 1919–21 had taught the Fed that such an outcome could happen. It had revealed that even legitimate credit expansion could, by financing inventory overinvestment instead of production for final consumption, lead to an inflationary shortage of consumers' goods followed by deflation when the excess stocks of those goods finally flooded the market. But this inventory cycle proviso, with its implication that credit is put to speculative uses when it finances production for inventory rather than for consumption, is inconsistent with the real bills doctrine. The latter, of course, equates all production, regardless of its purpose, with the proper use of credit.

Finally, the qualitative test stated that money is optimally supplied when it passes the real bills test—that is, when it is extended on loan for productive purposes as evidenced by eligible paper in bank portfolios. Whereas the quantitative test, sheared of its inventory proviso, stated that money and credit cannot be overissued when they move one-for-one with the value of real output, the qualitative test assured that this outcome is automatically achieved when banks lend only on real bills— that is, when loan growth goes 100 percent to finance working capital needs and 0 percent to finance fixed capital investment and stock market speculation. The implication is that quantitative control can be attained through qualitative means. The Federal Reserve Board took this latter implication seriously. It largely abandoned quantitative tests after the mid-1920s when its concern shifted from accommodating production to stopping speculation in the stock market (see Reed 1930, 60, 63; Yohe 1990, 482).

Rejection of Quantity Theory Indicators

Having deployed their framework to champion real bills indicators, board economists Miller, Stewart, and Goldenweiser put it through its fourth developmental stage when they applied it to reject rival quantity

11. Hardy's statement of the inventory theory proviso is classic. The Fed's responsibility, he writes, is "not to check price increases [associated with expanding production] but to supply a volume of credit appropriate to the higher prices, so long as the latter are not interpreted as the evidence of speculative accumulation of inventories" (1932, 77).

theory indicators, specifically those of the price level and the money supply. Their doctrine taught them that money was demand determined, that real forces drive the price level, and that causation runs from prices (and real activity) to money rather than vice versa as in the quantity theory. Accordingly, when Congress held hearings in 1926–27 and 1928 on Kansas Representative James G. Strong's proposed legislation to make price level stability an explicit goal of monetary policy, they and other Fed economists who testified at the hearings expressed their opposition in no uncertain terms (see U.S. House 1928).[12]

Regarding the price level, Stewart, Miller, and Goldenweiser denied its reliability or usefulness as a policy guide largely on doctrinal grounds supplemented occasionally with some sketchy statistical evidence. First, the Fed, they claimed, cannot control the price level. Nonmonetary forces outside the Fed's purview or sphere of influence determine that variable. New York Fed Governor Benjamin Strong, who adhered to some strands of the real bills doctrine while rejecting others, voiced a variant of this argument. Even if money can influence the price level, he declared, it is but one of many factors doing so. Others include a variety of real shocks plus the state of business confidence and the public's expectations of the future, none of which the Fed controls (U.S. House 1926, 482). Quantity theorists including John R. Commons readily agreed with this point but still contended that monetary policy was powerful enough to offset these forces and stabilize the price level (Hardy 1932, 207).

But board economists Stewart and Miller countered that even if Commons were right and the Fed could indeed stabilize the price level, it nevertheless has no business doing so. The Fed has no right to interfere either with price falls caused by cost-reducing technological progress or with price rises caused by exhaustion of supplies of scarce natural resources. To this contention quantity theorists like Fisher replied that, in the absence of changes in the stock of money per unit of real output, costs of production, whether lowered by technical progress or raised by increased scarcity, influence only the relative prices of individual goods but not the absolute price level, or general average of all prices. For with the money stock and so aggregate spending held constant, cost-induced rises in the prices of some goods requiring consumers to spend more on those items would leave them with less money to spend on other goods

---

12. On Fed testimony in the stabilization hearings, see Hardy 1932, 207–18, Hetzel 1985, and Meltzer 1997, 66–79.

whose prices would accordingly fall. If so, then the rise in the first set of relative prices would be offset by compensating falls in the second set, leaving general prices unchanged. Only if cost shocks had an impact on the total volume of output or trade could they alter the price level associated with a given money stock. Fed economists offered no rebuttal to this argument. Instead they advanced another reason why the general price level is a poor policy guide, namely that the public would confuse it with the prices of specific goods and assume that a policy of price-level stabilization required stabilizing the prices of individual commodities (Hardy 1932, 207).

Finally, Board economists condemned price level indicators on purely technical and statistical grounds. Stewart used a chart showing the 1921–1926 behavior of the wholesale price index and its agricultural and non-agricultural components to dismiss aggregate indexes of the price level as meaningless averages masking diverse movements of their individual elements (U.S. House 1926, 741–77; see also U.S. House 1928, 40). And Adolph Miller, citing long lags in price adjustment, argued that the price level registers inflationary pressures too late for policy to forestall them (U.S. House 1926, 837–38). Longtime Fed board member Charles Hamlin added that there are many different measures of the price level, including wholesale price, retail price, and cost of living indexes, as well as Snyder's comprehensive composite index (U.S. House 1928, 393) (which, in addition to wholesale and retail commodity prices, included wages, rents, and stock prices as well) Each measure may behave differently—Hamlin noted the 12, 2, and 0 percent falls of the wholesale, cost of living, and Snyder indexes, respectively, for the period 1925–27—and call for a different stabilization action. What should the Fed do when confronted with alternative index numbers that are simultaneously changing at different rates? Which index should it choose?

As for the money stock, Stewart, Miller, and company likewise gave it short shrift as an indicator. It was, they claimed, useless as a policy guide because the Fed exercised no control over it. Instead, the public determines the money stock through its demand for bank loans, just as the needs-of-trade doctrine contended. The money stock was likewise useless as an indicator of inflationary or deflationary pressure because it did not determine the price level. Or at least it did not do so if created by way of loans made to finance nonspeculative activity. In this case the money stock adapted passively to the needs of trade valued at the prevailing price level, a price level whose path was determined by real considerations including technological progress, productivity growth, or growing resource scarcity. Miller said it all when he insisted that neither of the assumptions of the quantity theory—that Fed policy causes money stock changes and that money stock changes cause corresponding changes in the price level—is true (U.S. House 1928, 109).

The upshot was that Fed officials contended that all the foregoing considerations rendered the quantity theory and its money stock and price level indicators unfit for policy use. The Fed might collect data on those indicators and report them in its publications. It might even monitor them as background information from time to time. In no case, however, would it use them for stabilization purposes. To influential congressmen, economists, and bankers alike, the Fed's arguments proved convincing. Quantity theorists were unsuccessful in getting their price stability target enacted into law.

Incorporation of Open Market Operations

Ironically, the main challenge to the real bills doctrine came not from the quantity theory but rather from the Fed's own discovery in 1922–23 of open-market operations as a means of reserve control. In incorporating this new policy instrument into the real bills framework, Board economists evidently reconciled the irreconcilable. That is to say, they reconciled the instrument with a doctrine whose precepts it violated in at least three ways. First, open-market operations, involving as they did purchases and sales of U.S. government securities, conflicted with the notion that the Fed should deal solely in short-term, self-liquidating commercial paper. Government securities, according to the pristine version of the doctrine, represented speculative rather than productive use of credit. Second, when the Fed conducted open market operations, it did so at its own initiative. Such active intervention clashed with the principle of passive accommodation according to which the initiative for reserve provision should come not from the Fed but rather from member banks and their customers responding to the needs of trade. Finally, open-market operations contradicted the idea that additional means of reserve provision were superfluous since banks could always obtain sufficient reserves at the discount window. How could use of such an instrument be squared with the real bills doctrine?

The Fed's "great discovery" (Burgess 1964, 220) of the so-called scissors, or displacement, effect permitted the reconciliation.[13] The scissors effect referred to the tendency of compensating changes in discount-window borrowing to offset open-market operations, leaving total reserves unchanged (see Friedman and Schwartz 1963, 251, 272, 296; Yohe 1990, 483; U.S. House 1926, 749). W. Randolph Burgess and Benjamin Strong of the New York Fed and Miller, Stewart, and Winfield Reifler at the board discovered this phenomenon in 1922–23. To their surprise, they found that open-market sales, by removing reserves, tended to induce member banks to come to the discount window to recoup the lost reserves. Conversely, open-market purchases, by increasing reserves, enabled member banks to reduce their indebtedness to the Fed by the full amount of the purchases. In both cases, compensatory changes in member bank borrowing tended to counteract the reserve effects of open-market operations. Borrowed reserves varied inversely with open-market operations (as measured by changes in the Fed's holdings of government securities) in a one-for-one relationship.[14]

The scissors effect prompted two interpretations of open-market operations consistent with the real-bills doctrine. According to the first, voiced primarily by Miller and Stewart, such operations constituted a test of whether reserves and the deposit money they supported were in excess of the needs of trade (see Federal Reserve Board 1924, 13–14). Open-market operations were taken at the initiative of the Fed. But the initiative to borrow or repay at the discount window came from member banks seeking to accommodate the needs of trade. If so, then the extent to which banks borrowed to replace reserves lost through open-market sales measured the true, or real bills, demand for such reserves. And the open-market operations themselves tested, or revealed, the extent of this demand.

Let the Fed apply the test by withdrawing, via open-market sales, reserves from the banking system. If banks replenished all the lost reserves through increased borrowing at the discount window, this would prove that reserves and deposits were not excessive. Reserves were not excessive because banks, in borrowing them, had to rediscount real bills equal to them in dollar value. That banks were willing to do so was proof positive that the reserves and deposits were not excessive to the needs of

13. The appellation is due to Harold Reed (1930, 28), who coined it.
14. On the one-for-one, or dollar-for-dollar, relationship between discount-window borrowing and open-market operations, see Yohe 1990, 483 and Meltzer 1997, 184.

trade. Only if banks failed to recoup, via the rediscount of real bills, all the reserves lost through open-market sales would such reserves be proved excessive.

The second interpretation, expounded by Burgess, Strong, and Riefler, was the more extreme of the two.[15] It held that open-market operations could be employed to control the volume of discount-window borrowing. For if such borrowing varied in an inverse, dollar-for-dollar ratio with open-market operations as the scissors effect implied, then the Fed could control the numerator by regulating the denominator. Via open-market sales, the Fed could compel banks to borrow just as surely as it could, through open-market purchases, spur them to repay their indebtedness. True, the very notion of the Fed controlling discount-window activity through open-market operations clashed with the passive-accommodation principle of the real bills doctrine. Nevertheless, other strands of the doctrine were preserved. The Fed was still obliged to rediscount upon demand all the eligible paper offered it at any level of open-market operations. Morcover, banks still eliminated their reserve deficiencies and excesses by rediscounting and repurchasing, respectively, real bills at the discount window. Finally, business loan demands still drove the generation of credit and money, with the Fed supplying the necessary borrowed reserves, albeit using open-market operations to force banks to borrow. On these grounds, at least, the real bills doctrine was upheld.

Key Indicators Established

The upshot was to render member bank borrowing and market interest rates the chief indicators of policy. Burgess (1927) and Riefler (1930) saw both indicators as measuring the degree of policy tightness or case produced by open-market sales and purchases, respectively. With respect to the borrowing indicator, the inverse one-for-one relationship between it and open-market operations guaranteed that it would be an accurate indicator of the thrust or pressure exerted by the latter. Thus, when restrictive open market sales pressured banks to borrow, the magnitude of borrowing (in excess of the Fed's desired target level of borrowed

15. Karl Brunner and Allan Meltzer christened this interpretation the "Riefler-Burgess doctrine" after Winfield W. Riefler and W. Randolph Burgess, the two Fed economists who gave it its classic exposition. Governor Benjamin Strong of the New York Fed was a staunch proponent of the Riefler-Burgess doctrine.

reserves, which Benjamin Strong in 1926 suggested was $500–$600 million) would capture the degree of restriction. Conversely, when expansionary open-market purchases spurred banks to repay their indebtedness, the resulting reduction in borrowing (below the Fed's $500–$600 million borrowed reserve target) would indicate the extent of the ease. The inverse relation ensured as much.

As for market rates, they sent the same signal as member bank borrowing. They did so because borrowing was the chief influence determining them. When borrowing was high, banks, being reluctant to remain continually in debt with the Fed, would be under great pressure to reduce their indebtedness.[16] To obtain the funds to do so, they would call in outstanding loans and curtail further lending. The resulting reduction in loan supply would raise market interest rates. The greater the indebtedness and thus the urgency to repay it, the greater the upward pressure on rates and so the higher their level. Contrariwise, when borrowing was low and banks had repaid their indebtedness, they would be willing to expand their lending. The resulting expansion in loan supply relative to loan demand would put downward pressure on rates. In this way, market interest rates, varying directly as they did with the scale of member bank borrowing, supplemented the latter as an indicator of the degree of policy ease or tightness (see Meltzer 1976, 464–65).

Signals Flashed by the Indicators Early in the Depression

Relying on these indicators—member bank borrowing and market interest rates—the Fed judged its policy to be remarkably easy in the initial phase (October 1929–31) of the Great Depression. Their indicators signaled as much. By mid-1931, member bank borrowing and market rates, respectively, had fallen to one-fifth and one-third of their October 1929 levels (Wheelock 1998, 130–31, 133). By all accounts both rates were extremely low—borrowing averaging but $243 million from January 1930 to September 1931, the Treasury bill rate averaging less than 2 percent over that same period—suggesting that the Fed had already

16. Fed economists, notably Riefler (1930) and Burgess (1927), cited a so-called tradition against borrowing, or reluctance to borrow, that was supposed to make banks eager to repay their indebtedness. Allegedly, such reluctance held even when borrowing was profitable—that is, when a positive spread between bank loan rates and the discount rate indicated that the expected rate of return on the use of borrowed reserves exceeded the cost of such reserves. See Meltzer 1976, 464–65 for a concise summary of the reluctance hypothesis.

done all it could do to arrest the depression. It was these indicators that the Fed used to justify its policy of inaction.

By contrast, the rival quantity theory indicators—money stock, price level, and real interest rates—were flashing the opposite signal. Thus Lauchlin Currie's pioneering series of the M1 money stock showed falls of 3.7 and 6.3 percent, respectively, in 1930 and 1931. Currie's figures, later confirmed by Clark Warburton (1945, 1946), Lloyd Mints (1950, 38; 1951, 193), and Milton Friedman and Anna Schwartz (1963), were reported both in his Harvard Ph.D. thesis, which he wrote in 1929–30 and submitted in January 1931, and in his 1934 *The Supply and Control of Money in the United States*. Such figures were fully available to the Fed at the time and could have been computed from data it regularly collected from the banking system.

Likewise available to the Fed were measures of the price level, particularly indexes of wholesale commodity prices. They had, by 1931, fallen by more than a fourth of their 1929 level. As for the real interest rate (as measured by the short-term government yield minus the percentage rate of change of the wholesale price index, which was negative at that time), it had, by mid-1931, risen to a level of 10.5 percent, more than six percentage points above its 1929 level. Clearly here was evidence that monetary policy was extremely tight, not easy, and that expansionary measures should be taken immediately to prevent further contraction in real activity. But the Fed either disregarded these signals or interpreted them as indicating that the money stock was behaving correctly. Indeed, it interpreted falls in the money stock as entirely appropriate given the fall in prices and output. Monetary contraction in response to the decline in nominal income was precisely what the real bills doctrine called for.

Conclusion

History might have been different had the Fed incorporated quantity theoretic insights into its analytical policy framework in the 1920s and early 1930s. For the quantity theory model of the business cycle featured statistical indicators that would have signaled that monetary policy was too tight and needed easing in the early years of the Great Depression. Acting on those indicators, the Fed could have eased policy and so prevented the depression, or at least mitigated its severity. Instead, Fed officials adhered to an entirely different framework whose indicators signaled that policy was remarkably easy and that the central bank had already done all it could do to arrest and reverse the slump. Accordingly, the Fed did nothing and let the economy slide further into the depression.

The Fed's failure to act shows that its adherence to the real bills doctrine had deleterious consequences. These consequences might have been avoided had the Fed selected, at the outset, the state-of-the-art quantity theory framework rather than the alternative real bills framework. The moral is clear: accuracy and precision are not the only determinants of the usefulness of measurements in policymaking. The conceptual framework that defines and constrains what is measured and how it is measured establishes the effectiveness and usefulness of those measurements. In the early 1930s, the measurements emanating from the quantity theory framework might have accomplished what their real bills counterparts could not—namely, help the Fed alleviate the depression.

References

Burgess, W. Randolph. 1927. *The Reserve Banks and the Money Market*. New York: Harper.

———. 1964. Reflections on the Early Development of Open Market Policy. *Monthly Review* (Federal Reserve Bank of New York) 46.11:219–26.

Chandler, Lester V. 1958. *Benjamin Strong: Central Banker*. Washington, D.C.: Brookings Institution.

Chipman, John S. 1999. Irving Fisher's Contributions to Economic Statistics and Econometrics. In *The Economics of Irving Fisher: Reviewing the Scientific Work of a Great Economist*, edited by Hans-E. Loef and Hans G. Monissen. Northampton, Mass.: Edward Elgar.

Currie, Lauchlin B. 1934. *The Supply and Control of Money in the United States*. Cambridge, Mass.: Harvard University Press.

Federal Reserve Board. 1924. *Tenth Annual Report of the Federal Reserve Board Covering Operations for the Year 1923*. Washington, D.C.: U.S. Government Printing Office.

Fisher, Irving. 1896. Appreciation and Interest. *American Economic Association Publications*, 3d ser., 11.4:331–442.

———. [1911] 1913. *The Purchasing Power of Money*. 2d ed. New York: Macmillan.

———. 1923. The Business Cycle Largely a "Dance of the Dollar." *Journal of the American Statistical Association* 18.144:1024–28.

———. 1925. Our Unstable Dollar and the So-Called Business Cycle. *Journal of the American Statistical Association* 20.150:179–202.

———. 1926. A Statistical Relation between Unemployment and Price Changes. *International Labour Review* 13:785–92.

Friedman, Milton, and Anna J. Schwartz. 1963. *A Monetary History of the United States, 1867–1960*. Princeton, N.J.: Princeton University Press.

Hardy, Charles O. 1932. *Credit Policies of the Federal Reserve System*. Washington, D.C.: Brookings.

Hetzel, Robert L. 1985. The Rules versus Discretion Debate Over Monetary Policy in the 1920s. *Federal Reserve Bank of Richmond Economic Review* 71.6:3–14.

Kemmerer, E. W. 1907. *Money and Credit Instruments in Their Relation to General Prices*. New York: Henry Holt.

Laidler, David. 1991. *The Golden Age of the Quantity Theory: The Development of Neoclassical Monetary Economics*. Princeton, N.J.: Princeton University Press.

———. 1999. *Fabricating the Keynesian Revolution: Studies of the Inter-war Literature on Money, the Cycle, and Unemployment*. Cambridge: Cambridge University Press.

Meltzer, Alan. 1976. Monetary and Other Explanations of the Start of the Great Depression. *Journal of Monetary Economics* 2.4:455–71.

———. 1997. New Procedures, New Problems, 1923–29. Unpublished manuscript.

Mints, Lloyd W. 1945. *A History of Banking Theory*. Chicago: University of Chicago Press.

———. 1950. *Monetary Policy for a Competitive Society*. New York: McGraw-Hill.

———. 1951. Monetary Policy and Stabilization. *American Economic Review* 41:188–93.

Newcomb, Simon. 1885. *Principles of Political Economy*. New York: Harper.

Norton, John P. 1902. *Statistical Studies in the New York Money Market*. New York: Macmillan.

Persons, Warren M. 1908. The Quantity Theory as Tested by Kemmerer. *Quarterly Journal of Economics* 22.2:274–89.

———. 1911. Fisher's *The Purchasing Power of Money*. *Publications of the American Statistical Association* 12.96:818–29.

Reed, Harold D. 1930. *Federal Reserve Policy, 1921–1930*. New York: McGraw-Hill.

Ricardo, David. [1810–1811] 1951–55. Notes on Bentham's *Sur les Prix*. In *The Works and Correspondence of David Ricardo*. Vol. 3. Edited by Piero Sraffa. Cambridge: Cambridge University Press.

Riefler, Winfield W. 1930. *Money Rates and Money Markets in the United States*. New York: Harper.

Snyder, Carl. 1924. New Measures in the Equation of Exchange. *American Economic Review* 14.4:699–713.

U.S. House. 1926. Committee on Banking and Currency. *Stabilization: Hearings on H.R. 7895*. 69th Cong., 1st sess.

U.S. House. 1928. Committee on Banking and Currency. *Stabilization: Hearings on H.R. 11806*. 70th Cong., 1st sess.

Warburton, Clark. 1945. The Volume of Money and the Price Level between the World Wars. *Journal of Political Economy* 53.2:150–63.

―――. 1946. Quantity and Frequency of Use of Money in the United States. *Journal of Political Economy* 54.4:436–50.

West, Robert C. 1977. *Banking Reform and the Federal Reserve, 1863–1923*. Ithaca, N.Y.: Cornell University Press.

Wheelock, David C. 1991. *The Strategy and Consistency of Federal Reserve Monetary Policy, 1924–1933*. Cambridge: Cambridge University Press.

―――. 1998. Monetary Policy in the Great Depression and Beyond: The Sources of the Fed's Inflation Bias. In *The Economics of the Great Depression*, edited by Mark Wheeler. Kalamazoo, Mich.: W. E. Upjohn Institute for Employment Research.

Wicker, Elmus. 1966. *Federal Reserve Monetary Policy, 1917–1933*. New York: Random House.

Working, Holbrook. 1923. Prices and the Quantity of the Circulating Medium, 1890–1921. *Quarterly Journal of Economics* 37.2:228–56.

―――. 1926. Bank Deposits as a Forecaster of the General Wholesale Price Level. *Review of Economics and Statistics* 8.3:120–33.

Yohe, William P. 1990. The Intellectual Milieu at the Federal Reserve Board in the 1920s. *HOPE* 22.3:465–88.

Leontief and the U.S. Bureau of Labor Statistics, 1941–54: Developing a Framework for Measurement

Martin C. Kohli

In 1953, twelve years after his collaboration with the U.S. Bureau of Labor Statistics began, Wassily Leontief (1953, vii) noted that "the continual cooperative relationship with [the Bureau of Labor Statistics] has benefited our work most decisively," but he did not elaborate. While Leontief cited the forecasts the Bureau had made during World War II of surprisingly robust postwar demand for steel ([1951] 1986, [1985] 1986), he never provided a comprehensive account of the Bureau's role in the development of input-output analysis.

This left the door open for a number of interpretations. Tjalling Koopmans (1951) described the early work on input-output economics as "initiated, developed, and stimulated largely by Leontief and given statistical expression by measurements and tabulations produced by the Bureau of Labor Statistics," thus distinguishing between the theoretical work accomplished by Leontief and the presumably atheoretical data gathering done by the Bureau. His account and that of Dorfman (1973) suggested

Correspondence may be addressed to Martin Kohli, U.S. Bureau of Labor Statistics, 201 Varick Street, Room 808, New York, NY 10014. I would like to thank several people who assisted with this essay. Solidelle Wasser initiated the project, researched much of it, and commented on numerous drafts. Marvin Hoffenberg provided insights from the invaluable perspective of a participant in some of the events described herein. Estelle Leontief graciously permitted access to the Leontief papers in the Pusey Library at Harvard. I owe an important reference to Karen Polenske. Comments from Mary Morgan prompted me to investigate Leontief's methodological convictions, while those of Judy Klein led me to clarify the different purposes of the early input-output tables. However, the author alone is responsible for the form and content.

that the Bureau's relationship with Leontief was significant largely because it supplied the muscle to flesh out his ideas.[1]

A closer examination will show that the Bureau did more than supply resources. To begin with, the Department of Labor's interest stimulated the development of a theoretical scheme, later known as the open input-output model, which proved to be more useful for policymakers than Leontief's first formulation. The Bureau also made several changes to the framework—the concepts and classifications—underlying the tables. Many economists have little interest in such issues, but Leontief insisted on their importance. He argued that in order to succeed in empirical work, the economist needed to develop "an intricate system of basic definitions, classifications, and rules of measurement" (1958, 105). This essay will show that the Bureau's conceptual changes made possible several significant measurements, thus buttressing Leontief's argument.

After discussing Leontief's pioneering work, conducted during the 1930s, this essay focuses on the period from 1941, when the Bureau began its collaboration with Leontief, until 1954, when the relationship temporarily ended. In the United States the early 1940s were years when the imperative of waging war led to a further expansion, building on the New Deal, of both federal intervention in the economy and of innovations in federal efforts to measure economic activities. Duncan and Shelton (1978) documented several wartime innovations, including the first official estimates of the product-side components of the gross national product. Flavio Comim (this volume) recounts how the need to finance World War II spurred innovations in national accounting in the United Kingdom. This should be no surprise, since, as Theodore Porter (this volume) reminds us, the relationship between state building and development of quantitative methods is centuries old. With the end of the Korean War and the advent of the Eisenhower Administration, Washington reverted to a less activist policy stance, leaving the issue of federal support for input-output tables unresolved, which is where the story told here properly ends.

When the Kennedy Administration took office, the federal government resumed constructing input-output tables on a regular basis. That development had its origins in the events that occurred between 1941 and 1954. The story of the early years of the Bureau-Leontief relationship

---

1. Carter and Petri (1989) recognized that the Bureau did more than gather numbers, but they focused on Leontief's contribution.

raised the issue that would later prove decisive—namely, the interest of the federal budget office in having accurate measurements of national income and product.

Leontief's *Tableau Économique* for 1919

In 1932, freshly arrived at Harvard after a brief stint with the National Bureau of Economic Research, Leontief began the unusual project of constructing a *tableau économique* for the United States. He had conceived of this project several years earlier while at the University of Kiel, where he developed a method for estimating supply and demand curves. Unable to resolve what later became known as the identification problem, Leontief became dissatisfied with the use of these curves to infer structural parameters (Rosier 1986; Leontief 1987). In an effort to provide reliable measures of the parameters of a twentieth-century economy, Leontief turned to an unlikely source—the eighteenth-century ideas of François Quesnay.

In 1936 Leontief published his first *tableau*. What he found in the physiocratic tradition was the idea of "general interdependence among the various parts of the economic system"—an idea that Leontief ([1936] 1951, 9) hailed as "the very foundation of economic analysis." After lamenting that contemporary economists relied, as had Quesnay, on "fictitious numerical examples," he declared that he would remedy this deficiency by taking advantage of "the remarkable increase in primary statistical data" (9).

The article's second section, with the grand sounding title of "Fundamental Concepts," discussed the mundane topic of accounting. Though it may not have been obvious to the casual reader, the accounting scheme offered the conceptual apparatus by which Leontief intended to use the now abundant primary data to quantify the interdependence of the economy's sectors. He proposed to consider the consequences of an accounting system that covered the economic activity of "every business enterprise as well as each individual household" (11). The key account was the expenditure and revenue account. The expenditure side showed the flows of commodities and services as they entered the enterprise or household during a particular period; the revenue side documented outflows of commodities and services. For the purpose of understanding the development of input-output analysis, the key feature of this conceptual schema was that the expenditure account explicitly included "capital outlays" (12). In other words Leontief's accounting scheme did not discriminate between current-account and capital-account purchases. He recognized that capital accounts existed, but they raised issues, such as depreciation, which he could not solve with his simple system of registering transactions between accounting units (19).

Because the accounting system covered all enterprises and households, every transaction would be recorded twice: once in the unit selling the product or service, and once in the purchasing unit. Double counting would also hold for exchanges between industries. Since one industry's sales to another would be recorded as the latter's purchases from the former, the industry accounts could be represented in what we now call a transactions table. Table 1 provides part of what Leontief titled "Quantitative Input and Output Relations in the Economic System of the United States, 1919." As his praise of Quesnay and the table's title suggest, one of Leontief's favorite ways of characterizing the economy was as a system—a set of interdependent sectors that formed a complex whole.

The systematic character of the economy had, I believe, an implication for what Leontief thought was a desirable attribute of economic measurements. When he praised a *tableau économique* as "an internally consistent, quantitative" representation of the economy (1953c, v), he demonstrated the value he attached to consistency. The double-entry character of the accounting system assured that the recorded transactions of each sector were consistent with those of every other sector and that the tabulated characteristics of the whole, such as total expenditures and total receipts, could be derived from measurements for the parts. Comim (this volume) stressed the importance of consistency for Richard Stone, who also used double-entry accounting to achieve consistent measurements.

The detailed transaction tables for 1919 contained forty-four sectors, forty-one of which were industrial sectors. The forty-second sector was international trade. Its row showed the distribution of its product, which was imports, while the column recorded its inputs, which were exports. Leontief recognized that to treat trade as a sector was to use geography, rather than product homogeneity, as a classifying principle. The inputs, or consumption, of households, the forty-third sector, produced services, which were measured in dollars, as table 1 illustrates. The only formal difference between households and other sectors was that the

Table 1 Selected Cells from "Quantitative Input and Output Relations in the Economic System of the United States, 1919" (Leontief [1936] 1951)

	14. Iron and steel (outlays)	15. Automobiles (outlays)	42. Exports (outlays)	43. Consumption (outlays)	Total output
14. Iron and steel (output)	503	381	896	634	11,610
15. Automobiles (output)	—	997	152	1,773	3,305
42. Imports (output)	36	—	—	572	4,205
43a. Wages and salaries (output)	4,096	677	—	3,464	33,356
43b. Capital and entrepreneurial services (output)	866	207	—	5,382	30,937
43c. Total services (output)	4,962	884	—	8,846	64,293
Total outlays	12,482	3,488	7,890	52,362	205,576

Note: In millions of dollars. Numbers before the names of industries correspond to the cell numbers assigned to those industries by Leontief. A note on reading the table is perhaps useful. Take, for instance, the $381 million figure in column 2, row 1. This means that $381 million of the iron and steel industry's total production (output) was used by the automobile industry; of all the costs (outlays) the automobile industry incurred in producing its products, $381 million went to purchase iron and steel products.

transactions table showed two types of income: wages and salaries under one subtotal, and capital and entrepreneurial services under another.

Lacking data on government expenses, Leontief could not include government as a distinct industry. Instead it was implicitly included in the last sector, called "Undistributed," which reflected a lack of income-expenditure accounts for wholesale and retail trade, banking and finance, and nonrail transportation, as well as federal, state, and local governments. This sector functioned as an accounting balance. Since, for example, the automobile industry produced $3,305 million worth of cars in 1919 and the other sectors absorbed $2,922 million, $383 million was charged to the undistributed sector. Undistributed charges accounted for

19.8 percent of total output in the 1919 table, reflecting large lacunae in our factual knowledge of the economy.

Leontief on the Relationship between Theorizing and Measuring

Not content merely to describe, Leontief also wanted to analyze. Relying on distinctive methodological convictions, he developed a theoretical scheme that would allow him to understand how the economy would react to changes in industrial productivity and savings ([1937] 1951).

The distinctive feature of Leontief's convictions concerned the relationship between theorizing and measuring. Here Koopmans, who was also interested in methodology, offered a sharp contrast. Koopmans considered theory building to be solely a matter of deriving interesting conclusions, using logic and mathematical techniques, from a small number of postulates (1957). With a formalist's pride, he regarded the body of neoclassical theory as "an impressive and highly valuable system of deductive thought, erected on a few premises that seem to be well-chosen approximations to a complicated reality" (142). For him empirical work was a separate activity, with which the theorist as theorist did not need to be concerned. For Leontief, by contrast, "the unparalleled ability to integrate theory and fact is his hallmark; it shines through all of his writings on economics, scientific methodology and even social policy" (Carter and Petri 1989, 8). Leontief ([1954] 1985, 40) explained later that, when specifying variables, the theorist should "take advantage of the strengths and reduce the weaknesses of the observational data." In other words, a good theory—one which would have "masses of seemingly amorphous facts do the bidding of the orderly and ordering mathematical thought" (43)—would focus attention on parameters and variables that could be measured with confidence. Leontief regarded the articulated chains of deductive reasoning, so prized by Koopmans, as necessary but not sufficient.

Such disagreements about the relationship between measuring and theorizing were not confined to the economics profession in the 1950s. Roy Weintraub (this volume) points out that circa 1900 Felix Klein and Vito Volterra believed that the successful application of mathematics in applied disciplines depended on accurate measurements and modeling strategies within those disciplines. Leontief would have assented, while

Koopmans would have had no reason to agree. Tobin (1987) and Marcel Boumans (this volume) remind us that Irving Fisher's development of the quantity theory of money was informed by his painstaking efforts to measure velocity and the general price level, and that in turn his measuring efforts were shaped by a theoretically relevant accounting identity. The empirical works of Fisher and Leontief were not, however, typical. As Porter (this volume) notes, throughout the twentieth century the connection between much economic measuring and theory remained tenuous.

In 1937, however, Leontief's beliefs about theorizing-measuring relationships were still developing. His first presentation of an input-output theoretical scheme began with a set of equations, one for each sector, describing "a hypothetical state of simple reproduction which knows neither savings nor investment" ([1937] 1951, 35). Each sector produced a good or service, X_i, which was consumed by the different sectors:

$$
\begin{aligned}
(1 - x_{11})X_1 - x_{12} \quad & - x_{13} - \cdots - x_{1n} & = 0 \\
- x_{21} \quad + (1 - x_{22})X_2 - x_{23} - \cdots - x_{2n} & = 0 \\
\cdots \qquad & = 0 \\
- x_{n1} \qquad - x_{n2} \qquad - x_{n3} - \cdots + (1 - x_{nn})X_n & = 0,
\end{aligned}
\tag{1}
$$

where x_{ij} is the amount of product i consumed by sector j. A second set of equations, not presented here, focused on prices and stipulated that the value of a sector's output equaled the value of the inputs. Both of these equation sets functioned as equilibrium conditions: they described an ideal state towards which the economy was assumed to tend.

The third set of equations concerned behavioral relationships—the technologies used in production and the pattern of household consumption. Leontief posited that the quantity of input i consumed by industry j depended on the industry's output and a technical or direct input coefficient, a_{ij}:

$$
x_{ij} = a_{ij} X_j.
\tag{2}
$$

This way of representing production raised the question of how to measure the parameters. Leontief recognized that most of his theory-oriented colleagues preferred more general functional forms, but these typically involved parameters that could be estimated only through what Leontief (1953b, 7) called the methods of "indirect statistical inference" rather than of "direct observation." By the latter term he meant facts "observed by someone else rather than the economist" and "usually described in ordinary, everyday language or in the technical language, not of economics, but of some other discipline" ([1954] 1985, 54).

The belief that reliable measurements are built not solely on sophisticated statistical technique but rather on systematic, direct observation as well is one of the recurring themes of Leontief's post-Kiel career. In 1941 he chose as the epigraph for his first book a quotation from Quesnay, which concluded: "Dans la recherche de la verité par le calcul, toute la certitude est dans l'évidence des données [in the search for truth by calculation, all certainty is in the clearness of the data]" ([1941] 1951, 2). In 1953 he noted that there were two alternative ways of obtaining the production function for a particular industry: "directly through the collection of the relevant technical, engineering information or . . . indirectly by way of a rather intricate interpretation of the supply-demand reactions of the industry" (1953b, 6). In his judgment, "there can be little doubt that direct observation offers the indisputable advantage of operational simplicity and, because of that, greater reliability" (6). Doubting that some of the parameters in regression equations of production functions corresponded to any characteristics of technology observable by an engineer, Leontief ([1982] 1985) criticized the position held by many economists (and described in Porter this volume) that assumes that with a regression equation one can measure anything.

To return to the treatment of production in the original scheme: Leontief ([1937] 1951, 37) justified the fixed-coefficient form of equation (2) on methodological grounds, declaring that "the numerical values of all the parameters must be ascertainable on the basis of available statistical information." He did not deny that as a matter of fact some production technologies allowed for substitution. Instead, lacking direct observations of alternative technologies, he shaped his theoretical scheme according to his judgment about the reliable measurement of the parameters.

Leontief ([1937] 1951) modified equation (2) in two directions, one of which was motivated by his theoretical interest while the other was conditioned by his accounting scheme. The theoretical concern involved being able to analyze a particular form of technical change, the proportional variation of all the coefficients in an industry. So he introduced a productivity coefficient for industry j, A_j, with an initial value equal to 1. The second change was to extend the model beyond the state of simple reproduction to incorporate the fact, embodied in his accounting data, of investment spending. If expenditures exceeded revenues, a sector was said to be investing, regardless of whether or not it increased its inventories or acquired fixed capital goods. To represent this phenomenon, he introduced a sectoral savings coefficient, B_j, whose initial value was the ratio sectoral receipts/sectoral expenditures. Because the level of sectoral investment would depend on macro variables such as the interest rate, he also introduced ß, an index for the overall level of investment in the economy, with an initial value of 1. Inserting these into the input equation (2) yielded:

$$x_{ij} = (a_{ij} X_j)/(A_j B_j ß). \tag{2'}$$

Substitution into the balance equations (1) produced a system of equations for the sectoral outputs:

$$
\begin{aligned}
X_1 &- (a_{11} X_1)/(A_1 B_1 ß) - (a_{12} X_2)/(A_2 B_2 ß) \\
&- (a_{13} X_3)/(A_3 B_3 ß) - \cdots - (a_{1n} X_n)/(A_n B_n ß) = 0 \\
- (a_{21} X_1)/(A_1 B_1 ß) &\quad + X_2 - (a_{22} X_2)/(A_2 B_2 ß) \\
&- (a_{23} X_3)/(A_3 B_3 ß) - \cdots - (a_{2n} X_n)/(A_n B_n ß) = 0 \qquad (3) \\
\cdots & \\
- (a_{n1} X_1)/(A_1 B_1 ß) &\quad - (a_{n2} X_2)/(A_2 B_2 ß) \\
&- (a_{n3} X_3)/(A_3 B_3 ß) - \cdots + X_n - (a_{nn} X_n)/(A_n B_n ß) = 0.
\end{aligned}
$$

A separate set of equations, not presented here, showed how relative prices were determined by the same direct input coefficients.

The question then arises of what one can do with this theoretical scheme. Leontief wanted to answer what-if questions: how would the systems of relative prices and quantities respond to different values for the industry productivity and savings parameters? Deploying his formidable powers of analysis, Leontief was able to derive formulae and to calculate how the price and quantity systems would, in theory, respond, using the parameters from the 1919 table.

By 1939 Leontief had completed the table for 1929. The Industrial Committee of the National Resources Committee, a New Deal agency, later known as the National Resources Planning Board, published this table in an appendix to National Resources Committee 1939, although the text offered no discussion of the table. Isador Lubin, the commissioner of Labor Statistics, served on the Industrial Committee, and this experience could have been his first exposure to Leontief's ideas.

In 1941 Harvard University Press published Leontief's first input-output articles, supplemented with additional material, and the tables for both 1919 and 1929. Academic economists provided a tepid reception. Neisser (1941) and Rothbarth (1943) criticized the assumption of fixed coefficients. Unlike Neisser, Rothbarth acknowledged Leontief's measurement-based reasons for choosing the fixed-coefficient functional form, but he thought that the theoretical disadvantages outweighed any possible advantages. Sales of *The Structure of American Economy, 1919–1929* were so slight that Harvard University Press wrote to Leontief to discourage any hopes for a second edition (Malone 1942).

Overcoming the Limitations of Leontief's Original Concepts and Theory

Leontief attributed the impetus for his relationship with the Bureau to the White House ([1985] 1986). According to him, President Roosevelt asked Secretary of Labor Frances Perkins, what would happen to the economy after the war.[2] In April 1941, before the United States officially entered the war, Commissioner Lubin requested $96,500 from Congress to fund a study of the economic effects of demobilization. The assignment was given to Donald Davenport. Davenport had recently left Harvard, where he had known Leontief, and had joined the Bureau's Postwar Division. Davenport suggested to Dal Hitchcock, another member of the Division, that an approach to the problem could be found in Leontief's recently published book (Battelle Memorial Institute 1973).

Leontief's theoretical scheme had not included government, let alone any policy levers, and this could have been seen as a liability in a tool for analyzing policy. Moreover, even if the scheme had included taxing and spending policies, these would have determined only relative prices and quantities. Thus Davenport's suggestion could have appeared unpromising. As it turned out, however, the limitations for policy analysis of Leontief's original framework did not prove to be permanent.

The Bureau's positive reaction to Leontief's early work illustrates how government and leading academic economists occasionally have

2. In an interview with Duncan Foley (1998), Leontief referred to a letter that Secretary Perkins had written to him. Taking a different point of view from Leontief, Battelle (1973) traced the relationship back to the Congress. Duncan and Shelton (1978) and Goldberg and Moye (1985) follow the Battelle account. This account is not inconsistent with Leontief's, since the appropriation could have resulted from a request from the executive branch.

different priorities. Untroubled by the absence of substitution in Leontief's scheme, the Bureau quickly hired him, opened an office of its Postwar Division in Cambridge, Massachusetts, and began work on a ninety-five-sector table for 1939. By 1943 the Bureau's staff had completed one version of the table, and the work was winding down. Senior managers had to decide whether they wanted to continue to support the project. Jerome Cornfield, an economist then working in the wholesale price division, reviewed the work accomplished thus far and concluded that Leontief's technique was "a useful tool" ([1964] 1981), reflecting a bureaucratic pragmatism. Around this same period, some academic economists wanted the Bureau to redefine its measure of consumer prices as a ratio of expenditures needed to hold utility constant. As Spencer Banzhaf (this volume) notes, the Bureau and other academics were more concerned with the observable characteristics of goods—a stance that reflected a belief, held by Leontief and discussed above, that direct observation was the foundation of reliable measurement.

Leontief ([1944] 1951) published a transactions table for 1939, which differed in several ways from its predecessors. The article presenting the table began with a question: "How will the cessation of war purchases of planes, guns, tanks, and ships—if not compensated by increased demand for other types of commodities—affect the national level of employment?" (139). This was a what-if question of the general type that Leontief's theoretical scheme was intended to answer. However, because of data and conceptual limitations, Leontief could not have used the first tables and the original scheme to answer this particular question.

This question concerned the effects of government spending. In the 1919 and 1929 tables, government had been consigned, because of a lack of data, to the undistributed sector. As an analytical category, government did not exist. In the 1939 table government stood alone in the eleven-sector version that Leontief published and in the forty-three-sector version included in the Bureau's unpublished study (n.d.), which was apparently completed in 1946. Even with the inclusion of government and trade, 15 percent of gross output was still charged to the undistributed account.

A second difference concerned the units of measurement. The question assumed that labor was measured not in dollars, as it had been in the first tables, but in employee years. This change, which was necessary if the table was to be used to analyze employment, marked a significant departure from the monetary measures Leontief had used in his first *tableaux*. As part of its work on the 1939 table, the Bureau also obtained data on output in physical units for at least fourteen other sectors. The use of these measures is discussed below.

A third change concerned the underlying conceptual scheme. Leontief ([1936] 1951) had pointed out the theoretical relationship between the transactions table and the national income. Under what he called "static conditions," meaning no savings and no investment, the national income, which was the sum of the entries in the household sector's row, equaled the national product, which was the sum of the sector's column entries. Following up on this idea, the Bureau sought to reconcile its 1939 transactions table with the national income accounts, which now included investment in the national product. Marvin Hoffenberg, the Bureau's expert on national accounts, had the responsibility for this work, and he realized the desirability of modifying Leontief's original accounting scheme. This scheme had been built on expenditure and receipt accounts that contained *all transactions* between accounting units. Hoffenberg assumed that firms kept separate accounts for current and capital spending and income. Purchases of capital goods were registered as expenses on the capital account, while depreciation charges counted as capital account revenue. Thus the 1939 table had an investment column, which showed how much of an industry's output was purchased for domestic private investment, and a row, which showed depreciation charges. The column sum was gross private investment, which Hoffenberg needed for his reconciliation, while the row sum was total private sector depreciation. After removing investment spending from the interindustry transactions and taking into account changes in inventories, the Bureau sought to impose the constraint on the industrial sectors that the value of output (the row sum) equaled the value of inputs (the column sum), although data limitations prevented the achievement of this goal in all industries.

Hoffenberg's reconciliation (in Bureau of Labor Statistics [1946?]) concerned only the income side, perhaps because the Commerce Department's product-side estimates were new and not well documented. The Bureau's estimates indicated that households received $61.2 billion in income from businesses and $10 billion from government for a total of $71.2 billion. The Bureau noted that the Department of Commerce estimate was $400 million, or 0.6 percent, less because of different treatments of contingency reserves, bad debt allowances, and inventory revaluations.

The motivating question for the 1939 table, regarding the effects of a decline in military spending, required a different theoretical scheme. In the original scheme all expenditures were determined endogenously, as table 2 shows. To answer a question about a change in spending, Leontief had to allow for a set of final demands determined outside the system of interindustry relationships. He began the revised theoretical scheme with balance equations that showed, for each industry, the distribution of output among the endogenous sectors, plus an amount available for final demand, Y_i. The flow of output can be represented as:

$$
\begin{aligned}
(1 - a_{11})X_1 - a_{12}X_2 \quad &- a_{13}X_3 - \cdots - a_{1n}X_n \quad = Y_1 \\
- a_{21}X_1 \quad + (1 - a_{22})X_2 - a_{23}X_3 - \cdots - a_{2n}X_n \quad &= Y_2 \\
&\cdots \\
- a_{n1}X_1 \quad - a_{n2}X_2 \quad &- a_{n3}X_3 - \cdots + (1 - a_{nn})X_n = Y_n.
\end{aligned}
\tag{4}
$$

In the input-output literature, this scheme is known as the open model (in the sense that it is open to sources of exogenous spending) of quantities, in contrast with the closed model in equation set (3). Both are systems of n equations in the n levels of output.

Leontief's revised theoretical scheme differs from the original one in several significant ways, however. First, it does not include the clutter of industry productivity and savings coefficients, which Leontief had used to accommodate the fact of investment spending into the Procrustean bed of static balance conditions. In addition, the open model includes the exogenous final demands where the closed model had zeroes. As table 2 shows, this changes the nature of the solution: where the closed model could be solved only for relative quantities, the solutions to the open scheme are absolute levels.

As Leontief noted, the open system was conceptually similar to the Keynesian theory of income determination ([1949] 1951). Both analytic tools relied on exogenous spending, combined with one or more equations that defined equilibrium or balance. The types of exogenous spending (typically, investment, government, and exports) and the resulting levels of output and income corresponded to magnitudes in the national income accounts. These features made both of them useful for policy analysis. The major difference, of course, was that the Keynesian theory, unlike Leontief's, was highly aggregated.

Table 2   Features of the Early Input-Output Theoretical Schemes

	Original (or Closed) Theoretical Scheme	Modified (or Open) Theoretical Scheme
Purpose	Illustrate hypothetical effects of changes in industrial savings and productivity	Illustrate effects of changes in exogenous spending
All spending endogenous?	Yes	No
Nature of solution	Relative prices and quantities	Absolute prices and quantities
Policy levers?	No	Yes

Note: "Original" refers to the scheme published in Leontief [1937] 1951; "Modified," to the scheme in Leontief [1944] 1951.

Forecasting the Effects of Peace and Other Early Applications

When the Bureau began constructing the 1939 table, it had intended to use the table to forecast postwar employment. In 1944, using assumptions about decreases in war spending and increases in personal consumption, it calculated its first comprehensive, albeit unpublished, forecasts of employment for the War Production Board. While this work was underway, the Bureau and other government agencies thought of a number of other uses for the table. These initial applications raised three measurement-related issues.

In 1944 the Office of Strategic Services (OSS) asked Leontief and the Bureau to create a table for Germany, using the U.S. table and a highly confidential German census of production. This project raised the issue of the extent to which parameters derived from accounting data, which would vary across nations with their systems of prices, would diverge from those representing technological relationships, which should be similar in countries at high levels of technological development. According to Jerome Cornfield ([1964] 1981), the German levels of output were consistent with coefficients from the U.S. table, except for the lumber and masonry products industries. The evidence of similar coefficients gave the Bureau's economists confidence in the parameters derived from the transaction table. If they were not the true structural parameters, they appeared to be at least good approximations. The OSS use of the table to guide its efforts to cripple the German economy and the Bureau's forecasts for the War Production Board were the first occasions on which government agencies applied Leontief's framework to specific problems.

In 1945 the Office of War Mobilization and Reconversion asked the Bureau to examine the postwar demand for capital goods. Since tanks, battle ships, and other military goods were steel intensive, it seemed likely that the steel industry would experience significant unused capacity. The concept of excess capacity involved two variables—a level of output measured in physical units and a maximum possible level of output, again measured in physical units, of the existing stock of fixed capital. Fixed capital had not appeared in Leontief's original static theoretical scheme. Nonetheless, as the employment forecasts had demonstrated, if one had input coefficients measured in physical units, the theoretical scheme could be used to predict the total quantities measured in physical units. For the 1939 table, the Bureau had measures of steel ingots in short tons. It was not feasible to measure capacity directly, so the Bureau examined levels of output over the 1919–44 period and treated the maximum level as full capacity. Assuming the existence of pent-up demand for construction, the Bureau concluded that the wartime increase in steel capacity might not prove adequate in the postwar years. Leontief ([1985] 1986, 35) commented that this was "a great surprise to experts who predicted a slump in steel—conventionally considered to be a 'war industry.'" This study, however, was not intended for public use.

An article in the *Monthly Labor Review* by Cornfield (1945) examined employment attributable, industry by industry, to U.S. exports in 1939 and was the Bureau's first published application of input-output analysis. This was also the first article by a government agency that examined the amounts of labor embodied directly and indirectly (in other words, in the intermediate inputs) in internationally traded goods. Leontief revisited the issue of trade and employment in considerably more detail ([1946] 1951). He introduced a conceptual distinction between competitive imports (which had domestically produced counterparts) and noncompetitive imports (which did not). This distinction had not been made in the 1939 table, and it played no role in the factual analysis.

The Bureau's first projections for the public examined whether, under plausible assumptions, the economy would achieve full employment in 1950 (Cornfield, Evans, and Hoffenberg 1947a and 1947b, which summarize the extensive treatment in Bureau of Labor Statistics [1946?]).

The input coefficients from the 1939 table, modified to incorporate expected changes in technology along with the assumed final demands, predicted 34.4 million private nonagricultural jobs, somewhat less than the 39.0 million that would have assured full employment. On the other hand, this level of employment was greater than many people had feared it would be. The Bureau economists then considered output levels for several products measured in physical units—tons of steel ingots, thousands of tractors, kilowatt hours of electricity—at full employment and found that in most cases the required level exceeded previous peaks.

According to Battelle (1973), the Bureau's projections, "alone among postwar predictions," did not foresee a depression. Moreover, by 1950 a number of industries had reached their capacity constraints.

Checking the National Income Accounts
with the 1947 Table

In 1947 W. Duane Evans, who had taken on the responsibility for the Bureau's input-output work, confronted two problems. First, he had decided that the 1939 table needed to be updated, a process that would require more resources. Second, the Truman Administration had decided to trim the Bureau's budget by 20 percent. The shortage of funds prompted him to search for money at better-funded agencies. In the same year Marshall Wood, who had an interest in techniques for coordinating training and materials procurement activities, became chief of the Planning Research Division of the Air Force. In 1948, with the Cold War growing chillier, Wood had the Bureau's input-output work included in an interagency project, funded by the Air Force, known as Project SCOOP (Scientific Computation of Optimum Programs). After the Korean War erupted in 1950, funding for Project SCOOP soared (see Judy Klein's essay in this volume). While the 1939 table was motivated by Roosevelt's concern with the economic effects of peacetime demobilization, the 1947 table was in large part motivated by Evans's desire to refresh his aging data and Wood's concern with possible obstructions to a wartime mobilization.

Wood was not the only upper-level government official who saw the value in input-output analysis. Ezra Glaser (1958), who represented the Budget Bureau (now known as the Office of Management and Budget) in Project SCOOP, believed that the government had an interest in understanding the potential consequences, such as capacity constraints or shortages of specialized labor, of possible changes in final demand. The

Table 3   Features of the Early Input-Output Tables

Feature	Table Year 1919 and 1929	1939	1947
Fundamental accounting concept	Revenue and expenditure accounts for establishments	Separate current and capital accounts for establishments	Separate current and capital accounts for establishments
Government sector	In undistributed sector	Separate sector	Separate sector
Unit of measurement for labor	Current dollars	Employee years	Employee years
Number of sectors	44	95	500
Imports	Classified by using sector	Classified by using sector	Classified by industry producing rival products

Budget Bureau regulated and coordinated the federal government's various statistical enterprises, so its support was not insignificant.

The result of the Pentagon's largesse was an unprecedented level of detailed information—450 industrial and 50 autonomous sectors (thus, 500 in all), as table 3 shows. In Leontief [1951] 1986, the first published version of the 1947 table, these were aggregated to 37 and 5 sectors respectively. The undistributed account declined to a mere 3 percent of gross output, a significant improvement over the 1939 table.

The Bureau also made an important change in how international trade was represented. As national income accountants recognized net exports as a component of the gross national product, it was natural to add to the final demand quadrant columns for exports and imports of goods and services that had domestic counterparts. Imports that had no domestically produced rivals had a separate row.[3] The classification of the competitive imports by industry allowed Leontief to compute how much labor and

3. This was how international trade was treated in the detailed tables. In the table published in Evans and Hoffenberg 1952, international trade was still represented by one row for imports and one column for exports.

capital would have been absorbed if the demand for those imports had been met by domestically produced goods (1953a). His principal finding, that U.S. exports were labor intensive compared with the import-competing goods, raised theoretical issues that lie beyond the scope of this essay. Since the focus of this study is the conceptual development of a framework for measurement, the important point is that, until imports were classified in this manner, it was not possible to measure how trade influenced the employment of factors.

During the development of data for construction, the Bureau became aware of a conflict between its estimates of the quantities of materials consumed by construction activities and the Commerce Department data on construction output, which were also used to measure investment in the national income accounts. The Bureau raised its estimate of construction output from $24.8 billion to $28.7 billion, thus making a judgment that the figures based on a consistent set of accounts were more likely to be correct (Evans and Hoffenberg 1952). Others who examined the issue came to the same conclusion. Participants at a 1952 conference on input-output analysis, organized by the National Bureau of Economic Research, discussed the issue. One of the organizers, Raymond Goldsmith (1958, 4), noted that "the need to fit data into a strict accounting mold . . . has led to the discovery of some gaps and deficiencies in our statistics," and he then cited "the major shortcomings" of the construction figures. According to Glaser, the reconciliation of the input-output table with the national income accounts revealed serious gaps and omissions in ocean transportation and services as well as construction (Battelle Memorial Institute 1973).

As Comim (this volume) reminds us, the use of detailed accounts to achieve consistent measurements of national income aggregates was one of Richard Stone's concerns. The U.S. experience with the 1947 estimates demonstrated that this was not just an academic issue.

In 1953 President Eisenhower took office. The following year, Secretary of Defense Charles Wilson, motivated in part by a concern that input-output tables could be used for central planning (he considered planning to be, as Carter and Petri [1989] put it, "even more frightening than the Russian menace"), eliminated all Department of Defense funding for input-output work.

While the work of constructing the tables halted, the issue of reconciling them with the national income and product accounts did not disappear. In 1955 Raymond Bowman became the Budget Bureau's assistant director for Statistical Standards. Determined to make the national income and product accounts the basic framework for federal economic statistics, he asked the National Bureau of Economic Research (NBER) to review these accounts (Duncan and Shelton 1978).[4] Goldsmith, who had been at the War Production Board when the Bureau produced its first forecasts of postwar employment and who had organized the 1952 NBER conference, chaired the review committee. In its report the committee examined ways of improving the accounts. Taking virtually the same position that Goldsmith had maintained earlier, the review committee declared, "it was work on the 1947 input-output table which pointed more conclusively than anything else to the shortcomings of the current construction statistics and gave impetus to the drive for improving these statistics" (1958, 146). This was one of the reasons the committee gave for recommending that the federal government resume producing the tables. Accepting this recommendation, the Budget Bureau decided to fund a 1958 table. In part because it wanted this table integrated with the national accounts, the Budget Bureau selected the Commerce Department to perform the work. After President Kennedy took office, the federal government resumed compiling Leontief's *tableaux* on a regular basis, and, using them, the Bureau of Labor Statistics resumed making detailed forecasts of employment by industry.

Developing a Framework for Measurement

According to several accounts, the Bureau of Labor Statistics was important in the development of input-output analysis because it secured the resources for the detailed 1947 table and its documentation. The Bureau did play that role. However, the initial passage quoted from Leontief referred to the "*continual* cooperative relationship" (emphasis added) as providing decisive benefits, suggesting that, as of 1953, the Bureau had played an ongoing role. This essay has attempted to buttress Leontief's contention by documenting three additional contributions made between 1941 and 1954.

---

4. Bowman's decision to make the national income and product accounts the central framework of the government's data-gathering activities meant that an increasing number of statistical series were integrated into the accounts and that the needs of the accounts increasingly determined which statistical series the federal government collected (Duncan and Shelton 1978, 100).

First, as Leontief recognized, the Bureau's wartime projections demonstrated that input-output analysis was a useful tool for government policymakers. Using Leontief's original theoretical scheme, such forecasts were impossible. This raises the issue of the Bureau's second contribution: prompting Leontief to develop what has become known as the open model. While Dorfman downplayed the differences between the 1936 and the 1944 theoretical schemes (1973), it is also possible to contend that these differences were significant. The latter model allowed government spending to be exogenous—a nontrivial feature during years in which Washington recognized the need for stimulative fiscal policies.

The Bureau's third contribution consisted of a series of conceptual developments of Leontief's framework. The most important of these was Marvin Hoffenberg's decision to take capital-account transactions out of the interindustry portion of the table. This made it possible to compile figures on the composition by industry of investment spending, figures which were necessary to reconcile the input-output table with the national income accounts. The second major conceptual refinement was treating competitive imports as subtractions from final demand, classified according to industries that produced rival products. This way of classifying imports made possible Leontief's path-breaking studies of the factor content of U.S. trade.

The importance of these findings brings us back to the methodological debate between Leontief and Koopmans. Earlier we saw that Koopmans regarded economic theory as a deductive system, the premises of which were "well-chosen approximations to a complicated reality" (1957, 142). Objecting to the frequent references to the degrees of the "realism" of premises, which assumed a uniquely describable reality, Leontief (1958, 105) contended that economic variables can only be measured "through an intricate system of basic definitions, classifications, and rules of measurement . . . without which a most rigorously constructed model can have no empirical significance of any kind." He held out a rosy scenario in which "an apt set of basic definitions" leads to an "effective theoretical formulation," which in turn permitted "sharper observations" (105). One can argue that the development of input-output analysis illustrates this dynamic: the progressive refinement of definitions and classifications by Leontief and his collaborators, including Cornfield, Evans, and Hoffenberg, along with the work of others, made possible more detailed models that motivated the development of new measurements.[5]

The development of Leontief's framework also exemplified the larger forces shaping the federal government's role in measuring the U.S. economy. As Duncan and Shelton (1978) documented, the need to plan and finance World War II created an urgent demand for accurate estimates of the national income and product and of their components. After the war ended, the interests of policymakers, government agencies, and professional economists in these measures did not disappear. What was once a wartime imperative became a peacetime routine, as the Budget Bureau recognized in 1955 when it made the national income and product accounts the central framework for federal statistics. Because the Bureau of Labor Statistics had demonstrated the value of Leontief's *tableaux* in measuring these aggregates accurately, the Budget Bureau was able, once the Kennedy Administration took office, to establish the making of input-output tables as an integral part of the government's measuring activities.

References

Battelle Memorial Institute. 1973. *Interactions of Science and Technology in the Innovative Process: Some Case Studies*. Columbus, Ohio: Columbus Laboratories.

Bureau of Labor Statistics. [1946?]. *Full Employment Patterns, 1950: The Structure of the American Economy under Full Employment Conditions*. Washington, D.C. Duplicated.

Carter, Anne P., and Peter A. Petri. 1989. Leontief's Contribution to Economics. *Journal of Policy Modeling* 11.1:7–30.

Cornfield, Jerome. 1945. Employment Resulting From United States Exports, 1939. *Monthly Labor Review* July: 37–38.

―――. [1964] 1981. Interview by Jonathan Grossman. Edited by Marvin Hoffenberg. Duplicated.

Cornfield, Jerome, W. Duane Evans, and Marvin Hoffenberg. 1947a. Full Employment Patterns, 1950: Part 1. *Monthly Labor Review* February: 63–190.

―――. 1947b. Full Employment Patterns, 1950: Part 2. *Monthly Labor Review* March: 420–32.

Dorfman, Robert. 1973. Wassily Leontief's Contribution to Economics. *Swedish Journal of Economics* 75.4:430–49.

5. Polenske (2000) offers a more detailed discussion of Leontief's critique of Koopmans. She also makes an argument, similar to the one in this conclusion, that Leontief's development of a theoretical model of interregional trade spurred important measurements of differences between regional economies.

Duncan, Joseph W., and William C. Shelton. 1978. *Revolution in United States Government Statistics, 1926–1976.* Washington, D.C.: U.S. Department of Commerce.

Evans, W. Duane, and Marvin Hoffenberg. 1952. The Interindustry Relations Study for 1947. *Review of Economics and Statistics* 34.2:97–148.

Foley, Duncan K. 1998. An Interview with Wassily Leontief. *Macroeconomic Dynamics* 2:116–40.

Glaser, Ezra. 1958. Comment. In *Input-Output Analysis: An Appraisal*, edited by Raymond Goldsmith. Studies in Income and Wealth, vol. 18. Princeton, N.J.: Princeton University Press.

Goldberg, Joseph P., and William T. Moye. 1985. *The First Hundred Years of the Bureau of Labor Statistics.* Washington, D.C.: U.S. Department of Labor.

Goldsmith, Raymond. 1958. Introduction to *Input-Output Analysis: An Appraisal.* Studies in Income and Wealth, vol. 18. Princeton, N.J.: Princeton University Press.

Koopmans, Tjalling C. 1951. Introduction. In *Activity Analysis of Production and Allocation: Proceedings of a Conference*, edited by Tjalling Koopmans. New York: John Wiley and Sons.

———. 1957. *Three Essays on the State of Economic Science.* New York: McGraw-Hill.

Leontief, Wassily W. [1936] 1951. Quantitative Input and Output Relations in the Economic System of the United States. *Review of Economics and Statistics* 18.3:105–125. In *The Structure of American Economy, 1919–1939.* 2d ed. Reprint, White Plains, N.Y.: International Arts and Sciences Press.

———. [1937] 1951. Interrelation of Prices, Output, Savings, and Investment. *Review of Economics and Statistics* 19.3:109–32. In *The Structure of American Economy, 1919–1939.* 2d ed. Reprint, White Plains, N.Y.: International Arts and Sciences Press.

———. [1941] 1951. *The Structure of American Economy, 1919–1939.* 2d ed. Reprint, White Plains, N.Y.: International Arts and Sciences Press.

———. [1944] 1951. Output, Employment, Consumption, and Investment. *Quarterly Journal of Economics* 58.2:290–313. In *The Structure of American Economy, 1919–1939.* 2d ed. Reprint, White Plains, N.Y.: International Arts and Sciences Press.

———. [1946] 1951. Export, Imports, Domestic Output, and Employment. *Quarterly Journal of Economics* 60.1:171–93. In *The Structure of American Economy, 1919–1939.* 2d ed. Reprint, White Plains, N.Y.: International Arts and Sciences Press.

———. [1949] 1951. Recent Developments in the Study of Interindustrial Relations. *American Economic Review* 39.3:211–25. In *The Structure of American Economy, 1919–1939.* 2d ed. Reprint, White Plains, N.Y.: International Arts and Sciences Press.

―――. [1951] 1986. Input-Output Economics. *Scientific American* 185.4:15–21. In *Input-Output Economics*. 2d ed. New York: Oxford University Press.

―――. 1953a. Domestic Production and Foreign Trade: The American Capital Position Reconsidered. *Proceedings of the American Philosophical Society* 97.4:332–49.

―――. 1953b. Introduction. In *Studies in the Structure of the American Economy*. Reprint, White Plains, N.Y.: International Arts and Sciences Press.

―――. 1953c. Preface. In *Studies in the Structure of the American Economy*. Reprint, White Plains, N.Y.: International Arts and Sciences Press.

―――. [1954] 1985. Mathematics in Economics. *Bulletin of the American Mathematical Society* 60.3:215–33. In *Essays in Economics: Theories, Theorizing, Facts, and Policies*. New Brunswick, N.J.: Transaction Books.

―――. 1958. The State of Economic Science. Review of *Three Essays on the State of Economic Science*, by T. C. Koopmans. *Review of Economics and Statistics* 40.2:103–6.

―――. [1982] 1985. Academic Economics. *Science* 217.4555:104, 107. In *Essays in Economics: Theories, Theorizing, Facts, and Policies*. New Brunswick; N.J.: Transaction Books.

―――. [1985] 1986. Input-Output Analysis. In *Input-Output Economics*. 2d ed. New York: Oxford University Press.

―――. 1987. Input-Output Analysis. In *The New Palgrave: A Dictionary of Economics*, edited by John Eatwell, Murray Milgate, and Peter Newman. New York: The Stockton Press.

Malone, Dumas. 1942. Letter to Wassily Leontief, 29 July.

National Bureau of Economic Research. 1958. *The National Economic Accounts of the United States: Review, Appraisal, and Recommendations*. Washington, D.C.: U.S. Government Printing Office.

National Resources Committee. 1939. *The Structure of the American Economy: Part I. Basic Characteristics*. Washington, D.C.: National Resources Committee.

Neisser, Hans P. 1941. Review of *The Structure of American Economy, 1919–1929*, by Wassily Leontief. *American Economic Review* 31.4:608–10.

Polenske, Karen R. 2000. Leontief's Magnificent Machine and Other Contributions to Applied Economics. Paper presented at the Thirteenth Annual International Input-Output Association Conference, 21–25 August, Macerata, Italy.

Rothbarth, E. 1943. Review of *The Structure of American Economy, 1919–1929*, by Wassily Leontief. *Economic Journal* 53:213–16.

Rosier, Bernard, ed. 1986. *Wassily Leontief: Textes et itinéraire*. Paris: Editions La Découverte.

Tobin, James. 1987. Irving Fisher. In *The New Palgrave: A Dictionary of Economics*, edited by John Eatwell, Murray Milgate, and Peter Newman. New York: The Stockton Press.

Richard Stone and Measurement Criteria for National Accounts

Flavio Comim

John Richard Nicholas Stone was a prolific and innovative writer. His contribution to economics covered a wide range of areas including empirical analysis of consumer behavior, economic growth, economic demography, and education. His work also covered topics such as index numbers, time series and cross-section surveys, environmental and sociostatistics, models of financial markets, and optimization problems related to economic growth. Stone's contribution to these topics was shaped by his concern with measurement, with integrating theory and facts, and abstract and practical reasoning and expressing results in a measurable form so that they could be used to solve concrete problems. In no other area did Stone's work achieve more recognition than in the field of national accounts (see Meade [1944–46] 1990, 62; Deane 1997, 389; Harcourt 1995, 153).

The origins of national accounting can be traced back to William Petty's early estimates of capital, income, and expenditure for seventeenth-century England and those of Pierre de Boisguillebert in France. Studenski (1958) provides a comprehensive discussion of the evolution of the national accounts that shows how the history of national accounts

Correspondence may be addressed to Flavio Comim, St. Edmund's College, Cambridge CB3 0BN, United Kingdom. I am especially grateful to Mary Morgan for her useful comments and kind assistance in the preparation of a final version of this essay. I am also grateful to Judy Klein, Geoff Harcourt, and the participants of the Age of Measurement conference for their comments and suggestions. I would like to express my gratitude to King's College Library, Cambridge, for permission to consult the manuscripts of Richard Stone.

could be classified into different periods: (1) early estimates (1571–1888); (2) the period 1900–1917; and (3) the period 1918–39, which Studenski calls the period of "the extraordinary flourishing of estimates" (1958, 149). It is within this last period that we can find the origins of the modern national accounting and of Stone's work.

The history of modern national accounting started with A. L. Bowley's, Colin Clark's, and Simon Kuznets's estimations of the principal macroeconomic accounting values for the United Kingdom and the United States, respectively, for some years in the 1920s and 1930s. Clark and Kuznets have been described as coauthors of 'the statistical revolution' that followed the revolution in macroeconomic theory of the 1930s (see Patinkin 1976, 1104; Arndt 1988, 2). Production of national statistics boomed during the 1930s in countries such as Hungary, Germany, Sweden, Canada, the Netherlands, the United States, and the United Kingdom (see Carson 1975 and Kendrick 1970). During the 1940s, when new institutions were created with the aim of calculating national statistics, many contributors, such as Milton Gilbert, Morris Copeland, George Luxton, E. F. Denison, O. Aukrust, and J. Tinbergen, to name just a few, helped the development of national accounting. Some of this work was aimed at the collection of national level data rather than national income data. Thus it was not uncommon to find a variety of diverse isolated statistics—such as those relating to production levels of food or minerals—being used to characterize the evolution of national income. Indeed, the beginnings of this 'statistical revolution' seem to be characterized by statistics being produced without much consistency.

In the history of the development of the national accounts, relatively little attention has been paid to the issue of what criteria should be used to assess the quality of measurement. Stone's contribution to the measurement of national accounts is particularly important in this respect and can be examined by looking at the different criteria to assess the measurement of these accounts that he developed in his work. The criteria suggested by Stone were influenced by a set of practical considerations, and this essay is about Stone's attempts to develop these practical criteria for national income accounts.

It seems that most of the criteria Stone developed over a period of about forty years were all originally conceived in his early work. In fact, the main criteria of logical consistency, flexibility, invariance, and standardized forms (as well as his error adjustment methods) were enumerated by Stone as early as in the beginning of the 1940s. Stone appeared to have thought of these criteria within a dynamic perspective according to which some criteria would have to be achieved first in order to provide a basis for subsequent extension of the accounts; in the new context, he expected other criteria to become more important.

This essay is organized into five parts. The first part examines Stone's contribution to the conceptualization and elaboration of a general structure of national accounts and his early views on measurement. The second part investigates the development of the criteria of flexibility and invariance. The third examines his work on standardization and the possibility of extensions such as regional accounts and demography. It argues that there was a tension in Stone's work between these different criteria to judge the effectiveness of the measurement of national accounts. The fourth part outlines Stone's work on errors in the measurement of national accounts, focusing on his answers to criticisms and development of adjustment techniques. The last part concludes.

From National Income to National Accounts:
The "Logical Consistency" of the Accounting Framework

Clark (1937) was the first to use the concept of "gross national product" and to elaborate all the "building blocks" to be used subsequently in national accounts. These included the estimates of income, output, consumers' expenditure, capital formation, saving, balance of payments and of government revenues and expenditures. He also discussed the importance of having comparable price indices for goods and services in different countries, the need to attempt qualitative estimates of the statistical accuracy of the national income figures for different countries, and the precise meaning of assembling figures with varying degrees of accuracy (1940).

Richard Stone began, like everyone else who worked with or on national accounts in the 1930s, by measuring different indices of industrial product and comparing them to other aggregate measures. When Colin Clark left for Australia in 1937, he bequeathed to Stone and Stone's first wife the editorial of a statistical supplement called *Trends* that appeared in the monthly *Industry Illustrated*. In *Trends*, Stone published statistics and graphs of British economic time series with occasional articles on a topical subject. The two Stones assembled information on movements in production from different sources and discussed the measurement problems involved in putting together statistics with different degrees of reliability. Their solution to these problems consisted in defining as a standard the material considered most accurate (for instance, the census and import duty inquiry data) and dismissing those that were extremely difficult to measure (e.g., the engineering group indices). Assessment of reliability of individual items was an intrinsic part of measurement. It was pursued directly, by confronting different indices that purported to represent the same things, and indirectly, by analyzing their logical significance. In the latter case, the accuracy of adjustments was of crucial importance. As they wrote when analyzing the adjustment of employment statistics, "It is often said that where approximate data are under consideration it is unsound to apply elaborate methods which are thought to be unduly refined, but it would seem incontestable that within broad limits it is better to estimate even roughly what we want to know, rather than to determine with comparative precision something which is seriously misleading" (Stone and Stone 1939, 481). Although adjustments are an intrinsic part of measurement, the Stones argued that they should be pursued within broad limits, and rough estimates should be used even when they were not very (relatively) precise—as long as they were accurate. In this work Richard Stone's concern was with the quality of individual series. "Confidence" and "creditability" were used as criteria of assessment of these individual and isolated series.

Partly as a result of Stone's work on *Trends*, he was invited to join the Ministry of Economic Warfare when world war became imminent in early 1939. In August 1940, by suggestion of Austin Robinson, he left the Ministry to join James Meade at the Central Economic Information Service of the Offices of the War Cabinet to work on national income accounts (see Pesaran and Harcourt 2000, F148). At that stage Meade had sets of categories but few numbers in them: Meade's system, as Deaton (1993, 477) puts it, "was a system of empty boxes."

Clark's assembly of the data was as comprehensive as possible but had been made without the help of a unified framework of analysis. Stone (1986a, 11) recognized this, commenting much later, "Although [Clark] did not set his figures in an accounting framework it is clear that they came fairly close to consistency." It is difficult to say to what extent the accounting framework was a creation of the innovative thought of Richard Stone, a simple formalization of insights developed by Colin Clark or James Meade, or an outcome of the need to provide information to be used strategically during the war. Though Meade had developed the original conceptual framework of national accounts, it was through Stone that this framework was operationalized. Meade and Stone worked together until April 1941. At that time a new budget split the Economic Information Service into an Economic Section, to which Meade was attached, and a Central Statistical Office (CSO), where Stone became responsible, thanks to John Maynard Keynes's intervention, for the national accounts.

It was during this period that a new conception of measurement emerged from the collaboration between Stone and Meade. This conception viewed the measurement of national income not merely as a quantification of isolated single magnitudes but as a quantification of an integrated accounting system in which magnitudes from different sources had to agree. Although Stone and Meade were not the first to create the concepts of national accounts or to estimate national aggregates, they were the first to put forward a notion of measurement based on criteria of systematization and consistency among aggregates.

At this early stage, the notion of accounts was not fully developed. Meade ([1944–46] 1990, 220) reports in his *Cabinet Office Diary* how in July 1945, on Stone's initiative, a joint committee between economists and accountants was created to discuss questions about the use of concepts common to both professions. Later the committee focused on issues concerning the definition and measurement of national account aggregates and alternatives to censuses of production. As suggested by Meade (300), these meetings were crucial to Stone's formulation of the system of accounts that appear in the work he did for the United Nations in the late 1940s. The group formed by economists (Stone, Meade, and J. R. Hicks) and accountants (Rees, Sewell Bray, and Norris) continued to meet regularly until June 1947.

To elaborate: In 1941, Meade and Stone put forward the notion of balance sheets as a method of clearing up some problems of definition that arose from the many different ways of defining national income. Agreement on definitions, such as those of net investment and direct and indirect taxes, became the first stage in the measurement of national accounts. Meade and Stone believed these definitions should be settled in ways that could be of interest and use to economists and allow statistical crosschecking. Main problems of definition should be solved in order to assure proper measurement. Proper measurement meant adopting principles of definitions, such as found in accounting systems, so that as a logical consequence all items are classified in only one place and the tables both balance and add up. The importance of settling definitions as the initial stage of measurement has been discussed by Martin Kohli (this volume), who describes how Wassily Leontief developed his input-output analysis by following a dynamic of progressive refinement of definitions and classifications. This conceptual step was widely acknowledged by Leontief and the U.S. Commerce Bureau as important in warranting consistency among different sets of indices and measures. It seems that Stone was not alone in emphasizing the issue of consistency in measurement.

Logical consistency as balance between different measures was achieved through the principle of double entry applied to a system of four accounts: domestic product account, income and outlay account, capital transactions account, and balance of payments account. Items on the debit side had also to be on the credit side so that equality between total incomings and outgoings was achieved. Because different sources were used to estimate different national totals, in practice the estimation depended on the residual errors to balance the totals. Logical consistency as aggregation was warranted by simple arithmetic equalization in a system of interlocking transactions and by the macroeconomic theory behind the choice of particular national totals, a theory which required that national income was equal to national expenditure and to national output.

Stone (1986a, 1986b, 1991) has commented upon and illustrated his own history of involvement with national accounts. Many other commentators have followed, including Meade ([1944–46] 1990), Deaton (1987 and 1993), Pesaran (1991), Harcourt (1995) and Pesaran and Harcourt (2000). The consensus is that the Meade and Stone 1941 essay represented a watershed in the literature of national accounts. While the previous focus on measurement criteria had been on the assessment of the reliability of individual series, Meade and Stone put forward the idea of considering all series together in a logical way. The tables of national income they produced were early versions rather than national accounts in the strict sense of the word, but they contained the measurement principle of logical consistency that would come to characterize, as argued here, the early stages of the contemporary development of national accounts.

The Measurement of National Accounts:
Definitions, Flexibility, and Invariance

It is important to note here that logical consistency as in the accounting sense used above was not the only criterion behind the formulation of national accounts. Because Stone was concerned with the *use* of national accounts, he tried to develop criteria that would help to adapt his framework of analysis to different realities. Consequently, he argued that national accounts should be formulated by using flexible or alternative definitions.

The differences between Kuznets's and Stone's approaches provide an immediate example. Interest in studying the variations in economic activity in a peacetime economy had led Stone, in 1943, to investigate U.S. figures. He joined the discussions between Simon Kuznets and the U.S. Department of Commerce on the definition and measurement of national accounts. Gilbert (1943, 76) at the Department of Commerce argued that the national product at market prices "is a more meaningful and fundamental aggregate than the sum of factor costs." He pointed out that the factor costs notion was confusing and obscure to the consumers of the estimates and that for this reason market prices should be used. In addition, he suggested that government interest is a transfer payment and that it should be excluded from the national accounts. His argument seems to rest upon an identification of government debt with unproductive uses of capital, such as those in the war.

Stone's discordances with methods used in American estimates revealed that in his view measurement criteria should not be decided a priori: if one were dealing with a situation facing consumers, he would agree with Gilbert's proposition and use market prices. However, if the situation to be analyzed were about productivity, then he would consider factor cost as a more relevant measure than market prices (see Stone 1943a, 82). Concepts should be rearranged according to the purpose at hand; for example, the measurement of government activity indicated people's attitudes toward government. Kuznets's interpretation of government as a commercial activity was rejected by Stone (1943b, 63) as being "a thoroughly inconvenient way of looking at the matter." It might be speculated that wartime experience provided a different perspective on government activities that influenced Stone's disagreement with the American (peacetime) position. Finally, Stone criticized Kuznets's use of maximum errors on the bases that (1) Kuznets did not define the range of his maximum errors and that (2) the reliability of estimates could be better assessed by using concepts analogous to probable or standard errors. Incomparability problems between American and British figures led Meade and Stone ([1944] 1988, 153) to emphasize the *"flexibility"* in the formulation of national accounts, according to which "there are many admissible ways of defining the national income, and that there is nothing absolutely right or wrong about any of these definitions. The national income must be measured according to the definition which is most suitable for the particular purpose in view."

A further illustration of flexibility and definitions is found in the memorandum entitled "Definition and Measurement of the National Income and Related Totals" that Stone wrote for the United Nations in 1947, in which he first proposed that the study of national income should be approached from the perspective of social accounting. Stone adopted, as his working system, definitions for three basic forms of economic activity: production, consumption, and accumulation—which became four when transactions with the rest of the world were added. By recording in four accounts all the incomings and outgoings of the basic forms of economic activity, Stone suggested a wider conceptual basis that provided a greater uniformity of content in the estimates for different nations. It also permitted Stone to advocate a change of emphasis from the measurement of individual aggregates to the measurement of structures of transactions. The basic forms of economic activity when put together would provide a display of the basic structure of an economic system reduced to its simplest terms but yet be wide enough to categorize most items correctly. The main message conveyed by the measurement framework of an accounting structure was of mutual interdependence among definitionally separate parts.

Flexibility about the level of aggregation was also an important feature of this wider system. In constructing and measuring a system of social accounts, the most important problem, as defined by Stone, consisted in combining accounts and transactions to obtain meaningful aggregates. A first balance must be looked for between the unmanageable detail of too many accounting entities and the potential lack of information inherent in one combined account. As Stone (1947a, 27) argued, "In the first case we should have no use for so much detail even if we could keep such elaborate records which, of course, we cannot; in the second we should have reduced all that was taking place in the economy to one single figure of very limited usefulness." After an adequate number of "accounts" had been selected, a second balance should be looked for between the further *subdivision* of accounts (to achieve a concrete picture of the economic system) and the aggregation of many different accounts (to select the most important variables of the system). Through the process of "simple consolidation," accounts could be aggregated and common entries could be deleted, providing economically meaningful aggregates. In addition, a sequence of operations could be carried out on the accounts in order to express identities in the system between sets of transactions. Measurement of national accounts would be completed when the balance between subdivision and consolidation provided a manageable and useful outcome.

Stone (1948) suggested that measurement and economic theory should be tailored to each other's needs. On the one hand, the social accounting system should preserve conceptual distinctions that are needed for economic analysis. On the other hand, economic analysis should restate its needs in a terminology that could be measured. These elements could be regulated through a process of selection and aggregation based on the notion of "equivalent subsets of transactions."[1] By using this notion, the general meaning of economic variables could be defined operationally in a way that makes measurement possible. Ultimately, the categories to be measured have to fit the economy itself, which has certain features of invariance or stability. Since there is no uniquely right way of combining accounts, flexibility could be used to establish the proper combination between subdivision and consolidation for each case. Yet, some types of account are never to lose their identity under consolidation. A degree of "invariance" was needed in order to cope with the complexity of irrelevant features of economic systems; invariance was of particular importance in the cases of nonmonetary transactions and systems of taxation, since it provides a very useful assumption of homogeneity that could be used to measure economies where a market basis exists. But this principle should not be pressed too far. As Stone (1948, 15) observes,

> There can be no doubt that the investigation of methods of obtaining aggregates which are invariant to various fortuitous features of

---

1. The concept of "equivalent subsets of transactions" is based on the balancing property of each individual account and the group property of subsets of transactions related to this. It comprises the substitution of the elements on one side of an account for different elements on the other side. Thus, accounts are transformed in subsets of transactions.

the situation should be encouraged. At the same time it is important in practical work not to become obsessed with the idea of invariance since its unremitting pursuit is likely to lead to an accounting structure which is quite unrecognisable by everyday standards and which in addition contains a large number of entries for which no satisfactory basis of estimation can be proposed.

Stone (1966) put forward a more elaborated proposal for multiple classifications in social accounting. According to him, a complete system of social accounts must be able to address transactors in their dimensions as producers, consumers, and accumulators. Classification of transactions is important because it allows a reduction in the number and variety of transactors to operational dimensions. The problem of choosing suitable criteria of classification could prima facie admit three solutions: (1) the "limited solution," where the transactor classification is removed or reduced to a minimum; (2) the solution of Procrustes, where a single classification of transactors is applied; and (3) the "proper solution," in which one can choose many classifications according to their usefulness (230–31). Stone claimed that only the accounting system with the proper solution could provide the system of classifications with some flexibility. And no doubt, flexibility was, for Stone, an essential element of proper measurement (see 231). How else could he explain and measure different systems of classification? How could he harmonize a consumers' classification of products with a producers' classification? Or to connect, for instance, government expenditures on health, education, and so forth with the different industries that are producing these goods?

Thus, a system of multiple classifications could transform theoretical distinctions into different ways of organizing the balance between subdivision and consolidation. The notion of a "classification converter" (for financial flows, for example) was also proposed by Stone in 1966. This new idea strengthened his view that flexibility increases the relevance of theoretical distinctions as an intrinsic part of measurement of national accounts. Ideally, data should be measured to fit parts of conceptual systems: they are intended to give life to those conceptual systems. In practical terms, the use of multiple classifications is tantamount to an adaptation of conceptual systems according to the practical relevance of empirical counterparts. In the national accounts, this implied a rejection of the use of supplementary tables, for they do not show in detail the structure of accounts, and of the imposition of a uniform and common classification, which is not suitable for all cases.

Now it is important to note that those flexibility criteria Stone suggested for measurement were not enough for the solution of all conceptual and practical problems involved in the actual measurement of national accounts. Two examples are illustrative here. The first concerns the measurement of nonmarket activities, such as household and amateur activities; the second concerns the measurement of depreciation of capital. Simply put, Stone argued for the exclusion of these former activities from the production boundary on grounds that their output does not have a measurable cost. In addition, he said that "these services are extremely numerous and in fact unrecorded; in the great majority of cases they are not even very well defined; and they merge imperceptibly into the activity of living, which can hardly be reduced to a number of measurable productive operations" (Stone and Stone [1961] 1977, 36). Stone was then forced to recognize that when measurement barriers cannot be overcome, conventions—in this case the convention of not including something—must be introduced, not as a matter of principle but of practice and convenience.

A different solution was proposed for the latter problem, the measurement of depreciation of capital. The basic problem in measuring depreciation is that it depends on the expected life of capital, on the estimate of the rate at which it will wear out and the sequence of prices in this wearing out. Estimates of the life span of different types of capital can never be certain; different methods can be used to account for depreciation, and the valuation of investment in stocks is in itself a very complicated issue, involving great difficulty in disentangling the investment in stocks from stock appreciation. Though recognizing such difficulties, Stone supported the inclusion of depreciation in the national accounts. Different sorts of practical conventions and assumptions were elaborated.

The solution for apparently unsolvable measurement problems involved the use of conventions. Yet two different classes of conventions seem to have been created: the convention of not including what is not potentially measurable and the convention of including what is uncertain but potentially measurable.

It must be noted that for Stone, flexibility criteria about the level of aggregation, definitions, and categories could not be applied mechanically, as in the case of criteria of logical accountancy consistency. Rather, these flexibility criteria should follow practical considerations related to economic theory and the relevant purpose of a particular system of national accounts, even when these considerations resulted in the use of conventions.

The Development of National Accounts:
Standardization versus Extension

In September 1945, during a visit to the Institute for Advanced Study at Princeton, Stone was invited by Alexander Loveday, the head of the Intelligence Department of the League of Nations, to write a report on national income statistics (see Pesaran and Harcourt 2000, F152). What followed was the beginning of a collaboration between Stone and the statistical office of the United Nations that lasted twenty-three years. Stone was responsible for the first basic framework for the national accounts, published in 1953, and its major revision and extension, requested in 1963 by Pat Loftus, head of statistics at the UN Headquarters, and concluded in 1968.

In general lines, the development of national accounts was characterized after 1947 by two broad tendencies. The first was the tendency of *standardization* of accounts and the second was of their *extension*. With the creation of the O.E.E.C in 1949 (later the OECD), further emphasis was given to the elaboration of comparable national statistics among countries. This progress in European research prompted the publication of the first *Standardized System of National Accounts* (first SNA), prepared by Stone for the UN in 1953. The SNA provided the framework for the *Yearbook of National Accounts Statistics*, which has been calculated since 1957. Standardization under the SNA: (1) required that all estimates should be expressed in money values of particular times and places, (2) introduced additional detail to connect the accounts to concepts of economic analysis, (3) determined standard feasible statistical calculations where relevant, and (4) established broad distinctions enabling definitions to acquire a fair degree of international comparability. A second version of the SNA was prepared in 1966 and finally, in 1968, a third version of the SNA appeared in which further advances were achieved. According to Johansen (1985, 5), this was "the last important step based on his [Stone's] work for the United Nations." It was only after 1968 that the second tendency, the extension of the SNA's boundaries, manifested itself with the development of regional accounts and sociodemographic statistics.

At the heart of the general development of national accounts there was a tension—that permeated Stone's work—between these two different tendencies. The first tendency concerned the formal aspects of national accounts and consisted in homogenizing definitions, classifications, and procedures, so as to narrow the variability of measurements. The second, apparently contrary, tendency concerned the human context of national accounts and consisted in extending the scope of measurement by the introduction of new dimensions of measurement of national accounts. These tendencies were relevant to Stone's choice of criteria for assessing the effectiveness of national accounts, and the tension between standardization and extension was manifested in the way Stone handled the inclusion of social and demographic variables into the general framework of national accounts.

In 1947 Stone wanted to introduce these variables directly as classifications in the economic accounts, but it was not until 1968 that he finally introduced them—and even then he treated them separately in independent sociodemographic accounts. This was not merely a question of convenience or flexibility of the systems as it could prima facie seem; rather, it was mainly a consequence of his emphasis on starting measurement from simplest structures and then complicating the picture by progressively adding new information. Because standardization preceded extension of SNAs, measurement techniques developed for the former were decisive for the constitution of the latter.

The tension between standardization and extension was evident in the 1968 revision of the SNA, which introduced a new structure for the system of accounts. This revision used a matrix approach to present the account model and halved the number of entries in the system. It also contained a new standard set of consolidated accounts, put forward new distinctions between accounts, and argued for uniformity in commodity valuation. The national accounts, including balance sheets, were subdivided into categories and subcategories, thus providing an amount of detail considered useful for analytical purposes (see Stone 1970, 167–69). For production, accounts were subdivided into commodities and activities. New assumptions—for instance, referring to the cost structure of industry—were introduced so that comparability among different industries could be made possible. Another assumption concerned uniformity of valuation between consumers and producers.

It appears that a price was paid for the measurement of detailed accounts in the form of further assumptions, since in practice it was barely possible to measure for each individual case—for instance, how costs are allocated to different commodities. The additional complication was that the classifications of items for consumers did not correspond with the classification of commodities for producers. A set of connecting matrices was then introduced to show how each of the consumer classifications would be transformed into the commodity classification.

Critics of the 1968 SNA focused on the uses of national accounting. The most outstanding criticism of the 1968 SNA—the Ruggles System—identified the following flaws (see Ruggles and Ruggles 1970 and Geary 1973), which might be thought to be associated with the move to standardization. For example, they claimed that the new consolidated accounts did not distinguish between government and household activities and that deconsolidation introduced a lot of unnecessary detail. The SNA was also criticized for proposing a "universal" accounting system that would not increase the explanatory power of national accounting; critics thought the system ineffective for this purpose anyway. Holub (1981), for instance, criticized the single universal system of accounts for asking questions that were not compatible with one another. He thought it unacceptable that in order to answer different questions, the SNA would require either different scales of measurement or that variables would give different values within the same scale of measurement.

As more details were added to the previous systems, a point was reached where measurement could only be dealt with by destroying the unity of the system. However, it was this unity that provided logical consistency for the collection of statistics. This is why Stone replaced the definition of a common system by a common set of interconnected subsystems in the 1968 SNA. His idea was that it would be impossible to homogenize alternative definitions and continue to use balancing sheets when so many different variables were introduced in the system. But now the underlying notion of consistency would have to be extended toward broader frontiers so as to guarantee the wider validity of the apparatus. The three main areas explored by Stone were regional accounts, demographic accounts, and educational planning. Rather than making new categories, however, the extension of SNAs appeared to involve more, rather than less, standardization of entries. His work on demographic accounts marked a tendency according to which he "gradually turned from accounting formulations towards the representation of national accounts in the form of a large 'social accounting matrix' or 'transaction matrix'" (Johansen 1985, 10).

It seems that extensions of the SNA, through the inclusion of regional and demographic accounts, would lead to an abandonment of the (formal) original principle of logical accounting consistency behind the concept of national accounts. The new formal basis of consistency lay in the matrix transformations which were designed to accompany the new bases of measurement. That is, the use of matrix algebra and transaction matrices replaced the former notion of accounts, providing the flexibility needed to assemble complex sets of information. With the extension and further development of national accounts, the use of the earlier single criterion of logical accounting consistency became insufficient to address the flexibility needed to incorporate new sets of information. More importantly, perhaps, a tension between alternative tendencies—standardization versus extension—seems to have pushed Stone into developing other harmonizing criteria.

The Accuracy of Measurement and Development of Adjustment Techniques

In no other area was the influence of experience on the elaboration of measurement criteria more evident than in Stone's development of adjustment techniques. It is interesting to note that the idea of measurement criteria as an extension of human experience had previously been put forward by Irving Fisher, as shown by Marcel Boumans (this volume). In his work on index numbers, Fisher suggested a sequence of practical criteria that aimed to give consistency (in Stone's wider sense) to the elaboration of indexes. This search for practical criteria of measurement and for compromises between theory and practice was a common characteristic between Fisher and Stone.

Stone's emphasis on the importance of adjustment techniques in assessing the quality of measurement of national accounts was present since his early writings, as his essay written with Champernowne and Meade (1941–42) illustrates. As they argued, there is an important practical element behind the idea of adjustment:

> It is not possible to work for long on material of this kind [national accounts] without forming some idea of the reliability of the estimates that go into making the final totals. Some of these estimates will be

accounting figures, for the geographical area required, of some element defined precisely as it should be; and they must for all practical purposes be considered accurate. . . . Still other cases will occur in which both prices and quantities are no more than guesses based perhaps upon a partial investigation relating to a single part of the country or on the results of a census now ten years out of date. Manifestly it would be absurd to give the same weight to all such measurements even though their precision cannot be estimated by the usual statistical methods. (1941–42, 112–13)

The Standard Adjustment Procedure, suggested initially by Stone, Champernowne, and Meade (1941–42), formalizes the simple idea of not changing the sources and initial estimates believed to be relatively accurate, and changing those believed to be inaccurate. They proposed the formation of subjective reliability ratings of the initial estimates in order to construct a variance matrix of the errors.

In other words, the variance matrix is a summary of the investigators' impressions about the accuracy and interdependency of the initial estimates. For instance, reliability categories, such as A, or "good," B, or "fair," and C, or "poor," could be elaborated. Subsequently they would be converted into numbers (e.g., $A = 0.01$, $B = 0.05$ and $C = 0.10$) that would be used to multiply the variances of the initial measures. Units and their relationships would then be used to correct for the logical and statistical errors. National accounts could be balanced by using variance matrices. Because this method, unlike the proportional adjustment method, is not mechanical, it can only rely on the systematic but tacit knowledge obtained by the investigator as the main source of adjustment. Stone saw statisticians' impressions of the relative soundness of data as a natural consequence of their experience of working with various sources of data. This is consistent with Stone's earlier statement that in the social sciences, it is difficult to obtain objective measures of error.

Later in his career, Stone, prompted by the difficulties of the 1968 SNA, devoted an unprecedented attention to adjustment techniques. He wrote a couple of methodological papers where he argued for the need for adjustment and discussed its practical importance as an essential element in the achievement of satisfactory measurement of national accounts. Stone argued that basic data, untailored by human hands, were incomplete, inaccurate, inconsistent, and subject to many types of errors. He recognized what he called the "problem of measurement" as pervasive in all sciences. In the natural sciences, Stone observed, this problem is constantly solved by appealing to adjustment for errors of measurement (1973, 1984). Nevertheless, he argued that "in the social sciences this is typically not the case, since measurements cannot usually be replicated" (1973, 30). That is, general problems of data collection are unavoidable. As Stone (1984, 191) observed, "In spite of the best endeavours of statisticians, national accounts contain statistical discrepancies, residual errors, unidentified items and other balancing entries, evidence of the difficulties arising from the fact that the information available is in some degree incomplete, inconsistent and unreliable." Quite often the problem of data collection is to organize the large quantities of economic statistics available. In concrete terms, as Stone (1986b, 454) argues, "we never start from a *tabula rasa* and the practical problem is not to devise an ideal data collection scheme *ab initio* but to introduce more design and coherence into the one that already exists." Measurement starts then with attention to the existing methods of collection and tabulation and the use of common definitions and classifications and standard dates and intervals. In addition, new types of data can be collected. Boundary regions should be delimited before what Stone, Champernowne, and Meade (1941–42, 111) called "the practical work of measurement" begins.

In a later formulation of the 1942 adjustment technique, Stone (1975) proposed the introduction of a matrix with direct and indirect constraints. By direct constraints he meant arithmetic constraints, constraints based on assumed knowledge and constraints arising in a stationary and stable population. By indirect constraints he meant those based on the lengths of age groups, life expectancies, mean times spent in given states, and mean age of entry. This new development aimed to allow researchers to differentiate more effectively between the relative reliability of (1) one's sources and (2) the individual estimates within each source.

An important distinction should be made here between what Stone referred to as *direct measurement* (the direct quantification of variables without considering their reliability and how they stand to other variables) and as *consistent measurement* (measurements achieved after proper adjustments). The "practical work of measurement" was a reference to the transformation of direct into consistent measurement. Because initial estimates could not alone produce a consistent and complete set of measures, the boundaries of measurement would have to include "the practical work" of transforming quantities into empirical facts. Many years after his initial paper on adjustment techniques, Stone (1984, 192) lamented that "even nowadays, it is not generally accepted that the task of measurement is unfinished until estimates have been obtained that satisfy the constraints that hold between their true values." So, there is a need for the adjustment of direct measurement of variables.

These constraints could be used to guide, but not determine, the impressions of the investigator. They would help him or her in assessing the reliability of the initial estimates and in constructing the variance matrix. The use of constraints is ultimately the decision of the investigator, or as Stone (1984, 200) puts it, "The question is what is the best way to do this and the answer is that it all depends on circumstances." Adjustments could be improved by refining reliability ratings, allowing for provisional estimates, introducing covariances, incorporating systematic errors, regrouping aggregates, studying the history of past revisions, and looking for the explanations behind the biases.

Despite Stone's best efforts, the adjustment method he proposed and its subsequent developments have not caught on. Stone acknowledged that this subject had 'bothered him for many years' and expressed his views that this method had not succeeded partly due to its use of subjective impressions as its major input (1975, 1). As he observed, "The notion of subjective estimates of error is repugnant to many people" (1970, 243).

Thus, the tacit knowledge factor of interpretative judgment was at the core of the development of adjustment techniques. Because of the importance of these techniques for the achievement of consistency, it could be said that what Stone called "the problem of measurement" became the problem of incorporating individual knowledge intuitions into figures.

Conclusion

Stone's contribution to the measurement of national accounts has been widely praised for giving the accounts internal and logical consistency (see, e.g., Geary 1973, 224, and Aukrust 1986, 111). Without rejecting the importance of this criterion in Stone's early work on the national accounts, it was argued that he aimed far beyond a systematic, logical bookkeeping approach to warrant consistency in national accounts. Rather, the evolution of Stone's development of criteria to judge the content and effectiveness of the national accounts followed practical considerations related to the use and purpose of these accounts.

In Stone's later work and unpublished papers, he associated the choice of measurement criteria with attempts at achieving "consistent" measures. When discussing the meaning of consistent projections in multisector models, Stone (1970, 35) considered consistency (1) in a restricted sense, in which certain logical identities must be satisfied and (2) in a wider sense, "to include consistency with everything we know, everything we expect, and everything we desire to achieve." In order to constrain this very broad definition, Stone formulated seven classes of consistency based on arithmetic identities, accounting identities, knowledge of past behavior and technology, expectations about future behavior and technology, transitional possibilities, all remaining aspects of the problem, and all long-term aims. Measurement structures will meet the different requirements in different degrees according to their uses. Stone did not discuss how a balance could be achieved among these different classes but observed that following theory might be a way of maintaining consistency.

Following this classification, it could be suggested in retrospect that Stone developed measurement criteria with the purpose of extending the notion of consistency toward broader frontiers so as to warrant wider validity for national account systems. It is interesting to note how Stone used the "restricted" notion of consistency in the beginning of his work and the "wider" notion at the end of his contribution to the national accounts. Although this could be viewed as simple ex post facto rationalization of his work, there is a descriptive element in Stone's classification that reveals a tension in his work between conflicting assessment criteria.

At the beginning of the "statistical revolution," when many figures on individual statistical series that did not relate to each other were produced, the criterion of logical consistency warranted by the use of balance sheets provided Stone with a key to reliable estimates. Subsequently, in the face of international comparability problems and extension of the basic core of national accounts, Stone stressed the importance of balancing the criteria of flexibility and invariance in order to achieve representative and useful estimates. Finally, as a result of his experience in the field and awareness of the limitations involved in the measurement of national accounts, he put forward a complementary set of criteria (or constraints) related to standardization and extension of accounts. It could be said that there was no unifying principle behind the choice of different criteria other than the practical imperatives related to the search for wider notions of consistency. The same practical imperative would determine the use of conventions and assumptions where measurement barriers could not be overcome. This conclusion seems to gain support from O'Brian's (1994, 242) argument that "the evolution of national accounting framework should be understood as a process of construction which reflects the historical context from which it emerged."

Stone's emphasis on the importance of adjustment techniques could be considered evidence for the relevance of consistency in the "practical work of measurement." Ultimately, consistent measurement—being an expression of the statistician's practice—would depend on circumstances and intuitive judgments. Otherwise, direct measurement could not become consistent measurement. Measurement for Stone (see n.d.b, 3) was about defining systems or stories that could "talk sense about the world." It could be suggested that in the face of the increasing complexity of the measurement of national accounts, the notion of practice (or practical imperative) ended up being an important element in Stone's development of measurement criteria.

References

Arndt, H. W. 1988. Colin Clark. In *National Income and Economic Progress: Essays in Honour of Colin Clark*, edited by D. Ironmonger, J. O. N. Perkins, and T. Van Hoa, 1–7. London: Macmillan.

Aukrust, O. 1986. On the Occasion of a Nobel Prize. *The Review of Income and Wealth* 32:109–12.

Carson, C. 1975. The History of the United States National Income and Product Accounts: The Development of an Analytical Tool. *Review of Income and Wealth* 12.2:153–81.

Clark, C. 1937. *National Income and Outlay*. London: Macmillan.

———. 1940. *The Conditions of Economic Progress*. London: Macmillan.

Deane, P. 1997. Comments. In *Some British Empiricists in the Social Sciences 1650–1900: Raffaele Mattioli Lectures*, by J. R. N. Stone. Edited by A. M. Cardani and G. Stone, 389–97. Cambridge: Cambridge University Press.

Deaton, A. 1987. Stone, John Richard Nicolas. In *The New Palgrave: A Dictionary of Economics*, by J. Eatwell, M. Milgate, and P. Newman. London: Macmillan.

———. 1993. Sir John Richard Nicholas Stone 1913–1991. *Proceedings of the British Academy* 82:475–92.

Geary, R. C. 1973. Reflections on National Accounting. *Review of Income and Wealth* 19.3 (September): 221–51.

Gilbert, M. 1943. U.S. National Income Statistics. *Economic Journal* 53 (April): 76–82.

Harcourt, G. C. 1995. *Capitalism, Socialism and Post-Keynesianism: Selected Essays of G. C. Harcourt*. Aldershot, U.K.: Edward Elgar.

Holub, H. W. 1981. Some Reflections on a Universal System of National Accounting. *Review of Income and Wealth* 27.3:333–38.

Johansen, L. 1985. Richard Stone's Contributions to Economics. *Scandinavian Journal of Economics* 87.1:4–32.

Kendrick, J. W. 1970. The Historical Development of National Income Accounts. *HOPE* 2.1:284–315.

Meade, J. [1944–46] 1990. *The Cabinet Office Diary 1944–46*. Vol. 4 of *The Collected Papers of James Meade*. Edited by S. Howson and D. Moggridge. London: Unwin Hyman.

Meade, J., and J. R. N. Stone. 1941. The Construction of Tables of National Income, Expenditure, Savings and Investment. *Economic Journal* 6 (June–September): 216–33.

———. [1944] 1988 *National Income and Expenditure*. In *The Collected Papers of James Meade*. Vol. 1, edited by S. Howson. London: Unwin Hyman.

O'Brian, E. 1994. How the "G" Got into the GNP. In vol. 10 of *Perspectives on the History of Economic Thought*, edited by K. Vaughn, 241–55. Aldershot, U.K.: Edward Elgar.

Patinkin, D. 1976. *Keynes's Monetary Thought*. Durham, N.C.: Duke University Press.

Pesaran, M. H. 1991. The *ET* Interview: Professor Richard Stone. *Econometric Theory* 7:85–123.

Pesaran, M. H. and G. C. Harcourt. 2000. Life and Work of John Richard Nicolas Stone 1913–1991. *Economic Journal* 110.461 (February): F146–65.

Reddaway, W. B., C. F. Carter, and J. R. N. Stone. 1948. British Output in 1942–46: Sustained Increase Due to Temporary Factors. *Times*

Ruggles, N. D. and R. Ruggles. 1970. *The Design of Economic Accounts*. New York: National Bureau of Economic Research, Columbia University Press.

Stone, J. R. N. n.d.a. Social Indicators. King's College Library, University of Cambridge. Autograph manuscript.

———. n.d.b. Theory and Observations with Assorted Econometric Calculations. King's College Library, University of Cambridge. Autograph manuscript.

———. 1943a. Comment. *The Economic Journal* 53:82–83.

———. 1943b. Two Studies on Income and Expenditure in the United States. *Economic Journal* 53:60–75.

———. 1947a. Definition and Measurement of the National Income and Related Totals. Appendix to *Measurement of National Income and Construction of Social Accounts*. Geneva: UN.

———. 1947b. The Social Accounts. Recovery in Consumers' Expenditure. National Income and National Budgeting, and Related Correspondence. King's College Library, University of Cambridge. Carbon typescript.

————. 1948. Social Accounting, Aggregation and Invariance. *DAE Reprint Series* 2. University of Cambridge.

————. 1966. *Mathematics in the Social Sciences and Other Essays*. London: Chapman and Hall.

————. 1970. *Mathematical Models of the Economy and Other Essays*. London: Chapman and Hall.

————. 1973. Statistics. Department of Applied Economics, University of Cambridge. Mimeographed.

————. 1974. What Is Wrong with the National Accounts? King's College Library, University of Cambridge. Autograph manuscript.

————. 1975. Direct and Indirect Constraints in the Adjustment of Observations. Department of Applied Economics, University of Cambridge. Mimeographed.

————. 1984. Balancing the National Accounts: The Adjustment of Initial Estimates—A Neglected Stage in Measurement. In *Demand, Equilibrium, and Trade*, edited by A. Ingham and A. Ulph. London: Macmillan.

————. 1986a. Nobel Memorial Lecture 1984, The Accounts of Society. *Journal of Applied Econometrics* 88.3:453–72.

————. 1986b. Social Accounting: The State of Play. *Scandinavian Journal of Economics* 1:5–28.

————. 1991. The *ET* Interview: Professor Richard Stone. *Econometric Theory* 7:85–123.

Stone, J. R. N., D. G. Champernowne, and J. E. Meade. 1941–42. The Precision of National Income Estimates. *The Review of Economic Studies* 9:111–25.

Stone, J. R. N. and G. Stone. [1961] 1977. *National Income and Expenditure*. 10th ed. London: Bowes and Bowes.

Stone, J. R. N. and W. M. Stone. 1939. Indices of Industrial Output. *The Economic Journal* 49.195:476–85.

Studenski, P. 1958. *The Income of Nations*. Pt. 1, *History*. New York: New York University Press.

United Nations. Statistical Office. 1968. *A System of National Accounts*. Studies in Methods, series F, no. 2, rev. 3. New York: United Nations.

Perspective
Making Measuring Instruments

Mary S. Morgan

In the mid-nineteenth century, economists had many numbers but relatively few measurements; by the mid-twentieth century, they began to take for granted that they had measurements for most of the phenomena about which they theorized. This is the change that marks the impact of the age of measurement, and my interest in this prespective essay is to provide an understanding of what this change entailed Out of many different economists' individual practical measuring projects around the late nineteenth and early twentieth centuries, there emerged a number of different kinds of measuring instruments, each carefully fashioned for economics. By looking carefully at the materials collected in this volume, we can discern that these instruments can be grouped according to the strategies or recipes that were followed in making such measuring instruments. As a historical development, first the instruments, then the strategies, served to connect the ambitions of economists seeking accurate scientific measures of their world with the practically necessary, sometimes mundane, but never trivial tasks of data collection.

Correspondence may be addressed to Mary S. Morgan, Department of Economic History, London School of Economics, Houghton Street, London WC2 2AE, U.K.; e-mail: m.morgan@lse.ac.uk. My thanks go to all the members of and contributors to the measurement workshops at the University of Amsterdam and the London School of Economics over the last few years and to the hard-working contributors to the *HOPE* workshop and this volume. I thank particularly Marcel Boumans, Harro Maas, and Hasok Chang for guiding my thinking about measurement issues. I acknowledge support from the British Academy for funding this work.

Both measuring instruments and measurement strategies are a consequence of the age of measurement, not a prerequisite for it.

Making measurements of economic entities requires instruments of a certain kind. The second broad historical thesis suggested by the essays in this volume is that the measuring instruments that economists built in this period were also analytical devices. These instruments embodied frameworks and techniques to turn observations into measurements and to organize the empirical data into particular types of arrangements so that economic phenomena might be arrayed before us. On one view, we can see this as a historical process of establishing facts about phenomena, paralleling the epistemological interests of Bogen and Woodward (1988).[1] On another view, this process can be seen, ultimately, as one of creating new categories of phenomena, paralleling the historical interests of Theodore Porter ([1994] 1996). I begin in the former tradition and will return to the latter interpretation.

Measuring Instruments

It is a conventional, and surely uncontested, claim that taking measurements requires instruments of measurement. From our childhood use of fingers and rulers to the technicalities of clocks and Geiger counters, we rely on tools to help us measure our world. Economics is no different, except perhaps in being relatively slow to develop such measuring instruments. The discipline did not develop such devices until the late nineteenth and early twentieth centuries, whereas there had been a dramatic increase in the number and range of measuring devices in the natural sciences in the seventeenth and eighteenth centuries (Heilbron 1990).

Economists of the late nineteenth century wanted to measure all sorts of things, from the close-up single choice of an individual to the aggregate price level changes in the economy as a whole. But they had few instruments that would allow them to do these things. Whereas some might suppose that economic measurement is merely counting "what is there," a similarly naive view would have us think that x-ray machines merely look through our flesh to reveal our bones. We don't see a macroeconomy, nor a consumer price index, nor an individual choice decision, hence fashioning measuring instruments in economics has been, in part,

---

1. Within this framework, the problem of differentiating facts from artifacts, and the role of measuring instruments in this process, are particularly finely treated in Franklin 1986.

a matter of developing ways of observing the economy. It is consistent with this to note, from the history of science, that the design and use of measuring instruments are often aligned to experimental investigations.[2] Our analogy continues with the advanced medical scanners, instruments of investigation that are designed and programmed to enable us to "see" certain things inside us by picking them out in a particular way. The ways in which the economic body is investigated and data are collected, categorized, analyzed, reduced, and reassembled amount to a set of experimental interventions—not in the economic process itself, but rather in the information collected from that process. Economic observations must not only be registered but also converted into measurements, and converted in ways which serve particular theoretical or empirical or bureaucratic purposes.

All this is to say that modern economics has rulers that are as complicated and as technical in design as those of modern medical science. Economic measurement requires counting and arithmetic on a grand scale according to certain procedures. Of course, those procedures involve bureaucratic regimes, clerical workers, automated information systems, and so forth. But they also require sets of instructions, provided, as Marcel Boumans (1999) has recently suggested, by certain mathematical models, or parts of models, that we can think of as constituting measuring instruments in economics. Using this important insight here, we can interpret the mathematical formulae, statistical formulae, and accounting rules, as well as the rules of data elicitation and manipulation, described in the essays in this volume in terms of measuring instruments. The appropriateness of such a labeling lies in the fitness and fruitfulness of the historical reinterpretations it prompts.

The terminology and concept of measuring instrument fit happily onto the work of several late-nineteenth-century masters of measurement. Marcel Boumans (this volume) uses his earlier insight to understand Fisher's index number formulae; Harro Maas (this volume) shows how William Stanley Jevons can be understood as using a "virtual balance"; and Franck Jovanovic and Philippe Le Gall (this volume) recount how

---

2. See for example, Chang 2001. Heilbron (1990, 6) suggests that the early scientific instruments can be labeled either as "measurers" (for example, the barometer) or as "explorers" (such as the air pump) which "produced artificial phenomena for demonstration, investigation, and measurement." This distinction might be difficult to maintain for instruments made by economists in the age of economic measurement, where the relation between these aspects of measuring instruments is very close.

instrument terminology was explicitly used by Lucien March to describe his "business barometers." When such economists wanted to solve a new measurement problem, they adapted, or fashioned anew, an instrument to make those measurements. These measuring instruments can now be grouped and typed according to certain general features. For example, this is a period when many different index number formulae are developed, each one offering a differentiated measuring instrument for a particular purpose. But we can also see that all index numbers follow a generic recipe or strategy of "weighted averages." For another example: we can understand how the umbrella strategy of "using causes to make measurements" can describe the various ways Jevons used assumptions about causes to make measurement possible, although the different ways might be thought of as different measuring instruments. Once such instruments are forged, they tend to be taken for granted, and once strategies are recognized, they provide recipes for new instruments. Each individual instrument has its own history, but the sum total of the age of measurement is the emergence of strategies for making such instruments.

Strategies for Making Measurements

Using Causes to Bootstrap Measurements

One strategy of measurement is to pay attention to causes. Since the 1920s or 1930s, econometrics has focused its energy on building models to represent relations in the economy. It then uses these models to establish which are the relevant causal factors and to measure the relevant strength of those factors in explaining certain economic phenomena represented in the models. This approach relies both on techniques, developed only in the twentieth century, to measure causal relations in statistical data and on the already established measurements of the variables in the relationships (see Morgan 1997). Econometricians practice a kind of indirect measurement of the causal connections in relationships based on their theoretical preferences and what are perceived, at best, as direct measures (or at worst proxies for those) of the elements to be related. But we find the role of causes was rather different in the measuring instruments of earlier times. Whereas twentieth-century econometricians assume measurements to access causes, nineteenth-century economists interested in measuring assumed causes to make measurements.

The problem as understood from Mill's time had been how to deal with multiple causes, some permanent and some accidental, and to pick out the effects of single causes from the multitude. Though it appeared possible in thought experiments to consider man as driven by a single motive of wealth acquisition, attempts to isolate and make measurements of single, even constant, causes in such circumstances were fraught with difficulty. Simple averages, the main statistical technique of the day, were thought to work on the assumption of many small disturbing causes which cancel out in the average, as in measurement errors. Sometimes these averages worked well, as in Jevons's measurement of the wear on coins discussed by Sandra Peart (this volume). Other times, as in Jevons's investigation of poverty, they were inappropriate—in such situations, often found in economics, each item involved in the aggregate is subject to many causes, all of them valid, and none necessarily small or assumed to cancel. We can also see these difficulties of multiple causes in Adam Smith's thinking about the value of money (in Kevin Hoover and Michael Dowell's discussion in this volume) and in Jevons's work on the same topic (as discussed by Hoover and Dowell, Peart, and Maas all in this volume).

The solution used by Jevons in his study of gold can be interpreted as assuming a cause (namely, variation in the supply of gold, which alters all prices equally) in order to bootstrap a measure of the change in the value of gold money, whereas later economists might start from measurements of money stock and prices and use these to measure the parameter relating the two as a test of the quantity theory. Jevons assumed that there was a reciprocal relationship between the value of gold money and the general level of prices, that the supply of gold would determine the general level of prices, and that other causes of individual price changes reflected in the data on individual prices were independent and would cancel out. He could then interpret the average change as attributable to variations in gold supply and thus provide a measure of the change in the value of gold: the assumptions about causes provided the basis for the measurement of the element of interest, namely, the change in the value of gold.

The kind of circularity inherent here, that of inferring a quantity on the basis of assuming a lawlike relation, is found in many fields, and need not necessarily be dismissed on the basis of its circularity, for as Chang (1995) argues, such circularity can be fruitful in concept building and inferences may mesh with other measurements obtained elsewhere.

The circularity would only become dangerous if Jevons's measure of the change in the value of gold was then followed by the kind of work undertaken in modern econometric practice in which such a measurement is used in a test of the quantity theory. It is to Fisher's credit that his work on this problem in the early twentieth century steered away from this measurement circularity in two connected steps: first, he represented the relation between money and prices in an equation of exchange which incorporated two other elements, velocity and trade; and second, he constructed independent measurements of all four elements in the equation.

Nevertheless, using causal assumptions to measure money changes remained fraught during the period from Jevons through the twentieth century. Thomas Humphrey's analysis (this volume) of the 1920s debate between Federal Reserve Board economists, who believed in the real bills doctrine of money, and the quantity theorists shows how intimately causes, concept definitions, and measurement structures (including the rules of the institution) are all bound together. The inextricable mixture of definitional questions and the use of causal claims with measurements represented in this episode might be considered common for the period between Jevons's usage of causes in constructing measurements and the methods generally accepted after the 1940s for establishing causal relations (assuming existing measurements of variables) which came with econometrics.

Adding with Weights to Make Index Numbers

Index number formulae conceived as measuring instruments are based on the strategy of aggregating in a way that allows each individual element to be assigned its due weight in the whole. Such a "weighted average" strategy provides a solution to a general problem in economics, namely that many concepts refer to aggregates of things which may be considered homogeneous in the dimension of prices or money value, but are nonhomogeneous in another dimension, namely amounts consumed or produced. The solution is to use weights to overcome the problem of how to average in a manner that takes account of both amounts and values.

The weighted averaging strategy of measurement that forms the basis of index numbers was developed in the late nineteenth century and became well accepted by the early twentieth century, although the problem of designing good index numbers is far from trivial and vibrant arguments remain over which particular design should be used in which circumstance. For example, the arguments recounted by Spencer Banzhaf (this volume) are concerned with the problem of taking into account a third dimension, namely quality, alongside quantity in the price index. In his account we see arguments from microeconomic theorists that index numbers should measure constant utility equivalents and complaints from aggrieved consumers (during times of price rises) that official indices did not measure price changes accurately because of hidden quality changes. The hopes of both groups were defeated by the practical problems about how to weight items to take account of quality changes—despite the advice of academics on committees of inquiry and the willingness of bureaucrats, who collect the data and construct the measurements, to take these problems seriously.

Measurement strategies, and the particular measuring instruments they spawn, often have an inherent design tension between satisfying consistency requirements and providing a measure of a concept that coheres with features of the empirical world. Instruments often embody both theoretical and empirical requirements in their design, creating two forms of internal consistency which ought to be met. Both these may place strain on the design and use of the instrument, a strain exacerbated by the desire for coherence. For example, it is well known that there is no perfect index number, just a very large set of possible ones. Some satisfy particular criteria from economic theory, others satisfy criteria which come from data rules. But the instrument design also needs to mediate between these two levels if it is to provide coherent measurements that link the empirical to the theoretical levels.

Boumans's detailed examination of Fisher's work (this volume) shows how, during his work on index number design, Fisher moved from a design focus on theoretical consistency, regarded as mathematical features of the index formulae, to a realization that since index numbers could not meet all such criteria at once, his tests would be better interpreted as ones of coherence—how well a particular index number captured the relevant theoretical concept in a way that minimized distortion of the aspect of the empirical world being measured. As Roy Weintraub (this volume) reminds us, mathematics connects to the other sciences in different ways as its image changes. The mathematical virtues of truth and exactness might sometimes be connected with measurement virtues of accuracy and precision, while at other times they might cut loose from them. Boumans (this volume) uses the history of mathematics to analyze Fisher's changing understanding of measurement: theory dictates the nature of possible measurement assuming the theoretical picture of the world is correct, but that world itself may be differently arranged. A parallel example comes from the early work on the "identification problem" in econometrics. Econometricians of the 1920s and 1930s were adamant that in order to measure the parameters in relationships, not only did the mathematical structure representing those relations need to have certain features, but the statistical data needed to have variability over the same features (see Morgan 1990). The issue of coherence between these two sets of conditions lay at the heart of the 1930s "pitfalls" debate.[3] The problem of coherence between theory and the world raises dangers for any measurement strategy.

Using Properties of the Balance

The strategy of using a balance for measurement purposes should come as no surprise: that is what a balance is for, and as Peart (this volume) shows, Jevons used a physical balance to measure the wear on coins. What is unusual in economics is that the balance is used not as a physical measuring instrument, but as a virtual instrument. We can see this in Maas's analysis (this volume) of Jevons's work both on the value of gold and on the measurement of individual feelings. In the former case, the balance analogy is used in a specific argument to structure the measurement problem and so to provide a solution to the problem of measuring the value of gold: here the measurement involves a weighing up procedure, and an averaging procedure, both of which, in their detail, depend on the properties of the balance. The measurement of feelings applies the idea of the balance to the individual and her perceptions of utility: here the mind is portrayed as the balance, the mind registers both moments of equality and the points at which the balance between two things tips in one direction. Jevons describes a procedure of measuring sufficient for the individual to decide action; there is a judgment of equality or inequality and no numbers are needed. Just as an hourglass can measure the passage of an hour without telling the time of day, the balance

3. See Hendry and Morgan 1995 for extracts from the debate and earlier papers on identification along with a commentary on these matters. The insights of those years were temporarily lost as "identification" came to be understood as a characteristic of the mathematical structure alone.

can judge the comparative heaviness of two things without telling their weights.

Accounting, Wholes and Parts

Accounting principles provide another generic strategy for economic measurement. Identities, accounting coventions and arithmetic identities defined by theory, hold things together and provide an important rule constraining the measured parts to fit together in a particular way: if two sides of the identity don't equate, something is missing or over-counted. Balancing requirements within accounting, either by the imposition of an equation or by using double-entry systems, provide another constraint available where theoretical structures stress equivalences of inputs and outputs as in the Leontief system (discussed by Martin Kohli in this volume), or the overall total equivalents of expenditure, output and income as in Richard Stone's national income accounts (discussed by Flavio Comim in this volume). These accounting elements provide both a strength and a weakness. Their summing and balancing requirements seem to ensure accuracy, whereas in reality they ensure only a type of precision. Everything that has to balance or add up must do so: precision, but this might be achieved at the cost of only partial coverage of the aggregate: inaccuracy. The strategy rewards consistency at the empirical and theoretical levels but shortcomings of coherence between the two may be neglected.

Another well-known advantage of the accounting strategy is that it is flexible to many different theoretical accounts of the economy, to different economic ideologies and to many different levels of application (see Morgan 2002). National income counting predated Keynesian economics and although it later became strongly associated with Keynesian theory, it has not, historically, been tied irredeemably to Keynesian concepts. Input-output accounts can be used within a Marxian economics framework and a planned economy accounting system as well as with a regulated or managed market economy. They can be constructed for fine- or coarse-grained measurement and analysis, for use with national income accounts or as part of a national budgeting system. This flexibility points to the fact that whatever accounting scheme is adopted is largely a matter of choice and is historically contingent, determined by the requirements of governments in war, the local economists hired to make the accounts, and so forth. Thus, in the same period, we see the Meade-Stone accounts developed to work out wartime expenditures in Britain; Leontief's input-output accounts used to predict future manpower levels and as a check on the national accounts developed by Simon Kuznets in the United States (see Comim's and Kohli's articles in this volume); and a particular form of national budgeting developed in Norway (see Bjerkholt [1998] 2000). The choice becomes a conventional one once national income accounts have been standardized under the auspices of international economic agencies in the later twentieth century and those agencies used their power to insist on their own measuring instruments.

Related to these accounting measures are strategies of measuring wholes and parts. One of the oldest and well-measured wholes is the population, with censuses becoming widely established just after 1800. The population might be considered something like a natural whole: difficult though it might be to count every person, in principle it is relatively easy to define the whole. Sybilla Nikolow's essay (this volume) shows how far early measurers in the German cameralist tradition could emphasize the importance of such population and geographical measures of the whole by using them to work out ratios of economic power and comparing different national results. With the twentieth-century development of macroeconomics, attempts to measure "the economy" taken as a unit whole (rather than an aggregate) proved much more difficult. Conventional definitions tend to cover only things which pass through the market place (including the government sector) and are thus accounted for in monetary terms. But this leaves out all sorts of economic activity ranging from neighborly exchanges to unpaid housework. Immediately, then, the strategy of what counts as part of the whole excludes some things and includes others in the count. The strategy of extending the accounts to wider wholes and breaking them down into narrower categories, or into different sets of parts, is associated with the accounting ideal along with a desire for classification and naming. But each such redefinition of wholes and reclassification of parts results in a complete revision of the measurement task. We can see this equally well in Comim's discussion (this volume) of Stone's desire to extend the accounts while standardizing them and in Kohli's discussion (this volume) of Wassily Leontief's difficulties in stretching the input-output accounts to focus beyond production.

Constructing Indicators

The measurement strategy which makes indicators to inscribe the path of the economy over time has often been derided as hopelessly empiricist, subject to "measurement without theory" jibes. Yet the creator of the French economic barometer, Lucien March, considered his task to be the extraction of regularities out of a complicated pattern of information, in much the same way as others had tried to extract measurements on one common cause out of the whole set of interlocking multiple causes. March referred to his indicators as "instruments of observation and analysis" (Jovanovic and Le Gall this volume). He characterized the numbers the barometer inscribed as "conventions," in the same way, we might add, as numbers registered by thermometers are conventions (either degrees Fahrenheit or Celsius), but nevertheless valuable for comparisons, and once the convention is known, for indicating absolutes.

Although called "index numbers" by March, these business barometer indicator measures had little in the way of principles dictating their construction compared to the weighted averages measures referred to above. Nor were they like the indicator diagrams produced in engineering and in psychology in which the indicators are a directly inscribed outcome of some physical process or some physiological reaction (see Brain and Wise 1999). The indicator diagrams of economics, seen in the Manchester Statistical Society's pursuit of a "weather glass" to indicate the "dark days" of the trade cycle (see Judy Klein's essay in this volume) and in March's business barometer of the early twentieth century, are both forerunners of the business cycle measurements of the 1930s. These measurements are the results of time-series data, carefully filtered and amalgamated according to different rules. Some rules are conventional (for example, detrending), some rules are driven by theories (for example, about which data series constitute the phenomena), and some are more ad hoc (for example, based on correlation measures). The indicators are then charted so as to trace out the movements of economic activity over time. This is a measurement strategy which depends heavily on quantitative techniques yet is barely bound by rules from accounting, balancing, or weighting conventions and makes little call on principles deriving from theory or knowledge of causes. More than other strategies, this strategy makes measurements without the benefit of any blueprint other than the techniques supplied by earlier makers of business barometers. This is ironic, for this measuring instrument is one of the

(handwritten margin note: Perhaps the ability to check its accuracy is important)

few in economics named after an existing scientific measuring instrument which is theory bound.

Though not shaped by strong principles, such time-series indicators have become one of the more well-used measuring instruments in twentieth-century economic life. Just as those who own a barometer read it on their way out the door, business people, investors, government ministers, and their economic advisors check the leading and lagging indicators of the economy to see where it is heading.

Social Surveys

Social surveys are perhaps the most easily conceived of as a strategy for measurement, for they embed the sampling principles and techniques from statistics alongside an open-ended, flexible observation and counting method which can be applied across a range of topics, depending on the historical context in which this demand for measurement is made and met. As Bradley Bateman (this volume) suggests, there were many examples of survey data being collected in economics in the late nineteenth century—on budgets, on insurance systems, on poverty and wages, and so forth. Though the survey went out of fashion in economics during the mid-twentieth century, replaced by the strategy of causal measurement in econometrics, it has since returned as an essential element of econometrics itself. Much of modern microeconometrics and microsimulation (which perhaps ought to be treated as a measurement strategy on its own) relies on data gained through surveys, and econometric techniques have had to be adapted to the measurements generated by such instruments.

The Components of Strategies

The development and adoption of strategies of measurement that I describe here may have been overlooked, but they have been no less effective for all that. Historians of economics have focused on individual cases of measurement history, and, taken individually, what we see is the development of specific measuring instruments, each of which might be described as a mixture of the conventional and the ad hoc. It is only when these developments are viewed together that we can discern and describe a history in terms of a few generic types of measuring instruments. The historical change that marks the age of measurement is not therefore to be understood just as a massive increase in the collection of numbers but as a set of processes that only begin with counting, and then go on to analyze, reduce, aggregate, and reform our measures of the economy in ways unthinkable in the early nineteenth century. It is these processes, taken together, and with hindsight, that reveal themselves as a set of measurement strategies.

What do I mean by the term *strategy* here? It may be defined as a method for making, doing, or accomplishing something. Its synonyms suggest an idea, plan, or design: a pleasing combination of practical and ideal, yet the terms are still too vague to describe what was happening in economic measurement during the period from the late nineteenth to the mid-twentieth century. Each economic measuring instrument can be understood as involving three elements, namely, of *principle*, of *technique*, and of *judgment*; but there is also an overall element of design which I call a strategy. A particular strategy constrains the choices and the combinations of the three elements, and these elements in turn shape the way individual measuring instruments are constructed and so the measurements that are made in economics. For example, we can characterize both accounting principles and the equations we get from economic theory as the kinds of principles or rules which are embodied in measuring instruments. Techniques also come in various forms: techniques for counting and calculating, for cleaning data of outliers and "noise," for choosing samples, for meshing observations, and so forth. Judgment plays a role in many places, but particularly where design decisions have to be made about classification, exclusion, and inclusion. These judgments or decisions are often determined by the purpose for which the measurement is made. But judgment, techniques, and principles are not freely chosen: in the case of each measuring instrument, they hang together within an overall strategy for making instruments of that particular kind.

Economists with as diverse aims and epistemological beliefs as Irving Fisher and Lucien March could both, at the beginning of the twentieth century, write seriously about the design of measuring instruments, their construction, and the criteria they should meet. Both indeed constructed "index number" measuring devices, but with very different principles and techniques. Because they were following different strategies, they constructed different kinds of instruments, and made different measurements. In contrast, the individual designs and constructions developed by Stone and Leontief can be recognized in terms of the same generic strategy—although, since Stone and Leontief judged different categories to be important, their measuring instruments were constructed to measure different things. Fisher, March, Stone, Leontief, and many others shared a strong commitment to the measurement ideal, and their measuring work forms the basis for now well-accepted measuring instruments.[4]

The Life of Measurements

I have painted an account of measurement strategies as epistemological instruments—to the neglect of the social, economic, and bureaucratic realms in which their history lives (see the essays by Klein and Porter in this volume). Yet the change wrought by the age of measurement is at least as evident in the way that we now habitually accept that the measurements provided by these instruments give us reliable representations of what is happening in the economy, and provide an impetus on which we as individuals, and on which our governments, act. The importance of numbers to social knowledge and action is made most evident in Bradley Bateman's essay. But Porter (this volume) emphasizes another aspect of the importance of numbers and reminds us of one of his cherished themes when he suggests that only in the period after 1900 did economists "systematically construct and analyse new entities through measurement." The measuring instruments discussed here are critical to this, for as Porter ([1994] 1996, 36) argues, "standardized quantitative rules have been almost as fertile as standard experiments and mass-produced instruments in the making of new things."

Measurement, maybe even more than theory, contributes to the making of new ontic furniture for the economic world. Porter reminds us, in his 1994 essay, that the history of science is riven with examples in which theoretical disagreements over the nature of things or lack of knowledge of causes failed to impede measurement; that quantities often displace concepts; and that quantitative "laws" have often been taken as evidence for the reality of elements in the laws. Though the wealth of the nation or the economic power of the national economy was an early category for discussion, it was only after 1950 that the Gross National Product (GNP)

---

4. One indication of the importance the profession attaches to these measurement strategies is to note that nine master craftsmen of measurement have been awarded Nobel prizes in economics: for the causal account (econometrics) strategy, by Jan Tinbergen, Ragnar Frisch, Trygve Haavelmo and Lawrence Klein; for the accounting strategy by Simon Kuznets, Richard Stone, and Wassily Leontief; and most recently to James Heckman and Daniel McFadden, who fashioned the econometric techniques which enabled economists to use survey data effectively.

moved from being a category of economic analysis to being a number of everyday concern to government. Its measurement, tied at some point to a particular theory of macroeconomics, broke away from its theoretical roots to become a theory-neutral (though not value-neutral) measure of the economy's progress and health. The monthly change in the consumer price index (CPI), like the daily temperature, is a regularly reported number in our newspapers and influences all sorts of decisions at all sorts of levels. Again, almost regardless of changing knowledge and theories about what causes the CPI to change, it is treated as a real quantity by the participants in an economy. Other categories of measurement are more limited in their circulation, being "real" for certain economists, officials, and businesses, but otherwise remaining technical terms that hardly touch the general consciousness.

As we have seen, these "real" quantities are constructed with measuring instruments that have become conventional quantitative tools of analysis yet whose starting point and reasoned development has often since been forgotten. Like thermometers, we need only to know how to use such instruments, not necessarily how and why they work. These measuring instruments report "facts" about phenomena for us, but the phenomena they describe have been constructed on instruments fashioned long ago from the experiments and choices made by scientists in the past (see Chang 2001). There is no "right" set of rules for GNP construction, one that fits naturally to our economic world. Like a new glove, awkward at the start, a new measurement gradually becomes comfortable, though it may never fit tightly. We choose our accounting conventions, and only after the passage of time does a measured concept like the GNP conform to our other knowledge and come to seem "real." If we do our own taxes, we make the same transition: tax authorities' accounting conventions rarely fit each human experience—our experiences have to be made to fit their conventions. This same process happens with economic measurement at other scales and with instruments other than accounting. Economic measuring instruments are not devices given by God for us to reckon his own preordained economy; they are the inventions of economists and we fit ourselves to their measures. As Werner, one of Goethe's fictional characters, remarked of double entry bookkeeping, "It is among the finest inventions of the human mind; every prudent master of a house should introduce it into his economy." The character of Wilhelm replied, "You begin with the form, as if it were matter: you businessmen commonly forget, in your additions and balancings, what the proper total of life is."[5]

References

Bjerkholt, O. [1998] 2000. Interaction between Model Builders and Policy Makers in the Norwegian Tradition. In *Empirical Models and Policy-Making: Interaction and Institutions*, edited by F. A. G. den Butter and M. S. Morgan. London: Routledge.

Bogen James, and James Woodward. 1988. Saving the Phenomena. *Philosophical Review* 97.3:303–52.

Boumans, M. 1999. Representation and Stability in Testing and Measuring Rational Expectations. *Journal of Economic Methodology* 6:381–401.

Brain, Robert M., and M. Norton Wise. 1999. Muscles and Engines: Indicator Diagrams in Helmholtz's Physiology. In *The Science Studies Reader*, edited by M. Bagioli. New York: Routledge.

Chang, H. 1995. Circularity and Reliabilty in Measurement. *Perspectives on Science* 3.2:153–72.

———. 2001. Spirit, Air, and Quicksilver: The Search for the "Real" Scale of Temperature. *Historical Studies in the Physical and Biological Sciences* (forthcoming).

Franklin, A. 1986. *The Neglect of Experiment*. Cambridge: Cambridge University Press.

Heilbron, J. L. 1990. Introductory Essay. In *The Quantifying Spirit in the 18th Century*, edited by T. Frängsmyr, J. L. Heilbron, and R. E. Rider, 1–24. Berkeley: University of California Press.

Hendry, D. F., and M. S. Morgan. 1995. *The Foundations of Econometric Analysis*. Cambridge: Cambridge University Press.

Jackson, M. W. [1994] 1996. Natural and Artificial Budgets: Accounting for Goethe's Economy Of Nature." In *Accounting and Science: Natural Inquiry and Commercial Reason*, edited by M. Power, 57–81. Cambridge: Cambridge University Press.

Morgan, M. S. 1990. *The History of Econometric Ideas*. Cambridge: Cambridge University Press.

———. 1997. Searching for Causal Relations in Economic Statistics: Reflections from History. In *Causality in Crisis: The New Debate about Causal Structures*, edited by V. McKim and S. Turner. South Bend, Ind.: University of Notre Dame Press.

---

5. I owe this wonderfully apt interchange to Jackson ([1994] 1996). The source is Goethe's *Wilhelm Meisters Lehrjahre* of 1795.

————. 2002. Economics. In *Modern Social Sciences*, edited by T. H. Porter and D. Ross. Vol. 7 of *The Cambridge History of Science*. Cambridge: Cambridge University Press.

Porter, T. H. [1994] 1996. Making Things Qualitative. In *Accounting and Science: Natural Inquiry and Commercial Reason*, edited by M. Power, 36–56. New York: Cambridge University Press.

"Facts Carefully Marshalled" in the Empirical Studies of William Stanley Jevons

Sandra J. Peart

William Stanley Jevons earned his well-deserved status as a "pioneer of modern economics" (Black 1981, 1) because of his role as a measurer and because of his contributions to economic theory. In both areas he struggled against the weight of John Stuart Mill's authority (Peart 1995, 1996a). This essay commences with the contrast between the mid-nineteenth-century method of Mill, who resisted using measurement techniques in economics, and that of Jevons, who endorsed measurement both in principle and by example. Mill allotted a rather inconsequential role to measurement in social science, one that precluded reliance on statistical data to establish causal relations. Jevons, on the other hand, generally regarded phenomena as governed by one (and, less often, several) "constant" cause, interfered with by "disturbances" ([1874] 1909, 339), and he urged the researcher to negate the influence of these disturbing causes by using techniques such as the method of means. In his own measurement projects, he maintained that omitted causes might

Correspondence may be addressed to Sandra Peart, Department of Economics, Baldwin-Wallace College, 275 Eastland Road, Berea, OH 44017. I am grateful to Mary Morgan and Judy Klein for encouraging me to embark on this project, for providing detailed comments on the paper, and for arranging such a wonderful conference. Participants in the Age of Measurement conference forced me to think more clearly and greatly helped me organize my ideas. Samuel Hollander, Jeffrey Lipkes, Neil De Marchi, Harro Maas, and Laura Mattos have provided helpful comments on the methods of John Stuart Mill and William Stanley Jevons. I would also like to thank David Levy and participants in the Seminar at the Center for the Study of Public Choice, George Mason University, for helpful comments and discussion when a very early version of this research was presented there.

be treated as "balancing" in the drawing of a mean (340), so that, for instance, the general variation of prices might be attributed to a single cause, the gold influx ([1865] 1884, 120).

Early proponents of statistical analysis, as opposed to those who used statistics for mere description, faced a major problem: they did not possess statistical measures of causal association (namely, measures of correlation). Nor did they have formal models to show how multiple causes might link in complex ways. Instead they relied on the analysis of tables and the taking of various kinds of averages to identify genuine causal relationships in their nonexperimental data (McKim 1997, 4; Morgan 1997, 74; 1990, 4; Klein 1997, chaps. 4 and 5). Although Jevons was well aware of the complexity of social and economic phenomena, he downplayed this complexity when he measured economic phenomena and presumed the existence of simple causal frameworks. There was also, as we shall see, continuing resistance to the sort of formal modeling that would be adequate for complex causal relationships. In order to situate Jevons's measurements in the context of contemporary work, we shall consider contemporary reactions to his measurements.

It is helpful in what follows to consider Jevons's empirical work along a spectrum: At one end we find those studies for which the causal framework was accepted before Jevons set out to measure the relationship. At the other are those projects for which he offered a less well accepted or new causal mechanism and which he tried to support with measurements. In cases where Jevons relied on established economic (or geological, or physical) relationships, he set out to confirm or measure the strength of the relationship and was able to apply his method of "wide averages" with relative success. In the case of proposed causal mechanisms less familiar to his contemporaries, we find him struggling to "marshall" the facts in support of his explanation.[1]

Mill and Jevons on the Role of Measurement

Since Jevons's *Principles of Science* (1874) was largely directed at Mill's method as set out in Mill's *Logic* (1843), it seems appropriate to commence with some brief remarks on Mill. In the *Logic* as well as in the 1848 and subsequent editions of the *Principles of Political Economy*,

---

1. See note 23 below for the full quotation in which he used the phrase "wide averages." I am grateful to Judy Klein for reminding me of the importance of the phrase "facts carefully marshalled."

Mill was reluctant to endorse the possibility of deriving empirical laws in social science ([1843] 1973, 908–9; [1848] 1965, 142–52; Peart 1995). Instead, Mill urged the scientist to investigate the existence and influence of all causal factors in the study of specific outcomes and to evaluate the merits of the theoretical framework in terms of its ability to explain that outcome (Hollander and Peart 1999). Measurement was not a means of inferring either the existence of causal relationships or the size of effects attributable to specific causes (Peart 1993, 1995).

In his *Principles of Science*, Jevons ([1874] 1909, 750, 759–60) also acknowledged that multiple causation created difficulties for the precise determination of laws in social science (see also Jevons [1871] 1911, 19). And, like Mill, he recognized the immense difficulties involved with experimentation in economics (see Harro Maas's article in this volume). But for Jevons ([1874] 1909, 271), theory was inseparably linked to measurement, and as science progressed, both measurements and theory become increasingly accurate. Evidence of the importance ascribed to measurement in this process is the arrangement of the *Principles of Science* into five sections: "Formal Logic, Deductive and Inductive"; "Number, Variety, and Probability"; "Methods of Measurement"; "Inductive Investigation"; and "Generalisation, Analogy, and Classification."

For Jevons, measurement was in principle *the* means of approaching the problem of multiple causation that so vexed Mill. Unlike Mill, Jevons ([1874] 1909, 274) thought it possible to measure the effects of single causes: "As every phenomenon is usually the sum of several distinct quantities depending upon different causes, we have . . . to investigate . . . the methods by which we may disentangle complicated effects, and refer each part of the joint effect to its separate cause."[2] He shifted the focus away from a Millian emphasis on "disentangling" many *equally significant* causes to measuring the effect of *one "significant"* cause disturbed by *"interfering causes"*:[3] one "endeavours to obtain that effect free from interfering effects" (339). The key task for the measurer

2. Jevons ([1874] 1909, 501) often assumed additive effects in economics, where observed outcomes were said to be "aggregates of an immense number of separate results." Mill also presumed additivity. For Marshall's similar position, see Stone 1980, 722.

3. Elsewhere Jevons refers to these as "constant causes" and "noxious errors" or "disturbances." His sense seems to be similar to that of Mill: constant is used to signify a general relationship, while a disturbing cause operates intermittently (Peart 1993).

is now said to consist of rendering the effects of "interfering causes" as negligible as possible (339; cf. 334, 335).

Jevons outlined five methods for this task: (1) avoidance, (2) the differential method, (3) correction, (4) compensation, and (5) the method of reversal (339–40). The first of these involved avoiding error altogether through careful experimental design; the second, the differential method, entailed comparing outcomes when errors were present with those when errors were absent. Correction called for estimation of the effect of error; compensation involved neutralizing the interfering cause by "balancing" it against "an exactly equal and opposite cause." The method of reversal entailed setting up an experiment so that the error cause worked in opposite directions for different outcomes, with the result that errors balance each other, "the mean result being free from interference" (340).

Invoking the work of Adolphe Quetelet (on whom, see Klein 1997, 163–64), Jevons maintained that measurement errors or errors reflecting ignorance of the full set of causal influences were inevitable.[4] He paid tribute to the Law of Error—"one of the most remarkable achievements of the human intellect"—which ensured that in the absence of known significant causes, the mean result was the most probable (385), and he urged social scientists to measure the probable error associated with their results (374, 387; cf. Stigler 1986).

Jevons urged that these procedures, which he termed broadly "inductive quantification," be directed toward "the raw materials of knowledge"—"numerical facts"—in order to "draw forth the principles of nature" (483).[5] In some instances, the scientist might only establish causality, although the precise relationship remained undetermined. Such cases might involve data established introspectively, for which interpersonal comparisons were not yet possible, as in the case of diminishing marginal utility (487). In most cases, however, the quantification of a precise cause/effect relationship was straightforward: "Take the mean of all those in which the effect to be measured is present, and compare it with the mean of the remainder in which the effect is absent, or acts in the opposite direction" (554).

4. Cf. Jevons [1874] 1909, 376–77. Like Mill, Jevons's conception of uncertainty reflected his conviction that laws were deterministic. Uncertainty arose from ignorance (Peart 1993). There are, however, some "cracks" evident in such determinism—as Hacking (1983; see Morgan 1997, 69) has pointed to in a different context.

5. See Peart 1993. Morgan (1990, 3) maintains that "Jevons even hoped statistics could be used to obtain the numerically precise (or 'concrete') laws thought to be typical of good physical science."

The "empirical formulae" resulting from application of these techniques to data are "only approximations to the results of natural laws" to be distinguished from "the true laws of nature" (489). Jevons remained cautious about the entire endeavour: "Human life may be subject at different ages to a succession of different influences incapable of reduction under any one law. The results observed may in fact be aggregates of an immense number of separate results each governed by its own separate laws, so that the subjects may be complicated beyond the possibility of complete resolution by empirical methods" (501).[6] But since this type of exercise led the scientist closer to "true" laws of nature (465), Jevons repeatedly called for the collection of data and the use of measurements in economics. In his 1870 opening address to Section F (Economics and Statistics) as president of the British Association for the Advancement of Science (BAAS), he urged social scientists to analyze, arrange, and explain economic facts ([1870] 1965, 194–95; cf. [1871] 1911).

Jevons's Measurements in Practice

The Condition of Coinage

Jevons played a major role in the controversy surrounding the state of the British coinage that played out in the House of Commons, the national press, the statistical societies, and the periodicals in the late 1860s.[7] In his view, this "practical, if not technical, subject" was related to the contemporary issue of an international coinage, something he advocated.[8] Along with the "cordial co-operation of many bankers and other gentlemen," he conducted a partial census of the coinage in order to measure the proportion of light coins in the United Kingdom (Foxwell 1884, xxxvi). The controversy that ensued arose in part due to the speech by the chancellor of the exchequer, Robert Lowe, in the House of Commons on 6 August 1869, which cited Jevons's measurement. Lowe then argued in favor of a 1 percent seignorage to meet recoining costs and urged that the gold

6. Aggregation is a key feature of Jevons's measurements (see the following section). I am grateful to Kevin Hoover for reminding me of this.

7. My aim here, in part, is to convey a sense of the breadth and variety of Jevons's empirical research. I neglect a number of important studies, including Jevons's early studies of periodicity (see Klein 1997) and muscular exertion (see White 1994).

8. Jevons recommended that a charge be imposed on banks to defray the costs of restoring the coin to its proper value. Such a charge, he argued, could be set at the internationally accepted rate (1972–81, 7:70–75).

content of coins be reduced so as to assimilate British coins into an international system. Jevons, J. B. Smith, Colonel J. T. Smith, Leone Levi, and Frederick Hendricks shared Lowe's views. They were opposed by J. G. Hubbard (later, Lord Addington), Thomson Hankey, Ernest Seyd, Sir John Herschel, and Lord Overstone (see Jevons 1972–81, 3:211).

Jevons's measurement relied upon an uncontroversial proposition that currency wear was proportional to use (proxied by age) (Jevons [1868] 1884, 258).[9] It remained to measure wear and tear on British currency and subsequently what proportion of the coinage was legally underweight. In 1867 Jevons asked bankers throughout the United Kingdom to record the date of issue for gold coins in a sample of one or two hundred sovereigns ([1868] 1884, 262–63). Response to his request came from 321 bankers from 213 localities, resulting in the enumeration of 90,474 sovereigns and 75,036 half-sovereigns, a sample that Jevons estimated contained at least one out of every 600 U.K. coins (263). Having examined the distribution of sovereign age in various parts of the United Kingdom, and using an estimate for the total number of sovereigns in existence, Jevons calculated the proportion of sovereigns minted in various years (274).

To estimate the average rate of wear, Jevons drew his own sample of 434 sovereigns and 178 half-sovereigns from the circulation at Manchester, each of which he cleaned and weighed (282).[10] He then calculated the average weight of sovereigns (122.71 grains) and the average date of issue (July 1854). Since the weight at issue was 123.26 grains, it yielded an average deficiency equal to 0.55 grains, in an average of 12.9 years; average wear per year was then 0.043 grains per year (284). At this rate coins would, on average, fall below the legal weight (122.5 grains) in about eighteen years (285).[11] Finally, Jevons estimated the proportion of sovereigns below the legal weight—that is, issued before 1850—at 31.5 percent (286).

9. The substance of the paper was read to the Manchester Statistical Society on 13 May 1868; the entire paper was read to the Statistical Society of London (later the Royal Statistical Society) on 17 November 1868. It was published by the Statistical Society of London in December 1868.

10. Here is an instance in which Jevons's detailed knowledge of the balance, obtained at the Mechanics Institute, was of great practical relevance. On the general significance of the balance in Jevons's thought, see Harro Maas's article in this volume.

11. The estimation did not require the use of least squares techniques since Jevons was interested in a single parameter, the rate of wear. But a least squares estimate would have been more precise (Kim 1995).

Jevons insisted that his conclusion pertained to the average and that exceptions to the eighteen-year prediction would occur due to "accidental circumstances" (285). While the age of any one coin might be a poor indicator of its weight, "the age of 1,000,000 or 1000, or even 100 coins drawn from the ordinary mixture in circulation, must be a very sure criterion" (285).[12]

Contemporary reactions to the work on coinage reveal that this study was perceived as particularly convincing and that Jevons's reasoning based on averages was rarely questioned. What was controversial, however, was Jevons's (and then Lowe's) policy recommendation that followed the measurement. Most commentators acknowledged the existence of a serious coinage problem and allowed the need for some remedy.[13] Whether that remedy should be a mint charge or not generated the substance of the ensuing debate. Those who favored the charge used Jevons's measurements as support for the policy, holding up the incontrovertible nature of his "facts" and the care with which the coinage experiments were conducted.

On the Value of Gold

The discovery of gold in Australia and the United States during the late 1840s and early 1850s generated an ongoing debate about the effects of the influx of gold on prices in the United Kingdom. The political economist Henry Fawcett raised the issue to national prominence in 1862 when he addressed the Newcastle meeting of Section F of the British Association for the Advancement of Science (BAAS). Arguments ensued in the *Times* and the *Economist* as to whether the effects predicted by what we now call the quantity theory had, indeed, materialized. Tied up in the controversy was a distributional concern: Cliffe Leslie, who, as we shall see, objected to Jevons's method in this context, feared that

12. Jevons used similar reasoning in the gold studies; see the section on the value of gold, below. Even in a sample of one hundred coins, "it is in the highest degree unlikely" that "accidental peculiarities of the history of any of those coins should influence appreciably the general average" ([1868] 1884, 285). Understandably (since sampling theory was not worked out until a generation later) Jevons did not elaborate on this statement. His failure to do so might be read as an assertion regarding sample size. In various instances he suggested that confidence in the measurement increases as the sample size increases.

13. See, for example, The "Untitled Article," 1869a, 502; Smith 1869. For an exceptional attempt to criticize Jevons's measurement, see Hubbard 1869. A debate ensued on the nature of the calculations ("Untitled Article" 1869b).

the effects of the gold influx would be unevenly distributed. Jevons entered the debate with an attempt to avoid "guess-work" and "groundless" argumentation through "facts carefully marshalled" (Foxwell 1884, xxiv–xxv). As Klein (1997, 103, 133–36) has noted, he relied here on the mercantile tool of arraying cross sections of data in relative time. *A Serious Fall in the Value of Gold Ascertained, and Its Social Effects Set Forth* (hereinafter *ASF*), published in 1863, constitutes a striking example of Jevons's use of this technique. Following its publication, political economists engaged in a debate about the method and assumptions underlying his analysis.

Kevin Hoover and Michael Dowell (this volume) correctly argue that the gold studies are steeped in a causal framework, the quantity theory of money. Jevons ([1863] 1884, 25) argued in *ASF* that the "value" of gold—its long-run, or "permanent" purchasing power—was determined by its cost of production. He attempted to measure the size of the depreciation and then offered this measured change as "proof" of the influence of the gold influx (21).[14]

Simple-minded observation was uninformative in the face of multiple causes, since for any one good a price change could be generated on the side of goods or gold (18–19). In addition, both gold and goods might be influenced by "temporary" as well as "permanent" forces. Temporary forces affected prices "due to varying demand, and dependent on the manias for permanent investment, and the inflations of credit," as well as the "natural variations of supply" (35). Permanent price alterations occurred because gold had become "more abundant and easily obtained" or "more scarce and troublesome to procure" (18; cf. [1865] 1884, 128; [1905] 1965, 149).

The measurement followed William Newmarch[15] by first attempting to eliminate cyclical influences on prices that were seen to leave the

14. Aldrich (1987, 240–41) is critical of *ASF* for failing to integrate the measurement and causation arguments. But for Jevons, the very measurement of the depreciation, coupled with the assumption that real influences on prices balance in the drawing of the mean, constitutes proof of the causal framework.

15. Newmarch (1820–1882) was a leading authority on historical statistics and price movements. He was secretary of the Globe Insurance Company, a prominent member of both the Statistical Society of London and the Political Economy Club, and president of Section F of the BAAS in 1861. He collaborated with Thomas Tooke on the *History of Prices from 1792 to the Present Time*, the last volume of which was published in 1857 and which expressed doubt as to whether the new gold had caused prices to appreciate. Newmarch published a series of papers on this in 1859, 1860, and 1861, which Black (Jevons 1972–81, 1:181n. 2) argues inspired Jevons's work.

permanent value of goods undisturbed (35). Using the rate of interest as an indicator of the cycle, Jevons selected 1844–50 as a trough to peak and drew the arithmetic mean price of each of thirty-nine goods in twelve product groups for these years, yielding, he argued, "the true or natural average according to the undisturbed value of gold" (43).[16]

Jevons then calculated the ratio of the post–gold discovery (i.e., after 1851), yearly price of each good to this six-year average. Having thus attempted to eliminate cyclical influences from his data, he argued that the ratios represented "the rise of prices above their former ordinary level," still, however, affected by "any temporary fluctuations" (43). To eliminate these, he grouped similar goods into categories (metals, cottons, and dyes, for instance) and found the geometric mean of price changes within groups ([1865] 1884, 126–27).[17] The average of these ratios was then found to reveal a 13 percent permanent rise in prices or, equivalently, depreciation of gold ([1863] 1884, 59).[18]

To reinforce the causal analysis, Jevons relied on two arguments. First, he maintained from the outset that it was eminently more reasonable that the values of all goods had changed for one (common) reason—a change in the value of gold—than it was to propose that values of *goods* had altered for disconnected reasons. This was especially true because the circumstances of gold production had recently altered ([1863] 1884, 22, 59; [1869] 1884, 157).[19] Second, in "The Variation of Prices," a paper

16. Because data were unavailable for 1844, Jevons used an average for 1845–50. In his essay "On the Study of Periodic Commercial Fluctuations," Jevons ([1862] 1884, 3) also acknowledged that the "revolution of the seasons" affected industry and commerce (cf. 6; see also [1866] 1884, 165–72; Klein 1997, 109–10).

17. Jevons ([1863] 1884, 23) insisted that the geometric mean constituted the correct method of averaging when the quantities of interest were ratios. Stigler (1982) notes that among the reasons Jevons provided for the geometric mean was the sound one that prices might be disturbed multiplicatively. On the importance of the balance in Jevons's choice of mean, see Maas this volume.

18. Recognizing that some of his goods were still susceptible to temporary supply fluctuations, Jevons ([1863] 1884, 54) constructed a second measure of price changes for 118 commodities. Mitchell (1928, 195) argues that Jevons "tested his result" with the larger sample (cf. Fisher, 1922, 459, 468). Since agricultural outputs were highly correlated, Jevons ([1863] 1884, 50) attempted to choose items "mostly distinct" from those in his smaller sample and "likely to vary independently of them and of each other." Aside from a suggestion that otherwise similar goods be produced in different geographical locations, he never elaborated on the criteria used to ensure this approximate independence.

19. Cf. [1869] 1884, 157: "The chances are 10,000 to 1 against a series of disconnected and casual circumstances having caused the rise of price . . . instead of the same general cause acting over them all."

read to the Statistical Society of London in May 1865 and published by the Society's *Journal* in June of that year, Jevons ([1865] 1884, 119) emphasized that the measured rise of prices *followed* the influx of gold, arguing that he had ascertained an "*unusual change* in the course of prices" following an "*unusual change* in the supply of gold." In his 1869 letter to the *Economist*, Jevons ([1869] 1884, 156) maintained that as long as the study were inclusive enough, with an almost "infinite" probability "a rise in one case will balance a fall in another" and that "the average then must in all reasonable probability represent some single influence acting on all the commodities."[20] He then calculated an average price rise of 16 percent, found the probable error of his result using ordinary least squares,[21] and constructed a confidence interval for the mean price increase (157).

Reactions to Jevons's work on the value of gold again reveal that his contemporaries for the most part accepted the causal (quantity theory) framework. Reviews split along two lines—those who accepted that changes in average prices could be used to measure the effect of gold and those who maintained that such a measurement was a chimerical exercise. In the latter case the method of means comes in for severe criticism.

The most detailed criticism emerged from the Irish proponent of the historical method, T. E. Cliffe Leslie.[22] Leslie (1879, 349) maintained that the new gold was only one of several causes affecting prices: "The method of averages fails in several ways. . . . By ascribing the whole rise of prices to the new gold, this method conceals the material fact that the gold is only one of a plurality of causes lately tending to raise them." He questioned Jevons's assumption that "the 'average must, in all reasonable probability, represent some single influence acting on all commodities'" (353). His own investigation focused on a "plurality of causes" and how

---

20. Jevons was struggling here with some of the most difficult measurement issues possible. For an examination of modern treatments, see the essays by Spencer Banzhaf and Marcel Boumans in this volume.

21. To my knowledge, this is the only instance in which Jevons used least squares methods. Stigler (1982, 362) has remarked on the "anomaly" that Jevons used least squares so rarely, given the accolades to the method in his *Principles of Science*.

22. Leslie (1825–1882) was Professor of Political Economy and Jurisprudence at Queen's College, Belfast. His relationships with Mill and Jevons were complex. Leslie was sympathetic to some of Jevons's work; in part because of Jevons's calls for the increased use and analysis of data, Leslie counts Jevons among those who favored the historical school (Peart 2001).

their influence differed across different goods (355).[23] In a paper that nevertheless argued strongly in favor of uniting economic science and statistics, Leslie presented a general criticism of the assumption that the average price change could be attributed to the gold influx:

> And we have in this matter an illustration of the defective character of that kind of statistical inquiry which confines itself to the collection of a multitude of instances of facts, without reference to causes. It must be allowed that the principles laid down by the illustrious Quetelet rather tend to foster the error to which we advert. He assumed that by enlarging the number of instances, we eliminate chance and arrive at general and stable laws or conditions. But a great number of instances does not give us their law, or justify us in any positive conclusion respecting the future. New conditions, for example, have been acting on prices during the last two years, and mere tables of prices for the last twenty or ten years, confound years in which those causes were in operation with years in which they were not. (382–83)

Even those who praised the gold studies took issue with Jevons's neglect of causes other than gold. J. E. Cairnes (1863a) praised *A Serious Fall*, finding "strong corroboration" in the different methods ("economic, as distinguished from statistical grounds") by which he and Jevons arrived at the conclusion of a depreciation. He did, however, object to Jevons's consideration of the depreciation "*without reference to the cause of the alteration*" (italics in original) and to the conclusion that the measured price change reflected the full effect of the new gold. He countered that the effect of the new gold was larger (and thus that the true depreciation was larger) than the measured alteration in prices, since significant and unmeasured causes (such as ongoing technological change) had served to counteract the effects of the gold discoveries.[24]

---

23. Jevons ([1863] 1884, 58) countered that "a searching inquiry into the conditions of supply and demand of every article would result in every one being thrown out as unworthy of reliance as a measure of the value of gold. It is only by ignoring all these individual circumstances, and trusting that in a wide average, such as that of 118 articles, all individual discrepancies will be neutralised, that we can arrive at any conclusion in this difficult question."

24. See the 1863 correspondence: Cairnes to Jevons, 28 May (Jevons 1972–81, 3:16–18); Jevons to Cairnes, 2 June (3:19–22); Jevons to Cairnes, 3 June (3:22–23); and Cairnes to Jevons, 4 June (3:23–25). In a 1 October letter to the *Times*, Cairnes (1863b) argued that the depreciation "may show itself partly in a rise of prices, partly in the absences of the natural fall in price where the cost of production has been cheapened." The *Economist* supported Cairnes ("Amount and Condition of the Gold Coinage" [1868]). Jevons saw Cairnes's argument as serving further to confirm his own (1972–81, 3:22).

Like Leslie, Cairnes (1863b) also focused on the "extraneous" causes—the "seasons, politics, the fashions"—that disguised the effects of gold.

Further objections were raised in this controversy on the grounds that Jevons failed to weight the goods in his sample. John Crawfurd (1863) argued Jevons failed to take account of goods of "smaller value," such as wine, and goods of greater significance, such as sugar and "ardent spirits."

On Coal

What Jevons called "the Coal Question" received widespread attention in the 1860s. In 1863 the engineer and entrepreneur Sir William Armstrong gave the presidential address to the BAAS, focusing on Britain's coal supplies. Armstrong shifted attention from the argument of the geologist Edward Hull that coal supplies were limited to the notion of increasing extraction costs as they relate to depth (White 1991). Theodore Porter (1986 and this volume) has argued that a growing interest in "Empire building" underscores measurement attempts at this time; the widely appealing link to national greatness was made in the context of the coal question sometime early in the 1860s. Given Jevons's disappointment in the reception of his work on gold (*ASF* was published at his own expense, at a cost of £43), he may have been trying to make his name with a work of broad interest (White 1991). *The Coal Question* (*TCQ*) undoubtedly secured his reputation as an applied economist. The prime minister, W. E. Gladstone, was particularly taken with the argument. John Stuart Mill, the most influential economist at the time, spoke on the work in the House of Commons.[25] Both the popular press and the periodicals published reactions to the work throughout the late 1860s.

Jevons's *Coal Question* provides a rare instance in which he set out to "measure" an economic law, the "Law of Social Growth." Although his name for this law sounds grandiose, it aptly reflects his sense that the fate of British manufacturing supremacy rested on his measurement. His procedure consisted of appropriating a key measurement from Hull and then forming an estimate of annual coal consumption. Again attempting

---

25. "It appears to me . . . that Mr. Jevons' treatment of the subject is almost exhaustive. . . . " (*Hansard* 3s, 182:1525). Jevons was also pleased that Sir John Herschel found the work convincing. Peart (1996a, 21–23, 38–39) discusses Jevons's early disappointment and the responses to *TCQ*.

to take account of the cycle, Jevons corrected for fluctuations in his estimate of the annual growth rate of coal consumption. Using data from the Mining Record Office for the years 1854 through 1863, he observed cyclical maxima in 1854 and 1861 and found the average annual rate of increase over the interval to be 3.7 percent. Using 3.5 percent as a "cautious" estimate and presuming this rate would remain unchecked, he then estimated total consumption would be 102,704 million tons over the next 110 years, 1861–1970. Allowing for the possibility that 1861 was a maximum, Jevons settled on an approximation of 100,000 million tons.[26] Comparing this to Hull's estimate of 83,000 million tons of remaining coal in Britain within a depth of 4,000 feet, Jevons ([1865] 1906, 274) predicted that a century at an annual growth rate of 3.5 percent would deplete the mines to a 4,000 ft. depth and that the price of fuel must rise "to a rate injurious to our commercial and manufacturing supremacy." Since, consequently, Britain's economic standing in the world would deteriorate, he argued that the appropriate policy response was to reduce the national debt.

As noted above, *The Coal Question* created something of a splash. A royal commission was formed. A debate ensued in Parliament and in the popular press. That debate split between the majority view, which accepted Jevons's reasoning and measurement and turned to his policy recommendation, and a few respondents who disputed that Jevons had in fact measured the "true" law of social growth.

Once again many of the responses focused on the policy context of *TCQ* as opposed to Jevons's measurement itself. A *Manchester Examiner* article ("Our Coal Supply and the National Debt" 1866) accepted both the argument that coal supplies would eventually be obtained at increasing cost as well as Jevons's predictions and the recommendation that as a consequence the nation should pay off its debt. The *Times* covered the issue in articles appearing on 4 and 5 May and in a 7 May 1866 editorial. These focused entirely on reducing the national debt, a policy endorsed by the *Times*. The link to British supremacy was also a common theme in these responses.

When criticisms of the work were raised, Jevons's contemporaries argued that he had underestimated Britain's greatness, that the 4,000 foot depth underestimated stores of workable coal in the nation, or that the

---

26. However, Jevons clearly underestimated the increasing importance of substitute energy supplies, so that, according to Black (1981, 16), actual coal consumption in 1961 was 192 million tons.

technological change which drove the recent growth of coal consumption had been extraordinary. Vivian Hussey, who moved in a 12 June 1866 parliamentary speech to form the Royal Commission to inquire into the state of the British coalfields, strongly opposed Hull's 4,000 foot estimate on the grounds that it neglected some 24 billion tons of workable coal in South Wales alone (*Hansard* 3s, 182:243). Hussey called for geological surveys to measure the amount of coal in existence (274–75). He also contended that Jevons's projections, based on data from the 1850s—a period of extraordinary railway growth—were unreliable: "We find ourselves involved in this absurdity that, according to the theory of geometric progression, we must, year by year, go on making, not alone the number of miles of railway that we have heretofore made, but as many more miles of railway as geometrical progression imposes upon us. . . . The whole question of the consumption of coal or anything else, or the rolling up of money by geometrical progression, must break down, and always does, when it comes to be tested by plain common sense" (267).[27]

Cyclical Fluctuations

Throughout the latter half of the nineteenth century there is evidence, especially in the research presented at the statistical societies, of a growing recognition of the cyclical nature of economic activity.[28] Research focused initially on dating economics cycles and the apparently decennial nature of fluctuations. In 1857 a Manchester banker, founder and later a president of the Manchester Statistical Society, William Langton, presented a paper to the society in which he argued that fluctuations were linked to "moral causes" and occurred with a periodicity of ten years (Peart 1996b, 139; see also Judy Klein's article in this volume). Another Manchester banker and later president of the Manchester Statistical Society, John Mills, relied on both arguments in 1866 and 1867 when he presented papers to the National Social Science Association and

---

27. An unsigned letter to the *Times* of 11 May 1866 reiterated each of Hussey's arguments against the coal question. The juxtaposition of "common sense" with "expert knowledge" is a common theme in the press on several of these issues. See the reference to the "black figures" in the section on mortality rates below.

28. My account agrees in substance with that by Morgan (1990). I include the sunspot research to emphasize the breadth of Jevons's interests as well as the links between Jevons, the bankers, and the meteorologists.

the Manchester Statistical Society. Jevons entered the debates by insisting that the fluctuations in what Mills called "commercial moods" were in turn triggered by variations in meteorological conditions—sunspots affecting harvest conditions in the United Kingdom and elsewhere.

In his attempts to establish a causal relationship between economic phenomena and sunspots, Jevons ([1878] 1884a, 228) announced himself "thoroughly biased in favour of a theory." The research took as its starting point work by J. A. Broun, Norman Lockyer, W. W. Hunter, and others and reveals the connections between Jevons and yet another group of measurers: the meteorologists.[29] It also reveals a tendency to think in terms of regularities in single variables as opposed to modeling or measuring the interactions among complex combinations of causes.

The underlying argument, outlined in "The Solar Period and the Price of Corn" ([1875] 1884) as well as in the *Principles of Science* and "The Solar Influence on Commerce" (1878, unpublished until 1981 in Jevons 1972–81, 3:90–98), was the "well-known principle of mechanics that the effects of a periodically varying cause are themselves periodic, and usually go through their phases in periods of time equal to those of the cause" ([1875] 1884, 194). Unlike the currency wear and gold studies, disturbing causes were now presumed to be largely absent instead of balancing. When he did find interfering causes, Jevons relied on the method of correction, arguing, for instance, that special circumstances might precipitate an early fluctuation.

Jevons faced a number of serious difficulties (Morgan 1990). The explanation for fluctuations involved vaguely defined variables (most notably, commercial "moods") for which data were simply unavailable. Neither the length of the sunspot cycle nor the record of economic fluctuations was well established; he was often forced to piece together evidence on fluctuations from various sources. Despite his attempts to ensure otherwise, interfering causes, to which he did not have access, affected the series.

Jevons's first attempt to find empirical support for his sunspot theory used James E. Thorold Rogers's data for the years 1259–1400 on

29. J. A. Broun (1817–1879), pioneer of meteorology, directed the Sir J. M. Brisbane magnetic observatory at Makestown, Dumfriesshire, from 1842 to 1849, and the observatory at Trivandrum from 1852 to 1865. Sir Joseph Norman Lockyer (1836–1900) was lecturer in astronomy at South Kensington in 1870 and professor of physics and director of the Solar Physics Laboratory, Royal College of Science. He became the founding editor of *Nature* in 1869. Sir William Wilson Hunter (1840–1900) was named director general of the Statistical Department of India in 1871.

wheat, barley, oats, beans, peas, vetches, and rye—data that appeared to be mostly free from the influence of major interfering causes. Using a technique borrowed from the physicists known as a Buys-Ballot table (Aldrich 1987), Jevons ([1875] 1884, 197) arrayed the price data on an eleven-year grid and then compared average prices for each of the eleven years of the sunspot cycle. Having calculated the mean price for each crop throughout the eleven-year period, he observed that "in every case" the maximum average price occurred in the third or fourth year, a result which, he argued, "is hardly conceivable" to be "accidental" (199). The correspondence reveals a considerable difficulty: "The same data would give other periods of variation equally well. The method of averages adopted seems delusive. . . . " (Jevons 1972–81, 4:188–89).[30]

Jevons continued working on commercial crises and sunspots, writing in 1877 that he was "more convinced than ever that there is some connection but it is a treacherous subject, and requires much care" (1972–81, 4:199). In August 1878, he presented "On the Periodicity of Commercial Crises and Its Physical Explanation" to the BAAS, in which he abandoned the attempt to correlate prices with stages of the cycle and attempted instead to establish that the length of the cycle corresponded to the length of the sunspot cycle, newly estimated by Broun at 10.45 years ([1878] 1884b, 215).

In an 1878 *Nature* article, "Commercial Crises and Sun-Spots," Jevons ([1878] 1884a, 230–31) established the following series containing several crises of a tentative nature, noted in parentheses: (1701?), 1711, 1721, 1731–32, (1742? 1752?), 1763, 1772–73, 1783, 1793, (1804–5?), 1815, 1825, 1836–39, (1837 in the United States), 1847, 1857, 1866, 1878. The elimination of tentative crisis years would have lowered his estimated cycle from 10.466 to 10.3 years (231).[31] In the second part of "Commercial Crises and Sun-Spots," published in an 1879 contribution to *Nature*, Jevons ([1879] 1884, 235–43; cf. 1972–81, 5:36) succeeded in finding support for his reasoning that the cycle was transmitted to England via famines in India.

---

30. Jevons evidently tried other periodicities as well: "Subsequent inquiry convinced me that my figures would not support the conclusion I derived from them, and I withdrew the paper from publication" ([1878] 1884b, 207). On the Buys-Ballot method, see Klein 1997.

31. Jevons first discarded, and then retained, weakly established crisis years and has been criticized for this both in his own time (Proctor 1880; "Sunspots and Commercial Panics" 1879) and since (Mitchell 1928, 384).

Among Jevons's contemporaries, his basic method—trying to measure "root causes" while acknowledging the existence of "accidental causes"—received wide support. Elijah Helm (1873, 26),[32] for instance, argued in a paper read to the Manchester Statistical Society in 1873 that Mills and Jevons had "laid bare the causes which lie at the root of all these disturbances, and it becomes possible to separate the accidental and peculiar features of all particular crises from those which are common to all."

What was widely criticized, however, and not surprisingly, given that the evidence of the connection between sunspots and economic activity was tenuous at best, was Jevons's choice of "root cause": sunspots. A 14 January 1879 article in the *Times*, "Sunspots and Commercial Panics," found the "most singular" argument to be wanting—and set out to discredit the inference using his own evidence of crises. In opposition to Jevons, the *Times* maintained that a "single decidedly unfavourable case (as 1804, 1815, 1837) does more to disprove such a theory than 20 favourable cases would do towards establishing it". The *Economist* similarly framed its 11 January 1879 discussion of Jevons's *Nature* article in terms of the causal inference ("The Periodicity of Panics" [1879], 32–33). Accepting the coincidence of the periods as established by Jevons, the *Economist* maintained that sunspots and crises need not be connected as cause and effect and offered an alternative explanation in the British banking system. Two difficulties with Jevons's inference are presented. First, the explanation lacked generality, since America, too, was subject to crises. In addition, Jevons's explanation for the connection—relying as it did on supposedly cyclical alterations in trade with India—is said to be lacking on the grounds that cyclical fluctuations occurred long before trade with the region became significant (33).

Mortality Rates

Jevons's final subject for empirical study reflects a long-standing interest in poverty that characterized his very early work (on slums in Sydney) and that continued through some of his last work, including the 1882 *State in Relation to Labour*. Not surprisingly, in the light of ongoing debates throughout the century on the Poor Law, the Irish question, and the

---

32. Elijah Helm (1837–1904), expert on the cotton trade, became president of the Manchester Statistical Society in 1879.

Factory Acts, this was a theme that resonated with his contemporaries. In his research on mortality rates, Jevons self-consciously attempted to support a hypothesis with empirical evidence. The work was influenced by the biometricians, and, not coincidentally, the hypothesis was very much in opposition to Mill's postulate of human homogeneity outlined in the *Principles* (Mill [1848] 1965, 319).[33] Jevons attributed what he regarded as unusual variation in death rates—in particular the very high rate in Liverpool—to racial variations in the makeup of city inhabitants. He was convinced that the proportion of Irish inhabitants was positively related to mortality rates—due to excessive drunkenness on the part of the Irish (see "Inaugural Address as President of the Manchester Statistical Society," read 10 November 1869; [1870] 1965, 194–216; and Jevons Archive 6/33/4).

Jevons's mortality rate argument was strenuously resisted in work read before the Manchester Statistical Society in 1871. Another prominent banker, Thomas Read Wilkinson,[34] presented a paper in which he used data to refute Jevons's claim and to support a counterclaim that poverty, and not race, explained mortality rates. E. J. Syson presented a paper in the same session (11 January 1871) in which he argued that sanitation (drainage) and crowding were important determinants of mortality rates.

Jevons was ultimately unsuccessful in his attempt to directly collect data on rates of drunkenness by race or nationality (see Jevons Archive 6/33/4). Later in his career, his work in this area turned instead to the issue of married women working in factories. In his 1882 *Contemporary Review* article, "Married Women in Factories," his data now consisted of infant mortality rates for various urban centers ([1882] 1883). Considering Portsmouth to be representative of the "standard" town for infant mortality rates (159), Jevons estimated infant deaths in "excess" of Portsmouth at 24,000 per year and attributed this excess to women working in factories. The argument was not entirely novel, and Jevons relied on the Report of the Select Committee on the Protection of Infant Life in making it. This report maintained that excessive infant mortality among children "put out to nurse for hire" for more than twenty-four

33. This work by Jevons constitutes one example of the many ways that Mill's postulate of human homogeneity is undermined late in the century (Peart and Levy 2000). On the significance of race in Jevons's work, see White 1994.

34. Wilkinson (1826–1903) succeeded William Langton as managing director of the Manchester and Salford Bank in 1876 and was president of the Manchester Statistical Society from 1875 to 1877.

hours at a time may be attributed to "hand" as opposed to breast feeding. Jevons (162–63) took this reasoning a step further, suggesting that it also applied to children left for shorter, recurrent periods of time, as when a woman works in a factory. To strengthen the causal argument, he also relied on an "experiment" that allowed a "true and complete induction" as to the cause of excessive infant mortality (women's work). Observations of agricultural areas where women also increasingly worked implied that "the excessive mortality of Salford or Nottingham, we see, is not due alone to the bad sanitary condition of the courts and streets, for like infant mortality makes its appearance in the most rural parts. We have, in fact, *a true and complete induction, pointing to the employment of women away from their homes as the efficient cause of their children's decadence*" (164).[35]

Jevons concluded that women with small children should be prohibited from working in factories, and this policy argument (rather than the statistical work) generated most of the lively response that followed in the *Manchester Guardian*. Members of the Manchester and Salford Sanitary Association were leading figures in the debates. That infant mortality and pauperism were serious problems in Manchester and elsewhere was taken for granted. The discussions contained few attempts to measure the causes of infant mortality, consisting instead of claims that other—unmeasured—causes were also or instead responsible for high rates of infant deaths. A 14 January 1882 letter by the chairman of the Sanitary Association, Arthur Ransome, questioned the practical skill of the inspectors who supplied Jevons's "columns of black figures" and argued that Jevons's data were inconclusive in demonstrating that factory work caused excessive infant mortality. Another letter (18 January 1882, by F. H. A. Wright) took up Jevons's argument on improvident marriages and argued that early marriage should be discouraged. Many correspondents maintained that ignorance (of basic principles of hygiene, of the benefits associated with breast-feeding, and of the dangers associated with laudanum) was the primary cause of excessive deaths and advocated education to reduce infant mortality rates (Darbyshire 1882).

---

35. Jevons ([1882] 1883, 165–170) also offered anecdotal evidence in support of the women's work/infant mortality hypothesis, including remarks on "Godfrey," a substance made from opium, treacle, and sassafras, and a report on women working in Birmingham, where a "man" is said to have observed that infant mortality rates for women working in a factory were ten out of every twelve births (166).

Conclusion

To some extent Jevons's calls for the use of data and his measurement attempts reflected an ongoing and important controversy among social scientists, anthropologists, and biometricians at the time (Peart and Levy 2000). In 1876 Sir Francis Galton moved to have Section F removed from the British Association for the Advancement of Science (and placed with the Social Science Congress instead) because the members of the Section were "unscientific"—overly engaged in anecdotal argumentation and unwilling to analyze data for statistical regularities.[36] Jevons was active in the defense of Section F, and his response consisted largely of agreeing with Galton and then promoting the use of statistics in social science by example.

The dispute about the place of economics within the British Association as well as Jevons's support for Galton emphasize two additional and decidedly late-nineteenth-century features of Jevons's measurements. First, Jevons possessed an incredible ability to conduct research in many areas (Black 1981), and because of this he was able to bring measurement techniques that, earlier on, occurred mainly outside the economics profession (Peart 1999), into the economics discipline. In addition to the biometricians whose influence figured into Jevons's work on mortality rates (see previous section), we have seen the significance of the work of bankers and meteorologists, among others, for his research. Second, these developments provide evidence of the growing importance of the statistical and scientific societies late in the century (see Henderson 1996).

Perhaps the most striking commonality of Jevons's measurements is the close link that exists in all cases between his statistical work and policy recommendations. His preoccupation with the lot of the laboring poor was a motivating force for much of his work (Peart 1996a); this interest underscores his concern with economic growth (the section on coal, above), and infant mortality (discussed in the previous section). That such a concern motivated the use of measurement was not unusual at the time: William Farr, Charles Booth, and Florence Nightingale conducted even more detailed attempts to assess the well-being of

36. Galton (1877, 471) concluded that "few of the subjects treated of [in Section F from 1873–75] fall within the meaning of the word 'scientific.'" Jevons's 1875 paper on sunspots is said to be an exception. The Social Science Congress was regarded as the unscientific, policy oriented, organization (Henderson 1994). On Galton's pioneering biometric work, see Porter 1986; on Galton as cofounder of eugenics, see Peart and Levy 2000.

the laboring poor (see Stone 1997). Bradley Bateman (this volume) provides another instance of the importance of such motivations for ongoing attempts at measurement in America early in the twentieth century. More generally, the previous sections have demonstrated that Jevons's measurements were linked to policy analysis and recommendations, and that it was very often the policy recommendations—as opposed to the measurement itself—that informed contemporary reactions to his work.

In many ways Jevons was surprisingly modern; in our search for precursors and the legitimacy that precursors may bring to contemporary practitioners (Whitaker 2001), we may be predisposed to see modern conceptions of probability and hypothesis tests in his work. I think this is precisely wrong. While Jevons clearly moved a step away from Mill on the role of measurement in economics and in the hard work of attempting to measure economic phenomena, the foregoing reveals that he remained steeped in prestatistical thinking. Despite his calls for increased and improved use of measurement in economics and the increasing use of data and measurements by his contemporaries, Jevons was unwilling or unable fully to overthrow mid-nineteenth-century causal analysis.

But this is hardly surprising. And certainly Jevons conducted careful and extensive empirical studies on a wide array of topics. In fact, that variety—along with the strong case he made in the *Principles of Science* in favor of measurement—constitutes a major contribution.

In short, the examples above reveal that Jevons attempted in myriad economic settings to put into practice his recommendations for measurement outlined in the *Principles of Science*. In so doing, he was not content to rely on data for illustrative purposes only, but attempted instead to use data to infer causation and to establish relations empirically. While there were certainly other social scientists, noted above, who were attempting similar measurements, Jevons did so in an unusually wide variety of settings. He found creative ways to use these techniques, and he defended their use. He was also successful in using measurements to bring issues of policy to the attention of the policymakers and the public. Because he framed his measurements in the broader context of policy formation, Jevons's career constitutes a striking example not only of how to measure, then, but also and perhaps more importantly of how measurements might prove to be a powerful rhetorical device.

References

Aldrich, John. 1987. Jevons as Statistician: The Role of Probability. *Manchester School* 40.3:233–53.

Amount and Condition of the Gold Coinage. 1868. *Economist*, 12 December, 1412–14.

Black, R. D. C. 1981. William Stanley Jevons 1835–82. In *Pioneers of Modern Economics*, edited by D. P. O'Brien and John R. Presley, 1–35. London: Macmillan.

Cairnes, J. E. C. 1863a.. Have the Discoveries of Gold in Australia and California Lowered the Value of Gold? Letter to the editor. *Economist*, 30 May, 592–93.

———. 1863b. Letter to the editor. *Times*, 1 October, p. 10, col. 2.

Coal Question. 1866. *Times*, 11 May, p. 6, col. 6.

Crawfurd, John. 1863. Letter to the editor. *Times*, 6 October, p. 10, col. 2.

Darbyshire, W. 1882. Married Women in Factories. *Manchester Guardian*, 7 January, p. 5, col. 7.

Fisher, Irving. 1922. *The Making of Index Numbers*. Boston: Houghton Mifflin.

Foxwell, H. S. 1884. Introduction to *Investigations in Currency and Finance* [a collection of writings by William Stanley Jevons]. London: Macmillan.

Galton, Francis. 1877. Considerations Adverse to the Maintenance of Section F (Economic Science and Statistics). *Journal of the London Statistical Society* 40.3:468–73.

Hacking, Ian. 1983. Nineteenth Century Cracks in the Concept of Determinism. *Journal of the History of Ideas* 30 (July/September): 455–75.

Helm, Elijah. 1873. The American Financial Crisis of 1873. *Transactions of the Manchester Statistical Society*, session 1873–74: 25–37.

Henderson, James P. 1994. The Place of Economics in the Hierarchy of the Sciences: Section F from Whewell to Edgeworth. In *Natural Images in Economic Thought: "Markets Read in Tooth and Claw,"* edited by Philip Mirowski. Cambridge: Cambridge University Press.

———. 1996. Emerging Learned Societies: Economic Ideas in Context. *Journal of the History of Economic Thought* 18.2:186–206.

Hollander, Samuel, and Sandra Peart. 1999. J. S. Mill's Methodology in Principle and in Practice: A Review of the Evidence. *Journal of the History of Economic Thought* 21.4:369–97.

Hubbard, J. G. 1869. Gold Coinage. Letter to the editor. *Times*, 20 August, p. 7, cols. 5–6.

Jevons, William Stanley. Archive. John Rylands Library.

———. [1869] 1883. Inaugural Address as President of the Manchester Statistical Society. In *Methods of Social Reform*, 181–93. New York: Kelley.

———. [1882] 1883. Married Women in Factories. In *Methods of Social Reform*. New York: Kelley.

———. [1862] 1884. On the Study of Periodic Commercial Fluctuations. In *Investigations in Currency and Finance*, edited by H. S. Foxwell, 3–11. London: Macmillan.

————. [1863] 1884. A Serious Fall in the Value of Gold Ascertained, and Its Social Effects Set Forth. In *Investigations in Currency and Finance*, edited by H. S. Foxwell, 13–118. London: Macmillan.

————. [1865] 1884. The Variation of Prices and the Value of the Currency since 1782. In *Investigations in Currency and Finance*, edited by H. S. Foxwell, 119–50. London: Macmillan.

————. [1866] 1884. On the Frequent Autumnal Pressure in the Money Market, and the Action of the Bank of England. In *Investigations in Currency and Finance*, edited by H. S. Foxwell, 160–93. London: Macmillan.

————. [1868] 1884. On the Condition of the Gold Coinage of the United Kingdom, with Reference to the Question of International Currency. In *Investigations in Currency and Finance*, edited by H. S. Foxwell, 244–96. London: Macmillan.

————. [1869] 1884. The Depreciation of Gold. In *Investigations in Currency and Finance*, edited by H. S. Foxwell, 151–59. London: Macmillan.

————. [1875] 1884. The Solar Period and the Price of Corn. In *Investigations in Currency and Finance*, edited by H. S. Foxwell, 194–205. London: Macmillan.

————. [1878] 1884a. Commercial Crises and Sun-Spots. Pt. 1. In *Investigations in Currency and Finance*, edited by H. S. Foxwell, 221–35. London: Macmillan.

————. [1878] 1884b. The Periodicity of Commercial Crises and Its Physical Explanation. In *Investigations in Currency and Finance*, edited by H. S. Foxwell, 206–20. London: Macmillan.

————. [1879] 1884. Commercial Crises and Sun-Spots. Pt. 2. In *Investigations in Currency and Finance*, edited by H. S. Foxwell, 235–43. London: Macmillan.

————. [1865] 1906. *The Coal Question: An Inquiry Concerning the Progress of the Nation and the Probable Exhaustion of Our Coal Mines.* 3d ed. New York: Kelley.

————. [1874] 1909. *The Principles of Science: A Treatise on Logic and Scientific Method.* London: Macmillan.

————. [1871] 1911. *Theory of Political Economy.* 4th ed. Edited by H. S. Jevons. London: Macmillan.

————. [1870] 1965. Opening Address as President of Section F (Economic Science and Statistics). In *Methods of Social Reform.* New York: Kelley.

————. [1905] 1965. *The Principles of Economics and Other Papers.* Edited by Henry Higgs. London: Macmillan.

————. [1878] 1972–81. The Solar Influence on Commerce. In vol. 7 of *Papers and Correspondence of William Stanley Jevons*, edited by R. D. Collison Black. London: Macmillan.

————. 1972–81. *Papers and Correspondence of William Stanley Jevons.* 7 vols. Edited by R. D. Collison Black. London: Macmillan.

Kim, Jinbang. 1995. Cairnes versus Jevons on Exact Laws. In *Measurement, Quantification, and Economic Analysis*, edited by Ingrid H. Rima, 140–56. London: Routledge.

Klein, Judy L. 1997. *Statistical Visions in Time: A History of Time Series Analysis 1662–1938.* Cambridge: Cambridge University Press.

Leslie, T. E. C. 1879. *Essays in Political and Moral Philosophy.* London: Longmans, Green, & Co.

McKim, Vaughn. 1997. Introduction to *Causality in Crisis? Statistical Methods and the Search for Causal Knowledge in the Social Sciences,* edited by Vaughn R. McKim and Stephen P. Turner, 1–19. Notre Dame, Ind.: University of Notre Dame Press.

Mill, John Stuart. [1843] 1973. *A System of Logic: Ratiocinative and Inductive.* Vols. 7–8 of *Collected Works of John Stuart Mill,* edited by J. M. Robson. Toronto: University of Toronto Press.

———. [1848] 1965. *Principles of Political Economy.* Vols. 2–3 of *Collected Works of John Stuart Mill,* edited by J. M. Robson. Toronto: University of Toronto Press.

Mitchell, Wesley C. 1928. *Business Cycles: The Problem and Its Setting.* New York: National Bureau of Economics Research.

Morgan, Mary. 1990. *The History of Econometric Ideas.* Cambridge: Cambridge University Press.

———. 1997. Searching for Causal Relations in Economic Statistics: Reflections from History. In *Causality in Crisis? Statistical Methods and the Search for Causal Knowledge in the Social Sciences,* edited by Vaughn R. McKim and Stephen P. Turner, 47–80. Notre Dame, Ind.: University of Notre Dame Press.

Our Coal Supply and the National Debt. 1866. *Manchester Examiner and Times,* 8 May, p. 6, col. 5.

Peart, Sandra. 1993. W. S. Jevons's Methodology of Economics: Some Implications of the Procedures for "Inductive Quantification." *HOPE* 25.3:435–60.

———. 1995. "Disturbing Causes," "Noxious Errors," and the Theory-Practice Distinction in the Economics of J. S. Mill and W. S. Jevons. *Canadian Journal of Economics* 27.4:1194–1211.

———. 1996a. *The Economics of William Stanley Jevons.* London: Routledge.

———. 1996b. "Ignorant" Speculation and "Immoral" Risks: Macheaths, Turpins, and the Commercial Classes in Nineteenth-Century Theories of Economic Fluctuations. *Manchester School* 64.2:135–52.

———. 1999. Review of *Some British Empiricists in the Social Sciences 1650–1900,* by Richard Stone. *Economic Journal* 109.459:G772–773.

———. 2001. Theory, Application, and the Canon: The Case of Mill and Jevons. In *Reflections on the Classical Canon: Essays in Honor of Samuel Hollander,* edited by Evelyn F. Forget and Sandra Peart, 356–77. London: Routledge.

Peart, Sandra and David Levy. 2000. Denying Human Homogeneity: Neo-Classical Economics & "The Vanity of the Philosopher." Paper presented at the HES Conference, Vancouver B.C.

Periodicity of Panics. 1879. *Economist,* 11 January, 32–33.

Porter, Theodore. 1986. *The Rise of Statistical Thinking 1820–1900.* Princeton, N.J.: Princeton University Press.

Proctor, Richard Anthony. 1880. Sun-Spots and Financial Panics. *Scribner's Monthly: An Illustrated Magazine for the People* 20.2:170–78.

Ransome, Arthur. 1882. Married Women in Factories. Letter to the editor. *Manchester Guardian*, 14 January, p. 5, col. 7.

Smith, J. T. 1869. The Coinage. Letter to the editor. *Times*, 9 September, p. 4, cols. 5–6.

Stigler, Stephen M. 1982. Jevons as Statistician. *Manchester School* 50.4:354–65.

———. 1986. *The History of Statistics: The Measurement of Uncertainty before 1900.* Cambridge, Mass.: Harvard University Press.

Stone, Richard. 1980. Political Economy, Economics, and Beyond. *Economic Journal* 90.360:719–36.

———. 1997. *Some British Empiricists in the Social Sciences 1650–1900.* Cambridge: Cambridge University Press.

Sunspots and Commercial Panics. 1879. *Times*, 14 January, p. 4, cols. 5–6.

Syson, E. J. 1871. On the Comparative Mortality of Large Towns. *Transactions of the Manchester Statistical Society*, session 1870–71: 37–47.

United Kingdom. *Hansard Parliamentary Debates*, 3d ser., vol. 182 (1866), cols. 1524–28.

———. *Hansard Parliamentary Debates*, 3d ser., vol. 182 (1866), cols. 241–95.

Untitled Article. 1866a. *Times*, 4 May, p. 8, cols. 3–5.

Untitled Article. 1866b. *Times*, 5 May, p. 8, cols. 4–5.

Untitled Article. 1866c. *Times*, 7 May, p. 8, cols. 4–5.

Untitled Article. 1869a. *Economist*, 1 May, 502.

Untitled Article. 1869b. *Times*, 20 August, p. 6, col. 7; p. 7, col. 1.

Whitaker, John. 2001. Claiming and Reclaiming the Past: The Legitimizing Role of the Precursor Concept. In *Reflections on the Classical Canon: Essays in Honor of Samuel Hollander*, edited by Evelyn L. Forget and Sandra Peart. 386–99. London: Routledge.

White, Michael. 1991. Frightening the "Landed Fogies": Parliamentary Politics and *The Coal Question*. *Utilitas* 3.2:289–302.

———. 1994. Bridging the Natural and the Social: Science and Character in Jevons's Political Economy. *Economic Inquiry* 32 (July): 429–44.

Wilkinson, Thomas Read. 1871. Observations on Infant Mortality and the Death-rate in Large Towns. *Transactions of the Manchester Statistical Society*, session 1870–71: 49–55.

Wright, F. H. A. 1882. Married Women in Factories. *Manchester Guardian*, 18 January, p. 7, col. 4.

An Instrument Can Make a Science: Jevons's Balancing Acts in Economics

Harro Maas

23 May 1864

But we noticed also the letters RJ1845. There can be no doubt I think that they were carved upon the tree . . . by my excellent but unhappy brother[1] . . . I admired him & the things he made. I have some few of them yet, for instance the little set of grain weights, which he constructed for his chemical balance. The latter was ingeniously made of wood with a common knife edge; the movement & pans & weights were all complete, & he was able to make quantitative experiments with considerable exactness.

—Jevons, *Papers and Correspondence I*

In other branches of science, the invention of an instrument has usually marked, if it has not made, an epoch.

—Jevons, *Principles of Science*

Throughout his life, William Stanley Jevons showed a keen interest in scientific instruments. As witness, we may point to the eight entries he

Correspondence may be addressed to Harro Maas, Department of Economics, Room E 9.09, Roetersstraat 11, 1018 WB, Amsterdam, The Netherlands; e-mail: harro@fee.uva.nl. I would like to thank Mary Morgan and Judy Klein for their encouragement and for comments on an earlier version of this essay. Comments by the participants of the Duke workshop were very helpful in rewriting the paper; thanks especially to Kevin Hoover and Ted Porter, who pushed me to explicate my thoughts. Discussions with Ivor Grattan-Guinness, Hasok Chang, Marcel Boumans, and Jo Wachelder and comments of two anonymous referees finally helped me to reframe my argument in the present form. The usual caveat remains, of course.

1. In the introduction to Jevons (1972–81, 1:7), Black gives us the following information on Roscoe Jevons. Roscoe (1829–1869) was Jevons's elder brother. He turned insane at the age of about eighteen, shortly after their mother died in 1845.

wrote for the *Dictionary of Chemistry and the Allied Branches of Other Sciences* (1863–68), most of them on measurement instruments: balance, barometer, hydrometer, hygrometer, thermometer, volumenometer. Jevons wrote these entries in the early 1860s, the period in which his major statistical and logical studies came to fruition and his outline for a mathematical approach to economic theory was read to Section F of the British Association for the Advancement of Science.[2] In his *Principles of Science* [1874] (1958), he even devoted a separate section to measurement instruments to point out "the general purpose of such instruments, and the methods adopted to carry out that purpose with great precision" (284).

In highlighting the importance of measurement instruments for scientific practice, Jevons differed from many of his contemporaries. Neither *measurement* nor *instrument* is, for example, an entry in John Stuart Mill's highly influential *Logic* (1843). This was no accident, for the *Logic* was a book about proof, not about discovery, as Mill's friend and biographer Alexander Bain (1882) noted. Mill had no experience with, nor knowledge of, concrete scientific practice.[3] William Whewell's *Philosophy of Discovery* (1856) also had extremely little to say on the importance of measurement instruments, even though he included short autobiographical sketches of some of the great practical reformers of science—like Galileo, for whom instruments (such as the balance) were indispensable tools to disclose the laws governing the universe (Machamer 1998).

To depict Jevons's writings on philosophy of science as an "attempt to reconcile some of the disputes between Mill and Whewell on scientific methodology" (Schabas 1990, 54) therefore leads our attention away from the role Jevons attributed to measurement instruments in scientific discovery. Indeed, in the *Principles* ([1874] 1958), Jevons stressed the importance of scientific instruments for the formation of scientific disciplines, most notably for chemistry. Chemistry, he suggested, "has been created chiefly by the careful use of the balance" (272), a claim widely supported by historians of science (see, for example, Levere 1990; Wise

2. Another instance is Jevons's interest in the so-called arithmometer, a calculating device that the French engineer Colmar invented about 1820. In November 1878 Jevons gave a short presentation for the London Statistical Society on the gains in terms of depth and scope of research a statistician might make by the use of this instrument. On the influence of the Colmar arithmometer on Victorian scientific practice, see Warwick 1995 and Johnston 1997.

3. This was notably regretted by Mill himself in the *Autobiography*. See Mill 1981, 21.

1993; Wise and Smith 1989a, 1989b; also Theodore Porter's article in this volume).

For Jevons, measurement instruments were an indispensable part of scientific practice: they were analytical tools of investigation as well as practical tools to give numerical precision to conclusions. Jevons's daily use of these instruments shows, even more than the entries in the *Dictionary of Chemistry* or the attention paid to them in the *Principles*, the importance of using measurement instruments. For Jevons, this was the way to access the world. There is virtually no page in his diary in which he did not record his measurements together with other descriptions.[4] There was no walk in the country in which Jevons did not take his barometer with him to measure the height of the hills.

One instrument stood out in these accounts: the balance. Antoine-Laurent Lavoisier, Jevons's great predecessor in chemistry, had used the balance as the "most glorious weapon" in his battle against error,[5] and Jevons, I will argue, used it similarly. It was his weapon against those political economists, such as Mill and John Cairnes, who considered political economy to be an inexact science in contrast to the exact natural sciences and hence not accessible to the use of numerical tools of research. "In matters of this kind," Jevons (1871b, 9) wrote in the *Theory*, "those who despair are almost invariably those who have never tried to succeed." Jevons's own empirical and theoretical investigations form, by contrast, benchmarks for standards of accuracy and precision in economics. My aim in this essay is to show what role measurement instruments, such as the balance, played in this transformation of political economy. Focusing on measurement instruments brings out Jevons's essentially uniform approach to what we currently call distinct scientific disciplines.

The essay is organized into five sections. Jevons's entry on the balance in the *Dictionary* shows how it was both an analytical tool of investigation and a measurement instrument. These different functions will be addressed in the first two sections. The remaining three sections of the essay investigate how his analysis of exchange in analogy with the balance changed political economy. The third section considers Jevons's use of the balance to make a numerical causal inference about the fall in the value of gold. The fourth section explores how the balance was used as

---

4. Jevons's diary of his journey to the gold diggings at Sofala, for example, is preceded by fourteen pages of meteorological observations.

5. See especially Bensaude-Vincent 1992 on Lavoisier's revolutionary use of the balance.

an analytical tool in the *Theory* in a way that restructured economists' thinking about the "laws of supply and demand."

The Balance as a Tool of Analysis

The balance played a pivotal role in Jevons's attempts to improve standards of precision in economics. Jevons's educational background in the natural sciences has of course been noticed in earlier accounts (see especially Black's introduction to Jevons 1972–81 and Schabas 1990, chap. 2), but it cannot be emphasized enough. He attended first the Liverpool Mechanics Institute High School, and then—after an interlude of two years at a private grammar school which was not to his liking—he studied at the preparatory school for University College London and then at the college itself.[6] Jevons's family background was also important for his early inclination toward the natural sciences. He came from a Unitarian and solidly middle class background (Schabas 1990, 12) and shared in the "superb confidence of the Victorian middle class" (Thompson 1978, 264) in the promises of rational argument and the advancement of science for the public good. Middle class Unitarians in Lancashire had been influential both in the establishment of Mechanics' Institutes designed for the education of the higher working class in the principles of the natural sciences and in the formation of the various literary, philosophical, and statistical societies (Kidd and Roberts 1985, 10–11). Advancement of society was the goal, progress of science the means.

After their initial creation in the early nineteenth century, the Mechanics' Institutes spread rapidly throughout Britain.[7] The range of topics taught, in many cases by outstanding specialists in their fields, was

6. The importance of the educational structure for the development of political economy has been extensively discussed for the French case. See, for example, Porter 1991 and 1995. The obvious reference for the relation of French engineering to the development of neo-classical theory is Ekelund and Hébert 1999. In the English context, the influence of educational structure on the methodological and doctrinal developments in economics has to my knowledge not been systematically addressed.

7. The Mechanics' Institutes find their basis in John Anderson's "Anti-Toga class" at Glasgow University, an experimental course in natural philosophy. Anderson explicitly allowed the general public to attend the lectures that were taught with experiments, models, and little formal mathematics so that even a laborer could understand their content. See Katoh 1989 for a short and helpful overview on the emergence of Mechanics' Institutes as a means for adult education. Inkster (1975) and Shapin and Barnes (1977) emphasize the political role of these institutes. Their thesis is critically examined in Watson 1987. On the educational effectiveness of these institutes, see Stephens and Roderick 1972 and more positively Inkster 1975.

extremely broad, ranging from the first principles of mechanical philosophy to lectures on Milton, German customs, or phrenology (see Stephens and Roderick 1972, 355; also Parssinen 1974). George Birkbeck, the founder of the London Mechanics' Institute, focused on the education of the craftsman, to "keep him abreast" of the technological changes that affected the machines, tools, processes, and materials he worked with rather than the education of the mere operative "doing a routine and mechanical job" (Stephens and Roderick 1972, 352). In some instances schools for the education of youth were affiliated with these adult education institutes, as was the case for the Liverpool Mechanics' Institute.

Mechanical philosophy formed an important part of the curriculum. By close study of diagrams, students learned to comprehend the mechanical principles of a number of contrivances, ranging from the balance to the steam engine. According to Henry Drougham, an early advocate of scientific education of the people, "enough will be accomplished, if they are made to perceive the nature of geometrical investigation, and learn the leading properties of figure" (Shapin and Barnes 1977, 49, quoting Brougham). The practical use of an instrument, such as the balance, for measurements may have been part of the education of the youngsters, though I have been unable to find evidence for this.[8]

Whether or not in general the youthful pupils gained practical experience, there is no doubt about it in Jevons's case. When he was still very young, he conducted experiments with his brother Roscoe and his cousin Harry Roscoe (later professor of chemistry at Owen's college, Manchester) in which they used a wooden balance with a fair amount of precision. His cousin Harry recollects in his autobiography the "delights" of making "fireworks for the 5th November" (Jevons 1972–81, 1:7, Black quoting Harry Roscoe). Jevons got even better acquainted with the secrets of the balance when trained as a gold assayer by his professor of chemistry at University College London. His daily use of the balance as gold assayer in Sydney ensured its principles became part of Jevons's second nature. It is no surprise that Jevons framed his empirical and theoretical work in accordance with these principles: the balance, for Jevons, was not just a metaphor, it was a genuine means to disclose the mechanics of the world—the physical and, as we will see, the mental.

---

8. The literature on the Mechanics' Institutes tends to focus on their role in adult training to the neglect of their importance in establishing opportunities for secondary education for the higher working class and middle class youth.

It was therefore natural that Jevons be asked to contribute several entries to the *Dictionary of Chemistry and the Other Allied Branches of the Sciences* (1863–68) on, among others, the topics of the balance and gold assaying in a period when dictionaries were an important aid in the diffusion of scientific knowledge (Layton 1965). From Jevons's entry on the balance, we get an extremely rich and detailed description not only of the balance itself, but also of the intricacies of its use and the precautions that should be taken to get significant results. The reader is struck by the effort Jevons makes to spell out all possible difficulties in making an accurate measurement with a balance and how to circumvent these difficulties. His entry was, in this respect, an effort to express tacit knowledge and give practical guidance in using the balance.

Jevons's entry contains a description of the geometry of the balance, a description of the actual instrument and how it should be used with care in practice. His geometrical account nicely captures the aim of such dictionaries to convey useful knowledge without troubling readers with notations they may not know.[9] One of his drawings (reproduced as figure 1) gives a detailed geometry of the balance, showing how the different forces acting on the balance were interrelated. It can be easily seen that the geometry of the balance is identical to that of a lever. Figure 2 shows how the effect of an additional weight, p, added to a balance at rest, may be understood by conceiving of the balance as a compound pendulum, where the greatest velocity of the beam (proportional to θ) gives an indication of p.

The Balance as a Measurement Instrument

Given its role in Lavoisier's "chemical revolution," it is no surprise that Jevons (1863, 481) described the balance as "the chemist's most important instrument." As Sibum (1995, 74n. 4) notes, in Jevons's days *precision* and *accuracy* related to different aspects of scientific instruments. Precision referred to the tools and their quality, whereas accuracy referred to the skill of the user. Jevons discussed both these issues in his entries on the balance and on gold assaying. An image of a balance used in gold assaying, for which great precision and accuracy were required,

9. Even though the secondary literature Jevons refers to makes use of the principle of virtual velocities (Charles Knight's *English Cyclopaedia* of 1861 calls it "perhaps the most important generalisation in mechanics"), Jevons does not use this principle in his dictionary entry. I would like to thank Michael White for having drawn my attention to this.

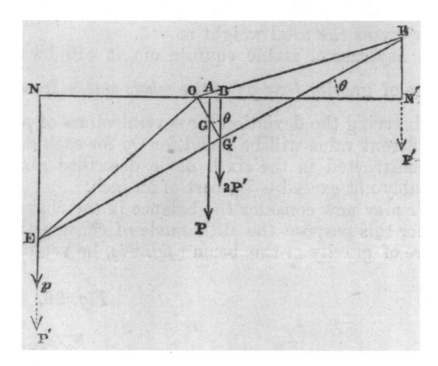

Figure 1 Jevons's drawing of the geometry of the balance. From Jevons 1863, 487.

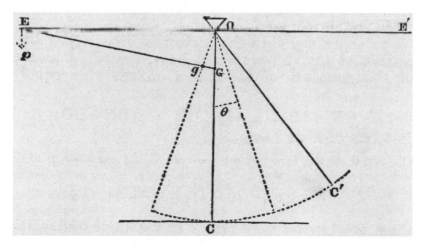

Figure 2 Jevons's drawing of the balance as a compound pendulum. From Jevons 1863, 488.

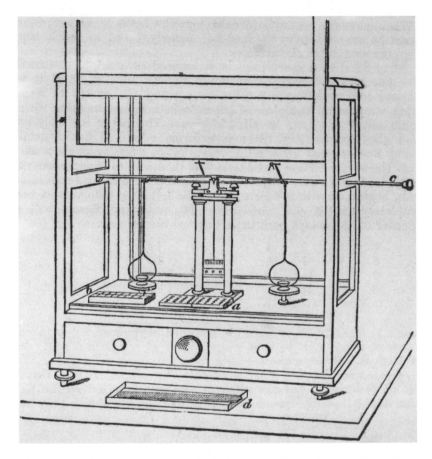

Figure 3   Jevons's drawing of a balance used in gold assaying. From Jevons 1864, 933.

accompanied his entry on gold assaying and is reproduced here as figure 3. If we take a look at this image of the balance, we see that it is depicted as in use in what looks like an experimental setting. At some points in his entries, Jevons indeed suggested that using the balance was the same as making an experiment (e.g., 482: "When a weighing is actually being made . . . retain [the planes on the edges] in the exact positions proper for a new experiment"). Such an experiment puts high demands both on the quality of the instrument and on the accuracy of the weigher.

Jevons provided criteria for the best materials for the balance, the weights used, and other technicalities concerning the construction of the instrument. The material the balance was made of, for example, should be such that as many disturbing causes as possible were excluded. These constructive requirements were intimately linked with the geometry of the balance. That is, the geometry of the balance enforced requirements for the construction of the actual contrivance: "In its most perfect form . . . it consists of a perforated brass beam, cast in a single piece, combining great strength and perfect inflexibility with comparatively small weight" (482). These requirements were not easily reconcilable in practice. Small weight, for example, could be obtained by the use of aluminium. However, aluminium was highly corrosive and flexible and thus a bad choice for this purpose. In practice the instrument necessarily fell short of the ideal requirements.[10] Other technicalities related to the adjustment possibilities of the beam or the edges. Screws— still known as precision instruments today—played an important role in adjusting the edges or the beam itself. The balance, Jevons wrote, should be enclosed in a "glass case, with convenient windows" to ensure that there were no "casual sources of mistake" (486).

Such casual sources of mistakes related to the inaccuracies on the part of the scientist, or weigher, and could not be known or corrected for in advance. Jevons gave the example of a "scrupulously exact gold-assayer led into serious mistakes by a small fly, which settled on his balance, unobserved at the time" (486). Even such an accurate assayer could be led astray by not taking proper care or not paying attention to all relevant details. In effect, Jevons wrote, "the casual sources of mistake are too many to mention" (486). To minimize these sources of inaccuracy, Jevons provided a list of "suggestions for the care of a balance" (486) which in fact urged the weigher to follow minutely fixed routines in handling the instrument so that when in doubt errors could be traced.

Even if the technical layout of the balance matched the highest standards of precision attainable and the instrument was handled by a skilled weigher, sources of error remained. In some of such sources of error, the geometry of the instrument came to the aid. The inequality of the arms

10. "All the instruments with which we perform our measurements are faulty" (Jevons [1874] 1958, 461). On the conflicting requirements of measurement instruments in relation to their mathematical ideal, see especially Boumans, this volume. Attempts to combine conflicting attributes created a separate discipline and literature on instrument making. Jevons was well read in this literature and refers to it throughout the *Principles*.

of the beam was a case in point, "for the extreme edges can never be adjusted at perfectly equal distances from the centre edge" (490). The geometry of the balance gave, however, a straightforward precept how to correct for this error. Jevons referred to Gauss, who, "by simply weighing the object alternately in one pan or the other" (490), had made use of the geometrical average of both measurements to obtain faultless results. It is easy to show that one obtains the true value of the required weight by this procedure. Another problem was the insensibility of the arms to very small differences between weights, but to turn the arm at all "some *definite* weight" was required. Once again, this type of error, Jevons argued, could be evaded by taking recourse to mean values instead of the read values (490).

We see then that the use of the balance involved a complex interplay of the actual instrument, its geometry, and its users. The balance imposed routines on its users; otherwise, accuracy could not be guaranteed. Its geometry imposed demands on the materials to be used and on the construction of the apparatus; otherwise, precision in the results was out of reach. These practical and analytical demands could not all be combined in practice (Marcel Boumans and Flavio Comim [both this volume] make a similar argument in their respective case studies). However, the very same geometry that put such high demands on construction (given the existing state of technology) also suggested solutions to measurement problems that could not be solved by the mere following of fixed routines and procedures. Finally, users needed a considerable degree of expertise and training. But even expert weighers could not just rely on these routines. At various moments in the weighing process, they relied on their judgment to get precise and accurate results.

As Jevons ([1874] 1958, 270) remarked in the *Principles*: "Measuring apparatus and mathematical theory should advance *pari passu*, and with just such precision as the theorist can anticipate results, the experimentalist should be able to compare them with experience." The balance served the same function for Jevons as it had for Galileo and Lavoisier: it was an engine of discovery.[11]

---

11. Even though the notion of an "engine of discovery" is somewhat Whiggish. See Wise and Smith 1989a; also 1989b, 434.

Balancing Disturbing Causes: "A Serious Fall in the Value of Gold Ascertained"

We have seen that, for Jevons, the imperfection of the measurement instrument—and the consequent occurrence of measurement errors—was the "normal state of things." In fact, he considered it even "one of the most embarrassing things" when "experimental results agree too closely" (357–58). In parallel to the usual argument in statistics—that small independent disturbances or errors will cancel out in the average—Jevons ([1874] 1958, 357) proposed in the *Principles* to "eliminate . . . the multitude of small disturbing influences . . . by balancing them off against each other." In other words, for Jevons, averaging and balancing ideas are connected, as we can see in his discussion of the different methods of error reduction found in chapter 25 of the *Principles*. Even when he faced situations in his statistical work where he acknowledged that causes were interconnected, he still argued that it was legitimate to treat them as "noxious" measurement errors that averaged out when as many causes as possible were included.[12] His famous gold study is the best case in point.

Once we see the importance of the mechanical balance for Jevons's approach to the problem (his most discussed innovation in this context), the use of index numbers to prove his point becomes obvious. Jevons used the mechanical balance as a tool of investigation: it was first a thinking tool to structure the analysis of the causal influence of a gold influx on prices, second, it served as a virtual, not a material, measurement instrument to attribute a number to the fall in the value of gold.[13] In using the balance in this way, he restructured the thinking of the political economists and statisticians of his day and made index numbers relevant in the computation of a measurement.

When Jevons undertook the gold study, it was considered to be impossible to give a numerical estimate of the influence of the new gold discoveries on prices. Cairnes's (1857, 95) views may serve as an example: "Now if Political Economy were an exact science, this question could be at once determined by calculating the effect of the causes assigned, and comparing the result of our calculation with the actual market price."

12. Statisticians of the day might have considered this as illegitimate. It gave Jevons, however, a possibility to circumvent the problem of multiple causation, which could not be addressed at that time (Morgan 1997). With regard to Jevons, see Aldrich 1987, 1992; Peart 1995a, 1995b; and Sandra Peart's article in this volume.

13. See Klein 1999 for a similar notion of scientific tools in classical chemistry.

But political economy was not then such an "exact science," so Cairnes considered this undertaking "impracticable." Even had accurate statistics been available, there were simply too many other causes involved to separate out the effect of the gold influx. Jevons's ingenuity lay in the use of the mechanical balance as an analytical tool first to circumvent the problem of multiple causation, and, second, to provide a numerical estimate for the fall of the value of gold.

Jevons ([1863] 1884, 18) started with the simple observation that "the comparative values of two articles are said to be altered when the proportion of the quantities usually exchanged in the market is altered." The ingenuity lay in the sequel. Drawing an analogy between an exchange on the market with the balancing of two weights at once simplified dramatically the problem other authors had faced: "This alteration may arise from circumstances affecting the supply or demand of either article, just as a balance may be disturbed by an upward or downward force, applied to either arm. There is nothing in the simple motion to indicate from which side the change comes" (18).

Jevons's recourse to the mechanical balance was, however, more than drawing an analogy or even invoking a metaphor; applying the balance argument restructured the way one should think about the problem of multiple causation in price formation, just as the analytical properties of the balance structured the way students at the Mechanics' Institutes were trained to understand the laws governing material objects. There was no need to go into the causes of all separate changes in prices of all the innumerable commodities involved, for the situation could be simply pictured like this: the price of gold was in one pan and the prices of all other commodities were in the opposite. The mechanics of the balance provided for an immediate connection between a change on the one side of the beam and on the other side: "It is obvious, in short, that an alteration in any one article is shown in its rate of exchange with all other articles, so that the fact of an alteration may be ascertained with a continual approach to certainty" even though "there always remains the alternative of a concurrence of causes affecting all other articles" (19). The balance mechanism structured the way we should think about the cause of price changes in relation to gold.

Jevons made only loose reference to probability arguments, since he supposed that everyone would agree that the odds were clearly against all the weights (prices) in one pan having altered in the same direction; it was far more likely that all these different changes would average out.

Thus, the cause of a movement of the beam must lie in the other pan—that is, in the factors affecting gold. Indeed, the more commodities involved, the more confidence one could have in this kind of reasoning.

Jevons then used the analytical properties of the balance to compute a numerical estimate of the fall in the value of gold. To ascertain this fall in value, one needed to ascertain the general rise in prices based on the idea that, departing from an initial equilibrium, all or at least a preponderance of prices would have risen against the price of gold. At this point, an average was needed. But of what kind? Jevons chose the geometric mean, a choice that lay at hand when calculating the average change in the ratios of prices. Perhaps this also followed naturally from his use of the mechanical balance to structure his investigation, since the balance measures ratios.[14]

Jevons's choice of the geometric mean to determine the fall in the value of gold was then, and has remained, something of an enigma.[15] Etienne Laspeyres interpreted Jevons as making an index number argument and queried the use of a geometric mean in that context. Jevons ([1865] 1884, 122) linked his choice for the geometric mean especially to his balancing argument in answer to Laspeyres's stated preference for the arithmetic mean:[16]

> [The geometric mean] seems likely to give in the most accurate manner such a general change in price as is due to a change in the part of gold. For any change in gold will affect all prices in an equal ratio;

14. At the turn of the nineteenth century some controversy arose as to whether measuring a ratio could be considered a measurement. See, for example, Carter 1907. I owe this reference to Judy Klein.

15. Arguments for the choice of the mean today are sought in the distributional characteristics of the observations. In the nineteenth century, errors were considered to average out with zero mean due to the "Law of Error." Only in the twentieth century has explicit recourse been taken to the distributional characteristics of observations. See, for example, Krüger et al. 1987 and Morgan 1990. In relation to Jevons, see Stigler 1982; Aldrich 1987, 1992; Kim 1995; Peart 1995a and this volume. Aldrich (1992, 674) rightly points out that "the overall impression from [Jevons's] writing is that the use of the geometric mean was divorced from any consideration of the distribution of price changes," but this does not make Jevons's choice the result of a "jumble of reasons."

16. Jevons passed over Laspeyres's argument for weighting the price changes in the arithmetic mean rather quickly. He had two other arguments for choosing the geometric mean. The first was that the geometric mean was to be preferred over the arithmetic or the harmonic (unweighted) averages because it lay in between the two, an argument that—as Marcel Boumans pointed out to me—would be repeated by Irving Fisher. The second argument was only for convenience. Jevons had a strong predilection for using logarithms, making the choice for the geometric mean the most natural.

and if other disturbing causes may be considered proportional to the ratio of the change in price they produce in one or more commodities, then all the individual variations of prices will be correctly balanced off against each other in the geometric mean, and the true variation in the value of gold will be detected.

Jevons's "proof" for the fall in the value of gold began with the average rise in prices of 39 commodities, and he subsequently enlarged the group of commodities to 118. Taking account of intricacies—such as the commercial tide—which could bias the outcome, Jevons's calculations led him to conclude that there had been a fall in the value of gold "by about 9 1/3 per cent" (54). This result convinced Jevons that he did not have to worry too much about causes on the other side of the balance, because the fall in the value of gold was so considerable that Jevons hardly doubted the influence of the new gold influx.

In his gold study, Jevons relied on common arguments used in his own experimental practices. Since he had shown that on average prices had risen, he argued that this rise "*is and constitutes* the alteration of value of gold asserted to exist" (21). Notwithstanding remaining problems—of which he was fully aware—Jevons had no doubt that his computations effectively established a fall in the value of gold, and they enabled him to give numerical evidence for the amount it had fallen in value.

Many of Jevons's contemporaries missed the novelty of his approach to the issue of multiple causation and argued that the causes of the change in prices for all commodities should be investigated one by one. Cliffe Leslie was one of them. Against Jevons's argument that "the average must in all reasonable probability represent some single influence acting on all the commodities," he countered: But why not a "plurality of causes"? (quoted in Peart this volume). Kevin Hoover and Michael Dowell (this volume) rightly compare the alternative method political economists like Cliffe Leslie suggested with Mill's Method of Residues. Such an approach stood in opposition to the setup of Jevons's inquiry. Jevons fully admitted that it would be possible to give causes for price changes in all individual cases. But if, on these grounds, one were to throw out the commodity in question from the inquiry, "the whole inquiry would be thrown into confusion by any such attempt . . . the impartial balance of the inquiry" would be "overthrown" ([1865] 1884,

58).[17] The reference to the impartial balance should here be taken literally. If one changes the weights in the balance during the process, the whole outcome is thrown in disarray, proving the investigator to be an inaccurate weigher.

Cairnes, in contrast to Leslie, acknowledged Jevons's accomplishment. He referred to it in a letter in the *Times* and used Jevons's results to substantiate his own conclusions in the same direction. In correspondence with Jevons, however, he underlined the complete differences in the methods they used to get the same results. Cairnes considered these differences advantageous—the argument was strengthened when similar results were obtained by completely dissimilar ways. Both Cairnes and Jevons were well aware that they used "entirely distinct methods of inquiry" (Jevons 1972–81, 3:17–18). In this case, it gave Cairnes no reason to dismiss Jevons's results. The situation changed, however, when it came to the use of the balance as a tool of investigation in the *Theory*.

Balancing Pleasures and Pains

In the middle of the nineteenth century it was a widely held opinion that tools and methods like mathematics and experiments, which could be so fruitfully applied to nature, were inapplicable to the phenomena of the mind, including political economy. Whewell, for example, had limited the sciences to the study of the natural, but not the moral, world even though he himself pioneered the use of mathematics in political economy. John Stuart Mill's famous essay on method (1836) and his *Logic* (1843) had made political economy as respectable as the natural sciences, yet its tools and methods were thought to exclude experiments and mathematics. In short, political economy was considered primarily as one of the moral or mental sciences, making a marriage with the tools and methods of the natural sciences hardly conceivable.

By the time Jevons began to devise a new approach to political economy, Mill's view had lost its status as self-evident truth. Developments within psycho-physiology, and the engineering type of mechanics that lead to the discovery of the conservation law in physics, created doubts over the categorical distinction between the phenomena of mind and matter. Physiologists such as William Carpenter argued for the so-called

17. To be able to make this argument, Jevons implicitly assumes uncorrelated price changes even though he knows they do not exist. This clearly made Jevons's argument flawed. See, for example, Aldrich 1987, 1992; Kim 1995; Peart 1995a.

principle of the "correlation of forces," in which motives were considered forces, just as forces work on matter. Similarly, the very idea that human labor could be examined in the same terms as the work performed by inanimate machines gained wide currency.[18] Margaret Schabas (1990, 84–89) rightly highlighted Jevons's consideration in the *Principles* that "the time may come . . . when the tender mechanism of the brain will be traced out, and every thought reduced to the expenditure of a determinate weight of nitrogen and phosphorus. No apparent limit exists to the success of scientific method in weighing and measuring, and reducing beneath the sway of law, the phenomena both of matter and mind" (Jevons [1874] 1958, 735–36). White (1994) examined extensively how Jevons's reading in the new developments in psychophysiology influenced his *Theory*. White in particular noted the influence on Jevons of Richard Jennings's *Natural Elements of Political Economy* ([1855] 1969), an eclectic mixture of associationist psychology and reflex physiology. Jevons wrote his new theory of exchange against this background.

The analogy of exchange with balancing of utilities is clearly expressed in Jevons's early version of the theory:[19] "Whether the exchange will take place or not can only be ascertained by estimating the utility of the objects on either side, which is done by integrating the appropriate functions of utility up to the quantity of each object as limits. A balance of utility on both sides will lead to an exchange" (1866, 284).

For Jevons, the laws of supply and demand were founded on the "laws of human enjoyment," and these laws obeyed the causal mechanism of the balance, leading to the surface event of exchange. Though Mill did not believe that the laws of human enjoyment bear upon market exchange, Jevons found these laws, as he said, in Jeremy Bentham's "springs of human action," our feelings of pleasure and pain. In the

18. A general account of this development can be found in Rabinbach 1990. For the physical context of this development, see Grattan-Guinness 1990, especially chap. 16, and Vatin 1993 with regard to French engineering; Wise and Smith 1989a, 1989b, and 1990 with regard to the developments in Victorian physics; and Mirowski 1989 for an account of the importance of the energy concept for the developments in economics. For the debates among Victorian physiologists and psychologists on the relation of mind and matter, see Daston 1978; Jacyna 1981 and 1983. Jevons's theoretical position in these physiological debates is examined in White 1994 and in the physical debates in White 1999.

19. The theory was part of *Notice of a General Mathematical Theory of Political Economy*, an essay that was read at Section F of the British Association for the Advancement of Science in 1862 and published in 1866 as the *Brief Account*.

Theory, Jevons wrote that Bentham had "thoroughly" understood the mathematical character of the subject and quoted his description of how to estimate the "tendency of an action": "Sum up all the values of all the pleasures on the one side, and those of all the pains on the other. The balance, if it be on the side of pleasure, will give the good tendency of the act . . . with respect to the interests of that individual person; if on the side of pain, the bad tendency of it upon the whole" (1871b, 12, quoting Bentham).

Bentham's balancing process, however, fell short in providing a genuine mechanism. This can be illustrated with a similar balancing procedure found in Benjamin Franklin's so-called *Moral Algebra*. In a letter to Joseph Priestley, Franklin had described his method of making difficult decisions by making up a balance of motives:

> To get over this [the uncertainty that perplexes us], my way is, to divide half a sheet of paper by a line into two columns; writing over the one *pro*, and over the other *con*; then, during three or four days' consideration, I put down, under the different heads, short hints of the different motives, that at different times occur to me, *for* or *against* the measure. When I have thus got them altogether in one view, I endeavour to estimate their respective weights; and when I find two (one on each side) that seem equal, I strike them both out. If I find the reason *pro* equal to some *two* reasons *con*, I strike out the *three*. If I judge some two reasons *con* equal to some *three* reasons *pro*, I strike out the *five*; and, thus proceeding, I find out where the balance lies; and if, after a day or two of further consideration, nothing new that is of importance occurs on either side, I come to a determination accordingly. And though the weights of reasons cannot be taken with the precision of algebraic quantities, yet, when each is thus considered separately and comparatively, and the whole lies before me, I think I can judge better, and am less liable to take a false step; and, in fact, I have found great advantage from this kind of equation, in what may be termed *moral* or *prudential algebra*. (Bain 1859, 463, quoting Franklin)

At first sight, Franklin's balancing procedure is about the care taken by a weigher when making measurements, adding new weights and quietly waiting until a new equilibrium is reached.[20] However, in contrast

---

20. I thank Mary Morgan, Hasok Chang, and Marcel Boumans for pushing me on this subject.

with a mechanical balance, the weights added are not homogeneous by nature. This highlights the importance of man's power of judgment. The estimation of weights relative to one another is in need of the constant interference of man's judgment. Franklin provides a prescriptive routine to aid judgment, not motive forces that drive the mind to equilibrium in accordance with mechanical principles. Franklin's procedure may be a useful routine, but it lacks the mechanics of a material balance. It is not, therefore, suited for applying the geometry of the balance, let alone the calculus, to demonstrate its properties.[21]

Jevons (1871b, 38–39) interprets Franklin's balancing procedure as if pleasures and pains are homogeneous quantities: "The algebraic sum of a series of pleasures and pains will be obtained by adding the pleasures together and the pains together, and then striking the balance by subtracting the smaller amount from the greater." To provide for a mechanism, however, it is not sufficient just to consider feelings of pleasures and pains as homogeneous quantities. Rather, pleasures and pains have to be considered as feelings that move the mind automatically, without the interference of judgment, in the same way that forces move the balance. To introduce the calculus in economics, Jevons not only considered feelings of pleasures and pains as homogeneous quantities, capable of "more or less"; he also considered man's deliberation process as moved by forces that escaped the interference of man's judgment.

In the *Theory*, Jevons interchangeably considers feelings of pleasure and pain as motives or as forces. In fact, this marks a major conceptual change. An individual acts not on an array of different motives that each have to be judged, but on forces that automatically move the individual in one of two directions. Jevons's term "feelings" applied equally to "physical pleasure or pain" and "mental and moral feelings of several degrees of elevation" (1871b, 29). When Jevons, in his original 1878 criticism of Mill's utilitarianism, refers to Bentham's procedure to estimate the "values of pleasures and pains," he adds that Bentham "obviously" meant by "*values* the quantities or forces" ([1890] 1971, 276, emphasis in the original). Jevons persistently framed the "laws of human enjoyment" in terms of natural forces instead of motives.[22]

21. One might argue that a system of double entry bookkeeping provides such a mechanism, but that was neither on Bentham's nor Franklin's mind.

22. Warke (2000) recently examined, from a different perspective than is pursued here, the mathematical fitness of Jevons's rendering of Bentham's felicific calculus.

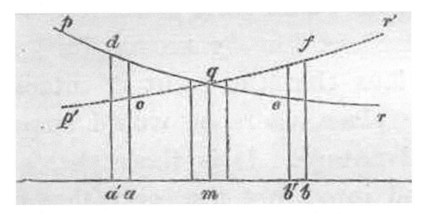

Figure 4   Jevons's diagrammatic representation of the utility adjustments of one individual (or trading body) to its optimum at m. The ver
tical axis (not drawn) depicts utility; the horizontal, two different commodities, apparently measured in the same quantities. The two curves
represent the utility functions for the respective goods, where the dotted
one $(p'qr')$ is superposed and inverted on the other (pqr). The ratio of
exchange is fixed at 1:1. From Jevons 1871b, 97.

Jevons's graphical illustration of how these different forces were interrelated for one person is reproduced in figure 4. In the diagram two utility curves are superposed and inverted upon one another; utility is measured on the vertical axis, commodities on the horizontal. Jevons showed
how this person would make a net gain in utility by extending trade from
a' in the direction of m and would lose in utility when trading beyond that
point. He constructed thus a genuine mechanism, akin to a mechanical
balance. An equilibrium would automatically emerge for this individual
at m. Jevons described our will, in consequence, with some justification
as a "pendulum" moved by pleasures and pains, "and its oscillations are
minutely registered in the price lists of the markets" (14).

Whether such an equilibrium would arise was, of course, dependent
on the form of the curves. Here the developments within psycho-physiology came to Jevons's aid, most notably Jennings's *Natural Elements* but
also the writings of physiologists like Carpenter (White 1994). For
Jevons, the "laws of human wants," in which "the basis of economy"
was to be sought, seemed to be grounded in mankind's "chemical and
physiological conditions" (1871b, 158). His own experiments on the exertion of muscular force convinced him that he was on the right track

for his theory of labor. From these sources Jevons took the idea that additional increments of commodity would lead to ever smaller gains in utility, an idea that was reflected in the form of the curves in the diagram. In a situation of exchange of one thing for another, such curves furnish a functional relation between the different sides of the individual's balancing of pleasures and pains. Jevons believed he had discovered a genuine mechanism explaining commodity exchanges, a *"mechanics of utility and self-interest,"* in contrast to authors like Mill who made reference to the "laws of supply and demand" without providing for a genuine mechanism explaining their workings.

Jevons's theory both provided for a mechanism of exchange based on the "laws of human enjoyment" and resolved the issue of how one might get at numerical estimates for utility, or feelings of pleasures and pains. Limiting himself to the static case, in which equilibrium was reached, Jevons rightly argued that there were in fact no numbers needed at all. Just as someone could roughly perceive the equilibrium of a balance with the eye, so the individual was able to judge the equivalence of pleasures and pains by paying attention only to their marginal increase or decrease. No assumption was needed as to whether the mind was able to judge accurately numerical quantities of utility. It was only necessary to assume that the mind could perceive a rough equivalence (or inequality) between them.[23] For the static case, Jevons's utility theory rested on measurement without numbers.[24]

The issue of the measurement of utility may need some extra discussion, if only for the extraordinary amount of intellectual energy that has been devoted to it in the past century. Many questions were immediately raised in response to the *Theory*. However, the measurement of utility only has an impact in those cases where equilibrium is not settled. In that case one should be able, one way or another, to assess the form of the individual (or average) utility functions in figure 4. This problem was intractable to Jevons, though he made several attempts to overcome it.[25]

23. See Peart 1995b for an extensive discussion of Jevons's approach to the measurement of utility in the *Theory*.

24. In this context, another set of experiments Jevons pursued are worth mentioning. In 1871 Jevons published a short note in *Nature* on the power of numerical discrimination. The upshot of his argument was that "the mind is unable . . . to estimate any large number of objects" but does better when a smaller number is involved (1871a, 281).

25. As Grattan-Guinness (2000) points out, Jevons was well acquainted with analysis of functional equations in which Augustus De Morgan, his mathematics teacher at University College, was an expert. In my view, Jevons's discussion on the King-Davenant "Law" of Demand

It is well known that Jevons's mechanics only worked when the ratio of exchange was fixed. As Fleeming Jenkin rightly pointed out in his famous letters on this issue, he saw "no motive power" tending to move two individuals toward an equilibrium rate of exchange, and he challenged Jevons to show how such an equilibrium rate would come about (Jevons 1972–81, 3:167–78). In the *Theory* Jevons circumvented the problem by taking recourse to his so-called law of indifference, which effectively amounted to saying that individuals adjusted their desired exchanges to a given exchange rate. His explicit "analogy" of the equation of exchange with the theory of the lever in the second edition implicitly clarifies the problem. If the ratio of exchange was not fixed, the fulcrum was not fixed, and the balance was essentially a defective instrument. Nevertheless, in using the mechanical balance as a thinking tool to disclose how exchange might be related to the laws governing the deliberations of an individual, Jevons paved the way for his successors.

Conclusion

In the introduction to the *Theory*, Jevons (1871b, 11) approvingly quoted Augustus De Morgan, his teacher in mathematics at University College London:

> Had it not been for the simple contrivance of the balance, which we are well assured (how, it matters not here) enables us to poise equal weights against one another, that is, to detect equality and inequality, and thence to ascertain how many times the greater contains the less, we might not to this day have had much clearer ideas on the subject of weight, as a magnitude, than we have on those of talent, prudence, or self-denial, looked at in the same light. All who are ever so little of geometers will . . . remember the steps by which this vagueness became clearness and precision.

It is perhaps hardly surprising that Jevons, who was a chemist and natural philosopher by training, made the balance his most important tool of research. It is surprising, I think, that this simple fact has escaped the attention of historians of economics for so long. This is no doubt because economists don't think of their subject as an "allied branch" of

---

relates to this issue of functional form and is therefore less of a digression than suggested in Creedy 1986. See also White 1995 and chapter 6 of my thesis (Maas 2001).

chemistry. Jevons did. In this essay we have seen how Jevons used the balance as a tool of investigation to enforce clearness and precision in economics. The result can be truly termed a revolution.

In his gold study, Jevons used the balance as a thinking and calculating tool to measure a fall in the value of gold and to make an inference as to the cause of the fall as well. Thinking with the balance structured the way one might conceive of the causal influence of the new gold influx on prices and focused attention on the rise or fall in the average level of prices as a numerical indicator for the amount by which gold had fallen in value. In his *Theory of Political Economy*, Jevons used the principles of the balance to reconstruct the process of human deliberation. He was thus able to relate the marginal utility considerations of individuals to exchange on the market. The balance thus restructured economists' thinking about the laws of supply and demand: by connecting exchange to the mechanics of the individual's mind, Jevons provided, in outline, an equilibrating mechanism for market exchange resting on what we today would call a preference ordering. These accomplishments fundamentally changed the research strategies of economists on both the theoretical and practical plane. From Jevons's work onward, it became feasible to ask for numerical estimates in answer to empirical questions. It became equally feasible to consider human deliberation in relation to price formation in terms of the calculus.

In the case of the gold study, Jevons's approach was extremely successful and widely approved. To understand mental deliberation itself as made by a mechanical balance involved, however, a shift in perspective on the phenomena of the mind that many of Jevons's contemporary economists were not prepared to make. An anonymous reviewer of the *Theory*[26] quickly spotted that the novelty of the book rested not primarily on Jevons's use of mathematics, but on his persistent comparison of man with an instrument:

> In what then, does Mr. Jevons's originality consist? First, in the fact that he approaches the subject from a new point of view; and, secondly, that this method enables him to express his conclusions in mathematical symbols. To explain the first statement we may remark that, for scientific purposes, human society may be considered as a vast

26. In the *Saturday Review* of 11 November 1871, possibly written by the mathematician George Wirgman Hemming, fellow of St. John's College, Cambridge, though the reviewer was in general quite sceptical to Jevons's undertaking in the *Theory*.

piece of machinery, in which the actions of the various parts is determined by the various forces which affect the will. Each man is regarded as an instrument moved by pain and pleasure; and the arrangements of society at large are determined by the aggregate impulses of all its individual members. (Jevons 1972–81, 7:152–53)

References

Aldrich, John. 1987. Jevons as Statistician: the Role of Probability. *The Manchester School* 55:233–56.

———. 1992. Probability and Depreciation: A History of the Stochastic Approach to Index Numbers. *HOPE* 24.3:657–87.

Bain, Alexander. 1859. *The Emotions and the Will*. London: John W. Parker and Son.

———. 1882. *John Stuart Mill: a Criticism with Personal Recollections*. London: Longmans, Green and Co.

Bensaude-Vincent, Bernadette. 1992. The Balance between Chemistry and Politics. *Eighteenth Century* 33.3:217–37.

Boumans, Marcel. 2000. How Economists Model the World to Numbers. *Research Memoranda in History and Methodology of Economics* no. 00/1. Amsterdam: University of Amsterdam.

Cairnes, John Elliot. 1857. *The Character and Logical Method of Political Economy*. London: Longmans, Brown, Green, Longmans and Roberts.

Carter, T. N. 1907. The Concept of an Economic Quantity. *Quarterly Journal of Economics* 21 (May): 427–48.

Creedy, John. 1986. On the King-Davenant "Law" of Demand. *Scottish Journal of Political Economy* 33.3:193–212.

Daston, Lorraine J. 1978. British Responses to Psycho-Physiology, 1860–1900. *Isis* 69.247:192–208.

The New English Cyclopaedia: A New Dictionary of Universal Knowledge conducted by Charles Knight 1854–1861. London.

Ekelund, Robert B. Jr., and Robert F. Hébert. 1999. *Secret Origins of Modern Microeconomics: Dupuit and the Engineers*. Chicago: University of Chicago Press.

Grattan-Guinness, Ivor. 1990. *Convolutions in French Mathematics: 1800–1840*. Basel: Birkhäuser Verlag.

———. 2000. "In Some Parts Rather Rough": An Unknown Manuscript Version of Stanley Jevons's Seminal "General Mathematical Theory of Political Economy." Forthcoming.

Inkster, Ian. 1975. Science and the Mechanics' Institutes, 1820–1850: The Case of Sheffield. *Annals of Science* 32:451–74.

Jacyna, L. S. 1981. The Physiology of Mind, the Unity of Nature, and the Moral Order in Victorian Thought. *British Journal for the History of Science*. 14.2:109–32.

———. 1983. Immanence and Transcendence: Theories of Life and Organization in Britain, 1790–1835. *Isis* 74:311–29.

Jennings, Richard. [1855] 1969. *Natural Elements of Political Economy.* New York: Kelley.

Jevons, W. Stanley. 1863. Balance. In vol. 1 of *Dictionary of Chemistry and the Allied Branches of Other Sciences*, edited by H. Watts, 481–91. London: Longman, Green, Longman, Roberts and Green.

———. [1863] 1884. A Serious Fall in the Value of Gold Ascertained, and Its Social Effects Set Forth, With Two Diagrams. In *Investigations in Currency and Finance*, edited by H. S. Foxwell. London: Macmillan.

———. 1864. Gold-Assay. In vol. 2 of *Dictionary of Chemistry and the Allied Branches of Other Sciences*, edited by H. Watts, 932–38. London: Longman, Green, Longman, Roberts and Green.

———. [1865] 1884. On the Variation of Prices and the Value of the Currency Since 1782. In *Investigations in Currency and Finance*, edited by H. S. Foxwell. London: Macmillan.

———. 1866. Brief Account of a General Mathematical Theory of Political Economy. *Journal of Statistical Society of London* 29:282–87.

———. 1871a. The Power of Numerical Discrimination. *Nature* 3:281–82.

———. 1871b. *The Theory of Political Economy*. London: Macmillan.

———. [1874] 1958. *The Principles of Science: A Treatise on Logic and Scientific Method*. New York: Dover.

———. 1884. *Investigations in Currency and Finance*. Edited by H. S. Foxwell. London: Macmillan and Co.

———. [1890] 1971. Utilitarianism: In *Pure Logic and Other Minor Works*, edited by Robert Adamson and Harriet A. Jevons. New York: Burt Franklin.

———. [1890] 1971. *Pure Logic and Other Minor Works*. Edited by Robert Adamson and Harriet A. Jevons. New York: Burt Franklin.

———. 1972–81. *Papers and Correspondence*. Vols. 1–8. Edited by R. D. Collison Black and Rosamond Könekamp. London: Macmillan.

Johnston, Stephen. 1997. Making the Arithmometer Count. *Bulletin of the Scientific Instrument Society* 52:12–21.

Katoh, Shoji. 1989. Mechanics' Institutes in Great Britain to the 1850s. *Journal of Educational Administration and History* 21.2:1–7.

Kidd, A. J., and K. W. Roberts. 1985. *City, Class, and Culture: Studies of Cultural Production and Social Policy in Victorian Manchester*. Manchester: Manchester University Press.

Kim, Jinbang. 1995. Jevons versus Cairnes on Exact Economic Laws. In *Numeracy in Economics,* edited by Ingrid H. Rima, 140–56. London: Routledge.

Klein, Ursula. 1999. Techniques of Modelling and Paper-Tools in Classical Chemistry. In *Models as Mediators*, edited by Mary S. Morgan and Margaret Morrison, 146–67. Cambridge: Cambridge University Press.

Krüger, Lorenz, Lorraine J. Daston, and Michael Heidelberger. 1987. *The Probabilistic Revolution*. Cambridge: MIT Press.

Layton, David. 1965. Diction and Dictionaries in the Diffusion of Scientific Knowledge: An Aspect of the History of the Popularization of Science in Great Britain. *British Journal for the History of Science* 27:221–34.

Levere, Trevor. 1990. Lavoisier. In *Nature, Experiment, and the Sciences*, edited by Trevor Levere and William Shea, 207–23. Dordrecht: Kluwer Academic Publishers.

Maas, Harro. 2001. Mechanical Reasoning: Jevons and the Making of Modern Economics. Ph.D. diss., Amsterdam University.

Machamer, Peter. 1998. Galileo's Machines, His Mathematics, and His Experiments. In *The Cambridge Companion to Galileo*, edited by Peter Machamer, 53–79. Cambridge: Cambridge University Press.

Mill, J. S. [1836] 1967. On the Definition of Political Economy; And on The Appropriate Method of Its Study. In vol. 4 of *Collected Works*, edited by J. M. Robson, 309–39. Toronto: University of Toronto Press.

——— . 1981. Autobiography and Literary Essays. In vol. 1 of *Collected Works*, edited by J. M. Robson. Toronto: University of Toronto Press.

Mirowski, Philip. 1989. *More Heat than Light: Economics as Social Physics, Physics as Nature's Economics*. Cambridge: Cambridge University Press.

Morgan, Mary S. 1990. *The History of Econometric Ideas*. Cambridge: Cambridge University Press.

——— . 1997. Searching for Causal Relations in Economic Statistics: Reflections from History. In *Causality in Crisis? Statistical Methods and the Search for Causal Knowledge in the Social Sciences*, edited by Vaughn R. McKim and Stephen P. Turner, 47–80. Notre Dame, Ind.: University of Notre Dame Press.

Parssinen, T. M. 1974. Popular Science and Society: The Phrenology Movement in Early Victorian Britain. *Journal of Social History* 8.1:1–20.

Peart, Sandra J. 1995a. "Disturbing causes," "Noxious errors," and the Theory-Practice Distinction in the Economics of J. S. Mill and W. S. Jevons. *Canadian Journal of Economics* 28.4b:1194–1211.

——— . 1995b. Measurement in Utility Calculations: The Utilitarian Perspective. In *Numeracy in Economics*, edited by Ingrid H. Rima, 63–86. London: Routledge.

——— . 1996. *The Economics of W. S. Jevons*. London: Routledge.

Porter, Theodore M. 1991. Objectivity and Authority: How French Engineers Reduced Public Utility to Numbers. *Poetics Today* 12:245–65.

——— . 1995. *Trust in Numbers: The Pursuit of Objectivity in Science and Public Life*. Princeton, N.J.: Princeton University Press.

Rabinbach, Anson. 1990. *The Human Motor: Energy, Fatigue, and the Origins of Modernity*. New York: Basic Books.

Schabas, M. 1990. *A World Ruled by Number: William Stanley Jevons and the Rise of Mathematical Economics*. Princeton, N.J.: Princeton University Press.

Shapin, Steven, and Barry Barnes. 1977. Science, Nature and Control: Interpreting Mechanics' Institutes. *Social Studies of Science* 7:31–74.

Sibum, Heinz Otto. 1995. Reworking the Mechanical Value of Heat: Instruments of Precision and Gestures of Accuracy in Early Victorian England. *Studies in History and Philosophy of Science* 26.1:73–106.

Stephens, Michael D., and Gordon W. Roderick. 1972. Science, The Working Classes and Mechanics' Institutes. *Annals of Science* 29:349–60.

Stigler, Stephen M. 1982. Jevons as Statistician. *The Manchester School* 50:354–65.

Thompson, E. P. 1978. *The Poverty of Theory and Other Essays*. London: Merlin.

Vatin, François. 1993. *Le travail: Economie et physique*. Paris: Presses Universitaires de France.

Warke, Tom. 2000. Mathematical Fitness in the Evolution of the Utility Concept from Bentham to Jevons to Marshall. *Journal of the History of Economic Thought* 22.1:5–27.

Warwick, Andrew. 1995. The Laboratory of Theory or What's Exact about the Exact Sciences? In *The Values of Precision*, edited by M. Norton Wise, 311–51. Princeton, N.J.: Princeton University Press.

Watson, Michael I. 1987. The Origins of the Mechanics' Institutes of North Yorkshire. *Journal of Educational Administration and History* 19.2:12–25.

Whewell, William. 1856. *On the Philosophy of Discovery, Chapters Historical and Critical*. London: Parker.

White, Michael V. 1994. The Moment of Richard Jennings: The Production of Jevons's Marginalist Economic Agent. In *Natural Images in Economic Thought: "Markets Read in Tooth and Claw,"* edited by P. Mirowski, 197–230. Cambridge: Cambridge University Press.

——— . 1995. "Perpetual Motion and Change": Statics and Dynamics in the Political Economy of W. S. Jevons. Mimeo.

——— . 1999. Edge of Darkness? Jevons's Formulation of the Post-classical "Economic Problem." Mimeo.

Wise, M. Norton. 1993. Mediations: Enlightenment Balancing Acts, or The Technology of Rationalism. In *World Changes: Thomas Kuhn and the Nature of Science*, edited by Paul Horwich, 207–56. Cambridge, Mass.: MIT Press.

Wise, M. Norton, and Crosbie Smith. 1989a. Work and Waste: Political Economy and Natural Philosophy in Nineteenth Century Britain. Part 1. *History of Science* 27:263–301.

——— . 1989b. Work and Waste: Political Economy and Natural Philosophy in Nineteenth Century Britain. Part 2. *History of Science* 27:391–449.

——— . 1990. Work and Waste: Political Economy and Natural Philosophy in Nineteenth Century Britain. Part 3. *History of Science* 28:221–61.

Perspective

Measurement, and Changing Images
of Mathematical Knowledge

E. Roy Weintraub

> To be sure, computation invites measurement, and every easily
> observed regularity of certain magnitudes is an incentive
> to mathematical investigation.
> —J. F. Herbart (in Moritz 1914, 251)

A number of essays at the conference touched on issues of mathematization, formalization, rigor, and axiomatization even as issues of measurement remained the focus of the discussions. Consequently the connection between the history of mathematics and the history of measurement
remained outside the direct view of the conference program even as that
history cast its shadows on histories of measurement. In this perspective
I suggest how in particular the changing "image of mathematics" may
provide one context for understanding the changing nature of measurement in economics.

As the historian of mathematics Leo Corry (1989, 411) has argued:

> We may distinguish, broadly speaking, two sorts of questions con-
> cerning every scientific discipline. The first sort are questions about
> the subject matter of the discipline. The second sort are questions
> about the discipline *qua* discipline, or second-order questions. It is
> the aim of the discipline to answer the questions of the first sort, but
> usually not to answer questions of the second sort. These second-order

Correspondence may be addressed to E. Roy Weintraub, Department of Economics, Duke University, Durham, NC 27708–0097.

questions concern the methodology, philosophy, history, or sociology of the discipline and are usually addressed by an ancillary discipline.

The first sort of question concerns the discipline's knowledge, while the second sort concerns the image of knowledge. Corry's (1996) argument is that to speak of change in mathematics is to speak not only of change in mathematical knowledge, in the sense of new theorems proved, new definitions created, and new mathematical objects described. But change in mathematics also involves changes in the image of mathematics, in, say, changed standards for accepting proofs, changed ideas about mathematical rigor and truth, and changed ideas about the nature of the mathematical enterprise. For Corry (1989, 418), "*It is precisely the task of the historian of mathematics to characterize the images of knowledge of a given period and to explain their interaction with the body of knowledge—and thus to explain the development of mathematics*" (emphasis added).

I urge the view that there were several shifts in the image of mathematical knowledge over the nineteenth century—the period out of which modern economics and its concerns with measurement developed—and those shifts are one context for understanding the development of economists' ideas about measurement. To fully detail this argument is beyond the scope of this short note,[1] so in what follows I will simply identify some of the issues and provide some of the references which can more fully indicate the nature of the claim.

From Geometric Certainty to Physical Representation

The first change in the image of mathematics was based on a new conception of what mathematical truth might mean. It occurred over the second third of the nineteenth century and was well incorporated in the Continental tradition in mathematics. That is, outside England there was a change in mathematics between the time of William Whewell's defense of mathematics in the educational process,[2] a defense based on

1. This argument is more fully developed in chapter 1 of Weintraub forthcoming.

2. "Early in the nineteenth century the loose Georgian approach gave way to a somewhat more rigorous academic structure. In a period of rising enrollments, examinations began to play an increasingly important role at both Cambridge and Oxford. At Oxford, the examinations were in classics, which focus was justified as a way of broadening young minds rather than as imparting specialized knowledge. The same kind of rationale was applied at Cambridge, where, however, the central examination was in mathematics. Until the middle of the century

the notion that mathematics (vide Euclid, Newton) was the paradigm of certain and secure knowledge (the time of Alfred Marshall's student days), and Marshall's later time as professor of political economy. The emergence of non-Euclidean geometries had made Whewell's argument about axiomatics and inevitable truth ring hollow long before the turn of the twentieth century. In the time of the new geometries, the difficulty of linking mathematical truth to a particular (Euclidean) geometry produced a real crisis of confidence for Victorian educational practice, a point well documented in Richards 1988. The roots of this crisis are linked to the unhealthy state of mathematics in England associated with the backward-looking mathematical tripos examination and its importance in the Cambridge institutional structures that were developed to define a fixed order of merit among honors graduates. This first crisis prepared the late Victorian mind for the new idea that mathematical rigor had to be associated with physical argumentation. And it was this new image of mathematics in science that helps us to understand the concerns of individuals like F. Y. Edgeworth and Vilfredo Pareto.

More precisely, the changes in mathematics in the last several decades of the nineteenth century were primarily changes in the image of mathematics as mathematicians reconstructed the nature of number, of proof, and of rigor. The early Victorian image of mathematical truth was that it was fixed and immutable, like analytic truth in the logicians' sense. But later in the century, mathematical rigor if not mathematical truth itself began to be identified with empirically grounded mathematical theories and arguments. A mathematical argument was only as strong as the connection of the mathematical ideas to the substrate of physical reasoning.

In order to get a fuller grasp of this alternative image of mathematics, consider how mathematicians were re-representing themselves and their enterprise in this period. What were they saying about the right way, the best way, to think about the nature and role of mathematics? What in other words was the context, in the community of mathematicians, for the views held by economists, at the time of the birth of the science of economics, on the role of mathematics in economics?

---

one needed a pass on this examination in order even to take the parallel examination in the classics. Even though the tripos became more and more mathematically demanding, the justification for requiring that the students study for it continued to be broadly humanistic rather than specific or professional. Throughout the century the center of England's mathematical education pursued the subject as a way to help students become fully formed human beings" (Richards 1991, 307–8).

When Felix Klein visited the United States in 1893 to deliver the Evanston lectures at Northwestern University (in conjunction with the Columbia exposition in Chicago), he was perhaps the most important "American" mathematician, even though he was German and his home was Gottingen. As is well documented, Klein had been the Ph.D. thesis advisor to almost an entire generation of American mathematicians, and so his invitation to come to the United States to provide a survey of mathematics was entirely appropriate (Parshall and Rowe 1994). Of special interest to us is his sixth lecture, delivered 2 September 1893, titled "On the Mathematical Character of Space-intuition and the Relation of Pure Mathematics to the Applied Sciences" (Klein 1894).

On the role of mathematics in the applied sciences, Klein noted, "From the point of view of pure mathematical science I should lay particular stress on the historic value in applied sciences as an aid to discovering new truths in mathematics. Thus I have shown . . . that the Abelian integrals can best be understood and illustrated by considering electric currents on closed surfaces . . . and so on" (46). In other words, the applied fields themselves nurture mathematics by providing a source for problems and ways of thinking about (models for) mathematical structures. The connections between mathematics and the sciences are not unidirectional, but rather flow both ways, as it is realization of Abelian integrals in terms of the electric currents that provide the logical foundation for those mathematical objects.

Klein continued by telling his audience that

> I believe that the more or less close relation of any applied science to mathematics might be characterized by the degree of exactness obtained, or obtainable, in its numerical results. . . . [But] it must not be forgotten that mathematical developments transcending the limit of exactness of the science are of no practical value . . . thus, while the astronomer can put to good use a wide range of mathematical theory, the chemist is only just beginning to apply the first derivative . . . for second derivatives he does not seem to have found any use as yet. (46–47)

This is a long way from Whewell but quite close really to an Edgeworth who sought to find quantitative measurements of pleasure and a Pareto who sought to describe the measurable characteristics of individual equilibrium. Mathematics for Klein is not really of much fundamental use in a science unless that science is able to constitute its basic concepts with "exact axioms" and precise numerical results. To truly imitate physics, a science of political economy would need to have measurable quantities of its conceptual building blocks and ways of measuring its "results." The prerequisite for having a mathematical science is to have exact measurements in that science. This is not the image of mathematics of "clear reasoning to certain conclusions."

In Klein's image of mathematics, the measurable and likely geometric structures that facilitate mathematical argumentation in any applied field require quantitative argumentation in that field in order to ground the analysis. The idea that one can have a useful mathematical theory of x, where x could be astronomy, economics, or forestry, would appear then to require physical modeling—mechanical modeling—in the manner of a successful mathematical physics. The success of any applied mathematical field would then be linked to a reductionist argument of the form "the nearness of field x to physics is an indicator of likelihood of successfully producing a mathematical theory of x." It was not that Klein himself developed such a reductionist perspective, but rather that no alternative appeared to be viable for him. His call for the study of mathematics together with its applications is our first hint that there was an alternative image of mathematics developing in the community of mathematicians. Near the end of the nineteenth century, Klein's vision looked backward to the successes of mathematics in physics. But those successes were to be questioned within a decade as Einstein and Max Planck called the reductionist mechanical program itself into question.

Klein of course was not alone among mathematicians in arguing that a mathematical science needed empirical grounding. Vito Volterra's (1906a) inaugural address as professor at the University of Rome[3] provided an opportunity for this gifted and distinguished international scientist to reflect on ways in which his own field, mathematics, could potentially enrich discourse and practice in the social sciences and biological sciences.

Among most mathematicians, however, comes the natural desire to direct their mind beyond the circle of pure mathematical analysis, to

---

3. The version which I shall examine is the translation by Ludovic Zoretti into French for *La revue du mois* of 10 January 1906, where the paper was called "Le mathematiques dans les sciences biologiques et sociales" (Volterra 1906b). In what follows, I shall use an English translation of this French version prepared by Caroline Benforado in December 1993.

work toward comparing the success of different methods that it holds
and to classify them based on applications in order to use its activity to perfect the most useful methods, reinforcing the weakest and
creating the most powerful. Curiosity is the most intense about the
sciences that math has ventured into most recently, I am, of course,
speaking mainly about the biological and the social sciences. It is all
the more intense because of the great desire to make sure that classical
methods which have given such clear results in mechanical-physical
sciences are likely to be transported with equal success into new and
unexplored fields which are opening before it. (1906b, 1–2)

Volterra's method is clearly stated.

First establish concepts in a way that allows the introduction of measure, and from those measures discover laws, from those laws work
back to the hypothesis, then by means of analysis, deduce from the
hypothesis a science which reasons in a rigourously logical manner
about ideal beings, compare consequences to reality, reject or transform the recycled fundamental hypothesis as soon as a contradiction
appears between the results of the calculation and the real world, and
in this matter succeed in guessing new facts and new analogies, or deduce once again from the present state what the past was and what the
future will be. This is, quite briefly, how one can summarize the birth
and evolution of a science which has a mathematical character. (5)

Volterra shows himself completely at ease with the emerging literature
in mathematical economics. He provides a lucid discussion of *homo eco-
nomicus* and Pareto's *ophelimite* and indifference curves. He cites Pan-
teloni, Pareto, Irving Fisher, Barone, Jevons, Whewell, Cournot, Gossen,
Walras, and even goes back to Ceva Giovanni of 1711. He notes that
"once our researcher has examined the logical method employed in obtaining the conditions of economic equilibrium, he will recognize the
reasoning which allows him to establish the principle of virtual labor.
And when he finds himself faced with differential equations of economics, he feels the urge to apply methods of integration to them" (8).

What we see for Volterra at this time of a century's new beginning
is the enthusiasm of a mathematician, who himself had done significant
work in mathematical physics, for the emerging theories in economics
and biology. Rigorous mathematics was founded on ideas of what we

would now call applied mathematical theory. Mathematics was importantly tied to applications of analysis, and those applications themselves had to be structured to facilitate answering questions of measurement and prediction. At a time when Marshall was calling for restraint in the application of mathematics to economics and was deeply suspicious of attempts to measure economic concepts like utility, we find Volterra suggesting that the work done was both interesting and potentially quite grand. For Volterra, as for Klein, the need in a field like economics was for measurement. For Volterra, as for Edgeworth, concepts had to be developed that would allow exact calculations, for that was the route to a mathematical science like physics, the paradigmatic mathematical science. Underlying Volterra's image of mathematics in economics in 1900 was a belief that it was possible for economics to develop in such a fashion. Indeed there was not really any other candidate perspective Volterra considered. Physics was the model. But neither Volterra nor Klein recognized that physics itself was losing its certitude.

From Physical Reductionism to Axiomatics

By 1900 the image of the best way to construct a mathematical science was again changing. Marshall's mathematics, the early Victorian tripos mathematics of Euclidean geometry, the drawing of cord segments and conic sections, and simple statics and dynamics and the like were thus to be twice removed from the concerns of mathematicians in the new century. The ideas of Volterra and Klein and the mathematical understandings of economists like Edgeworth and Pareto were themselves coming under attack because of the new ideas about axiomatics.

One of the central tropes found in many popular histories of mathematics, and indeed in many of the canonical histories of mathematics, concerns crises in mathematics and physics toward the end of the nineteenth century. These several crises are taken to be the causes of major changes in the way physicists and mathematicians conceived of their world. In mathematics, the crises were understood to concern the foundations of mathematics. I have argued that there was a change in the image of mathematics associated with the failures of Euclidean geometry to domesticate the non-Euclidean geometries. The end-of-century crises in mathematics concerned apparent inconsistencies in set theory associated with Georg Cantor's new ideas about "infinity" (i.e., transfinite cardinals and the continuum of real numbers) and apparent inconsistencies in the foundations of arithmetic and logic, associated with work by Friedrich Frege and Giuseppe Peano. Work done in response to these problems, it is often argued, left the community of mathematicians unsure of what was right and proper and true and lasting in mathematics. For example, one popular exposition argues that:

> Against the background of steady progress in the great scientific centers of England, France, Germany, Italy, and Russia, three sizzling developments in the last quarter of the 19th century prepared the ground for the massive explosion of new ideas in pure mathematics at the beginning the 20th century: The creation (basically, single-handed) of the theory of infinite sets by George Cantor (1845–1918); Felix Klein's (1849–1925) announcement in 1872 of the Erlanger Program which proposed geometry as a discipline concerned with the study of an abstract object invariant under given transformation groups; [t]he appearance in 1899 of *Grundlagen der Geometrie* by David Hilbert (1862–1943) axiomatizing Euclidean geometry. . . . All three came from Germany. They brought about a fundamental change both in the position of mathematics among other disciplines of knowledge, and the way mathematicians think about themselves. The aftershocks lasted well into the 1930s and beyond. . . . As a result, mathematics broke away from the body of natural sciences." (Woyczynski 1996, 107–8)

In the popular imagination, however, more critical was the failure of physics, particularly rational mechanics, to solve the new problems associated with blackbody radiation, quanta, and relativity. These problems led to a crisis in physics and a fortiori mathematical physics. That is, the kind of nineteenth-century mathematics based on differential equations—as well as both quantitative and qualitative properties of dynamical systems—was fundamentally linked to the problems in mechanics. If the deterministic mechanical mode of physical argumentation was to be replaced by an alternative physical theory, the mathematics too might have to be replaced. In any event, some established areas of mathematics were no longer connected to a canonical physical model.

Let me recapitulate the argument lest the main thread get lost in the details. Around the end of the nineteenth century, just as economists had begun to understand that constructing a mathematical science required basing argumentation on the physical reasoning of rational mechanics, and measurement of quantities to facilitate those reasoning chains, the image of mathematical knowledge was again changing.[4] Modeling the concerns of the new physics appeared to require a new mathematics, a mathematics less based on deterministic dynamical systems and more on statistical argumentation and algebra. Consequently mathematical physics was to link up with newer mathematical ideas in algebra (e.g., group theory) and probability theory (e.g., measure theory), as mathematicians took up the challenge to work on mathematical ideas which could facilitate understanding of the world.

Just as the objects of the physical world appeared changed—gone were billiard balls, newly present were quanta—the universe of mathematical objects too changed. Transfinite sets and new geometries, together with a recognition that the paradoxes of set theory and logic were intertwined, led mathematicians to seek new foundations for their subject. Analysis of those foundations of set theory, logic, and arithmetic, and thus the foundations of sciences based on mathematics, were to be based on axiomatic thinking.[5]

To summarize my argument: following a late nineteenth-century period in which mathematical rigor was to be established by basing the mathematics on physical reasoning, around 1900—as understanding of the physical world became less secure—mathematical truth was to be established not relative to physical reasoning but relative to other mathematical theories and objects. From a physical reductionism, mathematics moved to a mathematical reductionism[6] in the guise of one or another set of ideas about formalism: problems and paradoxes and confusions of the turn of the-century mathematics were to be resolved by a reconceptualization of the nature of the fundamental objects of mathematics. Even ignoring the mass of details which this argument appears to need in its support, looking at mathematical work done before 1900, work done later in the 1920s and 1930s, and work done in the 1950s, it is clear that the mathematical landscape had been transformed. The images of mathematical knowledge concerning ideas of rigor, truth, formalization, and proof changed over this period.

The story of measurement and its role in economics plays out against changing images of mathematics. These changing images are nowhere

---

4. This argument of course is central to Mirowski 1989.

5. This move was called for by Hilbert, among others. Using the metaphor of constructing a building (mathematics), Hilbert (1918) spoke of the axiomatic thinking as the method for constructing sufficiently strong foundations.

6. This argument is more fully developed in Ingrao and Israel 1990.

more apparent than in English-speaking countries whose educational practices were shaped, early in the nineteenth century, in part by the role of mathematics as the touchstone for logical, rigorous, and correct modes of argument. Thus as ideas of what constitutes "good" mathematics changed, so too did the mathematical underpinning of the nature and role of measurement in scientific, a fortiori economic, arguments.

References

Corry, L. 1989. Linearity and Reflexivity in the Growth of Mathematical Knowledge. *Science in Context* 3.2:409–40.

———. 1996. *Modern Algebra and the Rise of Mathematical Structures*. Boston: Birkhauser.

Hilbert, D. 1918. Axiomatisches Denken. *Mathematische Annalen* 78:405–15.

Ingrao, B., and G. Israel. 1990. *The Invisible Hand: Economic Theory in the History of Science*. Cambridge: MIT Press.

Klein, F. 1894. *The Evanston Colloquium: Lectures on Mathematics Delivered from Aug. 28 to Sept. 9, 1893 before Members of the Congress of Mathematics Held in Connection with the World's Fair in Chicago at Northwestern University, Evanston, Ill. Reported by Alexander Ziwet*. New York: Macmillan.

Mirowski, P. 1989. *More Heat Than Light*. New York: Cambridge University Press.

Moritz, R. E. 1914. *Memorabila Mathematica*. Washington, D.C.: Mathematical Association of America.

Parshall, K. H., and D. E. Rowe. 1994. *The Emergence of the American Mathematical Research Community, 1876–1900: J. J. Sylvester, Felix Klein, and E. H. Moore*. Providence, R. I.: American Mathematical Society.

Richards, J. L. 1988. *Mathematical Visions: The Pursuit of Geometry in Victorian England*. San Diego: Academic Press.

———. 1991. Rigor and Clarity: Foundations of Mathematics in France and England, 1800–1840. *Science in Context* 4.2 (autumn):297–319.

Volterra, V. 1906a. L'economia matematica ed il nuovo manuale del Prof. Pareto. *Giornale degli economisti* 32.2:296–301.

———. 1906b. Les mathematiques dans les sciences biologiques et sociales. *La revue du mois* 1 (10 janvier 1906): 1–20.

Weintraub, E. R. Forthcoming. *How Economics Became a Mathematical Science*. Durham, N.C.: Duke University Press.

Woyczynski, W. 1996. Appendix 1: Mathematics in Stefan Banach's Time. In *Through a Reporter's Eye: The Life of Stefan Banach*, R. Kaluza. Basel: Birkhauser.

Fisher's Instrumental Approach to Index Numbers

Marcel Boumans

> If contradictory attributes be assigned to a concept, I say, that
> *mathematically the concept does not exist.*
> —David Hilbert, "Mathematical Problems" (1902)

> Sometimes control with a single lens is impossible since some
> incompatible features are required and a compromise becomes necessary
> calling for further judgement on the part of the designer as to which error
> should be reduced and to what degree.
> —R. J. Bracey, *The Technique of Optical Instrument Design* (1960)

Since the beginning of the nineteenth century, a large number of price index number formulae have been developed, mostly named after their inventors, such as the Paasche and Layspeyres indexes. Parallel with the invention of new index formulae, criteria were developed for distinguishing between them. These parallel developments culminated in Irving Fisher's two classics on index numbers, *The Purchasing Power of Money* (1911) and *The Making of Index Numbers* (1922). In these, Fisher evaluated index formulae in a systematic way with respect to a number of "tests." Although these two volumes are considered the "Old and New Testament" of Axiomatic Index Theory (Vogt and Barta 1997, viii), the axiomatic approach originated from challenges to Fisher's system of

Correspondence may be addressed to Marcel Boumans, Department of Economics, University of Amsterdam, Roetersstraat 11, 1018 WB Amsterdam, The Netherlands; e-mail: Boumans@fee.uva.nl. I am grateful to Mary Morgan, Judy Klein, Ted Gayer, Roy Weintraub, Harro Maas, Mark Blaug, and an anonymous referee for their constructive comments.

tests on grounds of their inconsistency and the seeming arbitrariness of the choice of tests. That debate started with Ragnar Frisch in 1930, but the Axiomatic Index Theory only got its current name and shape—based on functional equation analysis—from Wolfgang Eichhorn in 1973. In Axiomatic Index Theory, the tests are considered as requirements on the functional form of the index number from which the index formula can be derived. If these requirements are inconsistent, no formula can be constructed. So although Fisher's work is seen as the forerunner of the Axiomatic Index Theory, his system of tests was much criticized because of its apparent internal inconsistency. The aim of this essay is to show that evaluating Fisher's work from an axiomatic perspective leads to a misconception of his empirically inclined approach to the assessment of index numbers. For a better understanding of his work on index numbers, his background in mathematics, his philosophical thinking, and his inventions of measuring instruments will all be examined.

The crucial problem behind the assessment of measurement formulae is that they are not theories and thus cannot be assessed as such. They cannot be tested in the usual way by comparing quantitative data generated by the formula with the quantitative data of the phenomenon to see whether they differ significantly. The reason is quite obvious: to obtain quantitative data of the phenomenon, we need to possess a measuring device. Of course such devices can involve theories, in a strong or loose sense; however, they are not built to explain or to make predictions about a phenomenon but to generate numbers about it. Nevertheless, we are not satisfied with any number; for example, we care about its representing quality. To attain this quality, measurement formulae should fulfill the relevant theoretical and empirical requirements with respect to the phenomenon concerned.

The assessment of the formulae depends not only on whether they fulfill certain theoretical and empirical requirements but also on how these requirements are fulfilled. That is, formulae are also assessed on the basis of how they are constructed, whether this construction is done in a rigorous way or not. And what is taken as rigor depends on the kinds of objects formulae are assumed to be, whether they are considered as formal concepts or as instruments. Although one usually associates instruments with physical devices, like a thermometer or a ruler, in economics they are immaterial. Despite their immateriality they still function as if they were empirical objects.[1] This treatment contrasts with the received or standard account of mathematical objects in which they are considered as formal axiomatic abstractions.[2] Both accounts will be considered to see whether they enable us to understand specific developments in the history of index number theory. It will be shown that the two quotations presented at the beginning of this essay, which characterize these two opposite accounts—from here on to be labeled as the *axiomatic* and the *instrumental* approach—reflect the difference between the Axiomatic Index Theory and Irving Fisher's work on index numbers. While one approach considers inconsistencies a capital sin, the other approach accepts that the best instrument sometimes has to be a compromise between incompatible requirements.

Because rigor and axiomatics are often seen as peers, one might tend to expect less rigor in Fisher's instrumental approach. This prejudgment is unjustified. Giorgio Israel (1981) and Roy Weintraub (1998) have shown that, in the history of mathematics, rigor has not always been identified with axiomatics.[3] Weintraub (1998, 235) showed, for example, that for Vito Volterra the "opposite of 'rigorous' was not 'informal' but rather 'unconstrained.'" This interpretation of rigor changed under the influence of the Axiomatization Movement. As a result of that movement, "a rigorous argument was reconceptualized as a logically consistent argument instead of as an argument that connected the problematic phenomenon to a physical phenomenon by use of empirical data. Propositions were henceforth 'true' within the system considered because they were consistent with the assumptions instead of being 'true' because they could be grounded in 'real phenomena'" (237). Israel discussed the distinction between rigor and axiomatics in relation to the "crisis of present-day mathematics," namely that the axiomatic trend has emptied mathematical research of any external determination and content to such an extent that its relationship to applications has been lost. Although the role of mathematics in applied sciences is growing rapidly—economics

1. This is closely related to Morrison and Morgan's (1999) model account. According to them, models function as "instruments of investigation," as quasi-empirical objects.

2. Note that mathematics is not equated with formal axiomatic abstractions, labeled by Lakatos (1976) as "formalism." Lakatos showed that mathematics grows as an informal, quasi-empirical discipline.

3. See also Roy Weintraub's essay in this volume. Two other case studies in this volume in which rigor is not equated with axiomatics are Flavio Comim's discussion of Stone's treatment of consistency in the measurement of national accounts and Martin Kohli's account of the development of Wassily Leontief's input-output tables.

is a good example—mathematics is still deeply separated from the applied sciences. "What appears to be missing, is a codification of the rules which should define and guide the use of mathematics as an instrument for the description, interpretation and control of phenomena" (Israel 1981, 219).

As we shall see, the rule implied by Fisher's instrumental approach can be well described as finding the best balance between theoretical and empirical requirements, even if these requirements are incompatible. Then, rigor is attained by making the instrument's performance as close as possible to a certain standard. In Fisher's case that standard was a specific geometrical form with which the geometrical representations of the candidate devices were compared so that the evaluation could be based on the judgment of the eye. Because of its visually appealing geometrical features, the triangle was Fisher's favorite standard of comparison.

The essay traces out the various characteristics of Fisher's instrumental approach to index numbers. Fisher's empiricist, rather than a priorist, inclinations can be traced back to the period in which he was educated as a mathematician, namely the period in which the rise of non-Euclidean geometry had a major influence on the foundations of mathematics. The impact of these developments in mathematics on Fisher's own view will be discussed in the next section. Fisher's habit was to solve a problem by approaching it as a design problem of an instrument. In the second section, I take a closer look at a specific invention that will help us to understand his typical approach in solving the index number problem, that in turn will be discussed in the third section. In his approach, rigor was not based on consistency; nevertheless, inconsistency was the main target of criticism of Fisher's work on index numbers. The contrast between the two approaches—instrumental versus axiomatic—will be clarified in the fourth section. Fisher's assessment of world maps, discussed in the fifth section, will provide a nice demonstration of his instrumental approach. The last section concludes with a brief reflection on the axiomatic and instrumental approach.

Non-Euclidean Geometry

Non-Euclidean geometry had a major influence on the foundations of mathematics at the end of the nineteenth century, the period that Fisher was educated as a mathematician. This new geometry obliged mathematicians to revise radically their understanding of the nature of mathematics and its relation to the physical world.[4] Until about 1800 all mathematicians were convinced that Euclidean geometry was the correct idealization of the properties of physical space and of figures in that space. But this conviction changed dramatically in the nineteenth century. Toward the end of that century, mathematicians and physicists understood that properties of space were not given a priori but had to be measured.

There is considerable evidence that Fisher was well informed about this development. In 1890 and 1891, in addition to the courses he was taking in graduate school, he started teaching geometry at Yale (which he continued to do for several years) (Allen 1993, 36). He even wrote a textbook on geometry, *Elements of Geometry* (1896), with Andrew W. Phillips of the Mathematics Department. Fisher also took courses under Josiah Willard Gibbs, one of his mentors at Yale (Allen 1993, 37), including one on multiple algebra (and so, vector analysis). But Fisher was also well aware of the philosophical implications of these developments in mathematics. Philosophy intrigued Fisher, and he had taken George Ladd's course in Kant (Allen 1993, 38). Geometry and philosophy were combined in an essay he wrote as a student during the period 1889–90. This handwritten and never published essay, "Mathematical Contribution to Philosophy; Attacking Kant's Theory of Geometrical Axioms,"[5] consisted of two parts. The first was a short history of the origin and development of non-Euclidean geometry, the second an "Application to Kant." Fisher's essay made no original contribution to philosophy or geometry; it was a further elaboration of Hermann von Helmholtz's "The Origin and Meaning of Geometrical Axioms" (1876, 1878). To explicate Fisher's understanding of the history and philosophical implications of non-Euclidean geometry, both will be expounded below in parallel to his own account.

Non-Euclidean geometry arose from attempts to prove Euclid's fifth postulate, the so-called parallel postulate or axiom. In fact, non-Euclidean geometry is a geometry in which the parallel postulate does not hold. Nikolai Ivanovich Lobachevsky (1792–1856) was one of the first who proposed to deny the parallel axiom and to see whether the resulting geometry would lead to a contradiction. It didn't, and the geometry he

4. Kline (1972) discusses this implication extensively.
5. Manuscripts and Archives, Yale University Library.

CYLINDER   SPHERE   PSEUDO-SPHERE

Figure 1   Triangles in three different spaces (Phillips and Fisher 1896, 52)

elaborated is now known as hyperbolic or Lobachevsky geometry. Carl Friedrich Gauss (1777–1855) arrived at the same conclusions and saw their most revolutionary implication, namely that non-Euclidean geometry could be used to describe the properties of physical space as accurately as Euclidean geometry does. Thus the latter is not the necessary geometry of physical space; its physical truth cannot be guaranteed on any a priori grounds. Gauss never published his views on the problem of the parallel axiom but he did publish his discussion of curved surfaces. Gauss introduced the concept of "measure of curvature," now known as the Gaussian curvature of a surface. For a surface of constant curvature, Gauss derived a simple formula relating curvature (K), area, and angular measure. He took a geodesic triangle $\triangle ABC$ with vertices A, B, and C and sides as geodesic segments. A geodesic segment between two points on a surface is the shortest path lying on the surface between those points. He determined that, if $\angle A$ denotes the measure of angle A, then

$$K \times \text{area } \triangle ABC = \angle A + \angle B + \angle C - 180°$$

The Euclidean space has constant zero curvature, the spherical space constant positive, and the pseudo-spherical space constant negative curvature. As a result, the sum of the angles of a triangle is respectively 180°, more than 180°, and less than 180° (see figure 1).

Besides this development, in which different kinds of geometries were worked out on the basis of a different parallel axiom, mathematicians started to think of the possible existence of more than three space dimensions. This notion of multidimensional space arose from multiple algebra (vector analysis), to which Josiah Willard Gibbs had made important contributions. Fisher, in his Josiah Willard Gibbs Lecture (1930), recalled Gibbs's response to German criticisms toward his violation of fundamental rules of algebra (such as the commutative rule that $a \times b$ is equal to $b \times a$), a consequence of his multiple algebra. Gibbs's comment was "that all depends on what your object is in making those sacrosanct rules for operating upon symbols. If the object is to interpret physical phenomena and if we find we can do better by having a rule that $a \times b$ is equal not to $b \times a$ but to minus $b \times a$, as in the multiplication of two vectors, then," he said, "the criticisms of the Germans are beside the point" (Fisher 1930, 231).

In the second part of his essay on Kant, Fisher discussed the consequences of these developments in mathematics for Kant's apriorism. Kant maintained that our minds supply certain modes of organization, so-called "intuitions," of space and time, and that experience is absorbed and organized by our minds in accordance with these intuitions. As a consequence, certain principles about space are prior to experience. According to Kant, these principles, which he called a priori synthetic truths, were those of Euclidean geometry. "We cannot say perhaps that Kant's doctrine of space as an a priori form of mental intuition is false but we can say without hesitation that the foundations on which he built his theory are false" (Fisher 1890, 6). Because the parallel axiom might be untrue, maybe "we do live in spherical or pseudo-spherical space. The illustration of the triangle which Kant makes so much use of is the most unfortunate one he could have chosen. For the proposition about the triangle rests directly on the parallel postulate. If this postulate be untrue then is it that the sum of the angles of a triangle are not exactly 180°" (6–7). Fisher's conclusion was an echo of Helmholtz's (1878, 214): "[Geometry] is not possible as a pure science. Its foundation truths are the accumulated consolidated experience of our race but no less experience. We must strip geometry of its pretended dignity of being pure and give it the greater dignity of being the most perfect of the physical sciences" (Fisher 1890, 9). Helmholtz's conclusion was in line with his general empiricist philosophy. He rejected the Kantian claim to look upon "the geometrical axioms as propositions given *à priori* by transcendental intuitions which no experience could either confirm or refute" (Helmholtz 1876, 320). All we know about space, he said, is what we have learned from experience. If we lived in a spherical or pseudo-spherical space, our experience of the world would dictate the adoption of the non-Euclidean geometries of (Georg Friedrich) Bernhard Riemann or Lobachevsky; nothing in our intuition would require us to adopt a "flat-space" Euclidean system. Thus the only useful test of the validity of the axioms lies in observation and measurement.

Developments like the creation of non-Euclidean geometry and *n*-dimensional geometry and a discovery like that of the non-commutative quaternions or vectors which challenged the accepted principles of numbers made mathematicians doubt the foundations of mathematics. As long as mathematics dealt with, or was considered to deal with, concepts that had physical meaning, rigor had an empirical basis. But because of the aforementioned developments, the view that all mathematical axioms are arbitrary prevailed by the end of the nineteenth century. David Hilbert's answer to this foundational crisis was to reintroduce rigor by the demand of consistency. As long as mathematics was regarded as truth about nature, the possibility that contradictory theorems could arise did not occur. When non-Euclidean geometries were created, however, their seeming variance with reality did raise the question of their consistency.

The Inventor

Besides being a mathematician and economist, Fisher was a "gadgeteer, an inventor of gadgets and widgets" (Allen 1993, 135), or as Tobin (1998, 371) worded it, "Fisher was, on top of everything else, an inventor." In his work as an economist, Fisher's approach had the same characteristics as that of a "great engineer" (Allais 1968, 483). Throughout his life Fisher sought an invention that would provide the foundation for a manufacturing enterprise that would make him rich. He began with the desk-opening-and-closing device that he invented while he was still in school. Next came the piano apparatus that he patented as a Yale freshman (Allen 1993, 135–36). Some of his inventions were accompanied with an article explaining and recommending their use. These included a tent for the treatment of tuberculosis (Fisher 1903), a mechanical diet indicator (Fisher 1906), and an icosahedral world map (Fisher 1943). His last invention was a portable stool (Fisher 1997, 301). But the only invention to pay off in a large way was the Index Visible Filing System (Fisher 1997, 282).

It was not only for money that Fisher invented and developed certain devices. He was convinced that visualization is essential for understanding a certain mechanism or phenomenon, "for correct visual pictures usually yield the clearest concepts" (1939, 311). Sometimes these pictures showed mechanical devices because he believed that a "student of economics thinks in terms of mechanics far more than geometry, and a mechanical illustration corresponds more fully to his antecedent notions than a graphical one" ([1891] 1925, 24). Fisher ([1891] 1925) used pictures of a hydrostatic mechanism to explain a three-good, three-consumer economy in this Ph.D. thesis.[6] He also used a mechanical balance to illustrate the equation of exchange and a hydraulic system "to observe and trace" important variations and their effects in the *Purchasing Power of Money* ([1911] 1963, 108).[7] On other occasions he used geometrical illustrations to visualize properties of a system. For example, he gave a description of a three-dimensional construction of the properties of production factors in his 1939 paper "A Three-Dimensional Representation of the Factors of Production and their Remuneration, Marginally and Residually" to help a student "to see, literally to see with his eyes" (311). He discussed a better method of graphical representation in his paper "The 'Ratio' Chart, For Plotting Statistics" (1917). There he recommended the ratio chart, in which only ratios are displayed and compared, because it "simply utilizes the natural powers of the eye. Consequently, when one is once accustomed to it, it never misleads, but always pictures a multitude of ratio relations at a glance, with absolute fidelity and without the annoyance of reservations or corrections" (1917, 600).

J. W. Gibbs may well have been influential in Fisher's efforts toward visualization. Gibbs's first two publications, "Graphical Methods in the Thermodynamics of Fluids" and "A Method of Geometrical Representation of the Thermodynamic Properties of Substances by Means of Surfaces" ([1873] 1961), dealt explicitly with this issue. In a biographical sketch, Henry Bumstead ([1906] 1961, xii–xiii) noted that

Professor Gibbs was much inclined to the use of geometrical illustrations, which he employed as symbols and aids to the imagination,

---

6. The hydrostatic mechanism had also actually been constructed twice. Photographs of both these models were reproduced in Fisher 1925.

7. Mary Morgan (1999) provides a detailed account of how Fisher, in his *Purchasing Power of Money* ([1911] 1963), by building and using models, learned about the monetary system.

Figure 2   Mechanical diet indicator (Fisher 1906, 430)

rather than the mechanical models which have served so many investigators; such models are seldom in complete correspondence with the
phenomena they represent, and Professor Gibbs's tendency toward rigorous logic was such that the discrepancies apparently destroyed for
him the usefulness of the model. Accordingly he usually had recourse
to the geometrical representation of his equations, and this method he
used with great ease and power.

While Gibbs saw geometrical illustrations mainly as aids to the imagination, Fisher stressed the role of visualizations because they helped one to
understand a system or phenomenon. It connected the unknown to something familiar, something with which one has experience. Fisher made
no principled distinction between geometry and mechanics, because geometry too was in his view "consolidated experience."

Fisher approached a problem by thinking of it in terms of building an
instrument. But this approach can only be fruitful when one also has the

skills of a designer. A proof of his ability as designer is his elegant "mechanical diet indicator," illustrated in figure 2 (Fisher 1906). The device was designed to "save labor and at the same time to *visualize* the magnitude and proportions of the diet" (418). It used a clever combination of mechanical and geometrical principles that also appeared to be very fruitful in the context of indexes.

The proposed method for indicating food values worked as follows. The first step was to measure food by calories instead of by weight and to take as the fundamental unit a standard portion of 100 calories. So, the value of each food is indicated by the amount of calories of protein, fat, and carbohydrate in the portion. The next step was to represent the food values geometrically in such a way that the portions of protein, fat, and carbohydrate form the coordinates of a point on an isosceles right-angled triangle. The third step was to use this geometrical representa tion for determining the constituents of combinations of different food. The point representing the combination of any number of different foods was obtained by taking the center of gravity of the points representing the respective foods, each being weighted in proportion to the calories or standard portions which enter into the combination. Since the resultant point was indeed the center of gravity, it could also be obtained by a mechanical method. The cardboard with the right-angled triangle on which points were located to represent the various foods employed was the essential element of the mechanical indicator. At points representing foods eaten, pins with heavy heads were thrust through the cardboard. When the card was placed in a "basket" and suspended on the standard, one could easily find the center of gravity.

The Making of Index Numbers

The Index-Number Problem

Fisher's original interest in index numbers arose from the problem of determining the purchasing power of money. The purchasing power of money was defined as the reciprocal of the price level. A core element of Fisher's quantity theory was the equation of exchange:

$$MV = pQ + p'Q' + p''Q'' + \cdots = \sum pQ \qquad (1)$$

where the ps represent the individual prices and the Qs the individual quantities; M is money in circulation and V the velocity of its circulation.

The price level was obtained by the conversion of the right side into the form PT, where P is a weighted average of all the prices, representing price level, and T the sum of all the Q's, representing the volume of trade. So, the "principles" determining the purchasing power were represented by the now well-known equation of exchange:

$$MV = PT. \tag{2}$$

As a result, the price level had to be consistent with the above equation of exchange.

P and T were connected with each other by the relation

$$PT = \sum pQ. \tag{3}$$

In other words, every form of P implied via equation (3) a corresponding, or in Fisher's ([1911] 1963, 385) terminology, a "correlative form" of T and vice versa. To find an adequate formula for P, Fisher suggested starting with T. T was the sum of all the Qs, but the various Qs were measured in different units. Fisher proposed to take as the unit for measuring any goods the amount which constitutes a "dollar worth" at some particular year called the base year. As a result, T was defined as:

$$T = \sum p_0 Q, \tag{4}$$

where the subscript zero indicates the base year. This definition implied the "correlative form" of P:

$$P = \frac{\sum pQ}{T} = \frac{\sum pQ}{\sum p_0 Q} = \sum w \frac{p}{p_0} \tag{5}$$

where

$$w = \frac{p_0 Q}{\sum p_0 Q}.$$

In other words, for the purpose of commensurability, P had to be seen as the weighted average of *price ratios*. Thus in general, Fisher had to consider P not as a price level but as a price index.[8]

The above "strict algebraic statement" (Fisher [1911] 1963, 24) of the equation of exchange was preceded by an "arithmetical illustration" and a "mechanical illustration" (21). The mechanical illustration was a visual

8. A price level depends only on prices of a relevant year, whereas in a price index the prices of two years are compared. Although this distinction might seem trivial, it is essential. Eichhorn and Voeller (1976, 59) show that "the version of Fisher's equation of exchange considered in most textbooks is not correct"; namely, equation (3) does not hold, as P is interpreted as a price level instead of a price index.

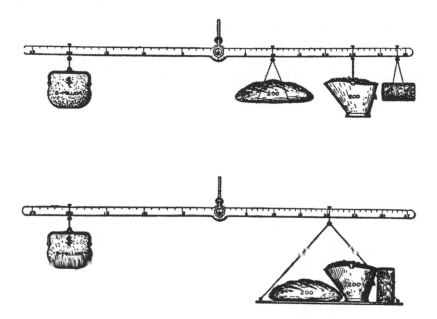

Figure 3   Mechanical balance (Fisher [1911] 1963, 21, 23)

representation, a picture of a mechanical balance in equilibrium, the two sides of which symbolized respectively the money side and the goods side of the equation of exchange (see figure 3). The weight at the left, symbolized by a purse, represented the money in circulation; the arm or distance from the fulcrum at which the purse is hung represented the velocity of circulation. In the top illustration (his fig. 2, 21) on the right side of this balance were three weights—bread, coal, and cloth, symbolized respectively by a loaf, a coal scuttle, and a roll of cloth. The distance of each from the fulcrum represented its price. Because of Fisher's interest in the price level, in the lower illustration (his fig. 3, 23) all the right-hand weights were hung at one point, symbolized by a basket containing the loaf, coal scuttle, and roll of cloth, so that the distance from the fulcrum now represented the average price.

According to Ragnar Frisch's (1936, 3) survey article on index numbers, the latter part of the analogy was "dangerously misleading." In the mechanical analogy, it is only because of the common physical unit of the three commodities, namely their weights, that the average price (distance to the fulcrum) can be determined. So he concluded that "it

is precisely the *absence* of this physical commensurability that constitutes the index-number problem" (3). In other words, for the index to be
defined as a weighted average, the main problem was to determine its
proper weighting system. The analogy with a mechanical balance seems
to mask that problem. Frisch was right about the nature of the index
number problem, but his judgment that Fisher's approach is "misleading" was wrong. Fisher was well aware of this commensurability problem, and his engagement in index numbers stemmed from it. In looking
for a common unit, Fisher proposed to take that amount of a good that
constitutes a "dollar worth." This change in unit shifted the meaning of
P in the equation of exchange from being the average price level to the
average of price ratios, the price index. As in the case of the mechanical
diet indicator, changing the standard unit made commensurability possible. The right-hand basket of the mechanical balance was constructed
according to similar principles as the diet indicator.

Tests of the Index Formulae

Index formula (5) was consistent with Fisher's equation of exchange. But
Fisher didn't stop here. Before he finally declared this index number formula as the best, he first submitted it to several "tests." In the appendix
to chapter 10 of his *Purchasing Power of Money* ([1911] 1963), Fisher
reviewed eight tests, including "all the tests which have been hitherto
applied in the study of index numbers and some others" (400). Each test
consisted of a general and a particular version. In the general case the
test should be fulfilled for any two years, indicated by the subscripts 1
and 2; in the particular case it should only be fulfilled when one of the
years is the base year, indicated by the subscript 0. Thus the particular
version was a weaker version of the general one.

1. Test of proportionality as to prices (F1). A formula for the price index
should be such that the price index will agree with all individual price
ratios when these all agree with each other.

Given $p_1/p_2 = p'_1/p'_2 = \cdots = k$, then
General: $P_{0,1}/P_{0,2} = k$
Particular: $P_{0,1} = k$

2. Test of proportionality as to trade (F2). The "correlative formula" for
the trade index should be such that the trade index will agree with all

individual trade ratios when these all agree with each other.

Given $Q_1/Q_2 = Q_1'/Q_2' = \cdots = k$, then

General: $T_1/T_2 = k$

Particular: $T_1 = k$

Because the trade index and the price index were corresponding indexes ($PT = \sum pQ$), this test could also be considered as a test on the price index.

General: $\dfrac{P_{0,1}}{P_{0,2}} = \dfrac{\sum p_1 Q_1}{\sum p_2 Q_1} = \dfrac{\sum p_1 Q_2}{\sum p_2 Q_2}$

Particular: $P_{0,1} = \dfrac{\sum p_1 Q_1}{\sum p_0 Q_1} = \dfrac{\sum p_1 Q_0}{\sum p_0 Q_0}.$

3. Test of determinateness as to prices (F3). A price index should not be rendered zero, infinity, or indeterminate by an individual price becoming zero.

4. Test of determinateness as to trade (F4). The "correlative trade index" should not be rendered zero, infinity, or indeterminate by an individual quantity becoming zero.

5. Test of withdrawal or entry as to prices (F5). A price index should be unaffected by the withdrawal or entry of a price ratio agreeing with the index.

6. Test of withdrawal or entry as to trade (F6). The correlative trade index should be unaffected by the withdrawal or entry of a quantity ratio agreeing with the index.

7. Test by changing base (F7). The ratios between various price indexes (and therefore those between the correlative trade indexes) should be unaffected by reversing or changing the base (from zero to a so-called year 8).

General: $\dfrac{P_{0,1}}{P_{0,2}} = \dfrac{P_{8,1}}{P_{8,2}}.$

This test implies a particular version that, in turn, implies a weaker version. Because both played a more prominent role in Fisher's *The Making of Index Numbers* ([1922] 1967) and the axiomatic index literature that followed (see below), they will be labeled by the names that were later given to them.

> Particular versions:
>
> *Circular Test* (F7-C): $P_{1,2} \cdot P_{2,3} = P_{1,3}$
>
> *Time Reversal Test* (F7-T): $P_{0,1} \cdot P_{1,0} = 1$.

8. Test by changing unit of measurement (renamed in Fisher [1922] 1967 as the *CommensurabilityTest* [F8]). The ratios between various price indexes (and therefore those between the correlative trade indexes) should be unaffected by changing any unit of measurement.

> Given Q_1 and p_1 changed in inverse ratio, then
>
> General: $P_{0,1}/P_{0,2}$ unchanged
>
> Particular: $P_{0,1}$ unchanged

These eight tests were not considered to be of equal importance. The Paasche Index, $P_P = \sum pQ / \sum p_0 Q$ (see formula 5), was Fisher's favorite in his 1911 publication: "theoretically at least, the best form of P" (Fisher [1911] 1963, 201). It represented how prices will change on average in all cases of variation of M, V and the Qs, except when the Qs vary relatively to each other. This was shown with the aid of the equation of exchange, so that changes in one of the factors and their results can be rendered as follows:

$$\frac{MV}{M_0 V_0} = \frac{PT}{P_0 T_0}.$$

Note that $P_0 = 1$.

If Q remains invariable ($Q = Q_0$) and thus $T = T_0$, while M and/or V change, then P_P express how prices will change on average:

$$\frac{MV}{M_0 V_0} = \frac{\sum p Q_0}{\sum p_0 Q_0} = \frac{\sum pQ}{\sum p_0 Q} = P_P.$$

If the Qs all vary in a given ratio ($Q = k Q_0$),

$$P \frac{T}{T_0} = k \frac{\sum p Q_0}{\sum p_0 Q_0} = k \frac{\sum pQ}{\sum p_0 Q}.$$

This means that if $T/T_0 = k$ (required by Test 2), then P has the form of P_P, and therefore P_P is imposed by Test 2.

Because "the equation of exchange itself prescribes test No. 2" (404), it was considered by Fisher as "the most important of all the eight tests for prices" (406). None of the forty-four index numbers passed all eight tests, but if Test 2 were imposed, the Paasche index came out as being the best formula.

Test 2 was also important because "it is the only test which indicates the kind of *weighting* required" (406). However, Test 2 did not account for the case that the Qs do not vary proportionally.

> When the Q's vary unequally, however, there seems to be *no* perfectly satisfactory formula. Under these circumstances the two systems of weights—one in the terms of Q_1's, the other in terms of Q_0's—conflict with each other. But the conflict has been shown by Edgeworth to be slight. In fact, the weights are of much less importance in determining an index number of prices than prices themselves. (406)

F. Y. Edgeworth had shown (in the Reports of the British Association for the Advancement of Science for 1887 and 1888) that an "error" in the *weights* only makes an "error" one-twentieth as great in the resultant index number, while an "error" in the *prices* themselves makes an "error" in the resultant index number one-fourth or -fifth as great. From this result, Fisher concluded that "considerable variation in weighting is of comparatively little practical importance" (422).

Empirical Test of the Index Numbers

Fisher, as the author of the 1911 publication, can rightly be called an apriorist with respect to index numbers. The best index number form was the one that fulfilled the test prescribed by the equation of exchange (F2). The "chief object" of his *Purchasing Power of Money* was "to explain the causes determining the purchasing power of money" (13). Therefore he first "reconstructed" the quantity theory of money into the equation of exchange and then statistically verified this equation in the second part of his book. For this statistical verification, he needed an index number formula in accordance with the equation of exchange, and as shown above, in dealing with the commensurability problem he arrived at the Paasche index. The evaluation of the forty-three other index formulae on the basis of eight tests was not his primary interest and was relegated to an appendix. But in the years that followed, Fisher became more and more interested in developing the best index formula "for all purposes."

That is, he treated the best index number problem as an important problem in its own terms and as a problem with a more general application than verifying the quantity theory of money.[9]

Ten years after the publication of his *Purchasing Power of Money*, Fisher presented a paper, "The Best Form of Index Number" (1921), at a meeting of the American Statistical Association. The discussion of the best form was not based on any economic-theoretic assumption—in contrast with his *Purchasing Power of Money*. The point of departure was the ratio of money value, to which "there can be no ambiguity": "There is only one index number of value—the value itself" (Fisher 1921, 533). The problem was to find how far the ratio of money value of a certain year to the money value of a base year is a matter of inflated prices and how far it is a matter of increased quantities (volume of trade). In other words, if one tries to split this ratio of money values into two factors, P and Q (where capital Q now indicates the quantity index and lower case qs the individual quantities), that is,

$$P_{0,1} Q_{0,1} = \frac{\sum p_1 q_1}{\sum p_0 q_0} = V_{0,1},$$

then what is the best form for each factor, P and Q?

Instead of the eight tests, Fisher now suggested only two "supreme" tests. The first was the *Factor Reversal Test* (F9). "The formula should *work both ways* as to the two factors, prices and quantities" (534). If the quantity index is obtained by interchanging the prices and quantities in the price index formula, then the two indexes multiplied together should give the value ratio.

The second was the Time Reversal Test (F7-T):

$$P_{0,1} \cdot P_{1,0} = 1.$$

"The formula should *work both ways* as to time" (534). This test was in fact the weakest version of the "test by changing base" (F7) of his *Purchasing Power of Money*.

It appeared that the simplest formula conforming to both these reversal tests (F9 and F7-T) was the geometric mean of the Paasche and Laspeyres indexes, the so-called "ideal" index.

The paper itself was not published, although an abstract was printed together with the discussion that took place at the meeting. The most

9. A similar "measurement without theory" move was made by Fisher's French contemporary, Lucien March, discussed by Franck Jovanovic and Philippe Le Gall in this volume.

important critiques focused on Fisher's claim that his "ideal" index was the best form for *all* purposes. In countering these critiques, Fisher ended up not with a paper, but with a book of more than five hundred pages: *The Making of Index Numbers*, published in 1922. The reason for this enormous expansion was that Fisher examined more than a hundred formulae, using calculations from actual historical data.

> This book is, therefore, primarily an inductive rather than a deductive study. In this respect it differs from the Appendix to Chapter X of the *Purchasing Power of Money*, in which I sought deductively to compare the merits of 44 different formulae. The present book had its origin in the desire to put these deductive conclusions to an inductive test by means of calculations from actual historical data. But before I had gone far in such testing of my original conclusions, I found, to my great surprise, that the results of actual calculation constantly suggested further deduction until, in the end, I had completely revised both my conclusions and my theoretical foundation. Not that I needed to discard as untrue many of the conclusions reached in the *Purchasing Power of Money*; for the only definite error which I have found among my former conclusions has to do with the so-called "circular test" which I originally, with other writers accepted as sound, but which, in this book, I reject as theoretically unsound. (Fisher [1922] 1967, xii–xiii)

The reason to abandon the Circular Test (F7 C: $P_{1,2}$ $P_{2,3}$ = $P_{1,3}$) was because it is a multiple comparison, and according to Fisher, index numbers were only appropriate for dual comparisons. Note that the Time Reversal Test, being a weaker version of the Circular Test, is not a multiple but a dual comparison.

Fisher assumed that the only formulae that conform to the Circular Test are index numbers that have constant weights, and constant weighting was according to him "not theoretically correct" (275) because it did not take into account the differences between countries or times. "Such a formula would prove too much, for it would leave no room for qualitative differences. Index numbers are to some extent empirical, and the supposed inconsistency in the failure of (variably weighted) index numbers to conform to the circular test, is really a bridge to reality" (274).

In *The Purchasing Power of Money*, Fisher ([1911] 1963, 406) had maintained that "the weights are of much less importance in determining an index number of prices than prices themselves," but in his *Making of Index Numbers*, he took the opposite position: only a formula that would leave room for "qualitative differences" would be "a bridge to reality" (Fisher [1922] 1967, 274). From neglecting the importance of the index's sensitivity to variations in the weights, he shifted to a position in which he emphasized that index numbers should be susceptible to changes in the weight system. This shift was ignored in the axiomatic index literature that evolved from Fisher's work. In that literature the main conclusions of *The Making of Index Numbers* were disregarded: the Circular Test was treated as inseparable from Fisher's system of tests. And, although Fisher ([1911] 1963, 200) had admitted that "it seems theoretically impossible to devise an index number, *P*, which shall satisfy all of the tests we should like to impose," consistency of the tests became one of the central issues in the axiomatic index approach.

The Axiomatic versus the Instrumental Approach

Consistency of Fisher's Tests

Ragnar Frisch's "Necessary and Sufficient Conditions Regarding the Form of an Index Number Which Shall Meet Certain of Fisher's Tests" (1930) was the first publication to prove the impossibility of maintaining a certain set of tests simultaneously. It was the starting point for a whole series of publications in which the inconsistency of Fisher's tests were discussed.

Frisch's 1930 essay was actually a discussion of seven of Fisher's tests.

1. Identity Test: $P_{t,t} = 1$
2. Time Reversal Test (F7-T)
3. Base Test (F7)
4. Circular Test (F7-C)
5. Commensurability Test (F8)
6. Determinateness Tests (F3 and F4)
7. Factor Reversal Test (F9)

Frisch didn't discuss or mention either the tests of withdrawal or entry (F5 and F6). Neither did he discuss either of Fisher's tests of proportionality (F1 and F2); he discussed only a weaker version, namely the Identity Test mentioned above.

The aim of Frisch's essay was "to derive the general form which it is necessary and sufficient that an index number shall have in order that certain combinations of the above test [sic] shall be fulfilled" (Frisch 1930, 400). While Fisher's approach was to select among a number of index formulae by testing them, Frisch's method was to derive mathematically the appropriate form from these tests. By interpreting the tests as conditions on the functional form of the index number formula, Frisch was able to derive the unique index number formula satisfying the Commensurability Test (F8), the Circular Test (F7-C), and the Factor Reversal Test (F9). In addition, however, Frisch showed that the Base Test (F7) (or Circular Test, F7-C), the Commensurability Test (F8), and the Determinateness Tests (F3 and F4) could not all be fulfilled at the same time—they were "incompatible." So, according to Frisch, one has to select between the tests. Since he favored a chain index, the Circular Test was not questioned. The choice then lay between satisfying the Determinateness Tests and the Commensurability Test, and Frisch chose in favor of the Determinateness Tests.

To better understand Frisch's critique of Fisher's tests, one should first note that Frisch advocated the microeconomic approach based on individual choice theory (see Spencer Banzhaf's article in this volume).[10] In his survey on index numbers, Frisch (1936) developed a theory of price indexes from the viewpoint of utility theory; that is, the price index is the ratio of costs of achieving a given utility level in two situations so the result is a function of the utility level. His very first paper on an economic topic, "Sur un problème d'économie pure" ([1926] 1971) started with an axiomatic formulation of measurable utility. "Though this approach is so familiar today, after the work of von Neumann and Morgenstern, Frisch's paper is very possibly the first formulation of its type" (Arrow 1960, 176). It is considered a classic in the theory of consumer behavior because it, "apparently" for the first time, introduced the axiomatic approach into the theory of economic choice (Chipman et al. 1971, 326).

The main critique of Frisch's paper came from another advocate of the microeconomic approach, Subramanian Swamy. Frisch's result that Fisher's tests are inconsistent was never doubted, but Frisch's proofs

---

10. Diewert (1998) distinguishes four main approaches to index number theory: (1) statistical (2) test or axiomatic; (3) microeconomic, which relies on the assumption of maximizing or minimizing behavior; and (4) neostatistical. Note that Diewert equates the test and axiomatic approach, whereas in this essay they are treated separately.

were (unjustly) criticized—creating some confusion about Frisch's results. In a debate that took place over many years (Swamy 1934, Frisch 1934, Swamy 1940, Swamy 1965), both the correctness of Frisch's proofs and the economic interpretation and significance of Fisher's tests were discussed. The inconsistency of the tests called for a selection of the most essential tests. The question of which tests should be rejected "must be analysed within the framework of economic analysis" (Swamy 1965, 622). Swamy considered Fisher's approach with its "mechanical tests" (Samuelson & Swamy 1974, 576) economically unfounded; in particular, both the Determinateness Test (F4) and the Factor Reversal Test (F9) were considered to be "suspect."

Parallel to this debate, Abraham Wald, in his 1937 article "Zur Theorie der Preisindexziffern," also proved the inconsistency of Fisher's tests. Wald showed that there is no index that fulfills at the same time the Proportionality Tests (F1 and F2), the Circular Test (F7-C), and the Factor Reversal Test (F9). He saw the Factor Reversal Test as "economically completely unfounded" [ökonomisch vollkommen unbegründet]; that is, its economic meaning was not given (Wald 1937, 183). Wald concluded that the formal mathematical method was not well suited to the solution of the index problem, so the larger part of his essay concerned the economic approach to index numbers based on individual choice theory.

An important reason for economists to retain the Circular Test is that, if the test is fulfilled, an index number is freed from one base year. Another reason, crucial for the microeconomic approach, is that "so long as we stick to the economic theory of index numbers, the circular test is as required as is the property of transitivity itself" (Samuelson and Swamy 1974, 576). Moreover, the forms of the indexes Samuelson and Swamy provided contradicted Fisher's assertion that only fixed weights lead to satisfaction of the Circular Test.

The inconsistencies between tests (and how to prove such inconsistencies) were systematically treated by Wolfgang Eichhorn in the so-called axiomatic index theory based on functional equation theory. The functional equation theory is transferred into index theory by defining the price index as a positive function, satisfying a number of axioms. These axioms do not determine a unique form of the price index function. Several additional tests are needed "for assessing the quality of a potential price index" (Eichhorn and Voeller 1976, 29). Both axioms and tests are formalized as functional equations. Then the inconsistency theorems can be proven by showing that for the relevant combinations of functional equations, the solution space is empty.

The power of this approach was immediately demonstrated in Eichhorn's first publication on index theory, "Zur Axiomatischen Theorie des Preisindex" (1973). The paper discussed five of Fisher's tests:

1. Proportionality Test (F1)
2. Commensurability Test (F8)
3. Circular Test (F7-C)
4. Determinateness Tests (F3 and F4)
5. Factor Reversal Test (F9)

First, Eichhorn arrived at the same result as Frisch (1930)—namely, the functional form of an index fulfilling the Commensurability Test (F8), the Circular Test (F7-C), and the Factor Reversal Test (F9). But now this result was derived from functional equation theory, in particular by using Josef Aczél's (1966) generalization of the solutions of Augustin Cauchy's functional equations. Eichhorn also showed that the derived index fulfills the Determinateness Tests (F3 and F4) but not the Proportionality Test (F1).

The five tests are inconsistent, so one of them has to be abandoned. Because the economic significance of the Factor Reversal Test (F9) had long been considered controversial, Eichhorn also abandoned this test. Next he showed that the other four are independent but nevertheless still inconsistent. A set of tests is independent when any set minus one can be fulfilled by an index that does not fulfill the remaining test.

Eichhorn's paper was written in German and published in a mathematical journal. Three years later these results were published in English in *Econometrica* (1976), in which a weaker version of Fisher's system of tests was also discussed. However, even this weaker system was inconsistent. Eichhorn again demonstrated that this weaker set of five tests is independent, but if one wants to keep to five tests, the question is how far the tests must be weakened further to obtain a consistent set. It appeared that if one weakens only the Circular Test (F7-C), by replacing it with the Time Reversal Test (F7-T), then the system of five tests is consistent. In the end, Fisher's system of tests was proven to be consistent, but Eichhorn didn't notice.

Fisher's Instrumental Approach to Indexes

In the axiomatic index literature, the axioms are considered prescribed by economic theory. Inconsistency problems were solved by omitting those "tests" that had no economic meaning or where the economic meaning was dubious. Fisher diverged from this approach in two respects. First, he distanced himself further and further from economic theory in assessing index number formulae. Second, he did not consider inconsistency problematic. The index number "should be the 'just compromise' among conflicting elements, the 'fair average,' the 'golden mean'" (Fisher [1922] 1967, 10). Fisher ([1911] 1963, 200) compared the construction of an index with that of lenses:

> Although in the science of optics we learn that a perfect lens is theoretically impossible, nevertheless, for all practical purposes lenses may be constructed so nearly perfect that it is well worth while to study and construct them. So, also, while it seems theorctically impossible to devise an index number, P, which shall satisfy all of the tests we should like to impose, it is, nevertheless, possible to construct index numbers which satisfy these tests so well for practical purposes that we may profitably devote serious attention to the study and construction of index numbers.

The problem of specifying the most suitable lens for its intended purpose is in fact a discussion of the most important defects in each lens, namely its aberrations. When the aberrations are identified, means for their control must be found. In the case of a simple lens, control of all the aberrations is sometimes impossible, and a compromise becomes necessary (see epigraph). Using multiple lenses in an optical instrument, so that the errors of the lenses nullify each other, normally solves this problem.

Fisher's empirical approach comes clearly to the fore in his discussion of the Circular Test (F7-C). Although he could not use this test as an apriori condition because it was "theoretically unsound," he investigated how well it could be used as an empirical test. The "important" question is: "*How near* is the circular test to fulfillment in actual cases? If very near, then practically we may make some use of the circular test as an approximation [to both Reversal Tests (F7-T and F9)] even if it is not strictly valid" (Fisher [1922] 1967, 276). It appeared that for all index numbers that fulfilled both Reversal Tests, the discrepancies between a dual comparison and a multiple comparison were slight. The "circular gaps" were small and especially so in his "ideal" index, which fulfilled the Circular Test to within one fourth of one percent (284). Fisher noted that the Circular Test could be considered "at bottom, to be simply a triangular test" (295), and if one takes a "3-around" comparison, the drawn triangle was almost closed (see figure 4). "The lines return so nearly to the starting point in each case that the observer has to look [very!] closely to see the gap" (287). So, "practically, then, the test may be said to be a real test" (Fisher [1922] 1967, 291–92).

It is rather remarkable that Fisher on one hand expressly argued against taking the Circular Test as a theoretical requirement but on the other hand spent twenty pages using and recommending it as an empirical test for index formulae. Fisher had a very practical reason to do so. Unless one accepts constant weights, index number formulae only allow for dual comparisons. But in practice one would like to make a multiple comparison between countries or times. Using a fixed base system for each comparison between any two years requires calculating a specific index number, which would entail "very great labor and expense" (299). Using a chain system, it is only necessary to calculate the index numbers of two successive years and then chain them for any other comparison. For example, to compare year i and j, one can chain the following index numbers:

$$P_{i,j} = P_{i,i+1} \times P_{i+1,i+2} \times \cdots \times P_{j-1,j}.$$

In principle both sides of the equation are inconsistent because "*theoretically* the circular test ought not to be fulfilled," but empirically the inconsistency is "so slight as *practically* to be negligible" (303).

To understand Fisher's peculiar stance toward the Circular Test, it is illuminating to compare his ideas with those related to the rise of non-Euclidean geometry. One obvious way to measure the properties of physical space was to determine the sum of the angles of a triangle. There is a close relation between triangles that are not closed and triangles with sums of angles larger or smaller than 180°. As an empirical test rather than a theoretical requirement, the "triangular test" is analogous to the measurement of the sum of angles to find the properties of a space. It can be used to observe the properties of the index number space. The triangle test showed that Fisher's ideal index is an object of a slightly curved index number space, but the curvature is so slight that one can practically assume a flat, Euclidean space.

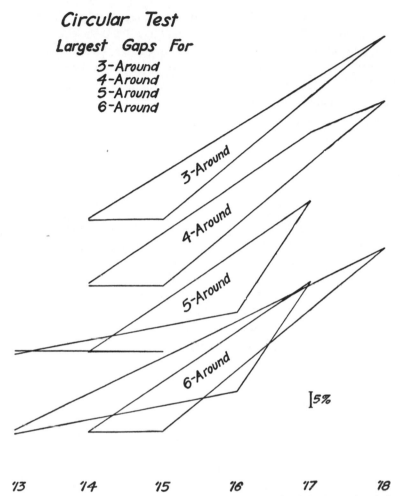

Circular Test

Largest Gaps For
3-Around
4-Around
5-Around
6-Around

3-Around

4-Around

5-Around

6-Around

|5%

'13   '14   '15   '16   '17   '18

CHART 52.   The circular test gap (at the left of each of the four circuits), even at its greatest, as here charted for Formula 353, is remarkably small in all cases.   It slightly increases as the circuit of year-to-year index numbers becomes more circuitous, reaching over one per cent in the 6-around circuit, 1913–'16–'17–'14–'15–'18–'13.

Figure 4   Triangle test (Fisher 1927, 286)

World Maps and Globes

Fisher was no sympathizer of the axiomatic movement nor of Hilbert's program of axiomatization. Being an inventor, he knew that while designing an instrument one sometimes has to compromise between contradictory requirements and that the eye is a reliable judge for assessing the best balance. A mathematically impossible object could still be devised in practice. To support the thesis of this essay—that this lifelong attitude was basically Fisher's approach toward scientific problems—I will now discuss his penultimate invention, the icosahedral world map.

Three years before he died in 1947, Fisher and O. M. Miller published *World Maps and Globes* to discuss the qualities desirable in world map projections and the methods by which these qualities can be obtained. The "map-projection problem" exists because of "the fact that every map, large or small, must have some distortions and that every *world* map must have interruptions" (Fisher and Miller 1944, 3). To flatten out a globe, one must stretch and/or shrink it in certain directions and tear it at several places. In particular, there is a tension between interruption and distortion: only by increasing the interruptions of the map can we lessen distortion.

In a chapter titled "The Four 'Cardinal Virtues,'" the problem was stated in terms of objectives:

1. to have *distances* correctly represented;
2. to have *shapes* correctly represented;
3. to have *areas* correctly represented (that is, square mileage);
4. to have great circles represented by *straight lines.*
   (Fisher and Miller 1944, 27–28)

It is a geometric impossibility on a flat surface to have all four of these virtues and to have them in every part. So, "projections are confessedly compromises, being perfect in none of the four ways but balancing the different kinds of errors against one another" (34).

To find a proper balance between the different kind of errors, Fisher and Miller suggested using a triangular grid for evaluating various map projections. Conventional maps have a grid of latitudes and longitudes; however, the areas bounded by these grid lines are not all the same size on a sphere, and comparisons between different map projections are therefore not easy to visualize (see figure 5). "The triangular grid (shown on almost all the maps in this book) will be found an easy means of making these comparisons by eye" (87–88).

Fisher advocated the icosahedral projection as the "most satisfactory" world map. The icosahedron is the fifth and last platonic body: namely, it is a regular polyhedron having the largest number of faces (twenty) which are equilateral triangles. Because it has the largest number of

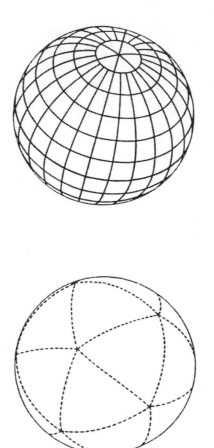

Figure 5   Triangular grid (Fisher and Miller 1944, 10)

faces, it has the smallest average distortion of all the regular polyhe-
drons. It had to be a *regular* polyhedron because "symmetry plays an
important part in conveying to the eye the relation between the flat map
and the globe (or its approximations) and this is accomplished only when
all the faces are of the same size and shape" (100).

Fisher copyrighted this idea of an icosahedral world map. The map itself, with instructions for folding the map into an icosahedron, was published in the *Geographical Review* in 1943.

Conclusion

There is a tacit but strong belief in economics that axiomatization leads to better theories. One finds the same kind of conviction in measurement theory—a standard work in measurement theory, *Foundations of Measurement* (Krantz et al. 1971), is exemplary for that conviction. But the axiomatic approach is also dominant in index number theory. Whether this conviction is justified or not, even the most authoritarian axiomatizer of economics, John von Neumann, warned against too much "de- empirization," as axiomatization was called by him: "at a great distance from its empirical source, or after much 'abstract' inbreeding, a mathematical subject is in danger of degeneration" (1961, 9). According to von Neumann, the "prime" reason why of all Euclid's postulates the fifth was questioned was its unempirical character (3). He found it "hardly pos sible to believe in the existence of an absolute, immutable concept of mathematical rigor, dissociated from all human experience" (6).

Fisher's instrumental approach to constructing index numbers gives us a nice example of how rigor and human experience can work together. Inconsistencies between the theoretical requirements do not stop us from rigorousness. As his work on converting the three-dimensional globe into a two-dimensional flat world map illustrated, if the perfect instrument is an impossibility, we still can aim at well-founded approximations. Fisher's rule was that an instrument's performance should approximate a standard within a satisfactory margin. The assessment whether the approximation was satisfactory should be something that the eye—as a reliable judge—could do, but mathematical considerations of consistency could not. Which standard is appropriate should depend on the case under consideration, but the standard itself should be concerned with fit to the empirical world.

References

Aczél, J. 1966. *Lectures on Functional Equations and Their Applications*. New York: Academic Press.

Allais, Maurice. 1968. Irving Fisher. In *International Encyclopedia of the Social Sciences*, edited by D. L. Sills. New York: Macmillan and The Free Press.

Allen, Robert Loring. 1993. *Irving Fisher: A Biography*. Cambridge, Mass.: Blackwell.

Arrow, Kenneth J. 1960. The Work of Ragnar Frisch, Econometrician. *Econometrica* 28.2:175–92.

Bracey, R. J. 1960. *The Technique of Optical Instrument Design*. London: The English University Press.

Bumstead, Henry Andrew. [1906] 1961. Biographical Sketch. In *The Scientific Papers of J. Willard Gibbs*, edited by Henry Andrew Bumstead and Ralph Gibbs Van Name. New York: Dover.

Chipman, John S., Leonid Hurwicz, Marcel K. Richter, and Hugo F. Sonnenschein, eds. 1971. *Preferences, Utility, and Demand*. New York: Harcourt Brace.

Diewert, W. E. 1998. Index Numbers. In vol. 2 of *The New Palgrave: A Dictionary of Economics*, edited by John Eatwell, Murray Milgate, and Peter Newman, 767–80. London: Macmillan.

Eichhorn, Wolfgang. 1973. Zur Axiomatischen Theorie des Preisindex. *Demonstratio Mathematica* 6:561–73.

———. 1976. Fisher's Tests Revisited. *Econometrica* 44:247–55.

Eichhorn, Wolfgang, and J. Voeller. 1976. *Theory of the Price Index*. Berlin: Springer-Verlag.

Fisher, Irving. 1890. Mathematical Contribution to Philosophy; Attacking Kant's Theory of Geometrical Axioms. Fisher's Archives, Yale University.

———. [1891] 1925. *Mathematical Investigations in the Theory of Value and Prices*. New Haven, Conn.: Yale University Press.

———. 1903. A New Tent for the Treatment of Tuberculosis. *Journal of the American Medical Association* 26:1576–77.

———. 1906. A New Method for Indicating Food Values. *American Journal of Physiology* 15.5:417–32.

———. [1911] 1963. *The Purchasing Power of Money; Its Determination and Relation to Credit, Interest and Crises*. 2d rev. ed. New York: Kelley.

———. 1917. The "Ratio" Chart, For Plotting Statistics. *Quarterly Publications of the American Statistical Association* 15:577–601.

———. 1921. The Best Form of Index Number. *Quarterly Publication of the American Statistical Association* 17.133:533–37.

———. [1922] 1967. *The Making of Index Numbers; A Study of Their Varieties, Tests, and Reliability*. 3d rev. ed. New York: Kelley.

———. 1930. The Application of Mathematics to the Social Sciences. *Bulletin of the American Mathematical Society* 36:225–43.

———. 1939. A Three-Dimensional Representation of the Factors of Production and their Remuneration, Marginally and Residually. *Econometrica* 7:304–11.

———. 1943. A World Map on a Regular Icosahedron by Gnomonic Projection. *The Geographical Review* 33.4:605–19.

———. 1997. *The Works of Irving Fisher*. Vol. 13. Edited by William J. Barber. London: Pickering & Chatto.

Fisher, Irving, and O. M. Miller. 1944. *World Maps and Globes*. New York: Essential Books.

Frisch, Ragnar. [1926] 1971. On a Problem in Pure Economics. In *Preferences, Utility, and Demand*, edited by John S. Chipman, Leonid Hurwicz, Marcel K. Richter, and Hugo F. Sonnenschein, 386–423. New York: Harcourt Brace Jovanovich.

———. 1930. Necessary and Sufficient Conditions Regarding the Form of an Index Number Which Shall Meet Certain of Fisher's Tests. *Journal of the American Statistical Association* 25:397–406.

———. 1934. Reply to Mr. Subramanian's Note. *Journal of the American Statistical Association* 29.187:317.

———. 1936. Annual Survey of General Economic Theory: The Problem of Index Numbers. *Econometrica* 4.1:1–38.

Gibbs, J. Willard. [1873] 1961. *The Scientific Papers of J. Willard Gibbs*. Edited by Henry Andrew Bumstead and Ralph Gibbs Van Name. New York: Dover.

Helmholtz, Hermann von. 1876, 1878. The Origin and Meaning of Geometrical Axioms. *Mind* 1.3:301–21, 3:212–25.

Hilbert, David. 1902. Mathematical Problems. Lecture Delivered Before the International Congress of Mathematicians at Paris in 1900. Translated by Mary Winston Newson. *Bulletin of the American Mathematical Society* 8:437–79.

Israel, Giorgio. 1981. "Rigor" and "Axiomatics" in Modern Mathematics. *Fundamenta Scientiae* 2.2:205–19.

Kline, Morris. 1972. *Mathematical Thought from Ancient to Modern Times*. New York: Oxford University Press.

Krantz, D. H., R. D. Luce, P. Suppes, and A. Tversky. 1971. *Additive and Polynomial Representations*. Vol. 1 of *Foundations of Measurement*. New York: Academic Press.

Lakatos, Imre. 1976. *Proofs and Refutations: The Logic of Mathematical Discovery*. Edited by John Worrall and Elie Zahar. New York: Cambridge University Press.

Morgan, Mary S. 1999. Learning from Models. In *Models as Mediators: Perspectives on National and Social Sciences*, edited by Mary S. Morgan and Margaret Morrison, 347–88. Cambridge: Cambridge University Press.

Morrison, Margaret, and Mary S. Morgan. 1999. Models as Mediating Instruments. In *Models as Mediators: Perspectives on Natural and Social Science*, edited by Mary S. Morgan and Margaret Morrison, 10–37. Cambridge: Cambridge University Press.

Neumann, John von. 1961. The Mathematician. In *John von Neumann, Collected Works*, edited by A. H. Taub, 1–9. Oxford: Pergamon Press.

Phillips, Andrew W., and Irving Fisher. 1896. *Elements of Geometry*. New York: American Book Company.

Riemann, B. 1882. On the Hypotheses Which Lie at the Bases of Geometry. In William Kingdon Clifford. *Mathematical Papers*. Translated by W. K. Clifford; edited by R. Tucker, 5–69. London: Macmillan.

Samuelson, Paul A., and Subramanian Swamy. 1974. Invariant Economic Index Numbers and Canonical Duality: Survey and Synthesis. *American Economic Review* 64:566–93.

Swamy, Subramanian. 1934. On a Certain Conclusion of Frisch's. *Journal of the American Statistical Association* 29.187:316–17.

———. 1940. Compatibility of Fisher's Tests for Index Number Formulae. *The Mathematics Student* 8:124–27.

———. 1965. Consistency of Fisher's Tests. *Econometrica* 33.3:619–23.

Tobin, James. 1998. Irving Fisher. In vol. 2 of *The New Palgrave, A Dictionary of Economics*, edited by John Eatwell, Murray Milgate, and Peter Newman. London: Macmillan.

Vogt, Arthur, and János Barta. 1997. *The Making of Tests for Index Numbers; Mathematical Methods for Descriptive Statistics*. Heidelberg: Physica-Verlag.

Wald, A. 1937. Zur Theorie der Preisindexziffern. *Zeitschrift für Nationalökonomie* 8:179–219.

Weintraub, E. Roy. 1998. From Rigor to Axiomatics: The Marginalization of Griffith C. Evans. In *From Interwar Pluralism to Postwar Neoclassicism*, edited by Mary S. Morgan and Malcolm Rutherford. *HOPE* 30 (supplement): 227–59.

Quantifying the Qualitative: Quality-Adjusted Price Indexes in the United States, 1915–61

H. Spencer Banzhaf

While economists had taken up questions of the best way to calculate an index of the "average level of prices" in the nineteenth century, the increased application of these concepts in the twentieth century raised a number of new questions.[1] Not the least of these questions was how to use the various index formulae when goods appeared and disappeared from the market. A closely related question was how to account for more subtle changes in the quality of the goods. At the same time, questions were arising about the true purpose of a price index. The history of these related concerns provides an interesting case of otherwise abstract ideas hitting concrete barriers in the form of data unwilling to conform to constructed compartments, a confused public, and political interests.

This paper tracks this history in the United States, examining three snapshots corresponding to important reviews of the government's price indexes and interspersing these snapshots with new ideas imported from Europe. These reviews, in two cases during world war, are explicit examples of measurement as statecraft (see the article by Theodore Porter in this volume): making the indexes more fair and accurate would improve them as tools for negotiating wages and setting other payments.

Correspondence may be addressed to H. Spencer Banzhaf, Resources for the Future, 1616 P Street N.W., Washington, D.C. 20036. I thank Neil De Marchi, Craufurd Goodwin, V. Kerry Smith, Roy Weintraub, and the conference editors and participants for valuable comments.

1. Few historians have taken up the story of price indexes, and so far as I know none the story of quality change. Diewert 1993, Mudgett 1951, and Persky 1998 are useful overviews for this period.

(See Sandra Peart's and Marcel Boumans's essays in this volume for two other contexts for price indexes.)

I begin with a review by Wesley Clair Mitchell in 1915 of the U.S. wholesale price index and with the work of Irving Fisher of about the same period (1922). Mitchell led a second, more extensive review of the government's price indexes during World War II, when price changes were particularly severe. The third review, completed in 1961, was conducted by a committee of the National Bureau of Economic Research (NBER) chaired by George Stigler, which used work by Zvi Griliches on "hedonic prices" to adjust for quality change. These three episodes, plus two interludes, form the outline of this paper. In each case, the ways these authors characterized the problem of quality change—and hence also the ways they tried to overcome the problem—have paralleled the ways in which they have conceptualized the price index itself.

Mitchell and Fisher

I begin this story with two prominent American economists who left a long-standing mark on the study of index numbers, Wesley Clair Mitchell (1874–1948) and Irving Fisher (1867–1947). Both men brought a broader interest in the quantity theory of money and business cycles to their work on price indexes, which included both calculation of actual index number series and theoretical writings. They were also colleagues and friends.[2]

Early in his career, Mitchell had investigated issues related to the history of money and inflation, especially during the civil war era (Hirsch 1970). He was also a major contributor to the formation of the official price indexes of the United States. The first important contribution was his review of the U.S. Bureau of Labor's wholesale price index in 1915 (revised 1921), published as "The Making and Using of Index Numbers." Among other things, Mitchell suggested that the wholesale price index was not an appropriate tool for measuring the general purchasing power of money for consumers (24). This point became important when, during World War I, the Shipbuilding Labor Adjustment Board began to use price indexes to control wages.[3] Accordingly, the U.S. Bureau of Labor Statistics developed a new "cost-of-living index" which became

2. See, for example, Mitchell 1952 and Allen 1993.

3. It was not the first time war time conditions required a price index to determine cost-of-living adjustments (see, e.g., Persky 1998).

available in 1919. (At the time, the term "cost of living" did not imply a link to welfare economics as it does today, but meant loosely an index of consumer prices for the purpose of wage adjustments.) Mitchell also served as editor of the War Industry Board's *History of Prices during the War* (1919).

Like Mitchell, Fisher had firsthand knowledge of the making of index numbers.[4] In 1923 he founded the Index Number Institute to release promptly a weekly wholesale price index (Fisher 1923; Allen 1993, 173). He also published a bible for all future students of index numbers, the comprehensive survey *Making of Index Numbers* ([1922] 1923). In this book, Fisher compared some 170 index numbers, identifying their algebraic properties and documenting whether they passed certain tests of consistency. His aim was to reject some indexes using these tests and so arrive at acceptable indexes that were close to the "true" index number. To this end, he recommended what he called the "ideal index," a geometric cross of the Laspeyres and Paasche index numbers (see Boumans this volume for more on Fisher's work).

Fisher sought to measure one true entity, "the price level," approximated by various formulae (1921; [1922] 1923, 229–34). Mitchell sought averages of individual prices, with different formulae potentially answering different questions ([1915] 1921, 23–25, 113). In comparison to later abstractions involving preference relationships, both viewed the problem in relatively physical terms, making explicit analogies to height, weight, and motion.[5] For example, both used the analogy of measuring the trajectory of a bursting bombshell. Wrote Fisher ([1922] 1923, 2–3),

> If we look at prices as starting at any time from the same point, they seem to scatter or disperse like the fragments of a bursting shell. But, just as there is a definite center of gravity of the shell fragments, as they move, so is there a definite average movement of the scattering prices. This average is the "index number." Moreover, just as the center of gravity is often convenient to use in physics instead of a list of the individual shell fragments, so the average of the price movements, called their index number, is often convenient to use in economics. (see also Mitchell [1915] 1921, 15)

---

4. See Dimand 1998 for additional background and summary.

5. There was a tradition of such physical analogies in the price index literature. See in particular Walsh 1901.

Elsewhere, Fisher used an analogy to a mechanical balance, in which items of different weight (prices) are placed at different distances from the fulcrum (quantity weights), and whose average weight (price) can be assessed by balancing the same items at one point (1911, 21–23, figs. 2–3).[6] Mitchell compared the measurement of prices to other instances of scientific measurement such as the weight of the atmosphere and the velocity of sound ([1915] 1921, 10).

This understanding of price indexes in physical terms conditioned how Fisher and Mitchell viewed the problem of new goods and quality change, which they both saw as a pervasive problem.[7] They tried to track prices through time, but their plans were thwarted because the set of prices itself changes. To continue the analogy of the bursting artillery shell, it is as if some of the shell fragments disappear midflight and become unobservable, while others suddenly appear midflight.

Fisher viewed the problem in terms of designing an index whose *value* will be robust to such changes. For example, if a new good or variety comes into the index at the same price as the outgoing good, then the analyst faces no difficulty because the value of the index will not change ([1922] 1923, 311). If the new good does affect the level of the index, the analyst must make some adjustment, presumably to avoid attributing the effects of a new sample to inflation. For example, if the new sample increases the price index by two percent, the analyst can adjust the index down by this amount to smoothly "splice" it into the old index. Similarly, if a new good is simply to be added to the index (in an increase in the size of the sample) and no base year prices are observed, the analyst can splice the new good in by starting it out at the value of the index as a whole. The analyst can also minimize such problems by updating the base frequently (311–12).

Fisher wanted to measure changes in the price level as a distinct entity from other factors such as changes in quality. He recognized that the prices of new goods are not directly comparable to the prices of old ones, so some adjustment must be made to the index number formulae. But he made no attempt to measure quality itself or to adjust for it. Instead, he suggested adjustments that would neutralize the information from the changing good so that it would have no effect on the value of the index. Similarly, if price remains unchanged even when quality does change, he

6. For more on this metaphor, see Morgan 1999.
7. See Fisher [1922] 1923, 310 and Mitchell [1915] 1921, 33.

suggested no adjustment. Thus it seems he did not see quality changes as having any bearing on inflation, except as an empirical difficulty. The fact that Fisher did not argue that quality changes should be interpreted as part of a quantity change, despite the fact that a central concern of his was to factor expenditures into price and quantity components, is consistent with this point of view.

In contrast to Fisher, Mitchell focused on an individual formula as one average of underlying prices that addressed a specific question or purpose, with different purposes justifying different averages. Inferring the cause of price changes from changes in money might be one purpose (see the articles by Thomas Humphrey and by Kevin Hoover and Michael Dowell in this volume), evaluating changes in the cost of living another. In the latter context, focusing in particular on a fixed basket Laspeyres index made sense since that index held the standard of living constant, but quality changes created a difficulty because the basket in fact was then *not* fixed. Mitchell ([1915] 1921, 25) grouped this problem together with other types of heterogeneity:

> We commonly speak of *the* wholesale price of articles like pig iron, cotton, or beef as if there were only one unambiguous price for any one thing on a given day. . . . In fact there are many different prices for every great staple on every day it is dealt in, and most of these differences are of the sort that tend to maintain themselves even when markets are highly organized and competition is keen. Of course, varying grades command varying prices, and so as a rule do large lots and small lots; for the same grade in the same quantities, different prices are paid by the manufacturer, jobber, and local buyer; in different localities the prices paid by these various dealers are not the same; even in the same locality different dealers of the same class do not all pay the same price to everyone from whom they buy the same grade in the same quantity on the same day. To find what really was the price of cotton, for example, on February 1, 1920, would require an elaborate investigation, and would result in showing a multitude of different prices covering a considerable range.

Heterogeneity in quality together with price variation across localities, variation across types of dealers, and just plain randomness all raise sampling difficulties. To overcome these difficulties, the field worker must select from among all these different prices for each of his commodities the one or the few series of quotations that make the most representative sample of the whole. He must find the most reliable source of information, the most representative market, the most typical brands or grades, and the class of dealers who stand in the most influential position. He must have sufficient technical knowledge to be sure that his quotations are for uniform qualities, or to make the necessary adjustments if changes in quality have occurred in the markets and require recognition in the statistical office.[8] (25)

That is, the field worker must pick a representative (rather than random) sample of prices, as well as a sample with stable qualities. Often, the convention of the price quotation matters. For example, prices of cattle and hogs are better than those of horses and mules because the prices of the former are quoted by the pound, whereas the latter are quoted by the head (33). Here, quality differences between animals are in terms of size and can be accounted for with appropriate per unit prices. When quality change can not be avoided, as in manufacturing, Mitchell suggested one of the splicing approaches discussed by Fisher, in which when varieties overlap the ratio of the old variety can be used from years 0 to 1 and the ratio of the new variety in years 1 to 2.

Like Fisher, Mitchell viewed quality change as a difficulty in measuring individual prices. Yet he seemed to go further than Fisher in advocating sampling designs that hold quality constant. However, at least at this point, he did not seem to have seriously suggested measuring quality itself in order to obtain quality-adjusted prices.

Interlude: New Ideas from Europe

With the next world war, Mitchell would have to think harder about the problem of measuring quality change, as labor organizations and others questioned the validity of the government's price indexes in the face of widespread quality deterioration. Before that occasion arose, however, two new ideas about the purposes of price indexes were born, new ideas which would influence Mitchell's thinking and which would create some confusion over the objective of price indexes.

---

8. Note that it is not clear what sort of adjustment Mitchell has in mind. Later he mentions only linking methods such as those discussed by Fisher.

These new ideas were imports to America from Europe. The first approach was that of François Divisia (1889–1964), who argued that index numbers should describe a historic path of price and quantity changes (1925). Divisia began with an equation of exchange and took time derivatives for the price and quantity components to derive a differential equation that could be approximated with a chain index. Divisia wrote in French, however, and his work did not seem to have been known in America until a review essay by Frisch was published in 1936, and he had little influence until even later than that. (Nevertheless, he will appear in this story again via another European, Erland von Hofsten.)

A more critical import into the American discussions of the period was the indifference-defined index of Alexander Konüs (1895–1991), a member of the price index section of the Moscow Business Cycle Institute directed by N. D. Kondratiev. Written in 1924 in Russian, this article was not directly known to most English speakers until its translation into *Econometrica* in 1939.[9] However, it was known by reputation through two publications in English by Staehle (1934) and Frisch (1936), whose acquaintance was in turn based on a two-page description in German by Ladislaus von Bortkiewicz.

Konüs's ([1924] 1939) definition of the cost-of-living index is the ratio of expenditures needed to hold utility constant under two price scenarios. That is, if the individual achieves utility u_0 in the base period at prices p_0, and prices change in the comparison period to p_1, the cost-of-living function P is defined as

$$P_{01} = E(p_1, u_0)/E(p_0, u_0), \tag{1}$$

where $E(\ )$ is the solution to the expenditure minimization problem. At about the same time as the work by Konüs and others on the continent, similar ideas were taking shape in England. Without reference to Konüs, A. L. Bowley (1928, 223) and John Maynard Keynes (1930, 97) defined the price index problem in similar terms. In a more sustained argument, Allen (1933, 200) asserted that "the theoretical problem of the price of living is to discover what change in expenditure must follow a given change in the price situation in order to leave an individual as 'well off' as before."

9. Henry Schultz initiated the translation project and wrote a critical introduction to the translation.

The idea was quickly picked up by a number of economists, although by no means all. Ragnar Frisch summarized and championed the indifference-based index in an important review article in *Econometrica* (1936). J. R. Hicks (1940) and Paul Samuelson (1947) also took up the indifference approach. Indeed, much of the indifference-defined price index literature is closely connected to the new use of dual cost functions, the rhetoric of revealed preference theories, and the "new welfare economics" of the same period and by many of the same champions. However, the approach did not sweep the profession and was contested by a number of economists at least into the 1950s, when the various approaches to price indexes began to appear side by side—at times in the same author.[10]

War and the Second Review

For its part, the U.S. Bureau of Labor Statistics (BLS) at first ignored the new indifference approach and dealt with quality change through splicing methods such as those described by Fisher and Mitchell. It tended to follow Mitchell's position in trying to measure prices holding quality constant. On the eve of American involvement in World War II, the BLS had three lines of defense against quality change (1941, 7–8).

The first line is what the Bureau called "specification pricing," or carefully defining the item that was being priced in the index, a practice recommended by Mitchell ([1915] 1921, 33).[11] Such detailed instructions aided the BLS in keeping the basket of goods constant in quality over time. When a new variety did not fit within any preexisting specifications, the BLS resorted to its second line of defense, a splicing method such as discussed by Fisher and Mitchell. When prices of varieties overlapped, they could be entered in such a way as to hold quality constant. As also suggested by Fisher, entirely new goods were entered at the base value of the index so that their entry had no affect. On occasion, however, varieties did not overlap and the BLS resorted to dividing the price of the

10. A notable example is Mudgett 1951.

11. The BLS (1949, 285) gives an example for men's shirts: "*Shirt, work, cotton chambray*: 3.90 yards per pound before sanforizing, about 3.60 yards per pound after sanforizing, based on 36-inch fabric, sanforized shrunk; Full cut, clean workmanship, good quality buttons, collar interlined with chambray or equal grade of fabric, continuous nonrip sleeve facing, double- or triple-stitched seam, 2 plain pockets with or without flap, 30 to 31 yards per dozen based on 36-inch fabric and neckband size scale 14 to 17 inches. (Specify whether double- or triple-stitched)." See also U.S. House 1951, 232.

new good by the price of the old without quality adjustment. Durable goods were the most troubling case because firms timed new models to the clearance of the old, excluding the possibility of splicing (Hoover 1961, 1178). The BLS was uncomfortable with this last approach because with improvements "price, with regard to quality, might show a greater decline," but it did not see a way to overcome "the technical difficulties" in measuring qualities (1941, 8).

Economic disruptions during World War II and associated political pressures forced the BLS and the economists with whom it consulted into a new round of thinking about price indexes generally and quality change in particular.[12] Only in this case, the concern on everyone's mind was quality deterioration. At the beginning of the American involvement in the war, national labor unions and industry agreed with the National War Labor Board to use the BLS's cost of living index to adjust wage levels. As a result, the index came under close scrutiny, with labor charging that the index underestimated price increases by failing (1) to observe cost increases disguised as quality increases (as when formerly "small" eggs are packaged as "medium")—a process called "upgrading"; (2) to account for forced "uptrading" to more expensive varieties as cheaper ones disappeared; (3) to account for quality deterioration; (4) to observe black market prices; and (5) to use an appropriate sampling scheme that captured the largest price increases (e.g., Meany 1944).

As a result of these criticisms, the government initiated a complicated review process (see Ostrander 1944). This process began with the report of a special committee of the American Statistical Association chaired by Frederick Mills and including Margaret Reid and Theodore Schultz. Later, President Roosevelt appointed a committee of government (William Davis), labor (George Meany and R. J. Thomas), and industry (H. B. Horton and George K. Batt). In the end, each of these groups issued their own reports. All the parties relied closely on a further technical review committee of Mitchell, Reid, and Simon Kuznets, with a staff including Solomon Fabricant and Lloyd Metzler.[13] The committee

12. As Martin Kohli (this volume) shows, the BLS was at the same time experimenting with input-output tables to try to anticipate future disruptions *after* the war.

13. This wartime work by economists on the committee (and in the BLS) is related to, but conceptually and administratively distinct from, work by other economists in price control. See Homan 1946, 868 for a description of this related work and Fellner 1942 for an example. Fellner uses a quite different definition of inflation than that presented elsewhere in this essay, defining it as total nominal product per fixed unit of input. On this reckoning, quality change that does not lead to more units would not be inflationary (129).

reviewed all of labor's critiques but eventually focused on the first three listed above, all dealing with the issue of quality change.

It is interesting that the war occasioned this round of thinking. As noted previously, quality change had been identified before. Moreover, the BLS (1940) had just recently updated its 1917–19 market basket, first in 1934–36 and then again in 1939, adding automobiles, light bulbs, radios, vacuum cleaners, refrigerators, and more fresh foods. Of course, one thing was different about the changes in World War II: quality change was quality deterioration. By December 1942, so many resources were diverted to the war effort that the BLS dropped a number of goods from the index, many of which had just been added two years previously. These goods included automobiles, gas stoves, radios, refrigerators, sewing machines, washing machines, vacuum cleaners, studio couches, bedsprings, and silk goods. Because of rationing, it also decreased weights for fuel. At the same time, it increased weights on substitutes for these disappearing and rationed goods, including automobile repair, mass transit fares, and rayon clothing (U.S. Bureau of Labor Statistics 1948; Cavin 1945).

The other difference was that government and industry were increasingly applying the price index to wage adjustments. This was a sticking point. The American Federation of Labor (AFL) had "never agreed to the principle of basing wages on cost of living or on price inflation" (Meany 1944, 35). George Meany (1944, 35), the AFL's representative on the president's committee, argued that

> the established wage policy of this country has always been based on raising wages as increases in productivity made this possible. This is the only possible basis for an expanding economy with rising living standards. In wartime, however, we have been willing to meet the emergency with emergency measures. At every stage of wartime policy-making the American Federation of Labor has supported inflation control and has loyally supported the war administration even though our living standards have not been maintained and we have been denied fair compensation for work done.

Labor may have been willing to accept a temporary decline in wages relative to productivity, but not relative to the cost of living. And it was a decrease in the standard of living that labor saw everywhere, much of which the so-called "index of the cost of living" did not capture. Again Meany (1944, 26–27):

Our living habits have had to adjust to wartime conditions, often at greatly increased costs. Landlords no longer do the repair and redecorating work they did before the war and we are forced to pay these costs ourselves; rationing of meat has forced us to eat in restaurants at greatly increased cost; inferior gasoline, wear and tear on automobiles by ride-sharing to and from work, the use of worn-out cars requiring much repair have increased the cost of necessary transportation and are only partly accounted for by the BLS; families living in crowded war centers without equipment for home laundering must send their washing out at much higher cost. (see also Thomas 1944, 26–27)

Quality change was a crucial concern that raised fundamental questions about the purpose of the price index. As shaped in America by Mitchell and Fisher, it was a measure of prices distinct from quality and other considerations, and the BLS tried to implement this vision by holding quality constant as much as possible. But the index was called a "cost-of-living index," and the cost of living now quite clearly involved more than just prices. This disconnection created confusion at the popular level, but even at a professional level the new ideas of the indifference-defined index added to the mix. Thus, some interpreted "cost of living" to mean a measure of the cost of a fixed basket (which would of course entail a constant standard of living); some meant the minimum cost of obtaining a certain standard of living; and others (including, but not limited to, many in the popular culture) meant the cost of the standard of living at any given time (hence including changes in the standard).[14]

This was the climate in which the Mitchell committee had to evaluate the U.S. price index. In light of this confusion and the severe problems of quality change, it is not surprising that some of the language of the Mitchell committee was different from that of Mitchell [1915] (1921). Whether this is because Mitchell had changed his way of thinking in the intervening years or whether it is a reflection of the other voices on the committee is not possible to say. Whatever the case, the committee took tentative steps toward the indifference-defined index. It considered the potential merits of "an index measuring change in real price, that is, the cost of a given quantity of utility" (Mitchell, Kuznets, and Reid 1944, 286). But these tentative steps fall short of an endorsement. In the end,

14. See Mills et al. 1943, 100–101; Mitchell, Kuznets, and Reid 1944, 263. For a later but especially revealing example of this confusion, compare the testimonies of economists and other witnesses in U.S. House 1951, 1–2, 102, 172, 181, 389–92.

the committee argued that there is no satisfactory way of measuring such changes in "real prices" and that the BLS should not make unscientific guesses at intangible, unmeasurable factors. Nevertheless, the committee did undertake a sensitivity analysis of some of the factors to see how much difference any potential adjustments would make.

But the committee had more than practical objections to the indifference-defined index: it also stopped short of recommending it even as a theoretical goal. The committee did stress that the purpose of the index was to measure changes in the prices of goods—not the change in total expenses, which would include quantity changes. In the same way, one would not want to mix measures of a person's weight and height (Mitchell, Kuznets, and Reid 1944, 264–65). Thus nonpecuniary changes that might affect welfare would not be germane to the index. To better understand its position, consider in turn the committee's treatment of uptrading, upgrading, and quality deterioration.

Since the purpose of an index is to measure prices, *voluntary* uptrading (switching to a better variety) should be ignored, with new goods spliced into the index to show no price change, an approach consistent with BLS practices (286). Note that this approach is not consistent with the indifference-defined index, since voluntary switching to a new commodity is, in a revealed preference sense, evidence of an increase in utility, suggesting a ceteris paribus fall in the cost of living. The committee wrestled more with the case of *involuntary* uptrading but was in the end skeptical. It suggested some cases of supposed forced uptrading—for example, eating out more often because wives are working or because gasoline rationing makes it difficult to drive home for lunch—are often really due to an increase in income (274, 315, 335). In other cases, the committee suggested that uptrading is really sidewise trading for a more expensive equal-quality variety, which could be handled easily by splicing (286). Thus in the end it judged that "forced quality uptrading is very small, on the whole (286)" and essentially ignored it.

The committee was more willing to accept upgrading (mislabeling of varieties) as a source of bias. Although difficult to correct, upgrading was an easier problem to accept in principle since no matter how one thinks of the price index, mislabeling a product variety as another more expensive variety would create havoc with the intended measure. Thus, if grade A meat were $0.33 per pound and grade B meat $0.30 per pound in a first period, and in the second period grade B meat was labeled grade A and sold for $0.33, it would appear prices had not changed when in fact they had increased ten percent (320). As a kind of sensitivity analysis, the committee assessed the potential bias in different categories, especially food. But even here, it assumed that in some categories the government inspectors, although cut back during the war, effectively prevent upgrading.

Quality deterioration also posed a problem. We have seen it was also a problem, addressed by Mitchell and Fisher, from the perspective of physically measuring price changes, but the committee entertained the idea of going further than these earlier works. It considered the role of "color, form, flavor, texture, style, or other characteristic[s] that will give greatest pleasure per dollar spent" (277), important factors from the perspective of the indifference-defined index. But it argued that even measuring the individual characteristics is often impossible, let alone "combining qualities of various characteristics of a given commodity into a single measure" (277). For example, who is to say how much the "price of shorts has gone up because they have ties rather than elastic sides?" (287). Instead, the committee focused on quality deterioration associated with quantity decline—that is, quality deterioration that necessitates buying more units. In this case, "crude objective measures might be secured of the performance or serviceability . . . , for example, mileage per gallon of gasoline, length of wear from sheets, pounds of fruits and vegetables after subtracting waste on account of defects" (277; also 318–19). Note that this is also the case that could be accepted within the earlier framework. Indeed, Mitchell himself had argued for the pricing of livestock by the pound instead of by head for the sake of constant "quality" (interpreted as quantity).

In summary, the actions taken by the committee were tentative. It discussed a new theoretical aim in terms of constant utility but saw no way to make it operational, and did not even theoretically endorse its aim. Instead, it opted for a measure of prices only. In the end, the only adjustments it made besides the old splicing procedure was for the one case where adjustment would have been called for under the paradigm of physical measurement: a physical change in the item that can be thought of in terms of *quantity*. Its recommendation was to retreat from the term "cost of living" altogether. The committee wrote,

> We know no satisfactory way of measuring changes in "real prices"— that is, the prices of a given quantity of utility, usefulness, or service, such as occurs when poorer qualities are priced.

> We recognize . . . that the lower quality of some items is putting
> pressure on many families to buy a larger quantity and thus to in-
> crease their expenditures by more than the increase in prices shown
> in the index. . . . [But] it may not follow that the Bureau of Labor Sta-
> tistics could, or should, take account of the rather intangible factors
> we have stressed. An official fact-finding agency is properly reluctant
> to state conclusions it cannot support by evidence. . . . The Technical
> Committee does, however, venture one suggestion: the index should
> be given a less misleading name. (262–63)

In other words, a scientific approach cannot address the intangibles that
lie behind changes in utility, making it impossible to meet the requirements of an indifference-defined index. That recommendation was eventually accepted. Accordingly, beginning in June 1944, each month's report had a disclaimer that "the index does not show the full wartime
effect on the cost of living of such factors as lowered quality, disap-
pearance of low-priced goods, and forced changes in housing and eating away from home" until the name was changed to the "Consumers'
Price Index" in September 1945 (U.S. Bureau of Labor Statistics 1966,
7). Not an index at constant utility, but an index of prices holding quality
constant.

Labor and industry leaders were willing to agree to this, but this is as
far as the agreement went. Whereas the Mitchell committee argued that
it was appropriate to limit the index to price changes (Mitchell, Kuznets,
and Reid 1944, 260–65), labor argued that such a limitation invalidated
the index from being used to adjust wages (Meany 1944, 33; Thomas
1944, 29). Thomas conceded that it did not make sense to compensate
for increased expenditures that resulted from increased income, but he
defended compensation for expenditures caused by changes in lifestyle
related to external factors such as the war. Thus, he argued that changes
in the "manner of living" should be included, but not changes in the
"standard of living" (Thomas 1944, 26–28).

The ironic part of this story is that labor is the party arguing, against
economists, for the perspective closest to what today would be considered the "economic approach" to price indexes. In contrast, both analysts
in the BLS and those economists who were asked argued for a price-only
perspective on index numbers, a perspective in which quality change and
other changes in the economy (e.g., rationing) should be netted out so
that they do not affect the index.

Interlude: Swedish Commentary

The United States was obviously not the only country wrestling with quality deterioration during the war, nor was it the only country that thought about these problems in the context of its official price indexes. Commentary on the American indexes from a Swedish economist by the name of Erland von Hofsten (1911–1996) made the Swedish experience important for the United States. Hofsten was the chief of the Swedish Social Welfare Board, responsible for Sweden's cost of living index, from 1947 to 1962. After spending time in Washington in 1948 to study American methods, he published *Price Indexes and Quality Changes* (1952) in English, a book motivated by the contrasting treatment of quality changes in Sweden and America. This book is interesting in its own right as the most detailed treatment of quality change in the price index literature to that point, but also as an important source read by later commentators on price measurement in the United States.

From the outset Hofsten rejected Fisher's view that the aim of a price index is to measure prices in general (15). Hofsten suggested two alternative purposes and meanings for a price index: one the indifference-defined approach of Konüs, the other the integral approach of Divisia. From the perspective of the indifference-defined index, Hofsten began by evaluating two of the approaches to splicing and found them each potentially deficient. First, he noted that ignoring quality change in the presence of changing varieties (that is, taking the value of the index as $p_1{}^b/p_0{}^a$ for two varieties a and b) would be incorrect (68). Second, he showed that there are also problems with splicing over two time periods when goods overlap, $(p_1{}^a/p_0{}^a) \cdot (p_2{}^b/p_1{}^b)$. For such an adjustment to be correct, it must be the case that $p_1{}^b/p_1{}^a$ is proportionate to the quality difference between the two goods (50). It was argued at the time that this criterion might be met in a free market since equilibrium requires that the ratio of marginal utilities of two goods equal the price ratio.[15] However, Hofsten doubted that this criterion is in fact met (50). For example, minor changes in a variety often merely camouflage price increases (68, 53–56).

Hofsten suggested another approach: measure quality and make explicit adjustments. First, he took the case of objective, quantitatively observable definitions of quality, an approach used for milk in the Swedish

15. This point was made by Ulmer (1949, 65–69), an economist in the BLS who Hofsten later cites (59). See also Hoover 1961.

index during the war. In this example, the measure of quality was caloric content arising from variation in milk fat. In 1940, milk sold for 30 öre/liter and had a caloric value of 650 calories. In 1941, under a new standard, milk had a lower fat content yielding 600 calories, and the price fell to 29 öre/liter. The relative change in quality, denoted g, is 600/650. The quality-adjusted price index for milk is then

$$(1/g) \cdot (p_1^{b}/p_0^{a}), \tag{2}$$

which is $(650/600) \cdot (29/30)$ or 1.05, thus yielding a price increase instead of the decrease one would have obtained without quality adjustment. Note the similarity of this approach to that taken by the 1944 Mitchell committee, which also made adjustments based on quantitative interpretations of quality changes.

Hofsten was willing to consider going further than this, adding more structure to his interpretation of g as he adapted it into the indifference-defined index. He emphasized the case of perfect substitutes, in which the consumer purchased only one variety and relative quality can be measured by the consumer's willingness to substitute between them. For the two-good case, g is then the ratio of the intercepts of the straight-line indifference curves (chap. 5).

In the case of the Divisia index, Hofsten actually defined g similarly. However, he now raised all the bugaboos of utility theory. He raised the problem of observing the indifference curves (99–100, 107) and disparaged the approach of adding new goods by assuming they had already existed in the person's preference ordering in the past but at the choke price—the approach of Hicks (1940) (Hofsten 1952, 98, 111). In addition, he raised the problem of changing preferences, noting people's tastes for simple novelty and susceptibility to advertising. To Hofsten, allowing such whimsical taste changes to affect the value of the index is dubious (111–19). By now, Hofsten had clearly undermined the entire indifference approach to the price index problem, a fact that he was well aware of (120). Indeed, he backed off from the approach, concluding that the factor g should be based on the articles' function, or "the services which they offer." "Factors which are not of real utility should be left out of consideration. This means that it is after all legitimate to use 'objective' criteria for the quality comparisons" (120).

Thus in the end Hofsten returned to the original formulation of quality adjustment in which one uses observable, quantifiable criterion such as caloric value. Unfortunately, he had to concede that sometimes even this adjustment is not possible, so that careful splicing may be necessary (71–72, 121). He suggested that firm rules are not possible, that decisions must be made on a case-by-case basis. In many ways Hofsten returned to the same procedures used by the 1944 Mitchell committee. In other ways he also anticipated the future work of Zvi Griliches (1930–1999).

The Stigler Committee and Griliches's Hedonic Price Regression

In 1961 Zvi Griliches published an influential paper that began a sustained literature on *hedonics*, an approach using multiple regression to control for quality.[16] In standard literature reviews of quality adjustment, hedonic regressions are usually the beginning of the story. In contrast, I shall argue here that the hedonic approach shows continuity with past work in many respects.

Griliches's work was part of a third external review of the government's price indexes by the NBER. Although the economy was no longer in crisis, the BLS again turned to the NBER for advice on how to make the index as accurate as possible (U.S. House 1961). The NBER established a Price Statistics Review Committee chaired by George Stigler and issued its report in 1961 along with Griliches's and others' staff papers. Like Mitchell's committee in the previous external review, Stigler's emphasized the problem of new goods and quality change. Indeed, they referred to it as the biggest problem facing the index. According to the Stigler committee (1961, 37), some new products such as televisions are "radically different" from anything that existed before; others, such as nylon socks and filter cigarettes, are "simply new varieties of an older product." However, such changes of quality are still important. Indeed, "if a poll were taken of professional economists and statisticians, in all probability they would designate (and by a wide margin) the failure of the price indexes to take full account of quality changes as the most important defect of these indexes. And by almost as large a majority, they would believe that this failure introduces a systematic upward bias in the price indexes—that quality changes have on average been quality improvements" (35). Note that an optimistic view of quality improvement has replaced the wartime frustrations of quality decline.

16. Predecessors include Waugh (1929), Court (1939), and Stone (1956). Griliches freely admitted that his approach was not original.

But more importantly, the Stigler committee differed from the Mitchell committee in its interpretation of the price index and, hence, in its
interpretation of the difficulties that quality change poses. While the
Mitchell committee was at most ambivalent about the role of an indifference-based index, the Stigler committee thoroughly endorsed it (51–
52). This was a radical suggestion from the perspective of the BLS and
touched off much debate.[17] In some ways, it may also be said to be radical from the perspective of those who had first articulated the indifference approach, who, as previously noted, applied it only to a single individual. The similarity to the Chicago school's willingness to use consumer surplus in contrast to more purist strands in the profession during
the same period is suggestive.

In any case, the Stigler committee did not limit itself to abstract discussion of the objective of price measurement. Among other concrete
suggestions, it recommended that the BLS try to revise the basket of
goods more often. Including new goods earlier would at least capture the
usual decline in prices early in a product's life cycle, if not the benefits of
the new good itself (31, 52). The committee had three recommendations
for treating more subtle quality changes. First, in the case of a change in
a single, dominant characteristic, the price can be adjusted by the relative change in the characteristic. "For example, if the average duration
of a hospital stay for an appendectomy has fallen by half over a period,
then the effective cost of the hospital service should be halved relative to
the cost of a hospital stay of fixed duration" (36). Here, the committee's
recommendation matched the treatment by the earlier Mitchell committee and in the Swedish index. Second, the committee suggested that psychologists and other specialists could use surveys to appraise consumers'
perceptions of the relative qualities of varieties (37). Third, the committee recommended that, when there is more than one dominant characteristic, multiple regression analysis could be used to calculate the implicit
prices of the characteristics and so control for quality change. In support
of this recommendation, the committee cited, among other essays, the
new work by Griliches (1961) on "hedonic price indexes for automobiles."

17. As it happens, the BLS rejected the Stigler committee's recommendation and continued
to interpret the index in terms of price changes only (Jaffe 1964; U.S. Bureau of Labor Statistics
1966), although it resolved to study the suggestion (U.S. Bureau of Labor Statistics 1965). Only
recently has the BLS changed its position.

Following the earlier work by Andrew Court and Richard Stone, Griliches treated prices of a good as a function of their underlying characteristics. This allowed for a hedonic regression of the general form

$$p_i = p(x_i) + \varepsilon_i, \tag{3}$$

where p is the price of variety i and x is a vector of characteristics. For example, the price of an automobile might be a function of its horsepower, its size, the type of transmission, the presence of a radio, and so forth.

Consider the example of car models in light of the previous treatments of quality change. Splicing over intermediate years is not possible because models change almost every year. The BLS had recently begun to address the problem by netting out the value of features that became standard based on the list price for the option from the previous year, but this approach could not account for brand new features or qualitative improvements (Hoover 1961).

Griliches gave two renderings to the hedonic price index that allowed it to overcome these concerns. In the first rendition, he used the regression to impute prices for varieties in years in which the varieties did not actually exist. For instance, he estimated a hedonic regression on 1959 models. Using this method, he could predict the price a new 1960 model would have had in 1959 based on its characteristics. With this technique, one can calculate a price index by aggregating up individual price relatives in the usual Laspeyres fashion.

The second rendition has come to be called a "direct" hedonic price index. In this case, the regression (3) takes on the special functional form

$$\ln(p_i{}^t) = \alpha^0 D^0 + \alpha^1 D^1 + q(x_i{}^t) + \varepsilon_i, \tag{4}$$

where D^0 and D^1 are dummy variables for the base and comparison years respectively and the αs are the associated intercepts. Taking the exponent of both sides, it is clear that $e^{\alpha D^1}/e^{\alpha D^0}$ is a price index corresponding to the quantity index e^{q0}. The ratio is the parallel shift in the hedonic surface.

The hedonic approach seemed like a potential way to incorporate the multifaceted problems of "color, form, flavor, texture, style" that seemed so difficult to the Mitchell committee. But it was not clear if it did so in a way consistent with the indifference-defined index. Griliches (1961, 175) wrote that the "existence and usefulness" of a hedonic price function "is an empirical rather than a theoretical question." As he would later recall, "[The hedonic approach] did not pretend to dispose of the question of whether various observed differentials are demand or supply determined, how the observed variety of models in the market is generated, and whether the resulting indexes have an unambiguous welfare interpretation. Its goals were modest. It offered the tool of econometrics, with all its attendant problems" (Ohta and Griliches 1975, 326). In other words, the hedonic index was a model in search of an interpretation.

In retrospect, Griliches's two renditions of the hedonic regression had much more in common with the earlier treatments of quality adjustment than at first appears. The link between the hedonic and the older literature is especially apparent in the "imputation" rendition of the hedonic. Under this rendition, the hedonic approach is entirely consistent with measuring prices as one would measure the trajectory of shell fragments, while allowing one to overcome the problem of fragments that seem to appear or disappear midflight. Indeed, it is often described in terms of filling in missing prices.

As it turns out, the "direct" hedonic also has ties to the earlier quality adjustment literature. It did not take long for people to begin asking under what restrictions on preferences the direct hedonic would be consistent with an indifference-defined index. Fisher and Shell (1968) showed that they are so consistent only when preferences take on the form of "repackaging." Repackaging means that the preferences can be expressed in a form where the utility of the quantity of a variety multiplies a quality subfunction of all its characteristics. Intuitively, it means that quality is essentially the same as quantity, or like a change in units from ounces to pounds. It also means that varieties are perfect substitutes for each other, trading at the rate of their relative qualities. In other words, the direct hedonic is consistent with the indifference-defined index only when preferences conform to the case analyzed by Hofsten, albeit with the important advantage of being able to quantify several characteristics. It is also very similar to the earlier treatments of Mitchell et al., in which, for example, the price of meat is simply multiplied by an adjustment from a single variable instead of a subfunction. Perhaps Griliches had these types of questions in mind when he stated his preference for the imputation version because it avoided some of the "metaphysical problems involved in the notion of quality" (1961, 174).

The relationship between the new hedonic price index and broader conceptions of price indexes was thus ambiguous. It was advanced by a committee advocating use of the indifference-defined index and ana-lyzed in these terms;[18] evaluated on those terms, however, it proved to involve very restrictive assumptions. And yet these assumptions are en-tirely consistent with the context in which Griliches was working, in at least two ways. The first I have already noted—that the restrictive as-sumptions turn out to be identical to those discussed by Hofsten, who had "written the book" on quality change a decade before. The second context is Griliches's other projects during the previous few years up to and during his work on the price indexes for automobiles.[19]

In a series of papers, Griliches (1958, 1959, 1960a, 1960b, 1960c, 1963) studied agricultural productivity primarily as a function of three inputs, each of which had undergone technical change: fertilizer, labor, and farm machinery (including automobilon). In this work, he was try-ing to explain use of inputs as a function of their relative quality-adjusted prices using fairly aggregate models of the Solow variety. In the case of fertilizer and labor, Griliches saw the quality change problem in terms of either a single service flow or as a single characteristic. Thus, fertil-izer provided a single service of "plant nutrient" that had been increas-ing over time in such a way that farmers could obtain the same amount of nutrition with fewer tons. Consistent with this view, Griliches (1958, 1959) estimated an early hedonic regression of fertilizer prices on the nitrogen, phosphoric acid, and potash content of fertilizers, interpreting the coefficients as the marginal contribution of each chemical to plant nutrition. Similarly, he used average wages by education levels to adjust for workers' productivity (1960c, 1963).

The third type of input, farm machinery, was somewhat different from fertilizer and labor. Here, Griliches confronted a problem of deflating a measure of capital that was already in dollar terms. He found this task an easier one because he was willing to take for granted that the purchasing prices reflected quality changes (1960b, 190). Consistent with this prob-lem, he focused his energies on thinking about the deterioration in the productive services of a stock of capital over time (1960b, 1963). Thus once again Griliches had a case of a single measure representing produc-tivity for which varieties of tractors and so forth are perfect substitutes.

To summarize, the Stigler committee made the new and radical sug-gestion that the CPI be conceived as an indifference-defined cost-of-

18. In addition to Fisher and Shell, see Adelman and Griliches 1961.
19. See Griliches's recollection in his retrospective (1990, 185–88).

living index. Taking up a theme from the Mitchell committee, it also stressed quality change as an important factor for such an index and offered the work of Griliches (1961) as one way to tackle the problem. However, it was not clear how Griliches's hedonic model fit into the framework of a cost-of-living index. In hindsight, it was not as radically new as it might have appeared. While providing a way to incorporate multiple characteristics into a single index, it did so only by collapsing them into a single composite measure of quality and treating that composite in the same way as earlier treatments of the quality problem.

Conclusion

As war and its associated economic stresses brought it into the sphere of wage negotiations, the government increasingly relied on price indexes as an objective basis for its stance (another example of a theme described in Porter 1995). To ensure that the indexes would be objective—and perceived as such—government agencies tried to make them as fair and accurate as possible, turning to outside economists and statisticians in the three episodes described here, as well as to those inside government. After the war, government agencies continued this process, with the role of price indexes taking a well-established place in American statecraft.

Quality change and new (disappearing) goods were a continual source of difficulty in this process. But as economists wrestled with this problem over the period covered in this narrative, their responses evolved along with their view of what they were measuring. This evolution, though by no means smooth, began with relatively simple notions of measures of average prices by analogy to physical measurement, to a more abstract relationship involving household preferences. These new ideas led to new thinking about when to apply fixes such as splicing and even to some new fixes such as explicit quality adjustment either in a single dimension or, later, in a multidimensional bundle estimated from a hedonic regression. At the same time, the reverse was true: apparent problems of quality change led to rethinking about what a price index should measure.

But despite these changing conceptions, the types of adjustments for quality did not radically change. Throughout the period, adjustments for quality, when done at all, amounted to adjustments for quantity. Perhaps it is because the profession's focus on supply and demand creates a predisposition to thinking in terms of quantities of homogeneous, well-defined goods. Perhaps it is because actual indexes, however interpreted by the prevailing theories, have been in the form of a Laspeyres index requiring prices and quantities. Since prices are inherently numerical, quality adjustment to prices would have to be numerical as well. The profession has only recently tried to overcome this problem by taking a new level of abstraction: structural models that explicitly estimate individual preferences to directly derive the information for a Konüs cost-of-living index (e.g., Trajtenberg 1990).

References

Adelman, Irma, and Zvi Griliches. 1961. On an Index of Quality Change. *Journal of the American Statistical Association* 56:535–48.

Allen, R. G. D. 1933. On the Marginal Utility of Money and Its Application. *Economica* 13:200–209.

Allen, Robert Loring. 1993. *Irving Fisher: A Biography*. Cambridge, Mass.: Blackwell.

Bowley, A. L. 1928. Notes on Index Numbers. *The Economic Journal* 38:216–37.

Cavin, J. P. 1945. Aspects of Wartime Consumption. *American Economic Review, Papers and Proceedings* 35:15–36.

Court, Andrew T. 1939. Hedonic Price Indexes. In *The Dynamics of Automobile Demand*. New York: General Motors Corporation.

Diewert, W. Erwin. 1993. The Early History of Price Index Research. In *Essays in Index Number Theory*, edited by W. Erwin Diewert and Alice O. Nakamura. Amsterdam: North-Holland.

Dimand, Robert W. 1998. The Quest for An Ideal Index: Irving Fisher and *The Making of Index Numbers*. In *The Economic Mind in America: Essays in the History of American Economics,* edited by Malcolm Rutherford. London: Routledge.

Divisia, F. 1925. *L'indice monétaire et la théorie de la monnaie*. Revue d'Economie Politique 39:842–8612, 980–1008, 1121–51.

Fellner, William. 1942. *A Treatise on Inflation*. Berkeley: University of California Press.

Fisher, Franklin M., and Karl Shell. 1968. Taste and Quality Change in the Pure Theory of the True Cost-of-Living Index. In *Value, Capital, and Growth: Essays in Honour of Sir John Hicks,* edited by J. N. Wolfe. Edinburgh: University of Edinburgh Press.

Fisher, Irving. 1911. *The Purchasing Power of Money*. London: Macmillan.

———. 1921. The Best Form of Index Number. *Quarterly Publication of the American Statistical Association* 17:533–51.

———. [1922] 1923. *The Making of Index Numbers: A Study of their Varieties, Tests, and Reliability*. 2d ed. Boston: Houghton Mifflin.

————. 1923. A Weekly Index Number of Wholesale Prices. *Journal of the American Statistical Association* 18:835–40.

Frisch, Ragnar. 1936. Annual Survey of General Economic Theory: The Problem of Index Numbers. *Econometrica* 4:1–38.

Griliches, Zvi. 1958. The Demand for Fertilizer: An Econometric Interpretation of a Technical Change. *Journal of Farm Economics* 40:591–606.

————. 1959. The Demand for Inputs in Agriculture and a Derived Supply Elasticity. *Journal of Farm Economics* 41:309–22.

————. 1960a. Estimates of the Aggregate U.S. Farm Supply Function. *Journal of Farm Economics* 42.2:282–93.

————. 1960b. The Demand for a Durable Input: U.S. Farm Tractors, 1929–1957. In *The Demand for Durable Goods,* edited by A. C. Harberger. Chicago: University of Chicago Press.

————. 1960c. Measuring Inputs in Agriculture: A Critical Survey. *Journal of Farm Economics* 42:1411–33.

————. 1961. Hedonic Price Indexes for Automobiles: An Econometric Analysis of Quality Change. In *Price Statistics of the Federal Government*, prepared by the Price Statistics Review Committee of the National Bureau of Economic Research. New York: National Bureau of Economic Research.

————. 1963. The Sources of Measured Productivity Growth: U.S. Agriculture, 1940–1960. *Journal of Political Economy* 71.4: 331–46.

————. 1990. Hedonic Price Indexes and the Measurement of Capital and Productivity: Some Historical Reflections. In *Fifty Years of Economic Measurement*, edited by Ernst R. Berndt and Jack E. Triplett. Chicago: University of Chicago Press.

Hicks, J. R. 1940. The Valuation of the Social Income. *Economica* 7:108–24.

Hirsch, Abraham. 1970. Mitchell's Work on Civil War Inflation in His Development as an Economist. *HOPE* 2:118–32.

Hofsten, Erland von. 1952. *Price Indexes for Quality Changes*. Stockholm: Bokförlaget Forum.

Homan, Paul T. 1946. Economics in the War Period. *The American Economic Review* 36:855–71.

Hoover, Ethel D. 1961. The CPI and Problems of Quality Change. *Monthly Labor Review* 84.11:1175–85.

Jaffe, Sidney A. 1964. The Statistical Structure of the Revised CPI. *Monthly Labor Review* 87.8:916–24.

Keynes, John Maynard. 1930. *A Treatise on Money*. New York: Harcourt Brace.

Konüs, A. A. [1924] 1939. The Problem of the True Index of the Cost of Living. Translated by Jacques Bronfenbrenner. *Econometrica* 7:10–29.

Meany, George. 1944. Letter to President Franklin D. Roosevelt, November 13. In *Report of the President's Committee on the Cost of Living*. Washington, D.C.: U.S. Government Printing Office.

Mills, Frederick C., E. Wight Bakke, Reavis Cox, Margaret G. Reid, Theodore W. Schultz, and Samuel S. Stratton (Special Committee of the American Statistical Association). 1943. An Appraisal of the U.S. Bureau of Labor Statistics Cost of Living Index. *Journal of the American Statistical Association* 38:387–405.

Mitchell, Lucy Sprague. 1952. A Personal Sketch. In *Wesley Clair Mitchell: The Economic Scientist*, edited by Arthur F. Burns. New York: National Bureau of Economic Research.

Mitchell, Wesley Clair. [1915] 1921. The Making and Using of Index Numbers. Part 1 of *Index Numbers of Wholesale Prices in the United States and Foreign Countries*, Bulletin 284 of the U.S. Bureau of Labor Statistics, 7–114. Revised ed. Washington, D.C.: U.S. Government Printing Office.

————, ed. 1919–20. *History of Prices During the War*. U.S. War Industries Board, Price Bulletins nos. 1–57. Washington, D.C.: U.S. Government printing office.

Mitchell, Wesley C., Simon Kuznets, and Margaret G. Reid. 1944. Prices and the Cost of Living in Wartime—An Appraisal of the Bureau of Labor Statistics Index of the Cost of Living in 1941–1944. *Report of the President's Committee on the Cost of Living*. Washington, D.C.: U.S. Government Printing Office.

Morgan, Mary S. 1999. Learning from Models. In *Models as Mediators: Perspectives on Natural and Social Science*, edited by Mary S. Morgan and Margaret Morrison. Cambridge: Cambridge University Press.

Mudgett, Bruce D. 1951. *Index Numbers*. New York: John Wiley and Sons.

Ohta, Makato, and Zvi Griliches. 1975. Automobile Prices Revisited: Extensions of the Hedonic Hypothesis. In *Household Production and Consumption*, edited by Nestor E. Terleckyj. New York: National Bureau of Economic Research.

Ostrander, F. Taylor. 1944. The Mitchell Committee's Report on the Cost-of-Living Index: Comments. *American Economic Review* 34:849–56.

Persky, Joseph. 1998. Price Indexes and General Exchange Values. *Journal of Economic Perspectives* 12:197–205.

Porter, Theodore M. 1995. *Trust in Numbers: The Pursuit of Objectivity in Science and Public Life*. Princeton, N.J.: Princeton University Press.

Samuelson, Paul A. 1947. *Foundations of Economic Analysis*. Cambridge, Mass.: Harvard University Press.

Staehle, Hans. 1934. International Comparisons of Food Costs. In *International Comparison of Costs of Living*, Studies and Reports of the International Labour Office, series N, no. 20. Geneva.

Stigler, George, Dorothy S. Brady, Edward Denison, Irving B. Kravis, Philip J. McCarthy, Albert Rees, Richard Ruggles, and Boris C. Swerling. 1961. *The Price Statistics of the Federal Government*. New York: National Bureau of Economic Research.

Stone, Richard. 1956. *Quantity and Price Indexes in National Accounts*. Paris: Organization for European Economic Cooperation.

Thomas, R. J. 1944. Letter to President Franklin D. Roosevelt, November 13. In *Report of the President's Committee on the Cost of Living*. Washington, D.C.: U.S. Government Printing Office.

Trajtenberg, Manuel. 1990. *Economic Analysis of Product Innovation: The Case of CT Scanners*. Cambridge, Mass.: Harvard University Press.

Ulmer, Melville J. 1949. *The Economic Theory of Cost of Living Index Numbers*. New York: Columbia University Press.

U.S. Bureau of Labor Statistics. 1940. The Bureau of Labor Statistics' New Index of Cost of Living. *Monthly Labor Review* 51.8:367–405.

———. 1941. *Changes in Cost of Living in Large Cities in the United States 1913–41*. Bulletin no. 699. Washington, D.C.: U.S. Government Printing Office.

———. 1948. Consumers' Price Index: Relative Importance of Components. *Monthly Labor Review* 67.2:156–60.

———. 1949. Technical Notes. *Monthly Labor Review* 69.3:284–90.

———. 1965. Editor's Note. *Monthly Labor Review* 88.6:658.

———. 1966. *CPI: History and Techniques*. Bulletin no. 1517. Washington, D.C.: U.S. Government Printing Office.

U.S. House. 1951. Hearings before a Subcommittee of the Committee on Education and Labor. *Consumers' Price Index*. 82d Cong., 1st sess.

Walsh, Correa Moylan. 1901. *The Measurement of General Exchange Value*. New York: Macmillan.

Waugh, Frederick. 1929. *Quality as a Determinant of Vegetable Prices*. New York: Columbia University Press.

Contributors

H. Spencer Banzhaf is a Fellow in the Quality of the Environment Division at Resources for the Future. He received his Ph.D. in economics from Duke University in 2001. His historical interests include twentieth-century welfare economics and policy analysis, and economic thought in the Enlightenment.

Bradley W. Bateman teaches writing and economics at Grinnell College. He is the author, most recently, of *Keynes's Uncertain Revolution* (1996).

Marcel Boumans lectures on methodology and the history of economics at the University of Amsterdam. His field of research is marked by three Ms: models, mathematics, and measurement. His recent publications include "Built-In Justification," which appears in *Models as Mediators* (edited Mary S. Morgan and Margaret Morrison; Cambridge University Press, 1999), and "Lucas and Artificial Worlds," in *New Economics and Its History* (edited by John B. Davis; Duke University Press, 1998).

Flavio Comim is a research associate at Von Hugel Institute, St. Edmund's College, University of Cambridge. He received his Ph.D. from the University of Cambridge in 1999; his thesis was titled "Common Sense Economics: Essays on the Role of Common Sense in the History of Economic Thought." His areas of research are the history of economic thought and development economics (with an emphasis on poverty issues). His most recent works include "Marshall and the Role of Common Sense in Complex Systems," in *Complexity and the History of Economic Thought* (edited by David Colander; Routledge, 2000); "Keynes' Common-Sense Economics: A Criticism of Coates' Argument," in *Keynes, Post-Keynesianism, and Political Economy* (edited by Claudio Sardoni and Peter Kriesler; Routledge, 2000); and "The Scottish

Tradition in Economics and the Role of Common Sense in Adam Smith's Thought," forthcoming in the *Review of Political Economy*.

Michael E. Dowell is a graduate student at the University of California at Davis. He is also a lecturer at California State University, Sacramento, where he teaches courses in macroeconomics and the history of economic thought. His research interests are in the history of economic thought, macroeconomics, and monetary economics.

Kevin D. Hoover is a professor of economics at the University of California at Davis. He is the author of numerous articles on macroeconomics, monetary economics, economic methodology, and the philosophy of science. His most recent books are *Causality in Macroeconomics* and *The Methodology of Empirical Macroeconomics* (both Cambridge University Press, 2001). He is president-elect of the History of Economics Society, immediate past chair of the International Network for Economic Method, and an editor of the *Journal of Economic Methodology*.

Thomas M. Humphrey is a vice president and economist at the Federal Reserve Bank of Richmond, where he has worked for the past thirty-one years. He is the longtime editor of and frequent contributor to the bank's *Economic Quarterly*. His main research interest is the history of monetary theory and policy.

Franck Jovanovic is a research fellow in economics at the University of Paris I (Panthéon-Sorbonne) and is a member of the research group GRESE. He is finishing a dissertation on the history of the random walk model in finance.

Judy L. Klein is professor of economics at Mary Baldwin College. She is the author of *Statistical Visions in Time: A History of Time Series Analysis, 1662–1938* (Cambridge University Press, 1997). Her research interests include the experience and comprehension of seasonal commercial rhythms and the post–World War II nexus of economics, statistics, and control engineering.

Martin C. Kohli, after majoring in philosophy at Northwestern University, joined the Bureau of Labor Statistics in New York City in 1979. In 1984 he heard Wassily Leontief describe the serendipitous early days of his relationship with the BLS. Mr. Kohli earned his Ph.D. at the New School, where he used input-output tables to analyze trade between the United States and Japan. From 1990 through 1992 he was the assistant director of Governor Mario Cuomo's Commission on Competitiveness. In 1993 and 1994 he represented the New York State Department of Economic Development at public forums on economic and telecommunications policy, and in 1995 he rejoined the BLS. He has taught microeconomics, international trade, and quantitative methods at several colleges in the New York area.

Philippe Le Gall is a professor of economics at the University of Angers and is a member of the research groups GRESE (University of Paris I, Panthéon-Sorbonne) and GEAPE (University of Angers). His main research interests are the history of econometrics and of economic modeling.

Harro Maas lectures in history and the methodology of economics at the University of Amsterdam. He recently finished his thesis on William Stanley Jevons's methodological approach to economics: "Mechanical Reasoning: William Stanley Jevons and the Making of Modern Economics."

Mary S. Morgan is a professor of history of economics at the London School of Economics and a professor of history and philosophy of economics at the University of Amsterdam. She is an editor of two previous *HOPE* supplements: one in 1994, *Higgling: Transactors and Their Markets in the History of Economics* (with Neil De Marchi), and one in 1998, *From Interwar Pluralism to Postwar Neoclassicism* (with Malcolm Rutherford). Her current research is on the historical and philosophical implications of economics becoming a modeling science.

Sybilla Nikolow is a research scholar at the Institute for Science and Technology Studies, University of Bielefeld, Germany. Since completing her Ph.D. thesis on the disciplinary history of German social statistics she has been working on the history of graphical representations in the social sciences. She held several postdoctoral fellowships in Berlin, Paris, Bielefeld, and Cambridge. Her recent publications include "Displaying the Invisible: 'Volkskrankheiten' on Exhibition in Imperial Germany," written with Christine Brecht (*Studies in the History and Philosophy of Biological and Biomedical Sciences*, vol. 31, 2000), and "'Die Versinnlichung von Staatskräften': Statistische Karten um 1800" (*Traverse*, vol. 6, 1999).

Sandra J. Peart is an associate professor of economics at Baldwin-Wallace College. She is the author of *The Economics of William Stanley Jevons* (Routledge, 1996) and, with Evelyn L. Forget, coeditor of *Reflections on the Classical Canon in Economics* (Routledge, 2001). Her current research with David Levy (see www.econlib.org) focuses on attacks on the race-neutral analysis of classical economics and the use of images as models.

Theodore M. Porter is a professor of the history of science in the Department of History at UCLA. His books include *The Rise of Statistical Thinking* (1986) and *Trust in Numbers* (1995). Most recently he has edited, with Dorothy Ross, a volume on the modern social sciences (forthcoming in 2002) in the Cambridge History of Science series.

E. Roy Weintraub (Duke University) was trained as a mathematician although his professional career has been as an economist. In recent years his research on the history of the interconnection between mathematics and economics in the twentieth century has helped shape the understanding of economists and historians. He is the author of seven books and the editor of two others, and he has published a number of articles in professional journals and edited volumes.

Index

"Accidental causes," 268
Accounting prices, 132
Accounting systems
    measurement instruments, 243–44
    national accounting, United
        Kingdom, 213–34
    Tableau economique
        (Leontief), 192–95
Accuracy of measurement, 227–30
Achenwall, Gottfried, 30, 44
Adams, Henry Carter, 57
Addams, Jane
    Hull House Maps and Papers,
        62, 76
    Men and Religion Forward
        Movement, 58
Adjustment techniques, 227–30
Age of economic measurement,
    111–36
    agriculture, economic
        measurement, 114–16
    decline of nations, 111–14
    geometric landscape, 114–16
    linear programming, 128–33
    Manchester Statistical Society,
        investigations by, 116–21

municipal statistics, 121–24
    trade cycle chart, 124–28
Agriculture, economic measurement,
    114–16
Allen, R. D. G., 351
American Economic Association,
    founding of, 57–58
American economics
    quantification, early twentieth
        century, 57–85
American Federation of Labor (AFL),
    354
American Protestantism, 65–69
    turn away from, 74
American social science, 74–76
American Sociological Society, 77
American Statistical Association, 77,
    353
*Annual Financial and Commercial
    Review*, 124
Anthropomorphism, 104
Arithmetic, astronomy and, 8
Armstrong, Sir William, 263
Arnon, Arie, 154
Arrowsmith, A., 38
Astrology, 9

Astronomy
    Enlightenment period, 10–12
    1730, to, 8–9
Atomic bomb, 132–33
Aukrust, O., 214
Axiomatics, 309–12
    Axiomatic Index Theory, 314–15
        instrumental approach versus,
        332–38

BAAS. *See* British Association for the
    Advancement of Science
    (BAAS)
Baconian science, 6–7
Bain, Alexander, 278
Baker, Henry, 118–19, 121
Balance
    cause and, 255
    mean, drawing of, 253
    measurement instruments, 237,
        242–43, 277–302
        analysis, as tool of, 280–82
        compound pendulum, drawing
        as, 283
        generally, 282–86
        geometry of, drawing, 283
        gold assaying, balance used
        in, 284
        gold valuation, use in, 284,
        287–91
        mental state, applicability to,
        291–97
        tool of analysis, balance as,
        280–82
Balance sheets, 217
Bank Charter Act of 1844, 149
"Banking Statistics as a Measure of
    Trade" (Pownall), 118
Bank of England, 118–19, 149
    chart of balance of account, 120
    species payment and, 129
Banque de France, 94
    discount rate, 97

Banzhaf, Spencer, 200, 241, 345–70
Bateman, Bradley W., 52, 57–85, 121,
    246
Bentham, Jeremy, 292–94
Bernoulli, Daniel, 13
    wealth or power, on gauging, 23
Bernoulli, Johann, 15
Bevölkerung, 33
Biometrics and social sciences,
    differences, 95
Birkbeck, George, 281
BLS. *See* U.S. Bureau of Labor
    Statistics
Boisguillebert, Pierre de, 213
Bold hypothesis, 92
Boom-bust cycle, 1919–21, 179
Booth, Charles, 271
    social survey movement, 62
Boskin Commission. *See* Commission
    to Study the Consumer Price
    Index
Boston
    Educational and Industrial Union,
    122
Boumans, Marcel, 19, 197, 227,
    313–44
    index numbers, 237, 241–42
Bowley, Arthur L.
    national accounting, 214
    price indexes, 351
    trade cycle chart, 124, 127
Bracey, R. J., 313
Brahe, Tycho, 9
Brandes, Ernst
    table making debate, 44, 47, 48, 50
Brinton, Willard, 123
Britain. *See* England; Great Britain;
    United Kingdom
British Association for the
    Advancement of Science
    (BAAS), 258, 263, 271, 278
Broun, J. A., 266
Bryan, William Jennings, 58

Budget Bureau, 209
*Bulletin de la Statistique Générale de
la France*, 90
Bullion Committee of 1810, 140,
145–49, 151
Bumstead, Henry, 321–22
Bunle, Henri, 96
Bureau of Labor Statistics. *See* U.S.
Bureau of Labor Statistics
Burgess, W. Randolph, 183, 184
Burke, Edmund, 112
"Reflections on the Revolution in
France," 47
Büsching, Anton Friedrich
criticisms of, 43
Crome, guidance to, 30, 31
population accounts, 33
Business cycles
Federal Reserve System and, 163
March, Lucien, work of, 96–100
real rate movements and, 170

Cabinet Office Diary, 217
Cairnes, John F., 262–63, 279, 290
Calendars, astronomy and, 8–9
Calkins, John U., 172
Calories, 323
Cameralists, 12
Cantor, George, 309, 310
Carpenter, William, 291–92
Cattle, silver price of, 142–43
Causal relationships, 100–103
"accidental causes," 268
measurement, role in causal
relationships, 253
Causes
money, quantitative assessment of
value of, 137–61
use to bootstrap measurements,
238–40
Census, 1730–1830, 12–14
Center for Advanced Study in the
Behavioral Sciences, 6

Central Statistical Office (CSO), 217
Champernowne, D. G., 227–28
Charities and the Commons, 63–65
Chemistry, 1730–1830, 12
Chicago social scientists, 5
Children
factory work, United Kingdom, 270
Women and Children in Industry,
1870 to 1900, 61
China, astronomy, 9
Cholera epidemic, 1832, 117
Christianizing the Social Order
(Rauschenbusch), 68–69
Christian social service. *See* Men and
Religion Forward Movement
Circular Test, 331–32, 334, 336–37
gap, 338
Clark, Colin, 214–16
Clark, J. M., 76
The Coal Question (Jevons), 263–64
Coefficients of dependency, 94 n8
Cohen, Patricia, 121
Coinage, condition of and
measurement, 239, 256–58
Cold War, 205
government employment of
economists, 129, 131
Comim, Flavio, 191, 213–34
Commensurability Test, 328
Commercial and Political Atlas
(Playfair), 112
"Commercial Crises and Sun-Spots"
(Jevons), 267
Commission to Study the
Consumer Price
Index, 138
Committee of 97, 59
Committee of 100, 58–59
Committee of government,
World War II,
353–54
Commodities, books and maps on,
31–32

Commons, John R.
  American economics, influence in,
    76
  chair of sociology, 82
  improvements in social surveys, on,
    77
  institutionalism and, 81
  Pittsburgh Survey, 63–64
Comte, Auguste, 116
  formulation from, 4–5
Condorcet, Marquis de, 10, 11
  censuses, 13, 14
Consistency, 193, 229, 231
Constraints, use of, 230
Constructing indicators, 245–46
Consumer price index (CPI), 138,
    249, 358
Copeland, Morris, 214
Copernicus, 9
Corn
  silver price of, 142–44,
    152
  "The Solar Period and the Price of
    Corn" (Jevons), 266
Cornfield, Jerome, 200, 203–4
Corps de Mines, 87
Correlation, 93, 100–103
Corry, Leo, 303–4
Cost-of-living
  public servants, adjustments, 143
  World War I era, 346–47
Cournot, A. A., 16
Court, Andrew, 363
Cowles Commission, 129, 131
CPI. See Consumer price index (CPI)
Crawfurd, John, 263
Croly, Herbert, 72
Crome, August Friedrich Wilhelm,
    23–56, 114
  criticisms of work, 43–51
  demography, development of,
    32–33 ·
  Europens Produkte, 31

Produktkarte, 32
  state, study of, 23–28
  statistical work of, 28–43
    background, 28–31
    commodities, books and maps
      on, 31–32
    state crafting, 32–34
    statistical maps, 39–40
    strength of the state,
      measurement of, 37–43
    table making, debate, 43–51
    Verhältniskarte von Europa,
      34–43
  training as statistician, 30
CSO. See Central Statistical Office
    (CSO)
Currency
  Inquiry into the Currency Principle
    (Tooke), 151–52
  The Currency School, 151–52
Currie, Lauchlin, 186
Cyclical fluctuations, 96–99, 265–68

Dantzig, George B., 128–33
Davenant, Charles, 153–54
Davenport, Donald, 199
Davis, William, 353
"Death Calendar in Industry for
    Allegheny County," 64
Debate over table making, 43–51
Debs, Eugene V., 73
Decline of nations, 111–14
Decomposition of time-series, 127
"Definition and Measurement of the
    National Income and Related
    Totals" (Stone), 220
Delambre, Jean-Baptiste, 11
Demography, development of,
    32–33
De Morgan, Augustus, 297
Denison, E. F., 214
Dennison, Henry, 76
Dependency index, 122

Depression. *See* Federal Reserve System
Dictionary of Chemistry and the Allied Branches of Other Sciences, 278, 279, 282
Dictionary of Trade (McCulloch), 117
Die Lehre von der Wirtschaft, 137
"Digression Concerning the Variations in the Value of Silver" (Smith), 140–45, 152
Direct measurement, 229
Direct observation, 196–97
Divisia, Franois, 351, 359
Dorfman, Robert, 209
Dowell, Michael E., 99, 137–61, 239, 259, 290
Drift and Mastery (Lippman), 72
Drunkenness, rates by race or nationality, 269

East India Company, 117
Eastman, Crystal, 64
École Polytechnique, 87
Economic Information Service (England), 217
Economic Journal, 17
Economist, 17
Edgeworth, F. Y.
    mathematics, 305, 306, 309
    weights, 329
    transitional work, 18
Educational and Industrial Union, 122
Eichhorn, Wolfgang, 314, 334–35
Eisenhower, Dwight D., 207
Eisenhower administration, 191
Elemente der Staatskunst, 48
Elements of Geometry (Fisher), 317
Ely, Richard T.
    American Economic Association, 57–58
    Hull House Maps and Papers (Addams and Kelley), 62, 76
    individualism, on, 70

Library of Economics and Politics, 62, 76
Social Gospel, 71
England. *See also* Great Britain; United Kingdom
    economic decline, 112
    social survey movement, 62–63
Enke, Stephen, 132–33
Epistemological foundations of statistics, 100–106
    causality, 100–103
    correlation, 100–103
    historical time, 100–103
    lost world, measurement of, 103–6
Equally significant causes, 254
Euclidean geometry, 309
Eugenics, 90–91
Europe
    statistical representations, 1770–1830, 23–56
Europens Produkte (Crome), 31
Evans, W. Duane, 205
Evelyn, Sir George Shuckburgh, 112
Exactitude, ideals of (1830–1900), 14–18
Experimental method, 89
Extension, national accounting, 224–27

Fabricant, Solomon, 353
Factor Reversal Test, 330, 334–36
Factory Acts (United Kingdom), 268
Farr, William, 271
Fawcett, Henry, 258
Fechner, Gustav, 94–96
Fed. *See* Federal Reserve System
Federal Reserve Act (1913), 163, 173–75
Federal Reserve Board, 164
    real bills doctrine of money, 240
Federal Reserve System
    augmenting doctrine, 175–76
    boom-bust cycle, 1919–21, 179

Federal Reserve System
(*continued*)
collateral, 177
framework, 171–86
Great Depression, 164–66, 185–86
inventory theory, 178–79
key indicators, establishment of,
184–85
money stock, 178
New York Fed, 168, 176–77
officials, list of, 172
open market operations,
incorporation of, 182–84
operational doctrine, 176–78
original doctrine, reformulation,
173–75
overview, 162–66
policy guides, 178–79
price level indicators, 180–81
productive loans, defined, 176
quantity theory indicators,
rejection of, 179–82
Tenth Annual Report, 178–79
Fisher, Irving
cyclical price-level effects
of money, 169–71
Elements of Geometry, 317
food values, 323
human experience, measurement as
extension of, 227
index numbers, 19, 237, 241–42,
313–44
Axiomatic Index Theory,
314–15, 332–38
consistency of tests, 332–35
empirical test of, 329–32
"ideal" index, 330–31
index formulae, tests of, 326–29
index-number problem, 323–26
instrumental approach,
described, 336–38
inventions, 320–23
making of, 323–32

mechanical balance, 325
non-Euclidean geometry,
316–20
price ratios, 324
world maps and globes, 338–40
Index Visible Filing System,
320–21
The Making of Index Numbers, 313,
327–28, 331–32
"Mathematical Contribution to
Philosophy; Attacking Kant's
Theory of Geometric
Axioms," 317
measurement instruments, 247
money, quantity theory of, 196
price indexes, 97, 346–50, 355,
357–58
The Purchasing Power of Money,
167, 170, 313, 321, 329–31
quantity theory framework, 166–68
"The 'Ratio' Chart for Plotting
Statistics," 321
ratio charts, 127
transitional work, 18
tuberculosis, tent for treatment, 320
visualizations, on, 322
World Maps and Globes, 339
Flexibility, national accounting,
219–24
Flux, A. W., 118–19, 121
Food values, 323
Forecasting, 105–6
France
metric system, 11–12
national accounting, 213
population studies, 34
1730–1830, Enlightenment, 10
social statistics, 79–80
statistical thought, 86–110.
See also March, Lucien
stock market, 1910s, 96 n14
Franklin, Benjamin, 293–94
Frege, Friedrich, 310

French Revolution, 42
  metric system, 11–12
  table making and, 47
Friedman, Milton, 186
  price increases and wealth, 147
Frisch, Ragnar, 314, 325–26
  "Necessary and Sufficient
    Conditions Regarding the
    Form of an Index Number
    Which Shall Meet Certain of
    Fisher's Tests," 332–34
  price indexes, 351–52

Galileo, 6
Galton, Sir Francis, 271
  epistemological foundations, 105
Gauss, Carl Friedrich, 318
GDP. See Gross Domestic Product
    (GDP)
Gemeine Tabellenmachers
    (Ordinary table makers),
    43–51
General Theory (Keynes), 137
Geometric certainty, 304–9
Geometry, 8
  agriculture and, 114–16
  balance, drawing, 283
  non-Euclidean, 316–20
George, Henry, 63
Germany. See also Crome, August
    Friedrich Wilhelm
  mining, 1730–1830, 12
  statistical economics, 16–17
Gibbs, Josiah Willard, 317, 319,
    321–22
Gießen, University of, 29, 42
Gilbert, Milton, 214
Gillin, John, 76–77, 82
Gillispie, Charles, 11
Gladden, Washington, 58
Gladstone, W. E., 263
Glaser, Ezra, 205
Glass, Carter, 172, 173

Globes, world, 338–40
GNP. See Gross National Product
    (GNP)
Gold, study of, 128, 242, 298
  assaying, 282, 284
  balance, use in, 284
  Bullion Committee of 1810, 140,
    145–49
  measurement instruments, 239–40,
    253, 287–91
  A Serious Fall in the Value of Gold
    Ascertained, and Its Social
    Effects Set Forth (Jevons),
    155–59, 259, 262
  valuing, 258–63
Goldenweiser, Emanuel, 172,
    179–82, 183
Goldsmith, Raymond, 207, 208
Göttingen, University of, 26
Göttingische gelehrte Anzeigen, 45
The Grammar of Science (Pearson),
    102
"Graphical Methods in the
    Thermodynamics of Fluids"
    (Gibbs), 321
Graphic Method for Presenting Facts,
    123
Graunt, John, 13
  wealth or power, on gauging, 23
Great Britain. See also England;
    United Kingdom
  Mechanic's Institutes, 280–81
  trade cycle, World War I, 124–28
Great Depression
  Federal Reserve System and,
    164–66, 185–86
Greece, classical sciences, 8
Griliches, Zvi, 346
  hedonic price regression,
    361–66
Größenkarte von Europa, 34
Größenkunde, 32–34
Gross Domestic Product (GDP), 138

Gross National Product (GNP),
    248–49
Grundlagen der Geometrie (Hilbert),
    310
Guy, William, 114

Hacking, Ian, 15
    epistemological foundations, 100,
    105
Halle, University of, 28, 41
Halley, Edmund, 13
Hamilton, Walton, 76
Hankey, Thomson, 257
Harvard style, 97
Hedonic prices, 346
    hedonic price regression,
    361–66
Heeren, Ludwig
    debate over table making,
    44–50
Heilbron, John, 7, 11
Helmholtz, Hermann von,
    317
Hendricks, Frederick, 257
Herschel, Sir John, 257
Heywood Bank, 119
Hicks, J. R., 352
Hilbert, David, 310, 313
Historical time, 100–103
History of measurement,
    4–22
    1830–1900, 14–18
    exactitude, ideals of, 14–18
    historiography, themes, 4–8
    periodization, elements of,
    8–20
    1730, measurement to,
    8–9
    1730–1830, Enlightenment,
    10–14
    Twentieth Century, 18–20
History of Prices During the War
    (War Industry

Board), 347
History of Prices (Tooke),
    149–55
Hitchcock, Dal, 199
Hoffenberg, Marvin
    capital-account transactions,
    201, 209
Hofsten, Erland von,
    359–61
Hooker, Reginald
    March, Lucien, contrast,
    96 n14
    time-series decomposition, 95
Hoover, Herbert, 76, 290
Hoover, Kevin D., 99, 137–61, 239,
    259
Household consumption, 196
How to Pay for the War
    (Keynes), 129
Hoxie, Robert F., 76, 81
Hubbard, J. G., 257
Huber, Michael, 107
Hull, Edward, 263
Hull House Maps and Papers
    (Addams and Kellcy),
    62, 76
Human experience, measurement as
    extension of, 227
Hume, David
    regularity, on, 102
    specie-flow mechanism, 146
Humphrey, Thomas M.,
    162–89, 240
Hunter, W. W., 266
Hurwicz, Leonid, 129
Hussey, Vivian, 265

Ideal models, 92
Imaginary prices, 132
Indexation. *See also* Index numbers
    barometric, 96–100
    indices de dépendance, 101
Index Number Institute, 347

Index numbers, 19, 237–38
  adding with weights to
      make index numbers,
      240–42
  Axiomatic Index Theory, 314–15
    instrumental approach versus,
      332–38
  changing base, test by, 327
  Circular Test, 331–32, 334, 336–37
    gap, 338
  Commensurability Test, 328
  constructing indicators, 245
  determinateness as to prices, test
      of, 327
  Factor Reversal Test, 330, 334–36
  gold, study of, 289
  "ideal" index, 330–31, 347
  instrumental approach to, 313–44
    Axiomatic Index Theory versus,
      332–38
    consistency of tests, 332–35
    description of, 336–38
    empirical test of, 329–32
    index formulae, tests of, 326–29
    index-number problem, 323–26
    inventions, 320–23
    making of index numbers,
      323–32
    mechanical balance, 325
    non-Euclidean geometry,
      316–20
    price ratios, 324
    world maps and globes, 338–40
  money, quantitative assessment of
      value of, 158
  The Paasche Index, 328, 329, 330
  proportionality as to prices, test of,
      326
  proportionality as to trade, test of,
      326–27
  Time Reversal Test, 335, 336
  withdrawal or entry as to prices,
      test of, 327

Index Visible Filing System, 320–21
Indicators, constructing, 245–46
Indices de dépendance, 101
Indifference-defined index, 351
Indirect measurement, money, 139
Indirect statistical inference, 196
Individualism, 70
Inductive quantification, 255
Industrial accidents
    compensation to victims, 66
    Work Accidents and the Law
      (Eastman), 64
Industrial management, productivity
    and, 72
Industry. See specific topic
Industry Illustrated, 215
Infinity, 309
Ingénieurs économistes, 86
Input-output economics, 129, 131,
    190–91, 218
    early schemes, 203, 206
    measurement instruments, 244
    1947 tables, 205–8
    usefulness of, 209
Inquiry into the Currency Principle
    (Tooke), 151–52
Inquiry into the Nature and Causes of
    the Wealth of Nations
    (Smith), 111
INSEE. See Institut National de la
    Statistique et des Études
    Économiques
Institute for Research on Poverty, 81
Institutional economics, 79–82
Institutionalism, 75–76
    start of, 81
Institut National de la Statistique et
    des Études Économiques, 107
Instruments. See Measurement
    instruments
Interfering causes, 254
Invariance, national accounting,
    219–24

The Isolated State with Respect to Agriculture and Political Economy, 114
Israel, Giorgio, 105, 108, 315

Jakob, Ludwig Heinrich von, 41
Jefferson, Thomas, 112
Jenkin, Fleeming, 297
Jennings, Richard, 292, 295
Jevons, William Stanley, 16, 252–76
  "accidental causes," 268
  background, 280
  balance, 242, 277–302
    analysis, as tool of, 280–82
    compound pendulum, drawing as, 283
    geometry of, drawing, 283
    gold valuation, use in, 284, 287–91, 298
    measurement instrument, as, 282–86
    mental state, applicability to, 291–97
    tool of analysis, as, 280–82
  coal, on, 263–65
  The Coal Question, 263–64
  coins, measurement on wear of, 239, 256–58
  "Commercial Crises and Sun-Spots," 267
  commercial debt and, 121
  compensation, strategy of, 157
  cyclical fluctuations, 265–68
  Dictionary of Chemistry and the Allied Branches of Other Sciences, contributions to, 278, 279, 282
  drunkenness, rates by race or nationality, 269
  gold, study of, 128, 242, 298
    assaying, 282, 284
    measurement instruments, 239–40, 253, 287–91

  valuing, 258–63
  independence, assumption of, 157–58
  index numbers, 158
  inductive quantification, 255
  isolation, strategy of, 157
  "laws of human enjoyment," 296
  "laws of human wants," 295
  Manchester Statistical Society, 117
  "Married Women in Factories," 269
  measurement, role in causal relationships, 253–56
  measurement instruments, 237–38
    balance, 242, 277–302
  money, value of, 140
  mortality rates, 268–70
  "On Tabular Analysis" (Guy), discussion of, 114
  Papers and Correspondence, 277
  Principles of Science
    balance, 286–87
    invention, on, 277
    mental state, applicability of balance to, 292
    role of measurement, 253–54
    underlying argument, 266
    recommendations for measurement, 272
  ratio charts, 127
  residues, method of, 158
  A Serious Fall in the Value of Gold Ascertained, and Its Social Effects Set Forth, 155–59, 259, 262
  social astronomy, 99
  "The Solar Influence on Commerce," 266
  "The Solar Period and the Price of Corn," 266
  State in Relation to Labour, 268
  sunspot cycle, 267–68
  "Sunspots and Commercial Panics" (Jevons), 268

The Theory of Political Economy,
    279, 294, 297–98
transitional work, 18
utility adjustment of individual to
    optimum, 295
Joint Committee on Standards for
    Graphic Representation, 127
Jovanovic, Franck, 79, 86–110,
    237–38
Judgment, 247
Justi, Johann Heinrich Gottlob
    state officials, instructions to, 27,
    28

Kameralismus, 23–25, 27–28, 29, 41
Kant, Immanuel, 310
    "Mathematical Contribution to
        Philosophy; Attacking Kant's
        Theory of Geometric
        Axioms," 317
Kelley, Florence
    Hull House Maps and Papers,
        62, 76
Kellogg, Paul U., 63
Kemmerer, Edwin W., 166–67
Kennedy, John F., 208
Kennedy administration, 191, 210
Keppler, Johannes, 10
Keynes, John Maynard, 217
    aggregate demand price, 151
    General Theory, 137
    How to Pay for the War, 129
Keynesian economics
    income determination, 202
    measurement instruments, 243
Kiel, University of, 192
Kitchin, Joseph, 124–28
Klein, Felix, 195, 306–7
Klein, Judy L., 3, 95, 111–36
Knight, Frank, 4
Kohli, Martin C., 190–212, 218, 243
Kondratiev, Nikolai, 124, 351
Konüs, Alexander, 351, 359

Koopmans, Tjalling
    Cold War and, 129, 131
    economics as deductive system,
        209
    input-output economics, 190–91
    theorizing and measuring,
        relationship between, 195
Korean War, 191, 205
Koyré, Alexandre, 6
    scientific measurement, defined, 15
Krug, Leopold
    criticisms of, 43, 49, 50
Kuhn, Thomas S., 4
    classical sciences, 8
    quantification in physics, 6–7
    scientific measurement, defined, 15
Kurita, Keiko, 87
Kuznets, Simon, 353
    national accounting, 214, 219

Ladd, George, 317
Länderkunde, 32, 34
Land ownership, poverty and, 63
Langton, William, 118–19, 265
    Bank of England, chart of balance
        of account, 120
Laplace, Pierre-Simon de, 11, 12
    censuses, 14
Laspeyres, Etienne, 289, 330, 347
Lavoisier, Antoine-Laurent, 11, 12
    balance, 279
    political arithmetic, 13–14, 28
League of Nations, 224
Le Gall, Philippe, 79, 86–110,
    237–38
Lenoir, Marcel, 96
Leontief, Wassily, 190–212. *See also*
    U.S. Bureau of Labor
    Statistics
    accounting principles, 243
    behavioral relationships, 196–97
    direct observation, 196–97
    indirect statistical inference, 196

Leontief, Wassily (*continued*)
   input-output economics,
      129, 131, 190–91,
      218, 244
     early schemes, 203, 206
     1947 tables, 205–8
     usefulness of, 209
   limitations of concepts,
      overcoming, 199–203
   measurement instruments,
      247–48
   1947 table, 205–8
   "Quantitative Input and Output
     Relations in the Economic
     System of the United States,"
     193–94
   *The Structure of American
     Economy*, 199
   Tableau economique, 192–95
   theorizing and measuring,
     relationship between,
     195–99
Leslie, T. E. Cliffe, 258–59, 261,
   290–91
*Les représentations graphiques et la
   statistique comparative*,
   94–96, 101
Levi, Leone, 257
Library of Economics and Politics
   (Ely), 62, 76
*Life and Labour of the People in
   London* (Booth), 62
Linear arithmetic, 133
   decline of nations and, 111
Linear programming, 128–33
Lippman, Walter, 72
Liverpool Mechanic's Institute,
   280–81
*Lloyd's Lists and Wettenhall's Course
   of Exchange*, 147
Lobachevsky, Nikolai Ivanovich,
   317–18
Lockyer, Norman, 266

Loftus, Pat, 224
Logarithmic scale, 127
Logical consistency, 218
Logic (Mill), 253–54, 278, 291
London School of Economics, 124
London Statistical Society, 116
Lost world, measurement of, 103–6
Loveday, Alexander, 224
Lowe, Robert, 256, 258
Lubin, Isador, 198, 199
Lueder, August Ferdinand, 48–49
Luxton, George, 214

Maas, Harro, 237, 242, 277–302
Machesterthum, 17
*The Making and Using of Index
   Numbers* (Mitchell), 346–47
The Making of Index Numbers
   (Fisher), 313, 327–28, 331–32
Malthus, Thomas, 41
Mammonism, 69, 71
Manchester Examiner, 264
Manchester Guardian, 117, 127, 270
Manchester Statistical Society, 128,
   245, 265–66
   examinations by, 116–21
Maps, 338–40
March, Lucien, 79, 86–110, 238
   anthropomorphism, 104
   biometrics and social sciences,
     differences, 95
   causality, on, 100–3
   contributions to statistics, 93–100
     barometer, 98
     barometric indexation, 96–100
     business cycles, 96–100
     coefficients of dependency,
       94 n8
     socioeconomic time series,
      93–96
   correlation, on, 100–103
   epistemological foundations of
     statistics, 100–106

eugenics, 90–91
forecasting, 105–6
historical time, on, 100–103
indicators, constructing, 245
lost world, measurement of, 103–6
measurement instruments, 247
objective foundations, 91–93
observation, concept of, 90
"pseudo-realities," 104
results, determination of, 92–93
"Statistique," 86
variability, on, 103
view of statistics, 88–93
"Married Women in Factories"
    (Jevons), 269
Marshall, Alfred
    ratio charts, 127
    transitional work, 18
Marty, Martin, 65–67
Marxian economics, 243
Marxist Social Democratic
    Federation, 62
"Mathematical Contribution to
    Philosophy; Attacking Kant's
    Theory of Geometric Axioms"
    (Fisher), 317
Mathematical knowledge,
    measurement and, 303–12
    applied sciences, 306
    axiomatics, 309–12
    geometric certainty, 304–9
    physical reductionism, 309–12
    physical representation, 304–9
    second-order questions, 303–4
Mathematical relations and
    measurement, Enlightenment
    period, 10
Mathematization of physics,
    1830–1900, 14
Mathematization of science, 5–6
Mayo, Elton, 72
McCormick, Cyrus, 59
McCulloch, J. R., 7, 117

McDougal, James B., 172
McKinley, William
    assassination of, 70
Meade, James
    national accounting, 216–18, 220
        adjustment techniques, 227–28
        Standard Adjustment Procedure,
        228
Meany, George, 353, 354
Measurement, role in causal
    relationships, 253–56
Measurement instruments, 235–51
    accounting principles and, 243–44
    balance, 237, 242–43, 277–302
        analysis, as tool of, 280–82
        compound pendulum, drawing
        as, 283
        generally, 282–86
        geometry of, drawing, 283
        gold assaying, balance used in,
        284
        gold valuation, use in, 284,
        287–91
        mental state, applicability to,
        291–97
        tool of analysis, as, 280–82
    causes, use to bootstrap
        measurements, 238–40
    constructing indicators, 245–46
    consumer price index (CPI), 249
    gold, study of, 239–40, 242, 282,
        284, 287–91
    gold assaying, balance used in,
        284
    Gross National Product (GNP),
        248–49
    history, 236
    index numbers, 240–42, 246. See
        also Index numbers
    judgment, 247
    life of measurements, 248–50
    multiple causes, 239, 245
    principle, 247

Measurement instruments
(*continued*)
social surveys, 246
standardized quantitative rules, 248
strategies, components of, 246–48
strategies for making
measurements, 238–46
techniques, 247
terminology, 237
virtual balance, 237
weighted averaging strategy,
240–42
wholes and parts, 244
Méchain, Pierre-François, 11
Mechanic's Institutes (Britain),
280–81, 288
Men and Religion Forward
Movement, 58–62, 65, 68
Committee of 97, 59
Committee of 100, 58–59
Program of Works, 60
Publicity Committee, 79
Social Service Committee, 60
Women and Children in Industry,
1870 to 1900, 61
World War I and, 73
Mental state, applicability of balance
to, 291–97
Mercantile Public, 119
Metaphysics and Measurement
(Koyré), 6
"A Method of Geometrical
Representation of the
Thermodynamic Properties of
Substances by Means of
Surfaces" (Gibbs), 321
Metric system, 11–12
Metzler, Lloyd, 353
Mill, John Stuart
coal, on, 263
cyclical fluctuations, 265–66
Logic, 278, 291
measurement, role in causal

relationships, 253–56
monetary issues, 99
Principles of Political Economy,
253–54, 269
residues, method of, 290
Miller, Adolph G., 172, 179–82, 183
Miller, O. M.
World Maps and Globes, 339
Mills, Frederick, 353
Mills, John, 117, 121
Mineral classification, 12
Mines, administration, 12
Mining Records Office
(United Kingdom), 264
Ministry of Economic Warfare
(England), 216
Mints, Lloyd, 173, 186
Mitchel administration, 122
Mitchell, Wesley Clair
philanthropic organizations, 76
poverty, research on, 81
price indexes, 97, 346–50, 355,
357–58
recession, on, 124
War Production Board and, 176
Mitchell committee, 361, 366
Monetary policymakers, 1920s,
162–89
cyclical price-level effects of
money, 169–71
quantity theory framework, 166–71
Money
policymakers. *See* Monetary
policymakers, 1920s
quantitative assessment of value of,
137–61
Bullion Committee of 1810, 140,
145–49, 151
cattle, silver price of, 142–43
corn, silver price of, 142–44, 152
"Digression Concerning the
Variations in the Value of
Silver" (Smith), 140–45, 152

historical context, 159–60
History of Prices (Tooke),
    149–55
independence, assumption of,
    157–58
indirect measurement, 139
measurement, generally, 137–40
*A Serious Fall in the Value of
    Gold Ascertained, and Its
    Social Effects Set Forth*
    (Jevons), 155–59, 259, 262
signal extraction, 144–45
quantity theory of, 196
*Money and Credit Instruments in
    Their Relation to General
    Prices* (Kemmerer), 166–67
Moody, Dwight, 65–66
Moore, Henry, 99
Moral Algebra (Franklin), 293–94
Morgan, J. P., 59
Morgan, Mary S., 3, 18–19, 89, 101,
    235–51
Moritz, R. E., 303
Mortality rates, United Kingdom,
    268–70
Moscow Business Cycle Institute, 351
Müller, Adam, 47–48
Multiple causes
    measurement instruments, 239, 245
Multiple classifications
    accounting, 222
Municipal statistics, early twentieth
    century U.S., 121–24

Napoleon, 42, 47
Napoleonic Wars, 129
National accounting
    France, 213
    United Kingdom, 213–34, 243. *See
        also* Stone, John Nicholas
        Richard
    definitions, 219–24
    extension, 224–27

flexibility, 219–24
    general structure, 215–18
    invariance, 219–24
    logical consistency of
        framework, 215–18
    multiple classifications, 222
    standardization, 224–27
National Bureau of Economic
    Research (NBER), 107
    economic management, 76
    1947 input-output tables,
        207–8
    Price Statistics Review Committee,
        361
    quality change and, 346
Nationalökonomie, 41
National Resources Committee
    Industrial Committee of, 198
National Resources Planning Board,
    198
National Social Science Association,
    265–66
National War Labor Board, 353
*Natural Elements of Political
    Economy* (Jennings), 292, 295
Natural history, quantification of,
    14–15
NBER. *See* National Bureau of
    Economic Research
"Necessary and Sufficient Conditions
    Regarding the Form of an
    Index Number Which Shall
    Meet Certain of
    Fisher's Tests" (Frisch),
    332–34
Neisser, Hans P., 199
Neue Erdbeschreibung
    (Büsching), 30
Newcomb, Simon, 166
Newmarch, William, 259–60
Newton, Isaac, 10
New York Charity Organization,
    63

New York City
    municipal statistics, early twentieth
        century, 121–24
New York City Bureau of Social
    Statistics, 122
Nightingale, Florence, 271
Nikolow, Sybilla, 23–56, 57, 114, 244
1911 and 1912
    American economics,
        quantification, 57–85
Nineteenth century
    mathematical knowledge,
        measurement and, 303–12
Non-Euclidean geometry, 316–20
Norris, George W., 172
Norton, John Pease, 95
    *Statistical Studies in the New York
        Money Market*, 166
Notion-limite, 102

Objectivism, 78
Objectivity, 91–93
O'Brian, E., 232
Observation, concept of, 90
Office du Travail, 90
Office of Strategic Services (OSS),
    203
Office of War Mobilization and
    Reconversion, 204
"On Tabular Analysis" (Guy), 114
Ordinary table makers, 43–51
"The Origin and Meaning of
    Geometrical Axioms"
    (Helmholtz), 317
OSS. *See* Office of Strategic Services
    (OSS)
OT. *See* Office du Travail
Ottolenghi, Otto, 127
Overstone, Lord, 257

The Paasche Index, 328–30
Papers and Correspondence (Jevons),
    277

Parade of statistical exhibits,
    New York City (1913), 123
Pareto, Vilfredo, 305
    ratio charts, 127
    transitional work, 18
Patten, Simon Nelson, 57
Peano, Giuseppe, 310
Pearson, Karl, 94–96
    correlation, 101–3
    The Grammar of Science, 102
Peart, Sandra, 239, 252–76
Pentagon, 206
Perkins, Frances, 199
Persons, Warren M., 166
    Harvard style, 97
Petty, William, 12–13
    national accounting and, 213
    wealth or power, on gauging, 23
Philanthropin, 28–29, 31, 51
Phillips, Andrew W., 317
Philosophy of Discovery (Whewell),
    278
Physical reductionism, 309–12
Physical representation, 304–9
Physics
    mathematization of, 1830–1900, 14
    quantification in, 6–7
Pittsburgh Survey, 63–64
Planck, Max, 307
Platt, Thomas C., 69–70
Playfair, William, 34, 111–14
    "Universal Chart of Commercial
        History" (Playfair), 112–13
Pleasure and pain, 291–97
Poland, population studies, 34
Policymakers, United States
    monetary, 1920s, 162–89
Political arithmetic, 13–14, 28
Political economy, 5
Political journalism, 26
Poor Law (United Kingdom), 268
Population measurement
    England, 1821 to 1831, 117

focus of statistics, as, 52
France, 33–34
Poland, 33–34
1730–1830, 12–13
Porter, Theodore M., 4–22, 191, 248,
    263, 345
Poverty
land ownership and, 63
New York City, early twentieth
    century, 122–23
Poor Law (United Kingdom), 268
War on Poverty (United States), 81
Poverty: A Study of Town Life
    (Rowntree), 62
Pownall, George, 118
Price indexes, 97
heterogeneity, 349–50
indifference-defined index, 351
involuntary uptrading, 356
price level, 347–48
quality deterioration and, 357
specification pricing, 352
United States, 1915–61, 345–70
    hedonic price regression,
        361–66
    Stigler Committee, 361 66
    Swedish economist,
        commentary, 359–61
    World War II, 346, 350–58
voluntary uptrading, 356
Price Indexes and Quality Changes
    (Hofsten), 359
Price ratios, 324
Prices. *See also* Money
accounting prices, 132
changes, measurement, 149–55
History of Prices (Tooke), 149–55
imaginary prices, 132
increases, wealth and, 147
shadow prices, 132, 133
trade cycle, World War I, 124–28
Priestley, Joseph, 293
Princeton University

Institute for Advanced Study, 224
Principles of Political Economy
    (Mill), 253–54, 269
Principles of Political Economy
    (Newcomb), 166
Principles of Science (Jevons)
balance, 286–87
invention, on, 277
mental state, applicability of
    balance to, 292
role of measurement, 253–54
underlying argument, 266
recommendations for
    measurement, 272
Probability, 93
Productivity, industrial management
    and, 72
Produktkarte (Crome), 32
Prognostication, 9
Program of Works (Men and
    Religion Forward
    Movement), 60
Progressive Era, 123
Progressive politics, 69–74
Project SCOOP, 205
Promise Keeper's movement, 59 n1
The Promise of American Life (Croly),
    72
Protestantism
social surveys, 65–69
Prussia, collapse of, 47
"Pseudo-realities," 104
Psychology, 5
*Publications of the American
    Statistical Association*, 77
Public servants, cost-of-living
    adjustments, 143
The Purchasing Power of Money
    (Fisher), 167, 170, 313, 321,
    329–31

Qualitative mathematical model,
    130–31

Quantification
   economics, American, 57–85
   natural history, 14–15
   physics, 6–7
   1730–1830, Enlightenment, 10
   1830–1900, 14–18
Quantitative astronomy, 8–9
"Quantitative Input and Output
      Relations in the Economic
      System of the United
      States" (Leontief), 193–94
Quesnay, François, 192, 197
Quetelet, Adolphe, 17, 255

Ransome, Arthur, 270
"The 'Ratio' Chart for Plotting
      Statistics" (Fisher), 321
Ratio charts, 127
Rauschenbusch, Walter
   Christianizing the Social Order,
      68–69
   Mammonism, on, 71
   Men and Religion Forward
      Movement, 58
   Progressive Era, on, 70, 73
   scientific knowledge, on, 79
   social conditions, on, 69
   working women, on, 122
Real bills doctrine of money, 240
Recession, 124–28
"Reflections on the Revolution in
      France" (Burke), 47
Rehberg, Wilhelm
   debate over table making, 44–47,
      50
Reid, Margaret, 353
Reifler, Winfield, 183, 184
Religion Forward Movement, 52
Report of the Select Committee on the
      Protection of Infant Life, 269
Residues, method of, 158, 290
Results, determination of, 92–93
Reuben, Julie, 78

Revel, Jacques, 42–43
Review of Economic Statistics, 127
Ricardian tradition, 99 n16
Ricardo, David, 17, 140
Robins, Raymond, 68
Robinson, Arthur, 32
Robinson, August, 216
Rockefeller, John D., Jr., 59
Rodgers, Daniel T., 70–72
Rogers, James E. Thorold, 266–67
Romantic Movement, 47–48
Roosevelt, Franklin D.
   committee of government, 353
   economy, concerns regarding, 199
Roosevelt, Theodore, 69
"Root cause," 268
Röpke, Wilhelm, 137
Roscoe, Harry, 281
Ross, Dorothy, 75
Ross, E. A., 57, 82
Rothbarth, E., 199
Rowntree, B. Seebohm, 62
Royal Society of London, 13
Royal Statistical Society, 114
Rubinow, Isaac Max, 122
Ruggles System, 226
Ruml, Beardsley, 76
Russell Sage Foundation, 63, 78
Rutherford, Malcolm, 75–76, 81

Salford District Provident Society,
      119
Samuelson, Paul, 352
Schabas, Margaret, 280, 292
Schlettwein, Johann August, 29
Schlözer, August Ludwig
   limited numerical measurement, 44
   political journalism, 26
   table making debate, 50–51
Schultz, Theodore, 353
Schwartz, Anna, 186
Scientific Revolution, 10
"Scientism," 75

Seay, George J., 172
Second-order questions, 303–4
A Serious Fall in the Value of Gold Ascertained, and Its Social Effects Set Forth (Jevons), 155–59, 259, 262
1730, measurement to, 8–9
1730–1830, Enlightenment, 10–14
1770–1830, statistical representations, 23–56
Seyd, Ernest, 257
SGF. *See* Statistique Géneérale de la France (SGF)
Shadow prices, 132, 133
Shipbuilding, World War I, 129, 346
Shipbuilding Adjustment Board, 346
Signal extraction, 144–45
Silver
   "Digression Concerning the Variations in the Value of Silver" (Smith), 140–45, 152
Simplex method, 132
Slave trade, 117
Small pox, 13
Smith, Adam
   "Digression Concerning the Variations in the Value of Silver," 140–45
   freedom, concept of, 48
   Inquiry into the Nature and Causes of the Wealth of Nations, 111
   multiple causes, 239
   political economy, 12
   Tooke, Thomas, criticism by, 152–53, 159
   trends, identification of, 150
   von Thünen and, 114
   Wealth of Nations, 140–45
Smith, Fred B., 68
Smith, J. B., 257
Smith, Colonel J. T., 257
SNA. *See Standardized System of National Accounts* (SNA)

Snyder, Carl, 166, 168–69, 176
Social accounting
   multiple classifications, 222
Social astronomy, 99
Social Darwinism, 63
Social Gospel, 58, 65–73 *passim*, 76
   distancing from, 79
Social Investigation and Research at the London School of Economics, 122
Social science, American, 74–76
Social statistics, 7
   France, 79–80
Social survey movement, 62–65.
   See also Social surveys
   end of, 76–78
   "in the scientific spirit," 76–78
   Pittsburgh Survey, 63–64
Social surveyors, cartoon, 80
Social surveys, 57–85. *See also* Social survey movement
   American Protestantism, 65–69
   turn away from, 74
   American social science, 74–76
   improvements in, 77
   institutional economics, 79–82
   measurement instruments, 246
   Men and Religion Forward Movement, 58–62, 65, 68
   Publicity Committee, 79
   World War I and, 73
   progressive politics, 69–74
   "scientism," 75
   social survey movement, 62–65
   end of, 76–78
   "in the scientific spirit," 76–78
Société Française d'Eugénique, 91
Socioeconomic time series, 94–96
Sociology, 5
"The Solar Influence on Commerce" (Jevons), 266
"The Solar Period and the Price of Corn" (Jevons), 266

Specie-flow mechanism, 146
Species payment, 129
Staatswissenschaften, 24–30 *passim*,
    37–38, 41
*Standardized System of National
    Accounts* (SNA), 224–27
  adjustment techniques, 228
State
  place of statistics in study of,
    23–28
    academic system, 23–25
    empirical basis for descriptions,
      26–27
    ratio and proportion, 32–34
    territorial state, how to govern,
      27–28
    table making and, 47–49
State in Relation to Labour (Jevons),
    268
*Statistical Account of the British
    Empire* (McCulloch), 117
Statistical Breviary (Playfair), 34, 112
Statistical economics, Germany,
    16–17
Statistical representations,
    1770–1830, 23–56
Statistical revolution, 231
*Statistical Studies in the New York
    Money Market* (Pease), 166
Statistics. *See specific topic*
Statistik der Europäischen Staaten, 29
Statistique Générale de la France
    (SGF), 86–87, 90
  stock market fluctuations, 96 n14
"Statistique" (March), 86
Steel industry, Pittsburgh, 64
Stelzle, Charles, 68
Stewart, Walter W., 81
  Federal Reserve Board, 172, 176,
    179–82, 183
Stigler, George, 346, 361–66
Stigler, Stephen, 17
Stigler Committee, 361–66

Stone, John Nicholas Richard,
    213–34, 363. *See also*
    National accounting
  accuracy of measurement, 227–30
  consistency, 193
  Institute for Advanced Study, visit
    to, 224
  measurement instruments, 247–48
  national income aggregates, 207
  Trends, 215–16
Strategies, components of, 246–48
Strong, Benjamin, 178, 183–85
Strong, James G., 180
The Structure of American Economy
    (Leontief), 199
Studenski, P., 213
Subjective judgments, 91–92
Süßmilch, Johann Peter, 23
Sunspot cycle, 267–68
"Sunspots and Commercial Panics"
    (Jevons), 268
*The Supply and Control of Money in
    the United States* (Currie), 185
Supply and demand, law of, 292
Survey
  social surveyors, cartoon, 80
Surveys. *See* Social surveys
Swamy, Subramanian, 333–34
Sweden
  economics, 1730–1830, 13
  mining, 1730–1830, 12
Swedish Social Welfare Board,
    359–61
Syson, E. J., 269

Tabellenknechte, 48
Tableau economique (Leontief),
    192–95
Table making, early nineteenth
    century debate, 43–51
  laborers, statisticians as, 47–49
  response to criticisms, 49–51
  words versus tables, 45–46

Taft, William H.
    Progressive reform and, 70
Tarbell, Ida, 74
Taylor, Frederick, 72
*The Techniques of Optical
    Instrument Design*
    (Bracey), 313
Territorial state, how to govern,
    27–28
Theorizing and measuring,
    relationship between, 195–99
The Theory of Political Economy
    (Jevons), 279, 294, 297–98
Thomas, Norman, 73
Thomas, R. J., 353
Thomas, Woodlief, 176
Time Reversal Test, 335, 336
Time series
    decomposition, 95, 127
    representations of cyclical activity,
        96
    socioeconomic, 94–96
Tinbergen, J., 214
Tooke, Thomas, 140
    History of Prices, 149–55
    *Inquiry into the Currency
        Principle*, 151–52
    residues, method of, 158
    Smith, Adam, criticism of, 152–53,
        159
Trade cycle chart, 124–28
"Trade Cycles Chart: The Past as a
    Guide to the Future, A Study
    in Economics" (Kitchin), 124,
    125–26
Trends (Stone), 215–16
Triangles in three different spaces,
    318
Triangular grid, globes, 340
Trotsky, Leon, 124
Truman administration, 205
Turgot, Anne Robert Jacques,
    12, 13

"Two party" Protestantism, 65

United Kingdom. *See also* England;
    Great Britain
    coal, 263–65
    coinage, condition of and
        measurement, 256–58
    cyclical fluctuations, 265–68
    Factory Acts, 268
    gold, value of, 239–40, 242, 253,
        258–63
    mortality rates, 268–70
    national accounting, 213–34
    Poor Law, 268
United Nations, 224
United States
    American economics, early
        twentieth century, 57–85
    American Protestantism, 65–69
    Bureau of Labor Statistics. See U.S.
        Bureau of Labor Statistics
    Men and Religion Forward
        Movement, 58–62
    monetary policymakers, 1920s,
        162–89
    municipal statistics, early twentieth
        century, 121–24
    Pittsburgh Survey, 63–64
    price indexes, 1915–61, 345–70
        hedonic price regression,
            361–66
        Stigler Committee, 361–66
        Swedish economist,
            commentary, 359–61
        World War II, 346, 350–58
    social science, 74–76
"Universal Chart of Commercial
    History" (Playfair),
    112–13
Universal ethic of measurement, 5
U.S. Air Force
    Planning Research Division,
        205

U.S. Bureau of Labor Statistics,
190–212
concepts, overcoming limitations,
199–203
Federal Reserve System and, 174
framework for measuring,
development, 208–10
1947 table, national income
accounts and, 205–8
peace, forecasting effects of, 203–5
price indexes, 346–47, 358
U.S. Commerce Bureau, 218
U.S. Department of Commerce, 201,
219
Utility adjustment of individual to
optimum, 295

Van Kleeck, Mary, 76
Variability, 103
Veblen, Thorstein
American economics, influence on,
76
institutionalism and, 81
Verhältniskarte von Europa (Crome),
34–37
later version, 37–43
Vienna Congress of 1815, 37, 42
Virtual balance, 237
Visualizations, 322
Volterra, Vito, 195, 307–9, 315
von Humboldt, Alexander
quantification of natural history, 14
von Neumann, John, 130–32
von Thünen, Johann Heinrich,
114–16
equilibrium model, 131
wheat, price of, 115, 116

Wald, Abraham, 334
Walras, Léon, 18
Wanamaker, John, 59
Warburton, Clark, 186
War Cabinet (England), 216

Wargentin, P. W.
censuses, 14
War Industry Board, 347
Warner, Amos Griswold, 63
War on Poverty (United States), 81
War Production Board, 176
Wars. *See also specific war*
linear programming and, 128–33
Wealth
measurement, 1730–1830, 12–13
price increases and, 147
Wealth of Nations (Smith),
140–45
Weather glass, 245
Webb, Sidney
Social Investigation and Research
at the London School of
Economics, 122
Weighted averaging strategy,
240–42
Weintraub, E. Roy, 195, 241–42,
303–12, 315
Westman, Robert, 9
Wheat, price of, 115, 116
Whewell, William, 16, 278, 304–5
Wilkinson, Thomas, 116–17,
119, 269
Willis, H. Parker, 172, 173
Wilson, Woodrow, 70
Wisconsin, University of
Institute for Research
on Poverty, 81
Women
factory work, United Kingdom,
269–70
Women and Children in Industry,
1870 to 1900, 61
Wood, Marshall, 205
Work
concept of, eighteenth century, 16
Work Accidents and the Law
(Eastman), 64
Working, Holbrook

monetary policymaking and, 166,
   168–69, 171
World maps and globes,
   338–40
World Maps and Globes
   (Fisher and Miller),
   339
World War I
   Federal Reserve System and, 173
   Progressive Era and, 73–74, 79
   science and, 78
   shipbuilding, 129, 346
   Social Gospel and, 76, 79
   trade cycle, 124–28
World War II
   committee of government, 353–54
   government employment of

economists, 129, 131
Ministry of Economic Warfare
   (England), 216
price indexes, 346,
   350–58
U.S. Bureau of Labor Statistics,
   203–5

*Yearbook of National Accounts
   Statistics*, 224

"Zur Axiomatischen Theorie des
   Preisindex" (Eichhorn),
   335
"Zur Theorie der Preisindexziffern,"
   334
Zustand, 25